RULES
FOR
REASONING

Edited by

Richard E. Nisbett
University of Michigan

 LAWRENCE ERLBAUM ASSOCIATES, PUBLISHERS
1993   Hillsdale, New Jersey   Hove and London

Lawrence Erlbaum Associates, Inc., Publishers
365 Broadway
Hillsdale, New Jersey 07642

Library of Congress Cataloging-in-Publication Data

Rules for reasoning / edited by Richard E. Nisbett.
    p. cm.
  Includes bibliographical references and indexes.
  ISBN 0-8058-1256-3 (cloth). -- ISBN 0-8058-1257-1 (paper)
  1. Reasoning. I. Nisbett, Richard E.
BC177.R76 1993
160--dc20   92-39042
                                   CIP

Books published by Lawrence Erlbaum Associates are printed on acid-free paper, and their
bindings are chosen for strength and durability.

Printed in the United States of America
10 9 8 7 6 5 4 3 2

For Matthew and Sarah

Acknowledgments

The editor wishes to acknowledge with thanks the many journals that gave their permission to reprint the following articles in this volume.

Nisbett, R. E., Krantz, D. H., Jepson, C., & Kunda, Z. (1983). The use of statistical heuristics in everyday reasoning. *Psychological Review, 90,* 339–363.

Thagard, P., & Nisbett, R. E. (1982). Variability and confirmation. *Philosophical Studies, 50,* 250–267.

Jepson, C., Krantz, D. H., & Nisbett, R. E. (1983). Inductive reasoning: Competence or skill? *Behavioral and Brain Sciences, 6,* 494–501.

Fong, G. T., Krantz, D. H. & Nisbett, R. E. (1986). The effects of statistical training on thinking about everyday problems. *Cognitive Psychology, 18,* 253–292.

Fong, G. T., & Nisbett, R. E. (1991). Immediate and delayed transfer of training effects in statistical reasoning. *Journal of Experimental Psychology, 120,* 34–45.

Cheng, P., Holyoak, K. J., Nisbett, R. E., & Oliver, L. (1986). Pragmatic versus syntactic approaches to training deductive reasoning. *Cognitive Psychology, 18,* 293–328.

Larrick, R. P., Morgan, J. N., & Nisbett, R. E. (1990). Teaching the use of cost-benefit reasoning in everyday life. *Psychological Science, 1,* 362–370.

Larrick, R. P., Nisbett, R. E., & Morgan, J. N., (In press). Who uses the normative rules of choice? *Organizational Behavior and Human Decision-Making.*

Nisbett, R. E., Fong, G. T., Lehman, D. R., & Cheng, P. W. (1987). Teaching reasoning. *Science, 238,* 625–631.

Lehman, D. R., Lempert, R. O., & Nisbett, R. E. (1988). The effects of graduate training on reasoning: Formal discipline and thinking about everyday life events. *American Psychologist, 43,* 431–443.

Lehman, D., & Nisbett, R. E. (1990). A longitudinal study of the effects of undergraduate education on reasoning. *Developmental Psychology, 26,* 952–960.

Smith, E. E., Langston, C., & Nisbett, R. E. (1992). The case for rules in reasoning. *Cognitive Science, 16,* 99–102.

Contents

1 Reasoning, Abstraction, and the Prejudices of 20th-Century Psychology

R. E. Nisbett
University of Michigan

Twentieth-century psychology has had a strong prejudice against abstraction, that is, against the view that the world is understood by means of rules that transcend the perception of a particular physical stimulus or the comprehension of a domain of related events. In the United States, the prejudice has been bound up with behaviorism and its successor positions. Behaviorists were determined to find the equivalent of the reflex arc in physiology — stimulus-response linkages that could be described with precision by a physical description of the stimulus, the response, and the conditions of their co-occurrence during learning. So complete was their dedication to such physical description that they felt confident that the study of animals could substitute for the study of humans in building a complete theory of behavior.

Early in the 19th-century, the behaviorist E. L. Thorndike performed a series of experiments that satisfied two generations of American psychologists that abstractions were not importantly involved in learning how to perform skilled tasks. He asked his subjects to perform a particular task for varying amounts of time (e.g., cancelling Os from a sentence, and then switched them to another task; cancelling adverbs from a sentence). He found that "transfer of training" effects were slight and unstable. Sometimes he found that performance of the first task enhanced the second, sometimes that it made it more difficult, and, often, that it had no effect at all. One would, of course, assume that performance on the second task would be improved if subjects learned something general from performance of the first task. Since they so often failed to show improved training, Thorndike inferred that people don't, in fact, learn much that is general

1

when performing mental tasks. This meant that training was going to be very much a bottom-up affair, consisting of little more than slogging through countless stimulus-response associations.

This conclusion has suffused deeply into American psychology, cognitive science, and education. Newell (1980), based on some similar failed efforts to find training effects for reasoning tasks, has asserted that learned problem-solving skills generally are idiosyncratic to the task. Just as the earlier behaviorists took the evidence of weak transfer-of-training effects to buttress their case for the exclusive role of specific stimulus-response linkages, some modern cognitive scientists have used such evidence to support connectionism—the modern successor to behaviorism. To the connectionist, all learning is just a matter of adding strength values to an initially neutral "network" of highly specific elements. The connectionists have all the courage of the behaviorists' convictions — asserting that they can mimic the important details of learning and cognitive performance without the postulation of any rules whatever.

Other trends of modern psychology are opposed to abstract rules, though not necessarily to rules of all kinds. Devotees of case-based reasoning approaches to problem solving hold that people do little more when solving problems than perceive similarities between old and new problems and occasionally apply strategies of analogy construction. Biological and evolutionary theories of cognition are sympathetic to the notion that people operate using rules of limited generality, but these are usually assumed to be limited to relatively tight domains. Thus there are rules, even prewired rules, for language, or for physical causality, or for particular types of social relations, but these are limited to particular content domains and would never be used for understanding events outside those domains.

European psychology has never been so deeply antiabstractionist as American psychology. In fact, Jean Piaget, the European psychologist whose influence on world psychology has been greatest, explicitly endorsed the notion that there are abstract rules that guide thought and behavior. Piaget even thought that the very most abstract rules, those of formal logic, have their intuitive counterparts in the human cognitive repertoire. These rules, part of the equipment that Piaget called *propositional operations,* are used to acquire other, somewhat less abstract but still domain-independent rules in the course of development. These are the *formal operations,* which include the concept of proportionality, the notion that every action has a reaction, and what Piaget called the *probability schema,* but most people today would call the law of large numbers. Piaget believed that people possessed these highly abstract rules in a form in which they made contact with the most ordinary problems in everyday life. Indeed, many common problems could not be solved without the use of such rules, and it was the press of such requirements that pushed people toward their acquisition, by means of inductive procedures operating within the logical constraints of the propositional operations.

Despite his endorsement of abstract rules for reasoning, Piaget was quite firm in his opinion that such rules could not be explicitly taught—certainly not by abstract or formal means. Such rules are the common equipment of every adult, and everyone acquires them by virtue of being the kind of organism that each human is and by virtue of living in the kind of world that each human does. Given our native equipment and the kind of experiences we are going to have, we perforce learn the abstract rules we are going to need for purposes of deductive and inductive inference. But such rules are learned only by an inductive process of self-discovery; the day of their acquisition cannot be hastened either by abstract instruction in the rule system or by a forced inductive march through specific problems. Nothing, not even an abstract rule, is learned by abstract or top-down training procedures. Nor is there any point in trying to fool Mother Nature by excessive drilling on concrete problems. No rule will be learned before the organism is ready for it and learning is inevitable once the organism is ready—so long as it is not kept in a closet.

You will read Piaget in vain for any evidence for this extraordinarily influential theory of how rules for reasoning are learned. It was simply obvious to him that you cannot teach abstract rules of reasoning, and it became equally obvious to us largely because of his enormous prestige and persuasiveness. There are to be sure shreds of evidence available since Piaget's time that are consistent with his view: (a) solutions to the missionaries and cannibals problem do not generalize to formally identical problems; (b) accelerated learning of conservation of mass for clay does not seem to generalize to an understanding of conservation in general. And there remains Thorndike's work, showing that there can be little transfer of training even across tasks that require lower levels of cognitive skill than one would want to dignify with the term *reasoning*.

But what if Piaget and, even more so, the American psychological tradition, were mistaken about abstractions? What if you actually could teach people highly abstract rules of reasoning—and even do so by highly abstract and therefore efficient means? What if such instruction resulted in people being able to apply those rule systems potentially to the full range of problems in everyday life for which they are relevant? How would we think about the human mind then? How would we think about education?

This volume tries to answer those questions, coming up with some very surprising answers. Ten years ago, I held a version of the received views about reasoning. I was dubious that people had any abstract rules for reasoning and confident that even if they did, such rules could not be taught. Indeed, I had just completed 10 years of work that seemed to me to give substantial support to these views. I had worked on questions of reasoning about human social behavior, finding that people often violated the requirements of statistical, causal, and even logical rules of inference. This work was very much in the tradition of Kahneman and Tversky's research showing that people substitute simple judgmental heuristics for the more formal inferential rules that are necessary to solve the problems they gave their subjects. I believed not only that my subjects did not possess the necessary statistical rules, I believed that instruction in statistics resulted only in inserting a sterile set of formal rules that could make contact only with scientific problems or problems for which there existed some massive and probably ecologically uncommon cue triggering their use.

With Geoffrey Fong and David Krantz, I began what I thought would be a swift program of work establishing these points, namely that instruction in statistics does very little toward helping people to solve everyday problems that require a statistical solution. My very first attempt to look at this question showed me that I was wrong (or should have showed me — actually I didn't believe the implications at first). Kahneman and Tversky (1972) had developed a clever problem to show subjects' statistical weaknesses called the *maternity ward problem*. In this problem subjects are told that there is a town with two hospitals, one large and one small. At the large hospital, about 60 babies a day are born, and at the small hospital about 15. Subjects are then asked at which hospital they think there would be more days during the year in which 60% or more of the babies born would be boys. About one third of the undergraduates they studied believed it would be the larger hospital, about one third believed it would be the smaller, and about one third believed it would make no difference. The law of large numbers, of course, requires that it would be the smaller hospital, because deviant sample proportions are likely in inverse proportion to sample size. While teaching an upper level undergraduate class at the University of Michigan, I tried to duplicate these results in a classroom demonstration. To my surprise, most of the students got the problem right. I then asked students to indicate how much statistics they had had as well as their preferred answer. The results were clear-cut. The students who had had no statistics duplicated the pattern of the Kahneman and Tversky subjects, those who had had at least one course in statistics were unlikely to get the problem wrong.

Subsequent work showed there was no anomaly here. Problems that Kahneman and Tversky had looked at, as well as problems with more social content of the kind I had looked at, turned out to be highly influenced by statistical training. This was true even for problems without obvious statistical clues. For example, one problem we gave subjects asked why someone who had an excellent meal in a restaurant might be likely to complain about a less good meal the next time around. Untrained undergraduates almost always gave purely deterministic answers such as "maybe restaurants change their chefs a lot." But subjects who had had many courses in statistics usually gave statistical answers, such as "there are probably more restaurants where you can get an excellent meal some of the time than there are restaurants where you can get an excellent meal all the time, so a person who gets an excellent meal the first time has to assume it's likely that the next one won't be."

We then began seeing whether you could teach such statistical reasoning in short training programs. We found to our surprise that even very brief interventions could produce fairly pronounced effects on the sorts of answers subjects would give to problems of the Kahneman and Tversky type. Indeed, purely abstract training, in which we defined the terms *sample, population, parameter,* and *variance,* and explained the relations among *variability, N,* and sample–parameter accuracy, even had an effect on solution of problems with purely social content. Moreover, training in a given domain, for example, training on problems concerning sports transferred fully to another domain, for example, problems concerning ability tests. In several studies, we found literally no advantage for the trained domain over other domains so long as testing was immediate. Such results are consistent with the view that people can operate with very abstract rules indeed, and that the techniques by which they learn them can be very abstract. Abstract improvements to the preexisting intuitive rule system are passed along to the full range of content domains where the rules are applicable, and improvements in a given domain are sufficiently abstracted so they can be applied immediately to a very different content domain.

It is important to note that the sort of instructional effects we discovered in these studies are by no means limited to laboratory or academic settings. When subjects are contacted outside of such settings (e.g., in the context of an opinion poll), the trained subjects answer questions differently from the untrained. In one study, male college students who had either just begun or just finished their first statistics course were asked to participate in a poll on opinions about sports. After answering a number of questions about the National Collegiate Athletic Association rules and National Basketball Association salaries, they were reminded that the top batters in both baseball leagues typically have averages of .450 or higher at the end of the first two weeks of play, yet no one has ever finished the season with such a high average. The students were asked to explain why they thought this was the case. The students just beginning statistics nearly always responded with purely deterministic answers such as "the pitchers make the necessary adjustments." The students who had taken the course were twice as likely as novices to give a statistical answer, such as "two weeks isn't a very long time, so you get some atypically high (and low) averages; no one really has the ability to hit .450 over the long haul."

Over the next 10 years, I pursued the implications of these findings on trainability with different sets of colleagues who were expert in particular rule systems, including the self-selection concept critical to control procedures in the social sciences, "pragmatic reasoning schemas" for contractual relations such as permission and obligation, rules for assessing causality, and the cost-benefit rules of microeconomic theory. The generalizations below hold for these rule systems taken as a group. All of the generalizations have been tested on at least three different abstract rule systems; none are contradicted by any evidence I am aware of.

1. People have intuitive versions of these formal rule systems that they apply to at least some problems in everyday life. We know this because they solve problems that require use of the rule systems, because they articulate the rule systems in justifying their solutions, and because instruction in the rule systems increases the correct solution of the problems.

2. People at a given level of education, prior to formal instruction in a particular rule system, differ in the degree to which they understand the rule system and are able to apply it to solve concrete problems. Such individual differences are associated with verbal intelligence.

3. Formal education beyond secondary school produces dramatic differences in people's use of different rule systems. It is no exaggeration to say that people who have substantial knowledge of statistics, or of economics, view the world very differently from those who do not. All sorts of mundane problems are understood differently by people with differing levels of education in the relevant rule system.

4. The rule systems are embodied at a level of abstraction equal to that posited by Piaget for the so-called formal operations. The absence of domain specificity is a striking observation across training studies, as is the ability of investigators to "insert" the rules by purely formal and abstract instructional means.

5. Despite their abstract nature, the rules are not applied across all domains equally. The same student who has no trouble applying statistical rules to the behavior of random generating devices, such as dice, may apply statistical rules rarely or never to problems with social content. Problems differ a great deal in how transparent they are with respect to a rule system necessary for their solution.

6. A consequence of people's differential ability to apply rules in different domains is that training in coding a given domain in terms of the rule can have dramatic effects — making it possible for people to apply a rule they already have to a new domain where previously it was unlikely for them to use the rule.

The upshot of these findings is that modern cognitive science and modern educational theory must accommodate themselves to the existence of abstract inferential rules. Psychological theories that hold that there are no rules, or no domain-independent rules, for problem solving, are not tenable in the light of the work presented in this book. Educational positions that emphasize self-discovery and maturation must make room for the generalization that abstract techniques of instruction can be very powerful. Psychological and educational positions, as well as philosophical positions, that assume a universal adult competence with respect to reasoning must give way to the recognition that adult inferential competence is highly variable and highly dependent on educational history.

The rest of the volume presents work making these points in detail. Some of the chapters have been published before and some were written especially for this volume. (Reference styles are not consistent across the different papers. We chose to leave the previously-published material in the same form in which it appeared originally, minus their abstracts.)

Part I documents the existence of abstract, intuitive, and statistical rules. Chapter 2, by Nisbett, Krantz, Jepson and Kunda, shows that people without formal training in statistics solve problems using the law of large numbers and actually articulate the rule in justification of their answers. This chapter also shows that the presence of various cues about the partially random nature of the events in a given problem can dramatically affect the likelihood that people will apply the law of large numbers to the problem.

Chapter 3, by Thagard and Nisbett, proposes a solution to Hume's riddle of induction, namely "Why is a single instance, in some cases, sufficient for a complete induction, whereas in others myriads of concurring instances, without a single exception known or presumed, go such a very little way towards establishing a universal proposition?" The solution lies in the law of large numbers, coupled with real world knowledge about the variability of kinds of objects with respect to kinds of properties. A "single instance is sufficient for a complete induction" when we take it for granted that objects of the kind in question are invariant with respect to properties of the kind observed. For example, observing the color of a sample of a new chemical element leaves us in little doubt about the color of future samples. Myriads of concurring instances do not convince when we take it for granted that the kind of object is highly variable with respect to the kind of property observed. For example, observing a bird in the rain forest that is green does not convince us that the next bird we see of the same type will be green because we do not assume invariability of color for bird types.

Chapter 4 directly attacks the notion assumed by many philosophers and psychologists that there is a single human inferential competence. Some philosophers, notably Jonathan Cohen, have argued that empirical demonstrations of human inferential error are logically impossible since "Ordinary human reasoning—by which I mean the reasoning of adults who have not been systematically educated in any branch of logic or probability theory—cannot be held to be faultily programmed: It sets its own standards" (1981, p. 317). One wonders why it is untutored reasoning that Cohen presumes to be correct rather than tutored reasoning, but even if one accepts that untutored reasoning gets the normative nod, the position is untenable on empirical grounds. Untutored people differ dramatically in their preferred solutions for concrete inferential problems and in the abstract rules for inference that they endorse. Even within a given culture, people differ so much that it is impossible to identify a single competence and establish it as a normative standard.

Part II presents the evidence on alteration of statistical rules. It shows that both standard types of statistical training and various experimental versions can drastically change people's understanding of events characterized by random or partially random determination. Both top–down, abstract training and bottom–up training within a given domain have widespread effects on reasoning.

Parts III and IV of this volume address the question of whether people have abstract rules for deductive reasoning. More than 20 years ago, Wason and Johnson-Laird raised the possibility that people do not have deductive rules, at least not in a form that makes contact with everyday problems. They asked their subjects to perform a simple task. The subjects were shown four cards reading A, B, 4 and 7. Subjects were informed that the cards had letters on one side and numbers on the other and were directed to turn over as many cards, and only as many, as were necessary to find out whether the rule, "If a card has an A on one side, then it has a 4 on the other" is violated. Interpreting the "if-then" connective as the material conditional in standard logic, the correct answer in this example is to turn over the cards showing A and 7. The rule used in such problems is a conditional statement, "if p then q," and the relevant cases are p (because if p is the case it must be established that q is also the case) and not-q (because if it is not the case that q it must be established that it is also not the case that p). Fewer than 10% of college students can solve such problems. Yet, solving it merely requires the application of the material conditional—the cornerstone of standard logics.

Over the past two decades, many people have tried their hand at resolving the so-called *selection task* conundrum. The one favored in this book follows the lead of Cheng and Holyoak (1985), who proposed that people probably make little if any use of the rules of formal logic, certainly not of modus tollens (which states the equivalence of "if p then q" to "if not-q then not-p" and which is required to solve the abstract version of the selection task problem). What people do have are "pragmatic reasoning schemas"—highly generalized, domain-independent, but not purely syntactic rule systems. Such schemas include Piaget's formal operations such as the probability schema or the law of large numbers and generalized rule systems for analyzing causality (Kelley 1972, 1973). Cheng and Holyoak (1985) and Cheng and her colleagues in the present volume have argued that similar pragmatic reasoning schemas govern contractual relations such as permission and obligation. Thus the obligation schema ("if p occurs, one is obliged to do q") implies that one would have a violation in two of four possible cases: p occurs but q is not carried out and q is not carried out even though p occurred. These authors find that simply invoking the semantic notion of obligation allows people to solve with ease problems formally identical to the selection task. Moreover, formal instruction in how to solve contractual-schema problems is highly effective while instruction in formal logic is of no use for such problems.

The two chapters in Part IV try to extend the notion of pragmatic reasoning schemas to the case of rules for causality. Though Kelley proposed the existence of such schemas and many theorists have taken it for granted that they exist, rigorous evidence in support of such schemas has not been provided. Cheng and Nisbett (see Chap. 8) find some evidence that deductive reasoning about causal relations is influenced by pragmatic considerations concerning expectations about the relative probability of an effect given that a cause is or is not present. Morris and Nisbett (see chap. 10) find that graduate instruction in psychology, which emphasizes assessment of causality, improves students' ability to reason deductively about causal relations. Instruction in other graduate fields has little or no effect on students' ability to reason about causal relations. This suggests that deductive rules specifically governing causal relations exist and can be formally taught. Taken together, the two sets of studies suggest that, when deductive reasoning centers on specifically causal relations, specifically causal rules are invoked. These rules are highly abstract, in that they are completely independent of domain, but they are not as abstract as the rules of formal logic which are indifferent not merely to type of entities under consideration but to type of relationship.

Part V of this volume deals with rules for choice. Economists have long argued that all choice makes use of cost-benefit rules, which require people to assess values of possible outcomes as well as their probabilities, to note "opportunity costs" of their behavior (i.e., value lost by continuing a course of action rather than switching) and to ignore "sunk costs" (i.e., never to carry out some action simply because value has already been expended — tickets bought, etc.). Psychologists are of course quite predisposed to doubt the existence of such an abstract rule system. Moreover, many clever psychologists from Herbert Simon to Kahneman and Tversky have found it easy to show that people's choices often depart grossly from those that would be dictated by an application of cost-benefit rules.

Nevertheless, I present evidence here that people do possess a version of cost-benefit rules. It is just that, as with the law of large numbers, the rule system they possess merely overlaps with the formal, prescriptive one and is not identical to it. Indeed, people can be shown to endorse, and even to articulate spontaneously, a choice rule that is diametrically opposed to the sunk-cost rule. However, as with the other pragmatically useful rule systems discussed in this volume, cost-benefit rules can be taught. When they are, people subsequently reason differently about a huge range of choice problems. Economists make different choices than do biologists, undergraduates who have taken a course in economics reason differently than do those who have not, and even a brief session of teaching the sunk-cost rule causes people to make very different choices than those who have not had such training.

Part V also presents evidence that people are better off using the microeconomic rules of choice, a claim made from the beginning by economists but never tested by them. Professors who are more likely to apply the microeconomic rules of choice in their daily lives make more money than those who are less likely to apply them. I believe this is the case because sound choice principles make people more effective in their work, which is recognized by their higher salaries. Similarly, college students who are more likely to apply the microeconomic rules of choice have higher grade point averages than those who are less likely to apply them. This is not the case simply because brighter students are both more likely to know and use the rules and to get higher grade point averages. The relation between rule use and Grade Point Average is actually higher when intelligence (verbal Scholastic Aptitude Test) is partialled out of the relationship. Use of the microeconomic rules is thus associated with overachievement.

Part VI spells out the implications of the research for higher education. Twenty-five hundred years ago, Plato enunciated the educational doctrine that held sway in the west until this century. This was the view that instruction in formal rule systems improved people's ability to reason. "Even the dull," he said, "if they have had an arithmetical training . . . always become much quicker than they would otherwise have been" (cited in Jowett, 1875, p. 785). The Romans added the study of grammar to the study of arithmetic and geometry; the medieval scholastics added the syllogism and the humanists added the study of Latin and Greek, and this formed the core of the curriculum until well into the nineteenth century. The rationale was Plato's "formal discipline" theory: The study of abstract rules improves reasoning.

The first policy victory of modern psychology was to destroy the intellectual basis for the classical curriculum. William James mocked the theory as recommending mere exercise for the nonexistent "muscles of the mind." Thorndike's transfer-of-training findings provided all the empirical evidence that was needed against the notion that teaching one kind of rule in one kind of context with one kind of material could have the slightest effect in another context with another kind of material (and probably a different rule to boot).

The critique was entirely successful, and deserved to be. Learning Latin, in fact, probably does nothing for reasoning, arithmetic probably does nothing for any mental operations except the purely arithmetical, and even training in syllogisms probably does little good. Bertrand Russell (1960) had this to say of the syllogism:

> The inferences that we actually make in daily life differ from those of syllogistic logic in two respects, namely, that they are important and precarious, instead of being trivial and safe. The syllogism may be regarded as a monument to academic timidity: if an inference might be wrong, it was dangerous to draw it. So the medieval monks, in their thinking as in their lives, sought safety at the expense of fertility. (p. 83)

So the behaviorists probably were throwing out bathwater when they insisted that there was no general inferential benefit of much consequence from study of the classical curriculum. But there was also a baby in that bathwater, a baby unknown to pedagogues of yore, from Plato onward, but a baby nonetheless. That baby was the set of all pragmatically useful inferential rule systems whose use can be increased by explicit instruction. What rules are in that set? We don't know them all yet, but we can certainly identify some: the law of large numbers, the confounded-variable principle, causal schemas, social contract schemas, and cost-benefit rules of choice.

What we know about this list of rules is fairly impressive and more than justifies their inclusion in the curriculum:

1. People can make better inferences if they know these rules than if they don't.
2. Some people have a better grasp of each of these rules than others.
3. Everyone's grasp of these rules can be improved by instruction. Different graduate courses, and even different undergraduate majors, emphasize certain of these rule systems, and change students' inferential behavior differentially.
4. The instruction can be relatively economical. Perhaps precisely because of the abstract nature of these rules, abstract instruction is effective by itself.
5. Notwithstanding their abstract nature, the rules can be made more accessible by teaching examples of their use, and especially by teaching people how to decode the world in ways that make it more accessible to the rule system.
6. We can do a much better job of teaching these rule systems than we do.

Statistics is taught to most people, in most courses, as if the instructor were determined to prevent its escape from the narrow world of formal data analysis. Examples are restricted if at all possible to IQ tests and agricultural plots. To a greater or lesser extent, the same is true of most of the other pragmatically useful rule systems; when they are taught at all they are taught with little imagination or sense of conviction about their general relevance. I believe that we have only begun to scratch the surface both of the number of pragmatically useful rule systems that can be taught and the means by which they can be most effectively taught.

Finally, Part VII brings home the relevance of the work to the field of cognitive science. In a word, it is a mistake, at this date, to try to found a theory of mental life on mere associations or connections between concretely-defined elements. Organisms make use of rules of some generality; humans at least make use of highly abstract rules that are completely independent of any particular domain of events. Beyond that, new rules are incorporated gracefully into pre-existing systems of rules, something that is difficult to achieve even with most rule-based artificial-intelligence models, especially when, as this book shows to be empirically the case, those rules are inserted from the top rather than "grown" from the bottom. Holland, Holyoak, Nisbett, and Thagard (1986) presented a sketch of a system that gracefully accepts new rules. Somewhat ironically, the systems return to old devices of reinforcement characteristic of behaviorist models in attempting to account for rule modification. Whether this is the best route to go, I don't pretend to know. But any artificial intelligence model that purports to rest on a realistic theory of mind will have to deal with the facts presented in this book: highly general rules exist, and can even be inserted in top–down and highly abstract fashion.

REFERENCES

Cheng, P. W., & Holyoak, K. J. (1985). Pragmatic reasoning schemas. *Cognitive Psychology, 17,* 391–416.

Cohen, L. J. (1981). Can human irrationality be experimentally demonstrated? *Behavioral and Brain Sciences, 4,* 317–331.

Holland, J. H., Holyoak, K. J., Nisbett, R. E., & Thagard, P. T. (1986). *Induction: Processes of inference, learning, and discovery.* Cambridge, MA: Bradford Books/The MIT Press.

Jowett, B. (1875). (Ed.) *The dialogues of Plato,* Oxford: Oxford University Press.

Kahneman, D. & Tversky, A. (1972). Subjective probability: a judgment of representativeness. *Cognitive Psychology, 3,* 237–251.

Kelley, H. H. (1972). Causal schemata and the attribution process. In E. E. Jones, D. E. Kanouse, H. H. Kelley, R. E. Nisbett, S. Valins, & B. Weiner (Eds.), *Attribution: Perceiving the causes of behavior.* Morristown, NJ: General Learning Press.

Kelley, H. H. (1973). The process of causal attribution. *American Psychologist, 28,* 107–128.

Newell, A. (1980). One final word. In D. T. Tuma & F. Reif (Eds.), *Problem solving and education: Issues in teaching and research.* Hillsdale, N.J.: Lawrence Erlbaum.

Russell, B. (1960). *An outline of philosophy.* New York: Meridian.

ESTABLISHING THE EXISTENCE OF RULES FOR REASONING

2 The Use of Statistical Heuristics in Everyday Inductive Reasoning

Richard E. Nisbett
University of Michigan

David H. Krantz
Bell Laboratories

Christopher Jepson
Ziva Kunda
University of Michigan

It can be argued that inductive reasoning is our most important and ubiquitous problem-solving activity. Concept formation, generalization from instances, and prediction are all examples of inductive reasoning, that is, of passing from particular propositions to more general ones or of passing from particular propositions to other particular propositions via more general ones.

Inductive reasoning, to be correct, must satisfy certain statistical principles. Concepts should be discerned and applied with more confidence when they apply to a narrow range of clearly defined objects than when they apply to a broad range of diverse and loosely defined objects that can be confused with objects to which the concept does not apply. Generalizations should be more confident when they are based on a larger number of instances, when the instances are an unbiased sample, and when the instances in question concern events of low variability rather than high variability. Predictions should be more confident when there is high correlation between the dimensions for which information is available and the dimensions about which the prediction is made, and, failing such a correlation, predictions should rely on the base rate or prior distribution for the events to be predicted.

Because inductive reasoning tasks are so basic, it is disturbing to learn that the heuristics people use in such tasks do not respect the required statistical principles. The seminal work of Kahneman and Tversky has shown that this is so and, also, that people consequently overlook statistical variables such as sample size, correlation, and base rate when they solve inductive reasoning problems. (See surveys by Einhorn & Hogarth, 1981; Hogarth, 1980; Kahneman, Slovic, & Tversky, 1982; Nisbett & Ross, 1980.)

The above research on *nonstatistical heuristics* has been criticized on several grounds. Some critics have maintained that evolution should be expected to produce highly efficacious and generally correct principles of reasoning and that the research may therefore be misleading in some way (Cohen, 1979; Dennett, 1978, 1981, Note 1; Lycan, 1981). Others have maintained that the research does not demonstrate that people fail to apply correct inferential rules but rather that (a) it is the researchers themselves who are mistaken about the correct inferential rules (Cohen, 1981), (b) subjects have been misled by illusionary circumstances of little general significance beyond the laboratory (Cohen, 1981; Lopes, 1982; Dennett, Note 1), or (c) people's general inferential goals are such that at least some violations of statistical principles should be regarded as a form of *satisficing,* or cost-effective inferential shortcuts (Einhorn & Hogarth, 1981; Miller & Cantor, 1982; Nisbett & Ross, 1980).

We offer a different perspective on the incorporation of statistical principles into inductive reasoning, one that rejects the preceding criticisms but is, at the same time, fairly sanguine about people's statistical reasoning. Workers in the Kahneman and Tversky tradition have focused primarily on (a) establishing that people fail to respond to important statistical variables for a wide range of problems and (b) examining the inferential principles that people seem to rely on in solving such problems. There has been no comparable systematic effort to determine whether people do respond to statistical variables, either for problems that are easier than those examined to date or for problems of a different kind than those examined.

If it could be shown that people sometimes do reason using explicitly statistical principles, then the work to date on inductive reasoning, and the criticism of that work, would be cast in a different light. Rather than asking why the failures occur or whether the failures are real, it would seem more fruitful to ask questions such as the following. What factors encourage statistical reasoning and what factors discourage it? For what kinds of events and for what kinds of problems is statistical reasoning most likely to be used? Does purely formal training modify the untutored heuristics of everyday inductive reasoning? In addition, accusations that the work to date rests on a kind of experimental sleight of hand or that people are deliberately and advisedly setting aside statistical principles in favor of quicker and generally satisfactory procedures would seem less plausible. Instead, it would seem more likely that there are just difficulties — surprisingly severe difficulties to be sure, but difficulties merely — in people's use of statistical principles for inductive reasoning.

In this article we first summarize the recent work establishing failures to reason statistically. We then review anecdotal and experimental evidence indicating that people do sometimes reason statistically. Next we present original experimental work indicating some of the factors that influence statistical reasoning. Then we summarize research suggesting that people's ability to reason statistically about everyday life problems is affected by training in formal statistics. Finally, we speculate on the normative implications of people's ability and trainability for statistical reasoning.

STATISTICAL PROBLEMS AND NONSTATISTICAL HEURISTICS

In a succession of studies over the past decade, Kahneman and Tversky have shown that much inductive reasoning is nonstatistical. People often solve inductive problems by use of a variety of intuitive heuristics—rapid and more or less automatic judgmental rules of thumb. These include the representativeness heuristic (Kahneman & Tversky, 1972, 1973), the availability heuristic (Tversky & Kahneman, 1973), the anchoring heuristic (Tversky & Kahneman, 1974), and the simulation heuristic (Kahneman & Tversky, 1982). In problems where these heuristics diverge from the correct statistical approach, people commit serious errors of inference.

The representativeness heuristic is the best studied and probably the most important of the heuristics. People often rely on this heuristic when making likelihood judgments, for example, the likelihood that Object A belongs to Class B or the likelihood that Event A originates from Process B. Use of the heuristic entails basing such judgments on "the degree to which A is representative of B, that is, by the degree to which A resembles B" (Tversky & Kahneman, 1974, p. 1124). In one problem, for example, Kahneman and Tversky (1972) asked subjects whether days with 60% or more male births would be more common at a hospital with 15 births per day, or at a hospital with 45 births per day, or equally common at the two hospitals. Most subjects chose the latter alternative, and the remainder divided about evenly between 15 and 45. The law of large numbers requires that, with a random variable such as sex of infant, deviant sample percentages should be less common as sample size increases. The representativeness heuristic, however, leads subjects to compare the similarities of the two sample proportions to the presumed population proportion (50%); because the two sample proportions equally resemble the population proportion, they are deemed equally likely. The data indicate that, for this problem at least, most subjects used the representativeness heuristic and very few subjects used the law of large numbers.

In another demonstration, Kahneman and Tversky (1973) studied the prediction of an outcome for a target person based on various characteristics of that person or based on scores from various predictor tests. Subjects used the representativeness heuristic: In general, they predicted whichever outcome was most similar to the target person's characteristics or scores.

For instance, in predicting the grade point average (GPA) for a target person who is in the 90th percentile on a predictor test, about the same results are obtained — that is, prediction of a GPA well above average — whether the predictor is the score on a test of sense of humor (which subjects do not regard as very diagnostic of GPA), the score on a test of mental concentration, or the GPA itself (!). Such predictions diverge from those that would be obtained from statistical considerations in which the average accuracy of prediction would be taken into account. Subjects do not seem to realize that if accuracy is very limited, then it is far more probable that the target person's outcome will be equal to the modal outcome (or near the mean of the unimodal symmetric distribution) than that it will take some relatively unusual value that happens to match the characteristics on the predictor. This is the statistical principle of regression to the mean, or base rate.

Other investigations have confirmed and expanded the list of statistical failings documented by Kahneman and Tversky. The failings seem particularly clear and particularly important in people's reasoning about social behavior. Nisbett and Borgida (1975), for example, showed that consensus information, that is, base rate information about the behavior of a sample of people in a given situation, often has little effect on subjects' attributions about the causes of a particular target individual's behavior. When told that most people behaved in the same way as the target, subjects shift little or not at all in the direction of assuming that it was situational forces, rather than the target's personal dispositions or traits, that explain the target's behavior. In a typical experiment, Nisbett and Borgida (1975) told subjects about a study in which participants heard someone (whom the participants believed to be in a nearby room) having what seemed to be an epileptic seizure. Subjects' predictions about whether a particular participant would quickly help the "victim" were unaffected by the knowledge that most participants never helped or helped only after a long delay. Similarly, subjects' causal attributions about the behavior of a participant who never helped the "victim" were unaffected by consensus information. Subjects were just as likely to say that the participant's personality was responsible for his behavior when they knew that most other participants were similarly unhelpful as when they assumed that most other participants helped with alacrity.

Nisbett and Ross (1980) maintained that people fail to apply necessary statistical principles to a very wide range of social judgments. They claimed that people often make overconfident judgments about others based on small and unreliable amounts of information; they are often insensitive to the possibility that their samples of information about people may be highly biased; they are often poor at judging covariation between events of different classes (e.g., "Are redheads hot-tempered?"); and both their causal explanations for social events and their predictions of social outcomes are often little influenced by regression or base rate considerations.

STATISTICAL HEURISTICS

Selective Application of Statistical Reasoning

The foregoing work indicates that nonstatistical heuristics play an important role in inductive reasoning. But it does not establish that other heuristics, based on statistical concepts, are absent from people's judgmental repertoire. And indeed, if one begins to look for cases of good statistical intuitions in everyday problems, it is not hard to find some plausible candidates.

Even when judgments are based on the representativeness heuristic, there may be an underlying stratum of probabilistic thinking. In many of the problems studied by Kahneman and Tversky, people probably conceive of the underlying process as random, but they lack a means of making use of their intuitions about randomness and they fall back on representativeness. In the maternity ward problem, for example, people surely believe that the number of boys born on any particular day is a matter of chance, even though they rely on representativeness to generate their subjective sampling distributions. But consider the following thought experiment: If someone says, "I can't understand it; I have nine grandchildren and all of them are boys," the statement sounds quite sensible. The hearer is likely to agree that a causal explanation seems to be called for. On the other hand, imagine that the speaker says, "I can't understand it; I have three grandchildren and all of them are boys." Such a statement sounds peculiar, to say the least, because it seems transparent that such a result could be due just to chance — that is, there is nothing to understand. Such an intuition is properly regarded as statistical in our view.

The contrast between the statistical intuition in our anecdote and subjects' use of the representativeness heuristic in the maternity ward problem illustrates the selectivity with which people apply statistical concepts. The failure to do so in the maternity ward problem may be due to the use of "60%" in the problem, which evokes comparison between 60% and 50% and thence the dependence on the similarity judgment in choosing an answer. It may also be due to lack of concrete experience in thinking about samples in the range 15–45. As Piaget and Inhelder (1951/1975) put it, people seem to have an intuitive grasp of the "law of *small* large numbers," even though they may not generalize the intuition to large numbers.

People also seem to have an ability to use base rates for selected kinds of problems. Consider the concepts of *easy* and *difficult* examinations. People do not infer that a student is brilliant who received an A+ on an exam in which no one scored below A− nor that the student is in trouble who flunked a test that was also failed by 75% of the class. Rather, they convert the base rate information (performance of the class as a whole) into a location parameter for the examination (easy, . . ., difficult) and make their inference about the particular student in terms of the student's relative position compared to the difficulty of the exam. Indeed, laboratory evidence has been available for some time that base rates are readily utilized for causal attributions for many kinds of abilities and achievements (Weiner et al. 1972).

As Nisbett and Ross (1980) suggested, one suspects that many lay concepts and maxims reflect an appreciation of statistical principles. It seems possible, for example, that people sometimes overcome sample bias by applying proverbs such as "Don't judge a book by its cover" or "All that glitters is not gold." Perhaps people sometimes even manage to be regressive in everyday predictions by using concepts such as "beginner's luck" or "nowhere to go but up/down."

There is one inductive reasoning task in particular for which there is good reason to suspect that statistical intuitions are very frequently applied. This is *generalization from instances*—perhaps the simplest and most pervasive of everyday inductive tasks. People surely recognize, in many contexts at least, that when moving from particular observations to general propositions, more evidence is better than less. The preference for more evidence seems well understood as being due to an intuitive appreciation of the law of large numbers. For example, we think that most people would prefer to hold a 20-minute interview rather than a 5-minute interview with a prospective employee and that if questioned they would justify this preference by saying that 5 minutes is too short a period to get an accurate idea of what the job candidate is like. That is, they believe that there is a greater chance of substantial error with the smaller sample. Similarly, most people would believe the result of a survey of 100 people more than they would believe that of a survey of 10 people; again, their reason would be based on the law of large numbers.

As we shall see, there is reason to believe that people's statistical understanding of the generalization task is deeper still. People understand, at least in some contexts, that the law of large numbers must be taken into account to the degree that the events in question are uncertain and variable in a statistical sense. Thus they realize that some classes of events are very heterogeneous; that is, the events differ from one another, or from one occasion to another, in ways that are unpredictable, and it is these classes of events for which a large sample is particularly essential.

Randomizing Devices and the Ontogeny of Statistical Reasoning

Where do people's selective statistical intuitions come from? An extremely important series of studies by Piaget and Inhelder (1951/1975) suggests that the intuitions may arise in part from people's understanding of the behavior of random generating devices. Statistical reasoning is of course very commonly applied in our culture to the behavior of such mechanisms. Piaget and Inhelder showed that statistical intuitions about random devices develop at an early age. They conducted experiments in which children were shown various random generating devices and then were asked questions about them. The devices included different-colored marbles on a tilt board, coin tosses, card draws, a spinner, and balls dropped through a funnel into a box with a varying number of slots. Children were shown the operation of these devices and then were asked to predict outcomes of the next operation or set of operations and to explain why particular outcomes had occurred or could or could not occur. The work showed that even children less than 10 years old used the concept of chance and understood the importance of sequences of repeated trials.

In one study, for example, Piaget and Inhelder (1951/1975) spun a pointer that could stop on one of eight different-colored locations. The young children they studied (in general, those less than 7 years old) did not initially recognize their complete inability to predict the pointer's stopping place.

> He knows quite well that he is not likely to be able to predict the color on which the bar will stop, but he does believe in the legitimacy of such a prediction and tries to guess the result. . . . The child oscillates quickly between two solutions. . . . Either the bar will have the tendency to come back to a color on which it has already stopped, or it will, on the contrary, stop on the colors not yet touched (p. 61).

At this stage the children did not recognize the equivalent chances of the various stopping places, and when the pointer was made to stop at one color repeatedly (by using a magnet) they found nothing unusual in this. A satisfactory causal explanation usually was forthcoming: for example, "the pointer got tired."

By around the age of 7, the Piaget and Inhelder subjects began to understand the chance nature of the pointer's behavior. After a few demonstrations, they quickly came to doubt the predictability of single trials and came to see the distribution of possibilities and their equivalence. Between the ages of 7 and 10, their subjects came to understand the importance of repeated trials and long run outcomes.

E: If I spun it ten or twenty times, could there be one color at which it never stopped?

S: (age 7): Yes, that could happen. That would happen more often if we did it only ten times rather than twenty (p. 75).

E: Will it hit all the colors or not?

S: (age 10 years, 7 months): It depends on how long we spin it.

E: Why?

S: Because if we spin it often, it will have more chances of going everywhere (p. 89).

How does the child come to have an understanding of the concept of chance during this period? Piaget and Inhelder argue that *the child's understanding of uncertainty grows out of the child's understanding of physical causality.* To the very young child with little understanding of the causal mechanisms that produce outcomes in a physical system, every outcome is a "miracle" — that is, unanticipated — and, paradoxically, once the outcome has occurred, the child believes that it can be explained. As the child comes to understand, in terms of concrete operations, the causal mechanisms that produce outcomes, the child begins to recognize which sorts of outcomes are predictable (and explainable) and which are not. The outcomes that are not predictable are gradually understood to obey certain *non-causal rules.* In particular, the child comes to recognize some cases of the law of large numbers, for example, that the likelihood of any given outcome occurring is greater with a large number of trials than with a smaller number.

By the age of 11 or so, many children have — in addition to a clear conception both of fully deterministic systems and of random generating devices — a good understanding of non-uniform probability distributions. These are partially random systems in which causal factors are at work making some of the possible outcomes more likely than others. The child comes to learn that even though individual events are uncertain in such a system, aggregate events may be highly predictable. In such a probabilistic system, the child grasps the relevance to prediction of the base rate, that is, the distribution and relative frequency of the various outcomes.

This latter point is well illustrated by children's understanding of a device that allows balls to be dropped through a hole into one of a number of slots or bins beneath. Here the chances of a ball dropping into one slot versus another can be made quite unequal by the physical set-up. It is easy to build the device, for example, so that most balls drop into middle bins and fewer drop in the side bins, generating a crude bell curve. Children under 7 generally fail to use this distribution as a basis of prediction. Although they slowly come to recognize that central positions will collect more balls than peripheral ones, they cannot generalize this fact from a box with a particular number of slots to another box with a different number; they do not expect symmetry between slots that are equidistant from the center; and they do not recognize the role of the law of large numbers in making the central slots particularly favored over a long series of trials. All of these intuitions, in contrast, come easily to many 12-year-olds.

We may speculate that the older child's statistical conceptualization of the behavior of randomizing devices serves as the basis for a similar conceptualization of other kinds of events that may be seen as variable and uncertain. We discuss later just what characterizes events where an analogy to randomizing devices can be seen versus those where it cannot be seen.

The Intellectual History of Statistical Reasoning

The cultural history of statistical reasoning appears to parallel in some interesting respects the developmental course described by Piaget and Inhelder (1951/1975). This history has been traced by Hacking in his book *The Emergence of Probability* (1975). Hacking points out that although random generating devices have been used at least since Biblical times, the modern concept of probability was invented rather suddenly in the 17th century. This was true despite the popularity of games of chance in antiquity and the existence of sophisticated mathematics. (Hacking notes that someone with only a modest knowledge of modern probability could have won all Gaul in a week!)

Paradoxically, the major factor underlying the sudden emergence of the modern concept of probability was the change to a deterministic understanding of the physical world. In the Renaissance, the task of science was understood not primarily as a search for the causal factors influencing events but as a search for signs as to the meaning of events. These signs were clues and portents strewn about by the benign Author of the Universe. This sort of understanding of events encouraged a heavy reliance on the representativeness heuristic. The Renaissance physician, for example, adhered to the *doctrine of signatures*. This was the "belief that every natural substance which possesses any medicinal virtue indicates by an obvious and well-marked external character the disease for which it is a remedy, or the object for which it should be employed" (John Paris, cited in Mill, 1843/1974, p. 766). The representativeness heuristic thus could be derived as a rule of inference from the principle that the Author of the Universe wanted to be helpful in our attempts to understand the world.

A quite different way of understanding events became predominant in the 17th century. This was a new "mechanistic attitude toward causation" (Hacking, 1975, p. 3). Just as the development of concrete operations helps the child to recognize the irreducible ignorance and uncertainty that is left as a residue after causal analysis of a randomizing device, so the new attitude toward causation helped 17th century scientists appreciate the nature of uncertainty in probabilistic systems. "Far from the 'mechanical' determinism precluding an investigation of chance, it was its accompaniment . . . this specific mode of determinism is essential to the formation of concepts of chance and probability" (Hacking, 1975, p. 3).

Summary

In short, there is good reason to believe that people possess *statistical heuristics* — intuitive, rule-of-thumb inferential procedures that resemble formal statistical procedures. People apply these heuristics to the behavior of random generating devices at a fairly early age. The formal understanding of statistical principles — that is, of the rules governing the behavior of randomizing devices — increases at least until adolescence. The use of such heuristics, both individually and culturally, seems related to the growth of causal understanding of the physical world and to attempts to extend this causal understanding, by analogy, to wider domains. Although we know little at present of the growth in the child's or adolescent's ability to apply statistical heuristics to events other than those produced by randomizing devices, it seems clear that such growth does take place. Adults who are untutored in formal statistics seem to reason statistically about a number of events other than those produced by randomizing machines — such as performance on tests, sports, weather, and accident and death risks. In addition, it is hard to imagine that people could conduct the most basic of inferential tasks, namely, generalization from instances, without the application of at least a rudimentary version of a law-of-large-numbers heuristic.

FACTORS THAT AFFECT STATISTICAL REASONING

Despite ontogenetic and historical growth in the ability to reason statistically, contemporary adults do not reason statistically about a wide range of problems and event domains that require such reasoning, and they often do not do so even if they have substantial training in formal statistics (Tversky & Kahneman, 1971). Why is this? What factors make it difficult to apply statistical heuristics when these are required, and what factors can make it easier? Three factors that seem important are implicit in the preceding discussion.

Clarity of the Sample Space and the Sampling Process

Randomizing devices are usually designed so that the sample space for a single trial is obvious and so that the repeatability of trials is salient. The die has six faces and can be tossed again and again; the pointer can stop on any of eight sectors and can be spun over and over. Clarity of sample space makes it easier to see what knowledge is relevant. For randomizing devices, the most relevant knowledge is often just the observation of symmetry of the different die faces, spinner sectors, and so forth. The salience of repeatability makes it easier to conceptualize one's observations as a sample.

In the social domain, sample spaces are often obscure, and repeatability is hard to imagine. For example, the sample space consisting of different degrees of helpfulness that might be displayed by a particular person in a particular situation is quite obscure, and the notion of repetition is strained. What is it that could be repeated? Placing the same person in *different* situations? Or *other* people in the same situation? The probability that Person P will exhibit Behavior B in Situation S is abstract and not part of the inductive repertoire of most people most of the time. Even though people recognize the possibility of errors in their judgments of social situations, they do not try to construct probability models; rather, they rely on the representativeness heuristic.

Recognition of the Operation of Chance Factors

A second major factor encouraging the use of statistical heuristics is the recognition of the role of chance in producing events in a given domain or in a particular situation. We have already seen how Piaget and Inhelder (1951/1975) describe the recognition of chance in the operation of randomizing devices. The child comes to recognize the limitations of causal analysis for a spinner and the consequent residual uncertainty about the production of events. Something like the same transparent indeterminism exists for other sorts of events as well, even those involving human beings. For example, statistical understanding of some types of sports is undoubtedly facilitated by the manifestly random component in the movement of the objects employed: "A football can take funny bounces." The random component probably does not have to be physical in order for people to recognize it. It is possible to recognize the unpredictability of academic test performance by repeated observations of one's own outcomes. Even with one's own efforts and the group against which one is competing held constant, outcomes can vary. One may even recognize that one's performance on particular occasions was particularly good or poor because of accidents: "I just happened to reread that section because Jill never called me back"; "It was very noisy in the study area that night so I didn't get a chance to review my notes."

In contrast, cues as to randomness in the production of events are much subtler for other kinds of events, especially for many social ones. When we interview someone, what signs would let us know that a particular topic got explored just by chance or that the person seems dour and lackluster because of an uncharacteristic attempt to appear dignified rather than because of a phlegmatic disposition? In addition, as Einhorn and Hogarth (1978) have pointed out, the gatekeeping function of the interview may serve to prevent us from recognizing the error variance in our judgments: The great talent of some people not hired or admitted may never be observed. Daniel Kahneman (Note 2) has suggested to us that the "interview illusion" exists in part because we expect that brief encounters with a living, breathing person ought to provide a "hologram" of that person rather than merely a sample of the person's attributes and behaviors. In most situations, cues as to the fact that an interview ought to be regarded as a sample from a population, rather than a portrait in miniature, are missing. The same may be true for visits to a city, country, or university. One of us long believed that reports of raininess in England were greatly exaggerated because he once stayed in London for 10 days and it only drizzled twice!

Cultural Prescriptions

A third factor that may contribute to the use of statistical heuristics is a cultural or subcultural prescription to reason statistically about events of a given kind. Although Piaget and Inhelder focused on developmental changes in the ability to reason statistically about randomizing devices, from a historical perspective it is the young child's ability to reason statistically at all about such devices that is remarkable. It seems implausible that a medieval European child would have reasoned in such a sophisticated way as the Piaget and Inhelder subjects. Statistical reasoning is the culturally prescribed way to think about randomizing devices in our culture, and this general approach undoubtedly trickles down to children. Similarly, statistical reasoning has become (or is becoming) the norm for experts in many fields — from insurance to medical diagnosis — and is rapidly becoming normative for the lay novice as well in such domains as sports and the weather. Models of statistical reasoning abound for sports in particular, as the two examples below indicate.

> Baseball's law of averages is nothing more than an acknowledgement that players level off from season to season to their true ability — reflected by their lifetime averages. A .250-hitter may hit .200 or .300 over a given period of time but baseball history shows he will eventually level off at his own ability ("Law of Averages," 1981).

> The musky tends to be a deep water fish. Most fishing success is in shallow water, but . . . this misleading statistic [is probably accounted for in part by the fact that] sheer statistical chance dictates that fish will come from the waters receiving the most man hours of fishing pressure. Shallow water fishing for muskies is very popular, and very few fishermen work them deep (Hamer, 1981).

The statistical spirit embodied in these quotations reaches many fans. Thus, it is commonplace to hear lay people endorse the proposition that "On a given Sunday any team in the NFL can beat any other team." (Compare with "On a given Sunday, any parishioner's altruism can exceed that of any other parishioner"!)

In our view, these three factors — clarity of the sample space and the sampling process, recognition of the role of chance in producing events, and cultural prescriptions to think statistically — operate individually and, perhaps more often, together to increase people's tendencies to apply statistical heuristics to problems that require a statistical approach. If these factors are genuinely important determinants of people's ability to reason statistically, then it should be possible to find support for the following predictions.

In cases where the sample space is clear and the possibility of repetition is salient, people will respond appropriately to statistical variables. In particular, in the task of generalizing from instances, where the sample space is a clear dichotomy and the sampling process is just the observation of more members of a clearly defined population, (a) people will generalize more cautiously when the sample size is small and when they have no strong prior belief that the sampled population is homogeneous, and (b) people can be influenced to generalize more or less readily by manipulations that emphasize the homogeneity or heterogeneity of the sampled population.

The following predictions should hold both for generalization and for other, more complex, inferential tasks: (a) Manipulations designed to encourage recognition of the chance factors influencing events should serve to increase statistical reasoning. (b) People who are highly knowledgeable about events of a given kind should be more inclined than less knowledgeable people to apply statistical reasoning to the events — because both the distributions of the events and the chance factors influencing the events should be clearer to such people. (c) People should be disinclined to reason statistically about certain kinds of events that they recognize to be highly variable and uncertain — notably social events — because the sample spaces for the events and the chance factors influencing the events are opaque. (d) Training in statistics should promote statistical reasoning even about mundane events of everyday life because such training should help people to construct distributional models for events and help them to recognize "error," or the chance factors influencing events.

Generalizing From Instances

Generalization from observed cases is the classic concern of philosophers and other thinkers who are interested in induction. A number of instances of Class A are observed, and each of them turns out to have Property B. Possible inferences include the universal generalization *all A's have B,* or the near universal *most A's have B,* or at least the relinquishing of the contrary generalization, namely, *most A's do not have B.*

The untrammeled employment of the representativeness heuristic would lead people to make the above inferences from quite small numbers of instances, and, indeed, this is often found, both anecdotally and in laboratory studies (Nisbett & Ross, 1980, pp. 77–82). On the other hand, philosophers since Hume have puzzled about how these generalizations can be logically justified, even when very large numbers of instances are observed. The puzzle has been compounded by the fact that sometimes it seems correct to generalize confidently from a few instances. Hume (1748/1955) wrote, "[Often, when] I have found that . . . an object has always been attended with . . . an effect . . . I foresee that other objects which are in appearance similar will be attended with similar effects" (p. 48). The problem is that only sometimes do we draw such a conclusion with confidence. "Nothing so like as eggs, yet no one, on account of this appearing similarity, expects the same taste and relish in all of them" (p. 50). Mill (1843/1974), a century later, phrased the problem like this: "Why is a single instance, in some cases, sufficient for a complete induction, while in others myriads of concurring instances, without a single exception known or presumed, go such a very little way towards establishing a universal proposition?" (p. 314).

The statistical advances since Mill's time make it clear that a large part of the answer to his question has to do with beliefs about the variability or *homogeneity* of certain kinds or classes of events (cf. Thagard & Nisbett, 1982). Generalization from a large sample is justified in terms of one's beliefs that the sampling itself is homogeneous (i.e., that the distribution of possible sample statistics is the same as would be predicted by random sampling). And generalization from a small sample or resistance to generalization, even from a large sample, are justified in terms of prior beliefs about the homogeneity or heterogeneity of objects or events of a certain kind with respect to a property of a certain kind. If, for example, the object is one of the chemical elements and the property is electrical conductivity, then one expects homogeneity: All samples of the element conduct electricity or none do. But if the object is an animal and the property is blueness, one's prior belief does not favor homogeneity so strongly; color may or may not vary within a particular species.

In other words, there are cases where use of the representativeness heuristic is justified in terms of beliefs about homogeneity, which in turn may be soundly based on individually or culturally acquired experience with kinds of objects and kinds of properties. For other cases, simple representativeness cannot be justified, and there are indeed cases, as Mill claimed, in which a strong prior belief in *heterogeneity* properly prevents acceptance of a generalization even after quite large numbers of instances have been observed.

We attempted to demonstrate, in a laboratory study of judgment, that people do in fact temper the use of representativeness to a greater or lesser degree depending on beliefs about the variability of a kind of object with respect to a kind of property.

Study 1: Beliefs About Homogeneity and Reliance on the Law of Large Numbers

In this study, we simply guessed at the prevailing beliefs about homogeneity. We tried to obtain different degrees of heterogeneity by using conductivity of metals, colors of animals, and so on. Subjects were told of one instance or of several instances of a sampled object having a particular property and were asked to guess what percentage of the population of all such objects would have the property. The sample sizes used were 1, 3, or 20; in the latter cases, all 3 or all 20 of the objects had the property in question. We anticipated that subjects would generalize more readily from a given number of instances when the kind of object was perceived as homogeneous with respect to the kind of property than when the kind of object was perceived as heterogeneous with respect to the kind of property.

Method

Subjects were 46 University of Michigan students of both sexes who were enrolled in introductory psychology. (As sex did not affect any of the dependent variables in this or any of the other studies, it will not be discussed further.) Eighty-five percent of the subjects had taken no statistics courses in college. The questionnaire was presented as one of several in a study on judgment. It read as follows for the $N = 1$ condition:

> Imagine that you are an explorer who has landed on a little known island in the Southeastern Pacific. You encounter several new animals, people, and objects. You observe the properties of your "samples" and you need to make guesses about how common these properties would be in other animals, people or objects of the same type.
>
> Suppose you encounter a new bird, the shreeble. It is blue in color. What percent of all shreebles on the island do you expect to be blue?

(This and the subsequent questions were followed by

> "___ percent. Why did you guess this percent?")
>
> Suppose the shreeble you encounter is found to nest in a eucalyptus tree, a type of tree which is fairly common on the island. What percent of all shreebles on the island do you expect to nest in eucalyptus trees?

Suppose you encounter a native, who is a member of a tribe he calls the Barratos. He is obese. What percent of the male Barratos do you expect to be obese?

Suppose the Barratos man is brown in color. What percent of male Barratos do you expect to be brown (as opposed to red, yellow, black or white)?

Suppose you encounter what the physicist on your expedition describes as an extremely rare element called floridium. Upon being heated to a very high temperature, it burns with a green flame. What percent of all samples of floridium found on the island do you expect to burn with a green flame?

Suppose the sample of floridium, when drawn into a filament, is found to conduct electricity. What percent of all samples of floridium found on the island do you expect to conduct electricity?

The questionnaires for the $N = 3$ condition and the $N = 20$ condition were identical except that they specified larger samples of each object. For example, the first shreeble item for the $N = 3$ condition read as follows:

Suppose you encounter a new bird, the shreeble. You see three such birds. They are all blue in color. What percent of all shreebles on the island do you expect to be blue?

The reasons subjects gave for guessing as they did were coded as to their content. There were three basic sorts of answers: (a) references to the homogeneity of the kind of object with respect to the kind of property, (b) references to the heterogeneity of the kind of object with respect to the kind of property—due to the different properties of subkinds (e.g., male vs. female), to some causal mechanism producing different properties (e.g., genetic mistakes), or to purely statistical variability (e.g., "where birds nest is sometimes just a matter of chance"), and (c) other sorts of answers that were mostly based on representativeness or that were mere tautologies. Two independent coders achieved 89% exact agreement on coding category.

Results

Any one element is presumed by scientists to be homogeneous with respect to most properties. At the other extreme, most human groups are highly heterogenous among themselves in many attributes, including body weight. If educated lay people share these beliefs and if they reason statistically, then (a) they should exercise more caution in generalizing from single cases when heterogeneity is expected than when homogeneity is expected and (b) large N should be important primarily in the case of populations whom subjects believe to be heterogeneous with respect to the property in question.

Figure 2.1 presents subjects' estimates of the percentage of each population having the property associated with the sample as a function of sample size presented. It may be seen that subjects are quite willing to generalize from even a single instance of green-burning or electricity-conducting floridium and also from a single, brown, Barratos tribesman. The modal estimate for $N = 1$ (as well as for $N = 3$ and $N = 20$) in all of these cases is 100%. In contrast, generalizations are less extreme for even 20 instances of blue shreebles or eucalyptus-nesting shreebles or 20 obese Barratos. The $t(31)$ contrasting $N = 1$ for floridium attributes and Barratos color with $N = 20$ for shreeble attributes and Barratos obesity is 3.00; $p < .01$.[1]

Subjects' explanations for their estimates fully justify this pattern of inferences. It may be seen in Table 2.1 that subjects reported believing that elements are homogeneous with respect to color and conductivity and that tribes are homogeneous with respect to color. In contrast, subjects rarely expressed the belief that there is homogeneity for the other kinds of populations and properties and instead expressed belief in heterogeneity of

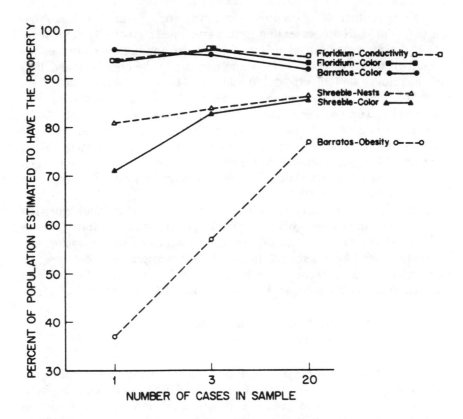

FIG. 2.1 Percentage of each population estimated to have the sample property as a function of number of cases in the sample.

TABLE 2.1
Number of Subjects Giving Each Type of Reason and Percentage of
Population Estimated to Have the Property

| Object and property | Reason | | | | | |
| | Homogeneity | | Tautology | | Heterogeneity | |
	n	%	n	%	n	%
Shreeble						
Color	6	95	17	83	22	75
Nests	8	96	19	84	19	78
Barratos						
Obesity	5	79	10	62	31	53
Color	31	98	7	94	8	80
Floridium						
Color	31	97	9	91	6	82
Conductivity	31	98	7	92	8	82

one sort or another for these objects and properties. Figure 2.1 shows that it is only for these latter cases that subjects reasoned statistically in the sense that they were more willing to assume that the population resembles the sample when N is larger. N affects the estimates of the obesity of Barratos and the color of shreebles ($p < .001$ and $p = .11$, respectively). In addition, a total of 10 subjects complained on one or more problems that the N was too small to give a good estimate. For nine of these subjects, the complaints were about one or more of the three problems where populations were presumed to be heterogeneous with respect to the property in question, whereas for only one subject was the complaint about a problem for which subjects in general believed populations to be homogeneous with respect to properties (exact $p = .02$).

Finally, an internal analysis of the Table 2.1 data for each question showed that those subjects who believed the population to be homogeneous with respect to the property estimated that a higher percentage of the population was like the sample than did those subjects who believed the population was heterogeneous with respect to the property. The lowest t resulting from the six comparisons yielded $p < .05$.

Study 2: Manipulating the Salience of Distribution Parameters

Study 1 established that people can apply statistical reasoning to one of the most basic of inferential tasks. It also established that beliefs about variability of the class of events in question can mediate the statistical reasoning. One other study in the literature made similar points. Quattrone and Jones (1980) proposed a version of the present view that beliefs about variability influence inductive generalizations in their important study on perception of ingroups versus outgroups. They hypothesized that "an observer's tendency to generalize from the behavior of a specific group member to the group as a whole is proportional to the observer's perception of the group's homogeneity" (p. 141). Because people are more familiar with the members of groups to which they happen to belong, they will recognize "the group's general variability, the extent to which its members . . . differ from one another when viewed over all dimensions" (p. 141). Because people are less familiar with outgroups, they are at liberty to assume that their members are relatively uniform. Thus people may generalize more readily from observations of the behavior of outgroup members than from observations of the behavior of ingroup members.

To test this hypothesis, Quattrone and Jones (1980) showed Princeton and Rutgers University undergraduates videotapes of male students who were allegedly serving as participants in psychology experiments. These students were asked to make choices such as to wait for a few minutes by themselves versus in the company of others or to listen to rock music versus classical music. Half of the subjects at each campus believed they were viewing Princeton men, and half believed they were viewing Rutgers men. After seeing the choice of one participant, subjects were asked to predict what the 100 participants in the study did. Quattrone and Jones found greater generalization from the participants' behavior to outgroup members than to ingroup members. Thus, Princeton subjects generalized more strongly to the behavior of the Rutgers population after observing the choice of the "Rutgers" participant than they did to the Princeton population after observing the choice of the "Princeton" participant.

If, as both we and Quattrone and Jones assume, generalizations about groups from the behavior of its members are mediated by assumptions about variability of group members, then it should be possible to manipulate those assumptions and therefore to influence the degree of generalization. People are inclined to think of (their own) university populations as being immensely variable—what with caftans here and exotic accents there, football players here and budding physicists there. In fact, however, university populations are not as heterogeneous as one might casually presume. Most students, even at multiversities, are, after all, bright young middle-class people of fairly homogeneous geographic and ethnic backgrounds. It seems possible that, if subjects were required to contemplate the central tendencies of their university populations before observing choice behavior like that presented to Quattrone and Jones's subjects, they might generalize more. This possibility was examined in Study 2.

Method

The procedure used by Quattrone and Jones (1980) was followed almost exactly, except that subjects were told that the videotapes were either of

University of Michigan or of Ohio State University students, and half of the subjects were exposed to a central-tendency manipulation before viewing the videotapes. Subjects were 115 University of Michigan undergraduates of both sexes enrolled in introductory psychology. They participated in small groups, seated around a table facing a .53-m (21-inch) video monitor. Subjects were told that the investigators were "studying how people make judgments about people—working from actual information they have about people to guesses about other aspects of people. One of our major interests is in how students perceive students at (their own/another) university."

At this point the central-tendency manipulation was delivered to experimental subjects, who were told that "we will be asking you several questions about students at (the University of Michigan/Ohio State University)" and were given the appropriate central-tendency questionnaire. Control subjects began viewing videotapes immediately.

The central-tendency questionnaire consisted of three questions that we expected would influence subjects' conceptions of the variability of a student population. Subjects were asked to "please list what you would guess to be the 10 most common majors at (the University of Michigan/Ohio State University)" and next to list the five most common ethnic group backgrounds and the five most common religious backgrounds at that university. Answering these questions might be expected to prompt subjects to recognize that the student body is not all that heterogeneous: Most students are, after all, white Protestants concentrated in a limited number of relatively popular majors.

Subjects viewed the Quattrone and Jones videotapes.[2] They were introduced as having been made during psychology experiments conducted at the University of Michigan or at Ohio State University. In each of the three tapes a male participant was shown being confronted with a decision, and he then chose one of two alternative behaviors offered. In the first scenario, a target person had to choose between waiting alone or waiting with other subjects while his experimenter fixed a machine. In the second scenario, the choice was between listening to classical music or listening to rock music during an experiment on auditory perceptual sensitivity. In the third scenario, the choice was between solving mathematical problems or solving verbal problems during an experiment on the effects of noise on intellectual performance. As the order in which scenarios were presented had no effect in the Quattrone and Jones study, it was held constant in our study.

The procedure was the same for each scenario. Subjects watched the target person being given instructions and being asked to make his decision. At this point the tape was turned off and subjects were asked to predict the target person's decision on a 21-point scale that had endpoints labeled with the two relevant options. The tape was then turned on again and subjects observed the participant make his decision. Half of the subjects saw the participants in the three scenarios make one set of decisions, and half saw the complementary set. Thus, subjects in Set A saw the target persons choose (a) to wait alone, (b) to listen to classical music, and (c) to solve mathematical problems. Subjects in Set B saw targets choose (a) to wait with others, (b) to listen to rock music, and (c) to solve verbal problems.

The dependent variable of interest consisted of the subjects' estimates of how many out of 100 participants in each of the three experiments chose each of the two options. (For the sole purpose of replication, subjects were also asked to indicate what they would have done and who they liked as people more — those who would prefer Option A or those who would prefer Option B.)

Results

Figure 2.2 presents subjects' generalizations about the University of Michigan and Ohio State University populations for control subjects and for subjects exposed to the central-tendency manipulation. *Generalization* is defined as the difference between population estimates for subjects presented with Set A choices versus those for subjects presented with Set B choices. The higher this index is, the more a group of subjects was influenced in their estimates by the behavior of the particular subject they witnessed. The index sums across all three types of choices, but the trends were the same for each of the three problems.

The difference between the control groups exposed to Ohio State

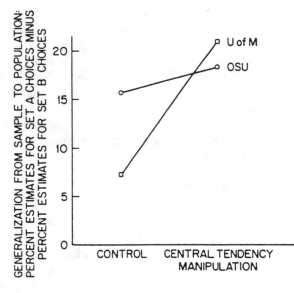

FIG. 2.2 Generalization from sample to population as a function of campus population and central-tendency manipulation. (U of M = University of Michigan; OSU = Ohio State University.)

University participants versus those exposed to University of Michigan participants provides a replication of the Quattrone and Jones finding. The magnitude of the difference is very similar to that found by them, though for our smaller sample it is only marginally significant, $F(1, 50) = 2.76$, $.05 < p < .10$).

The effect of the central-tendency manipulation was to increase the degree of generalization from the sample, $F(1, 107) = 4.23$, $p < .05$). It may be seen that the effect was largely due to the behavior of the University of Michigan group. This is not surprising because the judgments about the Ohio State students may have already incorporated central tendencies in the form of an outgroup stereotype. This explanation should be viewed with caution, however, inasmuch as the interaction failed to reach statistical significance.

Both findings provide support for the contention that concurrent representations of population variability mediate inductive generalizations. Familiarity with one's own group results in less willingness to generalize for them than for another group, although forced contemplation of central tendencies results in more willingness to generalize, at least for the familiar ingroup.

One other study, by Silka (1981), shows the importance for inductive reasoning of people's focus on variability versus central tendency. She asked subjects to examine a series of numerical values that were said to represent the mental health of several individuals. Some subjects were asked to remember the average of the values, and some were asked to remember the range. When subjects were asked, 1 week later, to assess the degree of change represented by a new value, subjects who had been asked to remember the average were more likely to infer that there had been a genuine change than those who had been asked to remember the range. The implication of Silka's finding, together with those of Study 2, is that inferences about continuity and change, and inductive reasoning generally, may be in part a function of arbitrary encoding and retrieval factors that accidentally emphasize either the homogeneity or the heterogeneity of events.

Study 3: Manipulating the Salience of Chance Factors

Study 2 establishes that manipulations of the salience of distributional parameters can influence subsequent generalizations. It should also be possible to influence generalizations by manipulating the salience of chance factors. One potentially interesting way of doing this would be to highlight for subjects the degree to which evidence about an object should properly be regarded as a sample from the population of the object's attributes. Such a reminder ought to prompt subjects to reason more statistically, deemphasizing evidence from smaller samples and placing greater weight on evidence from larger samples.

Borgida and Nisbett (1977) argued that people often ignore the judgments of others when choosing between two objects and substitute their own initial impressions of the objects as the sole basis of choice. People do this in part because they do not recognize the relevance of the law of large numbers when reasoning about events of the personal preference kind. When the objects are multifaceted and complex, however, the law of large numbers is applicable in two ways: (a) The reactions of other people to the object, especially if they are based on more extensive contact with the object than one has had oneself, generally should be a useful guide to choice (though, of course, it is possible to construct cases where other people's reactions would not be useful). (b) One's own experience with the object, especially if it is brief or superficial, may be a poor guide to choice because of the error that plagues any small samples, even those that happen to be our own.

It seemed likely that if people were made explicitly aware of the role of chance in determining the impression one may get from a small sample, they might place less faith in a small personal sample and more faith in a large sample based on other people's reactions.

Method

Subjects were 157 University of Michigan students of both sexes who were enrolled in introductory psychology classes. Eighty-seven percent had taken no statistics courses in college. Subjects participated in small groups. They were presented with two versions of the following problem.

David L. was a senior in high school on the East Coast who was planning to go to college. He had compiled an excellent record in high school and had been admitted to his two top choices: a small liberal arts college and an Ivy League university. David had several older friends who were attending the liberal arts college and several who were attending the Ivy League university. They were all excellent students like himself and had interests similar to his. The friends at the liberal arts college all reported that they liked the place very much and that they found it very stimulating. The friends at the Ivy League university reported that they had many complaints on both personal and social grounds and on educational grounds.

David initially thought that he would go to the smaller college. However, he decided to visit both schools himself for a day.

He did not like what he saw at the private liberal arts college: Several people whom he met seemed cold and unpleasant; a professor he met with briefly seemed abrupt and uninterested in him; and he did not like the "feel" of the campus. He did like what he saw at the Ivy League university: Several of the people he met seemed like vital, enthusiastic, pleasant people; he met with two different professors who took a personal interest in him; and he came away with a very pleasant feeling about the campus. Please say which school you think David should go to.

1. He should definitely go to the liberal arts college.
2. He should probably go to the liberal arts college.
3. It's a toss-up.
4. He should probably go to the Ivy League university.
5. He should definitely go to the Ivy League university.

Please indicate why you made the recommendation you did.

The remaining subjects were presented with an identical problem except that the possibilities for error in David L.'s sample were highlighted by having him draw up a list of all the things that *might* be seen on the two campuses and then selecting randomly from among them for his actual schedule. The following was added to the second paragraph of the no-cue version.

He proceeded systematically to draw up a long list, for both colleges, of all the classes which might interest him and all the places and activities on campus that he wanted to see. From each list, he randomly selected several classes and activities to visit, and several spots to look at (by blindly dropping a pencil on each list of alternatives and seeing where the point landed).

Open-ended responses to the probe question were coded (by a blind coder) as to whether subjects justified their choice by showing any recognition of the statistical questions involved—either the dubiousness of David L.'s impressions because of the quantity of his evidence or the superiority of his friends' testimony because of their greater experience. There was 90% agreement among coders as to the assignment of an answer to the statistical versus nonstatistical categories.

Results

When there was no sampling cue pointing to the probabilistic nature of David L.'s personal evidence base, 74% of the subjects recommended that David L. should go to the Ivy League university, which his friends didn't much like but where he enjoyed his day. When the sampling cue was present, this dropped to 56% ($\chi^2 = 5.38, p < .025$). Moreover, subjec.s in the probabilistic-cue condition were much more likely to refer to statistical considerations having to do with the adequacy of the sample. Fifty-six percent of probabilistic-cue subjects raised statistical questions in their open-ended answers, whereas only 35% of subjects in the no-cue condition did so ($p < .01$). Thus, when subjects are prompted to consider the possibilities for error that are inherent in a small sample of events, they are likely to shift to preference for large indirect samples over small personal ones, and their open-ended answers make it clear that it is statistical considerations that prompt this shift.

The findings of Study 3 are extremely ironic in that subjects are more likely to reject the superior personal evidence in the probabilistic-cue condition than to reject the inferior personal evidence in the control condition. This is because the same circumstances that serve to make the evidence superior in the probabilistic-cue condition also serve to make salient the extreme heterogeneity of the event population to be estimated and the small size of the personal sample of those events. It is important to note that when Study 3 is run with a "within" design, subjects assess the relative value of the personal evidence correctly; that is, they generally rate the quality of evidence in the probabilistic-cue condition as superior to that in the control condition. In two slightly different within-design follow-ups to Study 3, subjects rated the probabilistic-cue sample as being superior to the sample in the control version. In one of the follow-ups (where subjects read the control problem and rated the quality of the personal evidence, then read the cue paragraph and compared the quality of the evidence there with the control version) four times as many subjects preferred the probabilistic-cue evidence as preferred the control evidence. In the other follow-up (where subjects actually acted as subjects in the control condition and then were shown the cue version), 40% more subjects preferred the probabilistic-cue evidence than preferred the control evidence.

EXPERTISE AND STATISTICAL REASONING

Study 4: Recognition of a Regression Effect in Sports and Acting

The studies we have just described indicate that subjects reason statistically when they recognize the heterogeneity of the events in question and the samplelike nature of their evidence about the events. If people are capable of learning from experience that events of a given kind are heterogenous and are produced in part by chance, then it should be possible to show that greater expertise in a domain is associated with a greater tendency to reason statistically in that domain. The two domains we selected to test this proposition were sports and acting. We anticipated that experience with sports would facilitate recognition of a regression effect in sports and that experience with acting would facilitate recognition of a regression effect in acting. Subjects were told about a small sample of extreme behavior followed by a larger sample of less extreme behavior. It was anticipated that inexpert subjects would generalize from the small sample and then would be obligated to give a causal explanation for the discrepancy between the small sample and the large sample. Expert subjects were expected to generalize less and to recognize that the discrepancy could be due to chance factors making the small sample appear extreme.

Method

Subjects were the same as those in Study 3. The problem presented to them was one of several in a study described as being aimed at finding out "how people go about explaining and predicting events under conditions of very limited information about the events." Subjects were given one of two nearly identically worded problems. One concerned a football coach who usually found that the most brilliant performers at tryout were not necessarily the best players during the football season, and the other concerned a repertory company director who usually found that the most brilliant performers at audition were not necessarily the best actors during the drama season. The full text of the football version is presented below.

> *Football.* Harold is the coach for a high school football team. One of his jobs is selecting new members of the varsity team. He says the following of his experience: "Every year we add 10-20 younger boys to the team on the basis of their performance at the try-out practice. Usually the staff and I are extremely excited about the potential of two or three of these kids—one who throws several brilliant passes or another who kicks several field goals from a remarkable distance. Unfortunately, most of these kids turn out to be only somewhat better than the rest." Why do you suppose that the coach usually has to revise downward his opinion of players that he originally thought were brilliant?

The acting version of the problem was almost identical except that it was about Susan, the director of a student repertory company, who gets excited about "a young woman with great stage presence or a young man who gives a brilliant reading."

Subjects were asked which of the following explanations they preferred for the fact that the coach/director usually had to revise downward his or her opinion of the brilliant performers. The second alternative is the statistical one, suggesting that the explanation is simply that the tryout performances were uncharacteristically good for the "brilliant" performers.

1. Harold was probably mistaken in his initial opinion. In his eagerness to find new talent, he exaggerates the brilliance of the performances he sees at the try-out.
2. The brilliant performances at try-out are not typical of those boys' general abilities. They probably just made some plays at the try-out that were much better than usual for them.
3. The boys who did so well at try-out probably could coast through the season on their talent alone and don't put out the effort necessary to transform talent into consistently excellent performance.
4. The boys who did so well at try-out may find that their teammates are jealous. They may slack off so as not to arouse envy.
5. The boys who did so well at try-out are likely to be students with other interests. These interests would deflect them from putting all their energies into football.

Wording was altered very slightly for the acting version: "Boys" became "actors" and "try-out" became "audition."

Experience in sports was assessed by asking subjects whether they had played any organized team sports in high school or college. Those who had were defined as experienced. Experience in acting was defined as having had "more than a bit part" in a play in high school or college.

Results

It may be seen in Table 2.2 that experience affects the likelihood of preferring a statistical explanation for both the football version of the problem and the acting version. Most of the subjects with athletic team

TABLE 2.2
Percentage of Experienced and Inexperienced Subjects Who Preferred the Statistical Explanation for the Football and the Acting Problems

| | Subjects | | | |
Problem	Experienced	Inexperienced	χ^2	p
Football			3.10	.10
%	56	35		
N	52	26		
Acting			5.18	.025
%	59	29		
N	17	62		
Both versions			10.60	.001
%	57	31		
N	69	88		

experience (a majority) preferred the statistical explanation for the football problem, whereas most of the subjects without team experience preferred one of the other, deterministic explanations. Most of the subjects with acting experience (a small minority) preferred the statistical explanation for the acting problem, whereas most of the subjects without acting experience preferred one of the deterministic explanations.

We do not wish to infer from these results that experience in a domain will make statistical explanations more salient for *every* kind of problem. Expertise brings a recognition of the causal factors at work in a domain as well as a recognition of the remaining uncertainty. When the problem can be approached with this expert causal knowledge, the expert may give answers that are less statistical, at least in form, than those of the novice. We may speculate that expertise reduces reliance on the representativeness heuristic, which encourages unreflective assumptions that the future will resemble the past and that populations will resemble samples, and substitutes either statistical reasoning or reasoning in accordance with well-justified causal rules.

We should note also that it is possible that the tendency of experts to reason statistically may have less to do with knowledge of variability and uncertainty than with a subcultural norm for them to do so. The statistical answer may simply look more like a familiar, standard answer to the experts than to the nonexperts. For a correlational study such as Study 4, it is not easy to disentangle the undoubtedly related factors influencing statistical reasoning.

DOMAIN SPECIFICITY OF INDUCTIVE RULES

One of the major implications of the present viewpoint is that there should be a substantial degree of domain specificity of statistical reasoning. Its use should be rare for domains where (a) it is hard to discern the sample space and the sampling process, (b) the role of chance in producing events is unclear, and (c) no cultural prescription for statistical reasoning exists. We have noted that many of the studies showing people's failures in statistical reasoning examined judgments about events characterized by one or more of these factors. We have also noted that some of people's few demonstrated successes in statistical reasoning have been observed for people's reasoning about sports and academic achievements that seem to be characterized by clearer distributions for events, a more obvious role of chance, and, probably, cultural prescriptions as well. These observations were made across studies, across tasks, and across subject populations, however.

To demonstrate that the same subjects dealing with the same tasks in the same experiment are more likely to reason statistically for some events characterized by uncertainty than for others, Jepson, Krantz, and Nisbett (in press) presented subjects with two broad classes of problems. The first class of problems dealt with events that are assessable by objective means, such as abilities, achievements, and physical illness. The second class dealt with events that are assessable only by subjective means, for example, personal preferences among objects, assessments of leadership potential, and judgments about the need for sexual fidelity in relationships. It was reasoned that, in general, it is relatively easy to apply statistical reasoning to objective events because one is likely to have some idea of their distributions (or to be able to guess what the distributions might look like because the units of measurement and the sample space are likely to be relatively clear). In general, also, the role of chance is likely to be relatively transparent for those objectively assessable events that in fact have been observed under repeated, relatively fixed conditions. Finally, cultural prescriptions to reason statistically probably exist for many such events. In contrast, none of these things is true for most events that can be assessed only by subjective means. The first problem below is an example of the Jepson et al. *objective* problems; the second is an example of the *subjective* problems.

Championship Selection Problem

Two sports fans are arguing over which sport — baseball or football — has the best (most accurate) playoff system. Charlie says that the Super Bowl is the best way of determining the world champion because, according to him, "the seven games of the World Series are all played in the home cities of the two teams, whereas the Super Bowl is usually played in a neutral city. Since you want all factors not related to the game to be equal for a championship, then the Super Bowl is the better way to determine the world championship." Which procedure do you think is a better way to determine the world champion — World Series or Super Bowl? Why?

Class Selection Problem

It is the first week of the winter term. Henry has signed up for five classes, but plans to take only four. Three of these classes he knows he wants, so he must decide between the other two. Both are on subjects interesting to him. The student course evaluations indicate that Course A is better taught. However, he attended the first meeting of both classes this week, and found Course B's session more enjoyable. Which class should he take and why?

Subjects wrote open-ended answers to problems of each type. These were coded as to whether they reflected the use of statistical principles — chiefly the law of large numbers or the regression principle — or not. An example of a nonstatistical answer for the championship problem is the following: "Super Bowl, because of neutral ground and also a one shot deal. Either you make it or break it—one chance. The pressure is on to perform the team's best." An example of a statistical answer is the following: "World Series is better. Anyone can get lucky for one game, but it is harder to be lucky for four. Besides, being home or away is part of the game, you don't play on neutral ground during the season." An example of a nonstatistical answer for the class-choice problem is the following: "He's got to choose for himself." An example of a statistical answer is: "You can't tell from one time—thus a survey that is over a longer range is better. Although Henry's idea of a good class could be different from most students."

Statistical answers were much more common for problems about objective events than for problems about subjective events. Forty-one percent of the answers for the former were statistical; the range of mean percentage statistical answers across problems was 30%-93%. Only 12% of the answers to subjective problems were statistical; the range was 5%-16%.

The results also showed that subjects were consistent in their tendency to give statistical answers. Those who gave statistical answers for any given problem were more likely to give them for any other. This tendency was correlated with both verbal and mathematical scores on the Scholastic Aptitude Test.

The results of the Jepson et al. (in press) study show that the same subjects in the same context answering the same general kind of problem are more likely to give statistical answers for a set of problems dealing with abilities than for a set dealing with more subjective attributes. The results do not rule out the possibility that it is problem structure or the exact nature of the required statistical rule that produces the difference among problems rather than their content. To control for this, Fong, Krantz, and Nisbett (Note 3) developed five separate problem structures for which somewhat different versions of the law of large numbers were required to produce the most appropriate statistical solution. For example, in one structure a small personal sample of events had implications that were different from those of a large sample collected by someone else (as in the class-choice problem above). Subjects were asked to indicate which sample was the better guide to action and why. Another structure presented a simple regression problem in which subjects were asked to explain why an extreme outcome for a small sample was not maintained in a larger sample. For each problem structure, two or more problem versions were constructed, some dealing with objective events and others with subjective ones. With structure and required rule type thus controlled, there was still a marked difference in the percentage of statistical answers for the two kinds of events.

It should be noted that an alternative explanation still exists even for the Fong et al. (Note 3) results. This is the possibility that statistical answers are not as appropriate for the subjective problems as for the objective problems. This objection is not readily answerable with our present level of knowledge about the uncertainty of events. We can only urge our view that statistical answers were fully appropriate for all problems because all problems involved high degrees of uncertainty. But it must be acknowledged that other people having the relevant statistical training might not agree.

The Effects of Training in Statistics on Reasoning About Everyday Events

Perhaps the most important implication of the present view is that statistical reasoning about everyday events should be highly trainable. A major reason for optimism is that, as we have just demonstrated, people's intuitive reasoning skills include strategies that may be called statistical heuristics. Formal training in statistics, therefore, should represent less a grafting on of procedures than a refinement of preexisting ones. Formal training seems likely to improve reasoning for three distinct, but mutually supportive, reasons.

Training in Statistics is Apt to Facilitate the Recognition of Event Distributions and their Statistical Parameters. It can be difficult to apply rules such as the law of large numbers unless the units of evidence can be identified and, hence, the sample space and distribution of the event units. It seems likely that training in statistics could provide quite general skills in construing evidence in such a way that it can be properly unitized, the sample space identified, and parameters recognized. Training in probability theory, especially in permutations and combinations, should be particularly likely to be helpful in this regard as should test theory, which requires the student to recognize, for example, the different reliability of tests composed of different numbers of units—items, trials, occasions, and so on. But ordinary inferential statistics also introduces a fair amount of instruction in unitizing evidence: In order to measure the corn yield of a type of seed, for example, it is necessary to measure the yield for some unit of sampling (individual plot, individual farm, etc.). Statistics courses should also make it easier for people to think usefully about parameters of distributions—about central tendencies and about dispersion.

Training in Statistics in Apt to Facilitate the Recognition of the Role of Chance in Producing Events. A major concept of parametric statistics is that of error. Every inferential test features an estimate of error, and much of statistical training centers on questions of allocation of effects to the systematic category versus the random category. It seems possible that the focus on the concept of error in statistics might heighten the salience of uncertainty in daily life. A second major concept that might be helpful in recognizing uncertainty is the formal notion of sampling. This might be of general use in construing evidence as a (possibly small and inaccurate) sample from a (possibly heterogeneous) population.

Training in Statistics is Apt to Improve the Clarity and Accessibility of Statistical Rules and Should Expand the Repertoire of Statistical Rules. In effect, statistics training should hone intuitive heuristics into more precise tools. It seems clear that without training some statistical rules are poorly understood at any level of abstraction and in any context. Rules of covariation assessment and some versions of the regression principle are particularly difficult and may not even be represented in most people's intuitive repertoire. But even relatively intuitive rules such as the law of large numbers have nearly limitless corollaries and implications, some of which may be much easier to discern with formal training. Although people understand the "law of small large numbers," they may not be able to extend the principle to numbers of nonexperiential magnitudes without formal training. It may be the lack of a fully formal understanding of the law of large numbers that prevents people from applying it in the maternity ward problem, for example, where the sample sizes involved (15 and 45) are not often represented in people's everyday experience of sampling and variability.

The evidence indicates that statistical training does indeed have profound effects on people's reasoning about everyday life events. In one series of studies, Krantz, Fong, and Nisbett (Note 4) examined four groups of subjects differing widely in educational level. Subjects, who were college students with or without statistical training, graduate students with a fair amount of statistical training, or PhD level scientists with several years of training, were presented with one of a pair of restaurant problems. In each problem, a protagonist experienced a truly outstanding meal on the first visit to a restaurant but was disappointed on a repeat visit. The subjects were asked to explain, in writing, why this might have happened. A subject's explanation was classified as nonstatistical if it assumed that the initial good experience was a reliable indicator that the restaurant was truly outstanding and attributed the later disappointment to a definite cause, such as a permanent or temporary change in the restaurant (e.g., "Maybe the chef quit") or a change in the protagonist's expectation or mood. The explanation was classified as statistical if it suggested that meal quality on any single visit might not be a reliable indicator of the restaurant's overall quality (e.g., "Very few restaurants have only excellent meals; odds are she was just lucky the first time"). Statistical explanations were coded as to how articulate they were in indicating that a single visit may be regarded as a small sample and, hence, as unreliable. Explanations were thus coded as falling into one of three categories: (1) nonstatistical, (2) poor statistical, and (3) good statistical. The frequencies in each of these categories were used to define two dependent variables: *frequency* of statistical answers, defined as the proportion of responses in Categories 2 and 3, and *quality* of statistical answers, defined as the proportion of Category 2 and 3 answers that were Category 3.

The two versions of the restaurant problem differed. The probabilistic-cue version included a random mechanism for selection from the menu: The protagonist did not know how to read a Japanese menu and selected a meal by blindly dropping a pencil on the menu and observing where the point lay. The other version had no such cue. Within each group tested, half of the subjects received the cue and half did not.

The effects of training on both dependent measures were dramatic. College students without statistical training almost never gave an answer that was at all statistical unless the problem contained the probabilistic cue, in which case about half of the answers were statistical. In contrast, more than 80% of the answers of PhD-level scientists were statistical, whether or not there was a cue. Quality of statistical answers also depended on level of training. Only 10% of the statistical answers by untrained college students were rated as good, whereas almost 80% of the statistical answers by PhD-level scientists were rated as good. It is interesting that although the presence of the probabilistic cue was very important in determining whether less trained subjects would give a statistical answer, it did not affect the quality of statistical answers for subjects at any level of training. Apparently probabilistic cues can trigger the use of statistical heuristics, but they do not necessarily improve the quality of answers: the appropriate skills must be in the individual's repertoire to insure good quality.

The preceding study confounds training and native mathematical ability, but subsequent studies both avoid the confounding with ability and show that statistical training influences inductive reasoning outside the classroom and laboratory. Krantz et al. (Note 4) conducted a telephone "survey of opinions about sports." Subjects were males who were enrolled in an introductory statistics course and who admitted to being at least somewhat knowledgeable about sports. One hundred subjects were randomly selected and surveyed during the first 2 weeks of the term they were enrolled in statistics. Another 93 students were surveyed at or near the end of the term. In addition to filler questions on NCAA rules and NBA salaries, subjects were asked questions for which a statistical approach was relevant, as in the example below.

In general the major league baseball player who wins Rookie of the Year does not perform as well in his second year. This is clear in major league baseball in the past ten years. In the American League, 8 rookies of the year have done worse in their second year; only 2 have done better. In the National League, the rookie of the year has done worse the second year 9 times out of 10.

Why do you suppose the rookie of the year tends not to do as well his second year?

Most subjects answered this question in a nonstatistical way, invoking notions like "too much press attention" and "slacking off." Some subjects answered the question statistically (e.g., "There are bound to be some rookies who have an exceptional season; it may not be due to any great talent advantage that one guy has over the others—he just got a good year").

The statistics course increased the percentage of statistical answers and also increased the quality of statistical answers. The course also markedly influenced both the frequency and the quality of statistical answers to another question asking subjects to explain why .450 batting averages are common the first 2 weeks of the baseball season but are unheard of as a season average. In all, the course had a significant effect on three of the five questions asked.

Finally, Fong et al. (Note 3) showed that even a very brief training procedure can suffice to affect markedly subjects' answers to problems about everyday events. There were two major elements in their training package: One covered formal aspects of sampling and the law of large numbers and the other showed how to use sampling notions as a heuristic device in modeling problems. In the sampling instruction, subjects received definitions of population and sample distributions, a statement of the law of large numbers, and a demonstration (by drawing colored gumballs from a glass vase) that a population distribution is estimated more accurately, on the average, from larger samples. The modeling, or mapping, instruction consisted of three problems (in the general style of the restaurant problem and similar to the subsequent test problems), each followed by a written solution that used the law of large numbers and emphasized the analogy between amount of evidence and size of sample.

There were four major conditions: a control group given no instruction and three experimental groups—one given sampling training only, one given mapping training only, and one given both types of training. The subjects were adults and high school students. The test consisted of 15 problems. Five of these had clear probabilistic cues, five dealt with objective attributes such as abilities or achievements, and five dealt with subjective judgments. Training effects were marked for all three problem types, for both the frequency of statistical answers and the quality of statistical answers. Sampling training and mapping training were about equally effective, and in combination they were substantially more effective than either was alone. A particularly encouraging finding is that training showed no domain specificity effects. In a companion study, Fong et al (Note 3) showed that it made no difference to performance whether mapping training had been on probabilistic-cue problems, objective attribute problems, or subjective judgment problems. The latter finding suggests that training on specific problem types can be readily abstracted to a degree sufficient for use on widely different problem types.

The work on training should not be taken to indicate that a statistical education is sufficient to guarantee that people will avoid errors in inductive reasoning. Kahneman and Tversky (1982; Tversky & Kahneman, 1971, 1983) have shown repeatedly that statistical expertise provides no such guarantee against errors. On the other hand, it should also be noted that courses in statistics do not emphasize ways to use statistical principles in everyday life. Were they to do so, one might see much larger differences between the educated and the uneducated than we have found.

NORMATIVE CONSIDERATIONS

People can apply statistical reasoning to a wide range of problems of an everyday life sort. The use of statistical reasoning seems to be increased by greater clarity about the sample space and the sampling process, by recognition of the role played by chance, and by cultural prescriptions to apply statistical reasoning. As a consequence, statistical reasoning appears to be more prevalent for events that are assessed by objective means than for events that are assessed only subjectively. People apply statistical reasoning more frequently and more aptly after formal training in statistics.

Exactly what is the content of lay statistical heuristics? What is the range of problems to which they can be applied? Which statistical principles are well entrenched in the repertoire of formally untutored people and which are not represented or even counterintuitive? Is there an improvement or a worsening of statistical reasoning as one moves from laboratory studies of reasoning to studies of *in vivo* reasoning about analogous problems in their appropriate ecological context? Exactly how much improvement in people's ability to reason statistically could be expected from traditional formal education in statistics? How could educational practices be improved so as to amplify the real world consequences of training?

We refrain from speculating about these questions, despite their importance, because they are fundamentally empirical in nature. It would be more appropriate for us to sketch the normative implications of the work to date rather than to try to be prescient about future matters of fact. We have addressed many of the normative implications of the previous work on limits elsewhere (Krantz, 1981; Nisbett, 1981; Nisbett, Krantz, Jepson, & Fong, 1982; Stich & Nisbett, 1980; Thagard & Nisbett, 1983), and we have addressed at some length some of the normative implications of our work on individual differences (Jepson, Krantz, & Nisbett, in press), but it would be useful to summarize the general normative implications of the work presented in this review.

Ecological Representativeness of Problems Showing Errors

One criticism of the literature showing errors in inductive reasoning has been to argue that they are the result simply of examining people's judgment about particular kinds of problems, and in a particular kind of context, where judgments are particularly likely to be fallible (e.g., Cohen, 1981; Dennett, 1981; Lopes, 1982). The tenor of this criticism is that the studies show more about the cleverness of experimenters than they do about the real world failures of lay people.

The accusation that psychologists have been devising parlor tricks, which people are susceptible to in the laboratory context but either do not encounter or could solve in real world contexts, seems less plausible in view of the research reported here. First, for each problem we have reported, some of the subjects showed by their answers (and often by the rationales for their answers, subsequently elicited) an appreciation of the statistical principles that in previous work other subjects failed to appreciate. It seems more reasonable to explain the success of some of our subjects by saying that they are more skilled at statistical reasoning than the other subjects rather than to explain it by saying that they saw through the experimenters' tricks. Second, the factors that make statistical reasoning more or less likely, for example, recognition of heterogeneity and of the role played by chance, do not sound like factors that make people more or less dupable by experimenters but rather like factors that make the appropriateness of statistical reasoning more or less obvious. Third, statistical training markedly influences answers to the sort of problems we studied. This suggests that it is not problem- or context-produced illusions that make people unable to solve statistical problems but simply lack of statistical knowledge.

"Satisficing" in Decision Making and Inductive Reasoning

Since Simon's (1957) important work on decision making, it has been a standard part of normative analysis to point out that, because of time pressures and other constraints, it may be quite sensible for people to depart from formal decision models. This corner-cutting practice is called *satisfi-*

cing (in distinction to the presumed *optimizing* that would result from the formal procedures). This same defense is often applied to people's failures to reason statistically (Einhorn & Hogarth, 1981; Miller & Cantor, 1982; Nisbett & Ross, 1980). People who study inductive reasoning seem to have presumed that normatively correct inductive reasoning is usually more laborious and time consuming than is purely intuitive inductive reasoning, just as formal decision making is usually more time consuming than is intuitive decision making. The present work makes it clear that this presumption cannot be imported uncritically into the realm of inductive reasoning. Exclusively causal reasoning and the search for values on putatively relevant causal factors can be extraordinarily laborious. Statistical reasoning, once it is mastered, can be very rapid, even automatic. We found it striking, for example, to contrast the answers given over the telephone by subjects in the sports survey by Krantz et al. (Note 4). Some subjects doggedly persisted in causal explanations for problems such as the rookie of the year, sophomore slump ("Well, the success goes to their heads . . . and there's pressure to keep up the performance after the great first year . . . and . . ."), which did not seem to satisfy even the subjects who were generating them. Other subjects generated quick, crisp statistical explanations ("They just happened to have a first year that was better than their lifetime average") that still left them free to explore possible causal explanations.

It is also important to note that one has very little sense of subjects' *choosing* inferential strategies when one reads such protocols, in the sense that people may choose a formal decision-making strategy over an intuitive one. Rather, subjects either seem to spontaneously pursue a statistical approach or they do not. Formal decision-making procedures involve novel and counterintuitive practices such as drawing tree diagrams and multiplying probability and utility assessments. On the other hand, many statistical procedures, as we have shown, have their simpler intuitive counterparts in the equipment of everyday thought. There is no reason to presume that these will be any more cumbersome to use or will require any more conscious deliberation to access than will other intuitive approaches. Similarly, training in formal statistics may produce automatic, nonreflective transfer to everyday problems in a way that formal decision training would not.

Evolution and Inductive Reasoning

Many people have responded to the work demonstrating inferential errors by assuming that the errors are either exaggerated or that they are the incidental by-product of some overwhelmingly useful inferential procedure that happens to go astray under ecologically rare circumstances. This is essentially the argument from design, and several philosophers have endorsed it. (See, e.g., Cohen, 1979; Dennett, 1978, 1981, Note 1; Lycan,

1981. Einhorn & Hogarth, 1981, have presented several very compelling arguments against the design view, and we shall not repeat them here.)

Endorsement of the evolutionary, or design, view requires a rather static, wired-in assumption about the nature of inferential procedures. Philosophers are not alone in making this assumption, it should be noted. Psychologists who are wont to presume unlimited plasticity in social behavior often seem to presume complete rigidity in inferential rules, as if these could be influenced at most by maturation. In our view, there are few grounds for such a presumption. Whatever may be true for deduction, there are good grounds for assuming that inductive procedures can be changed. Renaissance physicians adhered to the doctrine of signatures, an inductive system with both descriptive and procedural components. Modern physicians have curtailed the scope of the representativeness heuristic in their daily inferential lives. (Although it is still relied on in interviews of applicants to medical schools. See Dawes, 1980, for a description of the doctrine of signatures at work in the admissions process for American universities.) Sophisticated causal analysis and statistical reasoning will eventually result in the further curtailment of simple intuitive heuristics, for physicians and for everyone else.

Although we see no merit in an evolutionary defense of the inferential behaviors that happen to characterize American college students in the latter part of the 20th century, we see a powerful argument in the work we have reviewed for the role of cultural evolution. It does not require unusual optimism to speculate that we are on the threshold of a profound change in the way that people reason inductively. The range of events that scientists can think about statistically has been increasing slowly but in a decided, positively accelerated fashion at least since the 17th century. The work of Kahneman and Tversky may be regarded as the most recent and one of the most dramatic inflection points on that curve.

We believe that, with a lag in time, lay people have been following a similar curve of ever-widening application of statistical reasoning. Most people today appreciate entirely statistical accounts of sports events, accident rates, and the weather; also, we found many subjects who gave statistical explanations even for subjective events such as disappointment about meals served by a restaurant; and Piaget's young subjects reasoned about the behavior of randomizing devices with a sophistication that seems quite unlikely for people of earlier centuries. Will our own descendants differ as much from us as we do from Bernoulli's contemporaries?

FOOTNOTES

[1]All p values are based on two-tailed tests unless otherwise indicated.
[2]We are indebted to George Quattrone for making these available.

REFERENCE NOTES

1. Dennett, D. C. *True believers: The intentional strategy and why it works.* Unpublished manuscript, Tufts University, 1983.
2. Kahneman, D. Personal communication, 1982.
3. Fong, G. T., Krantz, D. H., & Nisbett, R. E. *Improving inductive reasoning through statistical training.* Unpublished manuscript, University of Michigan, 1983.
4. Krantz, D. H., Fong, G. T., & Nisbett, R. E. *Formal training improves the application of statistical heuristics to everyday problems.* Unpublished manuscript, Bell Laboratories, Murray Hill, New Jersey, 1983.

REFERENCES

Borgida, E., & Nisbett, R. E. The differential impact of abstract vs. concrete information on decisions. *Journal of Applied Social Psychology,* 1977, *7,* 258–271.

Cohen, L. J. On the psychology of prediction: Whose is the fallacy? *Cognition,* 1979, *7,* 385–407.

Cohen, L. J. Can human irrationality be experimentally demonstrated? *Behavioral and Brain Sciences,* 1981, *4,* 317–331.

Dawes, R. M. You can't systemize human judgment: Dyslexia. *New Directions for Methodology of Social and Behavioral Science,* 1980, *4,* 67–78.

Dennett, D. C. *Brainstorms.* Montgomery, Vt.: Bradford Books, 1978.

Dennett, D. C. Three kinds of intentional psychology. In R. Healey (Ed.), *Reduction, time and reality.* Cambridge, England: Cambridge University Press, 1981.

Einhorn, H. J., & Hogarth, R. M. Confidence in judgment: Persistence of the illusion of validity. *Psychological Review,* 1978, *87,* 395–416.

Einhorn, H., & Hogarth, R. M. Behavioral decision theory: Processes of judgment and choice. *Annual Review of Psychology,* 1981, *32,* 53–88.

Hacking, I. *The emergence of probability.* New York: Cambridge University Press, 1975.

Hamer, C. *"Good-fishin'!"* (2nd ed.). St. Paul, Minn.: P.F., Inc., 1981.

Hogarth, R. M. *Judgement and choice.* New York: Wiley, 1980.

Hume, D. *An inquiry concerning human understanding.* Indianapolis, Ind.: Bobbs-Merrill, 1955. (Originally published, 1748.)

Jepson, C., Krantz, D. H., & Nisbett, R. E. Inductive reasoning: Competence or skill? *Behavioral and Brain Sciences,* in press.

Kahneman, D., Slovic, P., & Tversky, A. *Judgment under uncertainty: Heuristics and biases.* New York: Cambridge University Press, 1982.

Kahneman, D., & Tversky, A. Subjective probability: A judgment of representativeness. *Cognitive Psychology,* 1972, *3,* 430–454.

Kahneman, D., & Tversky, A. On the psychology of prediction. *Psychological Review,* 1973, *80,* 237–251.

Kahneman, D., & Tversky, A. On the study of statistical intuitions. *Cognition,* 1982, *11,* 237–251.

Krantz, D. H. Improvements in human reasoning and an error in L. J. Cohen's. *Behavioral and Brain Sciences,* 1981, *4,* 340–341.

Law of averages a reality for ballplayers. *Los Angeles Times.* June 7, 1981, Part 3, p. 6.

Lopes, L. L. Doing the impossible: A note on induction and the experience of randomness. *Journal of Experimental Psychology,* 1982, *8,* 626–636.

Lycan, W. G. "Is" and "ought" in cognitive science. *Behavioral and Brain Sciences,* 1981, *4,* 344–345.

Mill, J. S. *A system of logic ratiocinative and inductive.* Toronto, Ontario, Canada: University of Toronto Press, 1974. (Originally published, 1843.)

Miller, G. A., & Cantor, N. Book review of Nisbett, R., & Ross, L. Human inference: Strategies and shortcomings of social judgment. *Social Cognition,* 1982, *1,* 83–93.

Nisbett, R. E. Lay arbitration of rules of inference. *Behavioral and Brain Sciences,* 1981, *4,* 349–350.

Nisbett, R. E., & Borgida, E. Attribution and the psychology of prediction. *Journal of Personality and Social Psychology,* 1975, *32,* 932–943.

Nisbett, R. E., Krantz, D. H., Jepson, C., & Fong, G. T. Improving inductive inference. In D. Kahneman, P. Slovic, & A. Tversky (Eds.) *Judgment under uncertainty: Heuristics and biases.* New York: Cambridge University Press, 1982.

Nisbett, R. E., & Ross, L. *Human inference: Strategies and shortcomings of social judgment.* Englewood Cliffs, N.J.: Prentice-Hall, 1980.

Piaget, J., & Inhelder, B. *The origin of the idea of chance in children.* New York: Norton, 1975. (Originally published in 1951.)

Quattrone, G. A., & Jones, E. E. The perception of variability within in-groups and out-groups: Implications for the law of large numbers. *Journal of Personality and Social Psychology,* 1980, *38,* 141–152.

Silka, L. Effects of limited recall of variability on intuitive judgments of change. *Journal of Personality and Social Psychology,* 1981, *40,* 1010–1016.

Simon, H. A. *Models of man: Social and rational.* New York: Wiley, 1957.

Stich, S., & Nisbett, R. E. Justification and the psychology of human reasoning. *Philosophy of Science,* 1980, *47,* 188–202.

Thagard, P., & Nisbett, R. E. Variability and confirmation. *Philosophical Studies,* 1982, *42,* 379–394.

Thagard, P., & Nisbett, R. E. Rationality and charity. *Philosophy of Science,* 1983, *50,* 250–267.

Tversky, A., & Kahneman, D. Belief in the law of small numbers. *Psychological Bulletin,* 1971, *76,* 105–110.

Tversky, A., & Kahneman, D. Availability: A heuristic for judging frequency and probability. *Cognitive Psychology,* 1973, *5,* 207–232.

Tversky, A., & Kahneman, D. Judgment under uncertainty: Heuristics and biases. *Science,* 1974, *185,* 1124–1131.

Tversky, A., & Kahneman, D. Extensional vs. intuitive reasoning: The conjunction fallacy in probability judgment. *Psychological Review,* 1983, *90,* 293–315.

Weiner, B., Frieze, I., Kukla, A., Reed, L., Rest, S., & Rosenbaum, R. M. Perceiving the causes of success and failure. In E. E. Jones, D. E. Kanouse, H. H. Kelley, R. E. Nisbett, S. Valins, & B. Weiner (Eds.), *Attribution: Perceiving the causes of behavior.* Morristown, N.J.: General Learning Press, 1972.

3 Variability and Confirmation

Paul Thagard and Richard E. Nisbett
University of Michigan

> Why is a single instance, in some cases, sufficient for a complete induction, while in others myriads of concurring instances, without a single exception known or presumed, go such a very little way towards establishing an universal proposition?[1]

Hume left us with two problems of induction. The *strong* problem concerns the global justification of induction: how do we know that the future will be like the past? This problem seems to be insoluble, since no *a priori* justifications are forthcoming, and any *a posteriori* justification would be circular. We can do much more with the *weak* problem, which is to find a set of rules and principles which describe and justify, at least locally, our inductive inferential behavior. As Goodman pointed out, we can develop a set of inductive principles by paying attention to accepted inductive practice, while at the same time adjusting our inferential practice in the light of new principles.[2] The procedure of mutual adjustment of principles and practice is more complex than Goodman indicated,[3] but Goodman's general point, that the description and justification of inductive principles go hand in hand, provides a basis for pursuing Hume's weak problem.

Yet even the weak problem is very difficult. There has been limited progress in specifying the principles that describe and justify inductive practice. We believe that this is partly because many philosophers concerned with induction have assumed that inductive principles would be like deductive ones in being formulatable in terms of the syntactic structure of the premises and conclusions of inductive inferences. Whereas deductive principles can be based solely on the logical form of the relevant sentences, inductive rules must, we shall argue, make essential reference to the *content* of the premises and conclusion of the inference. The validity of inductive inferences depends in part on the nature of the objects and events about which one is reasoning. Inductive principles therefore are content relative in a way in which deductive ones are not.

We shall illustrate the contention that inductive rules are content relative by considering the classic problem that concerned Hume — the confirmation of generalizations by their instances. Much recent work on inductive reasoning has focused on giving a characterization of what it is for a generalization 'All F are G to be confirmed by an instance, 'Fa and Ga'.[4] As Mill noticed, the degree to which an instance confirms a generalization is highly variable. Some instances provide nearly decisive confirmation, whereas others hardly increase our confidence in a generalization at all. We shall argue that the degree to which an instance confirms a generalization depends primarily on very rich background knowledge about the *kinds* of entities and properties the generalization concerns. Specifically, our confidence in inferring a generalization 'All F are G' depends on background knowledge about how *variable* F's tend to be with respect to G's. This knowledge is based on F being a kind of K_1, G being a kind of K_2, and on the variability of things of kind K_1 with respect to things of kind K_2.

Section I contains experimental, thought-experimental and anecdotal evidence for the claim that this sort of background knowledge does in fact play a rôle in our inductions. Section II describes more rigorously how variability of kinds plays a rôle in confirmation. In III we briefly consider some of the philosophical problems concerning natural kinds, causality, and variety of instances which our account of confirmation raises. Section IV contrasts our account with more familiar models of inductive reasoning. The concluding Section V contains brief reflections on confirmation and on the methodology of using empirical work on inferential behavior as a guide to normative inductive logic.

I

Consider the following thought experiment. Imagine you are exploring a newly discovered island. You encounter three instances of a new species of bird, called the shreeble, and all three observed shreebles are blue. What is your degree of confidence that *all* shreebles are blue? Compare this with your reaction to the discovery of three instances of a new metal floridium, all of which when heated burn with a blue flame. Are you more or less confident of the generalization 'All floridium burns with a blue flame' than you were of the generalization 'All shreebles are blue'? Now consider a third case. All three observed shreebles use baobab leaves as nesting material, but how confident do you feel about the generalization 'All shreebles use baobab leaves as nesting material'?

Most people feel more confident about the floridium generalization than about either of the shreeble generalizations, and more confident about shreebles being blue than about their using baobab leaves as nesting material. Nisbett *et al* found that undergraduate subjects share such intuitions with professional philosophers and psychologists, and in fact often spontaneously articulate a version of the justification that we prefer.[5]

We know that metals tend to be quite constant with respect to such physical properties as flame color and electric conductivity, whereas we know that birds are more variable with respect to their color: different sexes of the same species can be different colors, and in some kinds such as parrots there is wide variation in color. Background knowledge also suggests that birds are even more variable with respect to what sort of materials they use for nests. This is why three shreebles' nests are so much less persuasive than three floridium flames.

It seems clear that people may differ in their background knowledge in such a way as to affect markedly the inductive generalizations they make from a given instance. This point has been illustrated in an experiment by Quattrone and Jones.[6] They found that subjects were more prone to make generalizations about members of an out-group than about members of an in-group. For example, Rutgers students were more likely to generalize about the behavior of Princeton students on the basis of the behavior of one Princeton student than were Princeton students, while Princeton students were more likely to generalize about Rutgers students after observing one Rutgers student than were Rutgers students. Quattrone and Jones conjecture that the reason for the discrepancy is the assumption by the in-group that members of the out-group are less variable in their properties than members of the in-group.

One implication of the Quattrone and Jones study is that the difference in people's beliefs about variability may be a function of the degree of their experience with events of the kind in question. For kinds of events that are characterized by high variability, the novice and the expert may thus make quite different generalizations. Nisbett *et al.* (op. cit.) found that people with a good deal of athletic experience were less willing to assume that a superb performance at a football try-out was indicative of generally superb abilities than were people who had less athletic experience. Similarly, people with acting experience were less willing to assume that a superb performance at an audition was indicative of generally superb acting abilities than were people who had no acting experience. Apparently the experienced subjects were more aware that a single instance of football playing, or of acting, may fail to reflect the individual's general level of ability.

The history of science provides examples of cases where a very limited number of instances proved to be decisive. We believe that these are well understood in terms of background knowledge about variability. For example, Einstein's general theory of relativity implied that light could be deflected by an intense gravitational field. Eddington's celebrated experiment during the 1919 eclipse set out to test the generalization that light is so deflected by considering whether starlight is bent by the sun. Only a few photographs sufficed to convince most scientists that light was indeed bent by a gravitational field.[7] Background knowledge tells us not to expect much variability in the behavior of light, so a few instances suffice. We do not crucially need to consider other eclipses, other light sources, other gravitational fields, or other mountain tops. Light is not the kind of thing for which these factors would matter. Compare the situation in social science, where variability is so great and we are so lacking in a coherent account of inductively reliable kinds of people and behavior, that we must constantly be wary of spurious correlations with no causal significance.

The above examples indicate that background knowledge about variability in kinds is important for confirmation theory. The importance has been largely unnoticed in recent philosophical work, which has followed Hempel in trying to give a general account of what it is for an instance to confirm a generalization, or Carnap in trying the build a formal model for quantitative confirmation.[8] Previous, less formal inductive logicians including Mill, Keynes, Russell, and Harrod noticed the relevance of background knowledge about variability and kinds but did not develop the insight.[9] We need a more rigorous and general account of how background knowledge about variability affects the degree to which a generalization can be confirmed by its instances.

II

That 'All floridium burns with a blue flame' is highly confirmed by a few instances is due to the fact that metals are highly invariant with respect to physical properties such as combustion. That 'All shreebles use baobab leaves as nesting material' is poorly confirmed by a few instances is due to the fact that birds are more variable with respect to the kinds of nesting materials they use. To make this precise, we need a formalism which enables us to compare the degree of variability in different kinds of things. Then we can make the claim that degree of confirmation is a function of degree of invariance.[10]

Let H be the hypothesis '$(x)(Fx \supset Gx)$', and let E be the evidence 'Fa and Ga'. Suppose F's are a kind of K_1 and G's are a kind of K_2; for example, shreebles are a kind of bird, and blue is a kind of color. Then if $C(H, E)$ is the degree to which H is confirmed by E, and $I(K_1, K_2)$ is the invariance of K_1 with respect to K_2, our basic claim can be represented:

$$C(H, E) = f(I(K_1, K_2)).$$

The claim needs to be fleshed out in two ways, by further characterizing the function f, and by indicating how the metric $I(K_1, K_2)$ is to be calculated. Confirmation is a function of more than just variability of kinds: full determination of $C(H, E)$ may require reference to other sorts of background information in addition to what we discuss, and of course degree of confirmation is partly a function of number of instances. But we maintain that how rapidly degree of confirmation increases with number of instances depends *primarily* on variability of kinds. Degree of confirmation is presumably a monotonic, negatively accelerated function of number of instances, but the rate of acceleration depends primarily on considerations of variability. With high $I(K_1, K_2)$, degree of confirmation increases very rapidly with only a few instances; but if invariance is low, degree of confirmation will increase only slowly as instances mount up.

How can we measure $I(K_1, K_2)$? In the metal case, estimation of $I(K_1, K_2)$ is based on our background knowledge that metals tend to be invariant with respect to physical properties like combustion and conductivity. This knowledge in turn is based on experience with many kinds of metals. We know that whatever particular physical property a few instances of the metal have, the other instances of that kind of metal will probably have it too. If one instance of aluminum conducts electricity, probably they all do. If one instance fails to take on a magnetic charge, probably they all do, given standard conditions. With birds, however, we can think of kinds which assume different colors and use different sorts of nesting material. There is a greater degree of association between kinds of metal and combustion properties than there is between kinds of birds and either colors or kinds of nesting material.

Various measures of association between classifications have been discussed by statisticians. Different measures are appropriate for different circumstances, but one particularly useful measure, discussed by Goodman and Kruskal,[11] is based on optimal prediction: degree of association of two

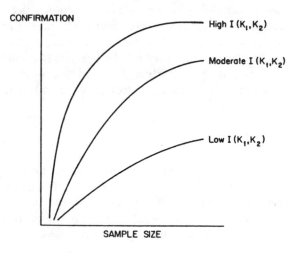

FIG. 3.1 Confirmation as a function of sample size and $I(K_1, K_2)$.

classifications into kinds is a function of how well knowing that something is of a kind from the first classification will enable you to predict its kind in the second classification, compared to how well you would predict without using the classifications. If kinds in the second classification are associated with high probability with specific kinds from the first classification, then knowing the classification will greatly improve prediction. For the formal details, see Goodman, and Kruskal footnote. It can easily be verified that their measure of association between classification can be adapted to provide a measure of degree of invariance between kinds, $I(K_1, K_2)$. In ordinary life, we do not have as part of our background knowledge a measure of invariance as precise as that calculated by Goodman and Kruskal, but their measure could be viewed as an ideal approximation to assessments of invariance such as people make in the metal and bird cases.

In assessing the degree of confirmation of *(x) (Fx ⊃ Gx)*, it is of course essential to consider the *relevant* kinds, K_1 and K_2. Normatively, selecting the relevant kind is analogous to the problem of selecting the appropriate reference class for a single object or event. To get an estimate of the probability that Fred will have a heart attack, we need to place him in the class such that subdivision is statistically irrelevant.[12] Similarly, we need to select a reference class for the class of shreebles; this is the broadest kind such that considering subkinds to which shreebles belong does not give a different estimate of variability with respect to color. The more one knows about a subject, the more relevant do subkinds become. Perhaps we should consider shreebles as a kind of waterfowl, or as a kind of Australian waterfowl, if these subdivisions give us a different judgment of variability from merely considering shreebles as a kind of bird. Placing shreebles in the most homogeneous class can make an enormous difference in the inferrability of generalizations. If our reference class is vertebrates, we have too much variability to be able to generalize usefully about color. We are reduced essentially to simple enumeration. At the other extreme, knowledge of the appropriate reference class can mean that a single case is "sufficient for a complete induction". Thus normally our inference making will be enormously more furthered by finding a narrower, more homogeneous reference class than by collecting more instances of shreebles.[13]

III

Philosophers accustomed to the syntactic austerity of Hempelian confirmation theory may find the above use of the notion of *kind* ontologically profligate. What are kinds, and how can we legitimately use such a vague notion in inductive logic? In responding to these questions, it should be noted at the outset that we already know from Goodman's grue problem and other paradoxes that a purely syntactic account of confirmation is impossible. Some background knowledge must be brought in, if only to select predicates which are *projectible* in Goodman's sense. The above discussion indicates that we also need knowledge about kinds, and we shall now try to show that the notion of kind possesses some psychological and philosophical respectability.

Much recent work in cognitive science concerns how human knowledge is organized with respect to kinds and categories. In cognitive psychology, the organization of objects into categories is considered to be critical to determining how humans store and process information.[14] Similarly, a standard technique in artificial intelligence is the organization of concepts into A-KIND-OF hierarchical networks.[15] Thus it is entirely plausible that people do naturally employ the organization in terms of kinds which our account of confirmation presupposes.

The notion of a kind is also philosophically important. There is more to saying that a robin is a kind of bird than just saying that all robins are birds. Simply to write *(x) (Rx ⊃ Bx)* would not bring out the information needed to run the model of confirmation described in Section II. As Quine points out in an important essay on natural kinds, kinds can be seen as sets, but not all sets are kinds. Quine claims that humans have an "innate similarity sense" which provides us with the initial ability to organize the world into kinds. However, natural selection has also endowed man with the ability to transcend this initial organization:

> He has risen above it by developing modified systems of kinds, hence modified similarity standards for scientific purposes. By the trial-and-error process of theorizing he has regrouped things into new kinds which prove to lend themselves to many inductions better than the old.[16]

Systems of theoretical kinds can be built up through inductive experience. Our model of confirmation makes use of such systems. Through past experience, we know a great deal about different kinds of metals and kinds of birds, and such knowledge cannot be neglected when analyzing degree of confirmation.

Quine describes important connections between the notion of a kind and more philosophically familiar notions of subjunctive conditionals: we can say that if *x* were a robin, it would be a bird. Kinds also are relevant to understanding singular causal statements: "To say that one event caused another is to say that the two events are of *kinds* between which there is invariable succession."[17] Mere sets will not suffice, since the two events might fall into any number of trivial sets which accidently overlap.

Talk of causality raises an important question for the account of confirmation we have given. We have described degree of confirmation in terms of background knowledge concerning kinds and variability. To what extent is this background knowledge *causal?* Certainly, we presume there are causal explanations of why metals behave as they do and why birds have the colors they do. If we were actually in possession of good causal explanations for these phenomena, our confidence in the degree to which we generalize from a given number of instances might increase. But we do not need this information in order to make inductive inferences. Although it is assumed that there is some causal underpinning to the classification into kinds, we do not need to know the full causal story in order to use the information about kinds and variability to assess degree of confirmation.

Much remains to be said about the philosophical and psychological bases for considering organization into kinds as a fundamental part of our understanding of the world, but we shall pursue that task no further here. The point of our discussion has been to show that the importance of the notion of a kind goes far beyond its rôle in our account of degree of confirmation.

IV

In this section we shall relate our discussion to several more general accounts of inductive reasoning—theory choice construed as inference to the best explanation, Hempel's qualitative confirmation theory, and Bayesian probabilistic confirmation theory.

Thagard has used case studies from the history of science to develop an account of scientific theory choice as selection of the best of competing explanations of the evidence.[18] This account departed from standard hypothetico-deductive accounts of theory confirmation by using a non-syntactic, highly contextual measure of explanatory power, taken from William Whewell.[19] Briefly, one theory is more *consilient* than another if it explains more classes of facts. The notion of a class of facts is highly pragmatic, depending on the organization of scientific knowledge at a given time. For example, refraction and reflection—the basic laws of each—constitute two classes of facts which optical theories must explain. Consilience is most relevant to assessing the explanatory power of *theories,* but it also has an application to generalizations. A generalization $(x) (Fx \supset Gx)$ is consilient if there is *variety* among the objects a such that Fa in conjunction with the generalization explains Ga. It is not the number of instances which matters so much as their variety.

That conclusion can be understood in terms of the account of confirmation given above. How do we assess "variety among instances"? Such an assessment requires background knowledge about the *kinds* of things involved. To test, for example, Snell's law of refraction, we would measure different substances at different temperatures, and so on, but not worry about such matters as the particular city where the results were achieved: the light and its media are not the kinds of things which are variable with respect to geographical location. When background knowledge tells us that F is of a kind K_1 which is variable with respect to K_2, of which G is a kind, then we know we need to find a variety of instances before we can infer that (x) $(Fx \supset Gx)$. Invariance based on background knowledge licenses not only restrictions to fewer instances, but also less concern about variety of instances. It is therefore background knowledge about the variability of kinds which enables us to assess the consilience of a generalization and infer it as the best explanation.

Variability in kinds is a consideration which goes beyond Hempel's syntactic account of confirmation,[20] but is of some help in understanding a well-known paradox in that account. It is a consequence of Hempel's conditions on confirmation that, because 'All F are G' is logically equivalent to 'All non-G are non-F', the first generalization is confirmed by anything which is non-G and non-F. Thus we get the paradoxical result that an instance of a white shoe confirms 'All ravens are black'. One popular resolution of the paradox is to grant that 'All ravens are black' is confirmed by a white shoe, but to point out that this confirmation is much *less* than that gained by an instance of a black raven.[21] The reason for the difference in degree of confirmation is that there are far more non-black things than ravens. Our model suggests that there is more to the difference in degree of confirmation than just the different numbers of ravens and non-black things. Our background knowledge tells us that ravens are kinds of birds, and black is a kind of color, and that birds are fairly invariant with respect to color. However, we have no analogous background knowledge about non-black things and non-ravens. 'Non-black' and 'non-raven' are not kinds of anything. With those properties, we are relegated to doing the kind of induction by simple enumeration which requires us to gather very many instances before we can have any confidence that we have more than an accidental correlation. In contrast, 'raven' and 'black' fit into our knowledge system in such a way that we can use information about variability of kinds to establish a high degree of confirmation on the basis of relatively few instances. This, in addition to size of the relevant classes, allows us to judge that 'All ravens are black' is much better confirmed by a black raven than 'All non-black things are non-ravens' is confirmed by a white shoe.

In probabilistic confirmation theory, $C(H, E)$ is generally identified with $P(H \mid E) - P(H)$.[22] The more a piece of evidence raises the probability of a hypothesis, the more it is said to confirm the hypothesis. $P(H \mid E)$ is generally calculated by means of Bayes' Theorem, a simple form of which is:

$$P(H \mid E) = P(H) \times P(E \mid H)/P(E).$$

There are numerous problems with Bayesian, probabilistic confirmation theory which we shall not attempt to review here.[23] But a discussion of our claims concerning the importance of variability to confirmation would not be complete without relating it to the Bayesian tradition.

At the top level, our variability model fits very well with probabilistic confirmation theory. Three instances of blue-burning floridium increase the probability of the relevant generalization more than three instances of blue shreebles increase the probability of 'All shreebles are blue', in some sense of probability. Hence degree of confirmation is greater in the former case. We might expect also that the background knowledge about what kinds of things are involved could play a direct rôle through Bayes' theorem, but the simple Bayesian model does not seem rich enough to bring out the relevant reasoning.

Three instances of blue-burning floridium give us a high probability for 'All floridium burns with a blue flame', but why? This is not due to high prior probability $P(H)$, because until we get the first instance of floridium, $P(H)$ would seem to be low, if we could sensibly give it a value at all. Moreover, high $P(H)$ cannot be the main contributor to high $P(H \mid E)$, since then $P(H \mid E) - P(H)$ and hence $C(H, E)$ would not be high. In addition, there seems to be no difference between the relevant values of $P(E \mid H)$ and $P(E)$ in the floridium and shreeble cases. Hence the Bayesian approach, narrowly construed, does not seem adequate to account for the variability effect.

A Bayesian could say that use of background information about variability is really deductive, and therefore need not be taken into account in a model of inductive reasoning. We might for example have the principle that any combustion property of a metal will be completely invariant. Letting 'MF' stands for 'F is a kind of metal' and 'CG' stand for 'G is a kind of combustion property' we could write the generalization:

$$(x)(y)(F)(G) [(MF \& CG \& Fx \& Gx \& Fy) \supset Gy].$$

This implies that once you have one instance of something which is both F and G, it follows deductively that the next F will be G. More generally, we can assume the presence in our background knowledge of information of the form:

$$(x)(y)(F)(G) \{P[Gy \mid (K_1 F \& K_2 G \& Fx \& Gx \& Fy)] = n\}$$

Using this information, we could deductively get from a single instance 'Fa & Ga' a high value for $P(Gb \mid Fb)$ and hence for $P((x)(Fx \supset Gx))$ and $P(H \mid E)$. Thus, it could be argued, the difference between the floridium and shreeble cases is that the former case gives a much higher value for n. Undoubtedly, some such construction could be made, but it does not go far in illuminating the logic of variability and confirmation. Perhaps the metal case is deductive, but the two shreeble cases, one involving color and the other nesting behavior, are clearly more complex. One instance would not generate a stable value for $P(Gx)$: getting extra cases *does* matter when confirming the generalizations that all shreebles are blue and that all shreebles use baobab leaves for nesting materials, and the important result to hang on to is that the extra case matters in different amounts to the two generalizations. Hence, we need the general relation $C(H, E) = f(I(K_1, K_2)$. So the existence of deductive relations is not enough to enable the Bayesian to take variability into account.

Mary Hesse has made a Bayesian proposal for accounting for the importance of variety of instances, which, we saw earlier in this section, is correlative to the problem of variability. It is indeed a problem for the Bayesian to explain why variety of evidence is inductively important. Hesse proposes that the concern for variety of instances is a corollary of eliminative induction.[24] Suppose $S = \{H_1, H_2, \ldots H_n\}$ is a set of finite, exhaustive, and mutually exclusive hypotheses. Then $P(H_1 \mid E) + P(H_2 \mid E) + \ldots P(H_n \mid E) = 1$, and any disconfirmation of any proper subset of S by new evidence increases the sum of the probabilities of the remaining subset. Variety of instances is then seen to be desirable, since greater variety will presumably lead to disconfirmation of more of the H_i, leaving the remaining ones better confirmed.

In the shreeble case, this might work as follows. Thinking deterministically, our alternative hypotheses, prior to any evidence, might be:

H_1 All shreebles are blue.

H_2 All shreebles are green.

$\cdots$

H_n All shreebles are brown.

Then if $P(H_1 \vee H_2 \vee \ldots H_n) = 1$, the observation of even one blue shreeble will eliminate all alternative hypotheses and establish that $P(H_1 \mid E) = 1$. Reference to variability and kinds would be unnecessary.

However, we have to consider the possibility that shreebles will vary in color. This possibility requires us to add:

H_{n+1} Shreebles come in various colors.

Then the observation of a blue shreeble will still rule out $H_2 \ldots H_n$, but we would have only the result: $P(H_1 \vee H_{n+1} \mid E) = 1$. If $P(H_{n+1})$, the prior probability that shreebles vary in color, is very high, then the probability that shreebles are blue will *not* be greatly increased by the evidence. Conversely, if shreebles are highly invariant with respect to color, then the probability of H_1 is greatly elevated. In order to get an objective estimate of

$P(H_{n + 1})$ we need a method for assessing invariance along the lines suggested above in Section II.

We do not doubt that our concerns about the relevance of variability to confirmation could be incorporated into some more elaborate Bayesian account of inductive inference. Our point has not been that there is any incompatibility between Bayesian inference to generalizations as we construe it, but rather that any confirmation theory including Bayesian will have to take into account the effects of variability on degree of confirmation.

V

Our account of confirmation illustrates our contention that inductive principles are content relative. Assessment of degree of confirmation must go beyond syntactic matters to consider the kinds of things under investigation. Further illustration of this principle could be found in the logic of theory choice, where the criteria for selecting the theory which provides the best explanation of the evidence are content relative, and in the logic of statistical analysis of data, where appropriateness of a particular statistical test in an empirical context depends on background assumptions about the nature of the relevant population.

In discussing the validity of deductive reasoning, we can abstract from the content of the sentences in question, since deductive validity is a function only of logical form. Even here, however, abstraction from content is unrealistic at the practical level. Since no finite reasoner has the time or resources to infer all the consequences of his or her beliefs, what actually gets inferred when must be a function of more than just what legitimately *may* be inferred by logical rules. The content of what we believe and the nature of our general concerns will determine what inferences are selected from the infinite number we could make.

In inductive reasoning, even which inferences we *may* make is in part a function of the content of our beliefs. Content can play a rôle in different ways. It affects what rules it will be appropriate to use. The rules for accepting theories, for adopting generalizations as well confirmed, and for accepting or rejecting statistical hypotheses, apply in different contexts. One needs to know what one is talking about in order to select the appropriate rules for the context. In addition, as our discussion of degree of confirmation showed, content affects how much evidence is needed before an inference becomes legitimate. Hence the validity of our inductive inferences depends on beliefs about the nature of the events in question.[25]

Since Carnap, most work on inductive logic has been highly analytical and mathematical, emphasizing syntactic constructions or Bayesian formalisms. In company with Goldman's approach to epistemology,[26] we recommend a more empirical approach to inductive logic. The inductive logician can take as data experimental results such as we described in Section I, or case studies from the history of science, or even the more informal anecdotal evidence that is usually all that logicians have considered. The empirical approach obviates distractions which arise from artificial constructs such as 'grue'.[27] Inductive logic is primarily concerned with how people actually do reason. Of course, there is no simple move from how people do reason to how people *should* reason, which is the concern of the normative discipline of inductive logic. But empirical results and reflection on them can contribute greatly to the development of normative models.[28] Empirical studies help us to identify pervasive features of human reasoning, and sound normative models must either account for those features, or explain why those features are not desirable parts of a normative model. We hope to have shown in this paper that any satisfactory normative model of confirmation must take into account the rôle of background knowledge concerning kinds and variability.

FOOTNOTES

*For helpful comments and suggestions, we are grateful to Jonathan Adler, Susan Carey, Lisbeth Fried, Daniel Hausman, John Holland, Keith Holyoak, David Krantz, Lance Rips, Glenn Shafer, Stephen Stich, and Stephen White.

[1]J. S. Mill: 1970, A System of Logic, Eighth edition (Longman London), Book III, Ch. III, Section 3.

[2]N. Goodman: 1965, Fact, Fiction, and Forecast, 2nd edition (Bobbs-Merrill, Indianapolis), p. 63f.

[3]See S. Stich and R. E. Nisbett: 1980, 'Justification and the psychology of human reasoning', Philosophy of Science 47, pp. 188–202; and P. Thagard: 1982, 'From the descriptive to the normative in psychology and logic', Philosophy of Science 49, pp. 24–42.

[4]See, e.g., C. Hempel: 1965, Aspects of Scientific Explanation (Free Press, New York); and R. Swinburne: 1973, An Introduction to Confirmation Theory (Methuen, London).

[5]R. E. Nisbett, D. H. Krantz, C. Jepson, and Z. Kunda; 'Intuitive models and statistical heuristics', (forthcoming).

[6]G. Quattrone and E. Jones: 1980, 'The perception of variability within in-groups and out-groups: implications for the law of large numbers', Journal of Personality and Social Psychology 38, pp. 141–152.

[7]R. Clark: 1972, Einstein, The Life and Times (Avon, New York), p. 290.

[8]Hempel, op. cit.; R. Carnap: 1950, Logical Foundations of Probability University of Chicago Press, Chicago).

[9]Mill, op. cit.; J. M. Keynes: 1921, A Treatise on Probability (Macmillan, London); B. Russsel: 1948, Human Knowledge: Its Scope and Limits (Allen and Unwin, London); R. Harrod: 1956, Foundations of Inductive Logic (Macmillan, London).

[10]We use the term 'invariance' rather than 'invariability' for reasons of euphony. Our notion of variability here is not the same as the statistical notion of variance of a sample or population, which is calculated by reference to a mean of some random variable. In our

qualitative cases, we have no mean value. Statistical variance does however have an effect essentially the same as our variability: if we know that the variance in a population is low, then only a very small sample suffices to give us an accurate estimation of the mean.

[11]L. A. Goodman, and W. H. Kruskal: 1954, 'Measures of association for cross classifications', Journal of the American Statistical Association 49 pp. 732–764, 740ff. Reprinted in Goodman and Kruskal: 1979, Measures of Association for Cross Classifications (Springer Verlag, New York).

[12]See Wesley C. Salmon: 1967, The Foundations of Scientific Inference (University of Pittsburgh Press, Pittsburgh), pp. 91ff. The sort of inference discussed by Salmon also will often require consideration of kinds. If we have complete statistical information, the appropriate reference class can be determined mathematically. But in the more common situations where information is limited, we will select a reference class for Fred based on what kinds of things we know him to be.

[13]It should be noted that there are ways of getting an estimate of variability other than by considering kinds. For example, we might have heard on the radio that Ford is economizing by making all its new subcompacts the same color. Then, deductively, we can infer from one observation of a blue Ford subcompact that all are blue.

[14]For surveys see: A. Glass, K. Holyoak, and J. Santa: 1979, Cognition (Addison Wesley, Reading, Mass.), Ch. 10; and E. Rosch and B. B. Lloyd (eds.): 1978, Cognition and Categorization (Erlbaum, Hillsdale, N.J.).

[15]See, for example P. Winston: 1977, Artificial Intelligence: (Addison Wesley, Reading Mass.), Ch. 7; and S. Fahlman: 1979, NETL: A System for Representing and Using Real World Knowledge (MIT Press, Cambridge).

[16]W. Quine: 1968, Ontological Relativity and Other Essays (Columbia University Press, New York), p. 128.

[17]Ibid., p. 133.

[18]P. Thagard: 1978, 'The best explanation: criteria for theory choice', Journal of Philosophy, 75, pp. 76–92.

[19]W. Whewell: 1967, The Philosophy of the Inductive Sciences, reprint of second edition (Johnson Reprint Corporation New York).

[20]Hempel, op. cit.

[21]See for example, J. L. Mackie: 1963, 'The paradox of confirmation', British Journal for the Philosophy of Science 13, pp. 265–277.

[22]Carnap, op. cit.; M. Hesse: 1974, The Structure of Scientific Inference (University of California Press, Berkeley).

[23]C. Glymour: 1980, Theory and Evidence (Princeton University Press, Princeton), Ch. III.

[24]M. Hesse, op. cit., pp. 137ff.

[25]For further discussion, see R. E. Nisbett, D. H. Krantz, C. Jepson, and G. T. Fong: 1982, 'Improving inductive inference', in D. Kahneman, P. Slovic, and A. Tversky (eds.): Judgment Under Uncertainty: Heuristics and Biases (Cambridge University Press, New York), pp. 445–459.

[26]A. Goldman: 1978, 'Epistemics: the regulative theory of cognition', Journal of Philosophy, 75, pp. 509–523.

[27]Goodman's (op. cit.) problem about grue does not arise in our account of confirmation. That all emeralds are green is highly confirmed by a few green emeralds, since we know that gems are highly invariant with respect to color. We have no similar information for assessing the degree of confirmation of 'All emeralds are grue', since grue is not a kind of anything represented in our background knowledge. Without background knowledge about the invariance of gems with respect to properties like grue, we cannot expect high confirmation of 'All emeralds are grue' by a few grue emeralds.

[28]See the articles cited in Note 3, and M. Friedman: 1979, 'Truth and confirmation', Journal of Philosophy 76, pp. 361–382. The relevant psychological discussions include: W. Edwards:

1968, 'Conservatism in human information processing', in B. Kleinmuntz (ed.): Formal Representation of Human Judgment (Wiley, New York); P. Slovic and S. Lichtenstein: 1971, 'Comparison of Bayesian and regression approaches to the study of information processing in judgment', Organizational Behavior and Human Performance 6 pp. 649–744; A. Tversky and D. Kahneman: 1974, 'Judgment under uncertainty: heuristics and biases', Science 185 pp. 1124–1131; R. E. Nisbett and L. Ross: 1980, Human Inference: Strategies and Shortcomings of Social Judgment (Prentice-Hall, Englewood Cliffs, N.J.).

4 Inductive Reasoning: Competence or Skill?

Christopher Jepson
University of Michigan

Richard E. Nisbett
University of Michigan

David H. Krantz
Bell Laboratories

In the study of inductive reasoning, there has been much debate about the standards for correct solutions to problems. Studies by psychologists have frequently used formalized statistical reasoning as the criterion, and have found the reasoning of ordinary adults to fall short of this standard in many cases. Others, however, have criticized this practice of applying formal standards to everyday reasoning. Some epistemologists have argued that inferential standards must be derived from the intuitions of ordinary adults (L. J. Cohen 1979; 1981, Dennett 1978; 1981; Lycan 1981) or that standards must take into account the trade-offs set by limitations of human capacity (Goldman 1978). The following quotations illustrate these views. "Our fundamental epistemic principles and habits, whatever ones they turn out to be exactly, are *good* principles, in that they are the ones that a wise and benevolent Mother Nature would have endowed us with, given Her antecedent choices of materials and overall anatomical structure" (Lycan 1981, p. 345). "Ordinary human reasoning—by which I mean the reasoning of adults who have not been systematically educated in any branch of logic or probability theory—cannot be held to be faultily programmed: it sets its own standards" (L. J. Cohen 1981, p. 317). "Advice in matters intellectual, as in other matters, should take account of the agent's capacities. There is no point in recommending procedures that cognizers cannot follow or prescribing results that cognizers cannot attain" (Goldman 1978, p. 510).

We believe that arguments such as those above are based upon a view of inductive reasoning that is too static and accords too small a role to learning processes and to individual differences. In our view, inductive reasoning is a process of accommodation: Mental models change in order to assimilate new data. The correctness of an induction depends not only on the adequacy of one's initial models but also on the conceptual tools one has available for extending or altering them. Changes in concepts and tools can therefore lead to different, and perhaps better, inductions. In other words, induction is a skill in which learning plays an important role. This perspective is at odds with those quoted above. Lycan's view attributes far too much importance to biological evolution and too little to cultural change. Cohen postulates far too broad a communality in the reasoning processes of the "untutored" adult. And although we agree with Goldman, we find it difficult to apply his criterion: New tools may be difficult to use at first but may lead to greater ease and efficiency after they are mastered.

One reason that many epistemologists have not thought of induction as a skill may be the existence of an analogy between inductive reasoning ability and the well-established concept of linguistic competence (Sober 1978). Cohen states this analogy as follows:

> To ascribe a cognitive competence . . . is to characterise the content of a culturally or genetically inherited ability which, under ideal conditions, every member of the community would exercise in appropriate circumstances. It states what people can do, rather than what they will do, much as the characterisation of a linguistic competence can be taken to describe what it is that native speakers must be assumed capable of recognising about the structure of morphophonemic strings. (1981b, pp. 321–22)

In our view, the analogy between language and inductive reasoning fails to recognize that there is far more to language usage than grammatical competence. Important cultural inventions, such as writing or new vocabulary, increase the effectiveness of language use. Some of these inventions, especially technical vocabulary, are acquired primarily through formal education. Frequent practice and emulation of good models can greatly increase the effectiveness of oral or written use of language. In addition, there are enormous individual differences in talent, that is, in the rate of improvement as a function of practice and exposure to models.

These aspects of language use fall outside the usual distinction between competence and performance. Improvements in vocabulary or in other aspects of language effectiveness, by a culture or by an individual, do not represent closer approximations to some ideal competence. Instead, there is potentially no limit to the invention of new concepts and new means to communicate them, or to the improvement of language skill.

We contend that effective inductive reasoning is also a skill; that it depends on cultural innovations, such as probability theory; and that it can be improved through education and frequent practice. We also suspect that there are large individual differences in talent, as well as in education and in practice, that affect inductive skill.

Previous work on inductive heuristics has left many theorists with the impression that subjects in reasoning experiments behave quite uniformly. For example, Kahneman and Tversky (1972) found no positive evidence that *any* subjects could apply the law of large numbers to the problems they presented, and they found (1973) that virtually all subjects ignore regression and fail to apply base rates. Because mistakes are made by almost all subjects in many experiments, the notion of "cognitive illusion" has been used to describe judgmental errors based on representativeness or other nonprobabilistic heuristics (Einhorn & Hogarth 1978; Kahneman & Tversky 1973; Nisbett & Ross 1980). It seems likely, however, that the universality of the errors demonstrated to date is simply a result of the fact that subjects have been presented with problems for which the investigators themselves felt drawn to the erroneous line of reasoning. If one is simply seeking to demonstrate errors, this is an efficient strategy. But normatively correct principles of reasoning apply not only to hard problems, that is, those that investigators themselves have difficulty with, but also to easy problems. By using somewhat easier problems, we can explore individual differences in the skill of inductive reasoning.

In the studies reported below, undergraduates without formal training in statistics were presented with problems in inductive reasoning for which statistical reasoning was required—use of the law of large numbers, regression, or base-rate principles. We tried to generate problems having a range of difficulty levels. Our view of inductive reasoning as a skill entails the following predictions:

1. For each problem, there will be a variety of approaches used by different individuals. There is no standard "lay" position, unitary and distinct from that of experts educated in probability theory.
2. Subjects will differ in their general strategies toward inductive problems: Some will consistently use probabilistic reasoning, others will do so infrequently.
3. Subjects' use of probabilistic reasoning will be correlated with their other mental skills.

STUDY 1: MATERIALS AND SCORING OF RESPONSES

Each subject completed a booklet containing 11 problems. Each problem required an open-ended answer. The order of the problems in the booklet was the same for all subjects.

The key factor common to all the problems was the inclusion of a sample of evidence that was fairly small to very small in size. A statistical solution depended upon conceptualizing the evidence as a "small sample" and applying the law of large numbers, which asserts that a large random sample is more likely to be representative of the population from which it was drawn than is a small one. Problems in which the sample, in addition to being small, was extreme in its value on the target attribute, could be solved by use of the principle of regression to the mean. People reasoning according to statistical principles should be reluctant to base inferences either on small samples or on samples yielding values that could be presumed to be extreme. The problems, together with examples of the answers given by subjects, are presented in the appendix.

Each answer was scored as either *statistical, deterministic,* or *intermediate,* depending on the predominating tenor of the subject's analysis of the problem. The analysis was scored as statistical if it contained an explanation based on the law of large numbers or, in some cases, on the principle of regression to the mean. Answers scored as statistical could include causal or other nonstatistical reasoning so long as a clear, correct statistical analysis was present. The analysis was scored as purely deterministic if it gave an exclusively causal interpretation of events or if it made no use at all of statistical principles or probabilistic reasoning. Most of these answers presumed, either tacitly or explicitly, that the sample was adequate and showed no recognition of the uncertain or probabilistic nature of events of the kind presented in the problems. Intermediate answers were those that mixed both types of reasoning or were ambiguous as to which type they were or made use of erroneous probabilistic reasoning such as the gambler's fallacy. The analyses given by 30 of the subjects were coded independently by two people, and intercoder reliability was assessed. Exact agreement on scoring category was obtained for 78% of responses. Responses coded as statistical by one coder and as deterministic by the other made up less than 2% of all responses.

In some problems, subjects were asked also to choose between two alternatives, one of which was favored on the basis of, a large sample and the other of which was favored by evidence from a small sample. Scoring of choices was straightforward: We simply recorded whether subjects picked the alternative indicated by the large sample or the alternative indicated by the small sample or neither.

The questionnaire originally contained eleven problems, but two of these were worded poorly, resulting in many subjects misunderstanding the questions being asked, and giving answers that could not be scored properly. These problems were therefore excluded from the analysis and are not presented in the appendix.

For purposes of data reduction, a numerical score between 2 and 6 was assigned to each response, with a higher score representing a more statistical answer. For problems that did not include choices, a deterministic analysis received a score of 2, an intermediate analysis a score of 4, and a statistical analysis a score of 6. For choice problems these analyses received scores of 1, 2, and 3 respectively, and the score for the analysis was added to the score for the choice: 1 for choice of the alternative indicated by the small sample, 2 for choice of neither, and 3 for choice of the alternative indicated by the large sample.

Subjects and Procedure

Subjects were 112 students in introductory psychology courses at the University of Michigan who participated in the experiment as a course requirement. Upon arrival, they were given the materials and asked to work on them individually. They were told that the investigators were interested in how people make judgments and choices under conditions in which information is not as complete as they might like. They were asked to go into as much detail as necessary in their responses, and to complete each problem before beginning the next. After finishing the problems, subjects filled out a questionnaire in which they indicated whether they had had any formal training in statistics, and recorded their Scholastic Aptitude Test (SAT) scores. Subjects were requested to allow the investigators to obtain their SAT scores from school records if they were not certain of them. Eight of the original subjects had had a statistics course in college and were not included among the 112 for whom data were analyzed.

Results

Table 4.1 presents the proportion of statistical, intermediate, and deterministic analyses given for each problem and, where applicable, the proportion of subjects choosing either the large sample alternative or the small sample

TABLE 4.1
Response Proportions in Study 1

Problem	Analysis			Choice		
	Statistical	Intermediate	Deterministic	Large no.	Undecided	Small no.
1. Lung cancer	.93	.02	.05			
2. Admissions	.50	.18	.32	.62	.06	.31
3. Championship	.49	.07	.44	.62	.13	.25
4. Batting avg.	.34	.28	.38			
5. 4.00 GPA	.30	.12	.58			
6. College choice	.16	.16	.68	.26	.01	.74
7. Fidelity	.13	.18	.69			
8. Job candidate	.12	.27	.61	.72	.01	.27
9. Class choice	.05	.06	.89	.19	.03	.79

From Jepson, Krantz, and Nisbett (1982).

alternative. The N for each problem ranges from 107 to 112. It may be seen that subjects are divided in their approach to the problems. Unanimity did not occur for any of the nine problems, and for four of the problems there was very great disagreement, with 30% or more of subjects favoring statistical answers and 30% or more favoring deterministic answers.

To determine whether individuals were consistent across problems, we examined the correlations between pairs of problems. The reliability (Cronbach's Coefficient Alpha) for this nine-problem test was .38, corresponding to a mean interitem correlation of .056 ± .017. This is low, but significantly different from 0 ($p \le .001$).[1]

Another way to examine consistency is to look at the best and worst subjects. Of the 100 subjects who completed all 9 problems (the other 12 each omitted one problem), 3 gave 8 out of 9 nondeterministic responses (i.e., statistical or intermediate), 6 more gave 7 out of 9, and 17 gave 6 out of 9. Under a hypothesis of no individual difference (statistical independence), the expected frequencies would have been 0.7, 4.4, and 14.2 respectively, in these upper categories. Similarly, 5 of these subjects produced 6 statistical responses apiece; the expected frequency of 6 or more statistical responses, under the null hypothesis of independence, would be only 1.8. Corresponding to these probabilistic subjects, there were also more subjects with poorer overall performance than would be expected by chance. One subject gave all deterministic responses, and 11 others gave all but 1 or 2 (under the null hypothesis, 7.5 would be the expected frequency of 0–2 deterministic responses, with 0.04 expected for all deterministic).

The relationship between the use of statistical reasoning and other mental skills was assessed by examining the correlation between subjects' total test scores and their verbal, quantitative, and combined SAT scores. Correlation coefficients were .35, .48, and .48 respectively. (A correlation of .25 is significant at the .01 level, for $df = 101$. Nine of the 112 subjects were not included in the analysis because SAT scores were not available for them.) Thus it was decidedly the case that subjects with higher aptitude scores were more likely to reason statistically. The size of these correlations is surprisingly high in view of the relatively poor reliability. Subtests of intelligence scales typically correlate with one another between .20 and .50, or with the full intelligence scale between .40 and .70.

Separate analyses were performed on two subsets of the data in order to check possible errors. The first source of potential error was in the SAT scores. We had obtained permission to check scores from only half of our subjects, for the rest, we were relying on the subjects' memory and honesty. We separately computed the correlation between SAT and total test score for only those subjects with verified SAT scores. The resulting correlations were .22 (verbal), .41 (quantitative), and .37 (combined), where a correlation of .34 was significant at the .01 level.

The other possible source of error was that we had not limited ourselves to subjects who were totally untutored in statistics. Subjects' responses to our questions following the experimental sessions revealed that roughly two-fifths of them had had some exposure to statistics in high school mathematics courses (usually in the form of a week or two of probability theory). To check whether such training might influence the pattern of responses, we performed separate analyses on the data for subjects who reported no training in statistics whatever. Patterns of response to the problems, Cronbach alpha, and SAT-total test score correlations were all virtually identical to those obtained for the entire sample of subjects.

Finally, it can be seen from examination of the problems and from the left half of Table 4.1 that statistical solutions were much more common for problems dealing with objectively measurable attributes (cancer, batting average, GPA) than for those dealing with subjective judgments (the need for fidelity in relationships, leadership qualities, liking for a college). This is consistent with the observation by Nisbett, Borgida, Crandall, and Reed (1976) that base rates are often applied well to events such as sports and other achievement situations in which the fixedness of the circumstances and the ability to observe large numbers of people serve to render central tendency and variability transparent. Aptitude scores were correlated with the tendency to give statistical answers for both objective attribute and subjective judgment problems. The correlation was .37 between total SAT score and tendency to give statistical solutions for the first five problems in Table 4.1 and .34 between SAT score and the last four problems in Table 4.1 (for both $p < .01$). These correlations indicate that mental ability is associated with the tendency to reason statistically both about problems for which such reasoning is generally popular and about problems for which it is deviant.

STUDY 2

Study 1 was highly successful in demonstrating two of the three anticipated results. For all of the problems presented, there was divergence of opinion among subjects as to whether a statistical solution was appropriate; and the tendency to provide statistical solutions was associated with other measures of intellectual ability. However, the tendency to provide statistical solutions was not shown to be a very consistent individual difference. It seemed possible that by increasing the number of items and the precision of the scoring system we might be able to show more clearly consistent individual differences than were found in Study 1. A total of 15 items was used in Study 2, and the scoring system was refined so as to distinguish among different qualities of statistical answers, ranging from poor to excellent. To increase the generalizability of the findings of Study 1 it also seemed important to replicate the study with different items.

Study 2 also allowed for a finer-grained analysis. The refined scoring system described below made it possible to determine whether aptitude is correlated with the overall frequency with which a statistical approach is taken to problems, or with the quality of statistical answers, or with both.

Method

The procedure was virtually identical to that of Study 1. Subjects were 41 University of Michigan introductory psychology students of both sexes. Responses to 15 problems were examined. The problems were similar in format and content to those used in Study 1, but only two of those problems, "Admissions" and "College choice," were repeated.[2]

Three categories of problems were generated, and subjects were given five problems in each category. Two categories were refinements of the "objective attribute" type (for example, the "Admissions" problem) and the "subjective judgment" type (for example, the "College choice" problem referred to in the previous section). The additional category dealt with objective attributes, but added a broad hint as to the probabilistic nature of the events described in the problem. This hint came in the form of a random generating process producing or influencing events — a lottery, a haphazard search through a jar of pennies, or an explicitly random selection procedure. An example of a problem in this "probabilistic event" category is presented below.

At Stanbrook University, the Housing Office determines which of the 10,000 students enrolled will be allowed to live on campus the following year. At Stanbrook, the dormitory facilities are excellent, so there is always great demand for on-campus housing. Unfortunately, there are only enough on-campus spaces for 5,000 students. The Housing Office determines who will get to live on campus by having a House Draw every year: Every student picks a number out of a box over a three-day period. These numbers range from 1 to 10,000. If the number is 5,000 or under, the student gets to live on campus. If the number is over 5,000, the student will not be able to live on campus.

On the first day of the draw, Joe talks to five people who have picked a number. Of these, four people got low numbers. Because of this, Joe suspects that the numbers in the box were not properly mixed, and that the early numbers are more favorable. He rushes over to the Housing Draw and picks a number. He gets a low number. He later talks to four people who drew their numbers on the second or third day of the draw. Three got high numbers. Joe says to himself, "I'm glad that I picked when I did, because it looks like I was right that the numbers were not properly mixed."

What do you think of Joe's reasoning? Explain.

The expectation was that the great majority of subjects would give statistical answers for the manifestly probabilistic events, while fewer would give statistical answers for the objective attribute problems, and only a minority would give statistical answers for the subjective judgment problems. If so, it should be possible to determine to what degree aptitude is related to the tendency to give statistical answers, and to the quality of the statistical answers that are given, both under circumstances in which most subjects model events in a probabilistic way and under circumstances in which most subjects do not.

Scoring of responses was similar to that in Study 1 except that four levels of quality were distinguished: (1) purely deterministic reasoning, reflecting no recognition of uncertainty or of the probabilistic nature of the events in the problem; (2) erroneous or unclear statistical reasoning; (3) a correct application of the law of large numbers, but perfunctory and incomplete and with no indication that the sampling "units" (e.g. encounters with different people in the college choice problem) had been correctly identified; and (4) correct application of the law of large numbers, including correct identification of sampling units. Exact agreement on scoring category was 80%. Agreement as to whether the answer was deterministic (category 1) or statistical (category 2, 3, or 4) was 94%.

Results

The pattern of results found in Study 1 was replicated. The percentage of subjects giving statistical responses for individual problems ranged from 90 on the easiest problem to 15 on the most difficult. For all problems, therefore, some subjects gave statistical answers and some gave purely deterministic ones. The Cronbach Alpha coefficient was .64, corresponding to a mean interitem correlation of $.100 \pm .016$ ($p < 10$), which would be a more satisfactory level for single items in a test of ability. (The difference between studies in mean interitem correlation is $.044 \pm .023$; thus, our claim of an improvement is not asserted with a great deal of confidence.) Correlations of total test scores with verbal, quantitative, and combined SAT scores were .48, .42, and .49 respectively, all significant at the .01 level.

As in Study 1, responses of those subjects having no statistical training in high school were analyzed separately. Results were entirely similar for these subjects. Separate analysis of subjects whose SAT scores were verified was unnecessary, since only five of the subjects had unverified scores.

Problem category had a very pronounced effect on the frequency of statistical responses. The first column of Table 4.2 shows the percentages of statistical responses (i.e. scores of 2–4) for the three categories, as well as the overall percentage for all 15 problems. The differences between

TABLE 4.2
Problem Categories and Statistical Reasoning Subscores

Problem category	% Statistical response	Correlation of scores with SAT		
		Frequency score	Quality score	Total score
Probabilistic	82	.33	.27	.37
Objective	57	.46	.32	.50
Subjective	26	.29	.01	.26
Combined	55	.49	.39	.49

Note: For $df = 39$, an r of 131 is significant at $p < .05$. (From Jepson, Krantz, & Nisbett 1982.)

categories are highly reliable. (There are about 200 responses for each percentage, 5 problems $\times$ 41 subjects, with occasional missing data.)

The second column of Table 4.2 shows the correlation of frequency of statistical responses with combined SAT score, across subjects, again breaking down the result by problem category. Clearly, this frequency score correlated with SAT, though the sample size is too small to make any assertion about the pattern of correlation across problem categories. We also examined the quality of statistical responses: For each subject, a quality score consisted of the number of 3–4 responses divided by the total number of statistical (2–4) responses. (The denominator of this conditional frequency fell as low as 1 in some cases.) Fong et al. (1982) have shown that this quality score does not vary with problem category. Column 3 of Table 4.2 shows that the quality score (combined across problem categories) also correlates with SAT score.

Discussion

The behavior that we report here might be called uninstructed use of probabilistic concepts. By this we mean that the subjects have little if any formal training in the use of such concepts and are not prompted or aided by others or by situational cues, other than cues in the problems themselves. The findings about this behavior may be summarized as follows.

1. Uninstructed use of probabilistic concepts is neither rare nor universal. Its frequency varies from problem to problem; it is higher for problems that allude to culturally designated "chance" mechanisms, such as slot machines, and lower for problems that deal with tastes or feelings. There is no "lay" standard for these problems: Subjects vary widely in their approaches to them.

2. Uninstructed use of probabilistic concepts varies reliably between individuals, at least for the particular university population and problems studied.

3. Uninstructed use of probabilistic concepts is correlated with other mental skills, at least for the particular university population and problems studied. (And it should be noted that the correlation for university students is probably lower, because of the truncated range, than the correlation in the general population.)

These facts seem consistent with the view that inductive reasoning, like other kinds of problem solving, and like language use, is a skill. "Ordinary human reasoning" does not "set its own standards"; rather, its standards are determined by the culturally evolved tools, such as probability concepts, that are available for use. Though our subjects were formally uninstructed, they had all learned at least a minimal concept of probability from our culture, and in Study 2, each of them applied it at least once.

These results do not pose problems for psychological competence theorists, most of whom would feel comfortable with the notion of individual differences in competence. The results do tend to undermine, however, any *normative* theory of inductive reasoning that presupposes a broad competence for inductive reasoning shared by all unimpaired members of the culture. Perhaps there is such a competence, but it remains to be identified. It cannot be inferred from observing ordinary people's solutions to inductive problems, since these solutions vary according to skill in using statistical concepts. If it is granted that future empirical work is likely to continue to reveal pronounced performance differences, suggestive of genuine underlying competence differences, normative philosophical competence theories will be confronted with an impasse. As Stich (1982) put it, "if there are *many* cognitive competences abroad in our society and in others, then there are *many* normative theories of cognition. But if there are many normative theories of cognition, then which is the right one?" Dropping the notion of "inductive competence" and thinking in terms of "inductive skill" lead to the view, which we think is reasonable, that inductive norms should be defined in relation to the best inferential tools available at a given time (see Thagard & Nisbett, in press). The normative advice to a person ignorant of or unskilled in the use of an inductive tool is simply that the person should learn (more) about it.

Inductive Reasoning as a Trainable Skill

The most important implication of the notion that inductive reasoning is a skill is that it should be highly trainable, just as other skills such as swimming, long division, and chess are. And in fact, Krantz, Fong, and

Nisbett (1982) have shown that training in statistics has a profound effect on the way people reason about problems of the kind we gave to subjects in the present studies. For example, they found that a single course in introductory statistics was sufficient to produce marked effects even on problems presented outside the academic context. Male students enrolled in statistics were called either at the beginning or end of the term and asked to participate in "a survey on opinions about sports." They were asked, among filler items, questions like the batting average problem from Study 1 (where subjects had to explain why .450 averages are common in the first two weeks but unheard-of over the whole season). Fifty percent of the answers for that question were statistical for subjects surveyed at the beginning of the term, while 70% of the answers were statistical for subjects surveyed at the end of the term. Other problems showed comparable effects of training (though it should be noted that some showed little or no effects).

Fong, Krantz, and Nisbett (1982) showed that even a half-hour training session is sufficient to influence subjects' answers to problems of inductive reasoning. Subjects were told about the law of large numbers in the abstract, were shown it concretely in operation by drawing various sized samples of colored gumballs from a vase, and were shown how to "model" various real-life events so that the law could be applied to them. This training had a marked effect on answers to problems of the kind presented to subjects in the present studies.

It is important to note that in all of the studies of Krantz et al. and of Fong et al., training affected not merely the likelihood of a statistical answer, but the quality of statistical answers as well. Training in statistics not only makes a statistical approach more salient, it also improves the quality of statistical reasoning.

Optimality

Since the early work of Simon (1957) on normative aspects of decisions, it has become conventional to demand of any decision or judgment procedure that it be cost effective. "Satisficing" solutions are often more rational than so-called optimal ones, if the latter are sufficiently costly or time consuming. Workers in the judgment area have tended to assume that more correct, statistical inferential procedures are more difficult and time consuming than intuitive procedures that do not entail probabilistic representations of events (e.g., Einhorn & Hogarth 1981; Nisbett & Ross 1980). This acknowledgment has then been taken as the basis for a normative critique of the judgment tradition on the ground that so-called normative judgments may sometimes be so time consuming as actually to be nonnormative (Einhorn & Hogarth 1981; Miller & Cantor in press; Nisbett & Ross 1980).

In the course of the present studies, however, we came to recognize that statistical thinking may in fact be quite cost effective. First, it was clear from an examination of representative answers to problems in Study 1 (appendix) that statistical answers are not necessarily longer than deterministic ones. Second, in supplementary studies, we presented students with oral versions of the problems in Studies 1 and 2 and asked them to respond verbally. It was clear from these conversations that statistical answers were not necessarily more time consuming to generate. To be sure, subjects who gave statistical answers sometimes fumbled around at length trying to find a probabilistic model that satisfied them, but sometimes their answers were crisp and instantaneous. It was not uncommon for subjects presented with the batting average problem, for example, to say unhesitatingly that of course unusually high or low averages could be found in any short span of time because of luck, but that luck plays less of a role as the number of times at bat increases. Conversely, some subjects who gave deterministic answers spent a long time pondering the problem, giving one causal explanation after another, none of which seemed to satisfy even the subject himself: "Well . . . the game favors the batters early on because the pitchers haven't had a chance to tailor themselves to individual batting styles . . . also the batters who are doing so great will have a natural tendency to slack off."

Whether statistical approaches to problems are generally more time consuming seems to us to be very much an open question. It is important to recognize that optimality is always relative to some current state of an individual's cognitive development. We may speculate that probabilistic concepts can be incorporated into virtually automatic processing strategies, resulting in an improvement in thinking even in terms of sheer speed of producing an answer. An analogy may be drawn with the speed-accuracy trade-off encountered in other domains of human performance. The usual theoretical relation is a negative one: If subjects are forced to go faster, accuracy is sacrificed. But when speed and accuracy are correlated across subjects, or across training levels or task conditions, the observed relation is generally a positive one. Greater speed is associated with greater accuracy, because both increase with greater aptitude and training of the subject and with easiness of the tasks.

The present evidence is therefore consistent with some very optimistic assumptions about human inductive reasoning. It is a skill; it is trainable; the culture improves in it as knowledge expands; and the benefits of change may far outweigh the costs.

FOOTNOTES

[1]All p values reported are based on two-tailed tests.

[2]The full text of all problems may be found in Fong, Krantz, and Nisbett (1982). They are the 15 problems categorized as having structures I–V.

REFERENCES

Cohen, L. J. (1979). On the psychology of prediction: Whose is the fallacy? *Cognition, 7,* 385–407.

Cohen, L. J. (1901). Can human irrationality be experimentally demonstrated? *Behavioral and Brain Sciences, 4,* 317–331.

Dennett, D. (1978). *Brainstorms.* Montgomery, VT: Bradford Books.

Dennett, D. (1981). Three kinds of intentional psychology. In R. Healey (Ed.). *Reduction, time and reality.* Cambridge: Cambridge University Press.

Einhorn, H. J., & Hogarth, R. M. (1978) Confidence in judgment: Persistence of the illusion of validity. *Psychological Review, 85,* 395–416.

Fong, G. I., Krantz, D. H., & Nisbett, R. E. (1982). The effects of statistical training on thinking about everyday problems. Unpublished manuscript, University of Michigan.

Goldman, A. I. (1978). Epistemics: The regulative theory of cognition. *Journal of Philosophy, 75,* 509–523.

Kahneman, D., & Tversky, A. (1972). Subjective probability: a judgment of representativeness. *Cognitive Psychology, 3,* 237–251.

Kahneman, D., & Tversky, A. (1973). On the psychology of prediction. *Psychological Review, 80,* 237–251.

Krantz, D. H., Fong, G. T., & Nisbett, R. E. (1982). Statistical training and reasonong. Unpublished manuscript, University of Michigan.

Lycan, W. G. (1981). Is and ought in cognition science. *Behavioral and Brain Science, 4,* 344–345.

Miller, G., & Cantor, N. (In press). Review of *Human Inference* by Nisbett and Ross. *Contemporary Psychology.*

Nisbett, R. E., Borgida, E., Crandall, R., & Reed, H. (1976). Popular induction: Information is not always informative. In J. Carroll & J. Payne (Eds.), *Cognition and social behavior.* Hillsdale, NJ: Erlbaum, 1976.

Nisbett, R. E., & Ross, L. (1980). *Human inference: Strategies and shortcomings of social judgment.* Englewood Cliffs, NJ: Prentice-Hall.

Simon, H. (1957). *Models of man.* New York: Wiley.

Sober, E. (1978). Psychologism. *Journal for the Theory of Social Behavior, 8,* 165–191.

Stich, S. (1982). On the ascription of content. In A. Woodfield (Ed.), *Thought and object.* Oxford: Oxford University Press.

Thagard, P., & Nisbett, R. E. (In press). Rationality and charity. *Philosophy of Science.*

APPENDIX: PROBLEMS AND EXAMPLES OF ANSWERS

The nine problems, and examples of each type of analysis for each problem, are presented below. The problems are presented in order of difficulty — that is, they are ordered by percentage of statistical analyses given, from highest to lowest.

Problem 1 ("Lung cancer")

Mr. Johnson said to a friend: "There seems to be a lot of evidence that the increase in lung cancer among women is caused by the increase in women's smoking. But my mother and my wife's mother have both smoked pretty heavily all their lives, and they're both in their eighties now, so I can't see it as that necessarily harmful." Criticize Johnson's reasoning.

Statistical Analysis

Johnson is basing his argument for the overall general effect upon entire populations upon two women. He does not take into his concern the numbers, percentages, and data done by research — but rather takes a narrow almost "egocentric" view of the entire issue.

Intermediate Analysis

She [sic] is just giving an excuse to smoke. But if his mother and his wife's mother haven't gotten cancer, then his chances of getting it are more or less better, even though being independent upon either woman. Since there is evidence that smokers get more lung cancer the law of probability should start to even out.

Deterministic Analysis

Smoking is not the only cause of lung cancer. Possibly the increase of women lung cancer victims is due to more pollutants in the air. Maybe there are more women [or] maybe more women are being exposed to "bad air."

Problem 2 ("Admissions")

The Psychology Department of the University of Michigan keeps records on the performance of all its graduate students and relates this performance score to all kinds of background information about the students. Recently there was a debate on the admissions committee about whether to admit a particular student from Horace Maynard College. The student's scores on the GRE and his GPA were marginal — that is, almost all students actually admitted to the department have scores as high or higher, while most rejected students have lower scores. The student's letters of recommendation were quite good, but none of the writers of the letters were personally known to any of the Michigan faculty. One member of the admissions committee argued against admission, pointing out that department records show that students who graduate from small, nonselective colleges like Maynard perform at a level substantially below the median of all Michigan graduate students. This argument was countered by a committee member who noted that two years ago Michigan had admitted a student from Maynard who was now among the three highest-ranked students in the department. Which committee member has the better argument and why?

Statistical Analysis

The first, because he has records of many accounts and the more examples you have the better it is to draw a conclusion. The second may have been merely one strange case.

Intermediate Analysis

The first due to the fact that you cannot judge apples with oranges. Just because the first Maynard grad did well does not mean the next guy will. You should look at each person applying objectively, and separately.

Deterministic Analysis

The second committee member. I do not think it is fair to go by what the first member said because many times a small school helps people better educationally because of more personalized attention.

Problem 3 ("Championship")

Two sports fans are arguing over which sport—baseball or football—has the best (most accurate) playoff system. Charlie says that the Super Bowl is the best way of determining the world champion because, according to him, "the seven games of the World Series are all played in the home cities of the two teams, whereas the Super Bowl is usually played in a neutral city. Since you want all factors not related to the game to be equal for a championship, then the Super Bowl is the better way to determine the world champion." Which procedure do you think is a better way to determine the world champion—World Series or Super Bowl? Why?

Statistical Analysis

World Series. Anyone can get lucky for one game, but it's harder to be lucky for four. Besides, being home or away is part of the game: you don't play on neutral ground during the season.

Intermediate Analysis

The home field is definitely an advantage so I would have to go with the Super Bowl. However, one game may not truly be representative of a team's football-playing ability.

Deterministic Analysis

I think Super Bowl, because of neutral ground and also a one-shot deal. Either you make it or break it—one chance. The pressure is on to perform the team's best.

Problem 4 ("Batting average")

At the end of the first two weeks of the baseball season, newspapers start publishing the top ten batting averages. The leader after the first two weeks normally has a batting average of .450 or higher. Yet no major league baseball player has ever finished the season with a better than .450 average. What do you think is the most likely explanation for the fact that batting averages are higher early in the season?

Statistical Analysis

The amount of times at bat versus the result is far greater earlier in the year than at the end of the year. If someone bats twice after two weeks and gets one hit his average is .500, but it may not be a true indication of how well he bats. The more frequently he bats the clearer the true information as to how well a batter hits.

Intermediate Analysis

Less amount of times at bat.

Deterministic Analysis

It's kind of funny that I think about the same question myself. I have had to explain it to myself in this way: As the season commences a player will, I think, become less motivated to impress people with a powerful bat — he is taking a sort of ho-hum attitude about it.

Problem 5 ("4.00 GPA")

The registrar's office at the University of Michigan has found that there are usually about 100 students in Arts and Sciences who have a 4.00 GPA at the end of their first term at the University. However, only about 10–15 students graduate with a 4.00 GPA. What do you think is the most likely explanation for the fact that there are more 4.00 GPAs after one term than at graduation?

Statistical Analysis

It is easier to get a 4.00 for one term than for eight terms. It is difficult to do the same thing eight times especially when it is a perfect score.

Intermediate Analysis

The people are taking easier classes, they have just come to the school and are ready to work. As time goes by, motivation decreases sometimes, or as more classes go by, the odds are you won't have something quite well enough for the A, or just make a mistake.

Deterministic Analysis

Students tend to work harder at the beginning of the college careers and not as hard toward the end.

Problem 6 ("College choice")

David L. was a senior in high school on the East Coast who was planning to go to college. He had compiled an excellent record in high school and had been admitted to his two top choices: a small liberal arts college and an Ivy League university. The two schools were about equal in prestige and were equally costly. Both were located in attractive East Coast cities, about equally distant from his home town. David had several older friends who were attending the liberal arts college and several who were attending the Ivy League university. They were all excellent students like himself and had interests similar to his. The friends at the liberal arts college all reported that they liked the place very much and that they found it very stimulating. The friends at the Ivy League university reported that they had many complaints on both personal and social grounds and on educational grounds. David initially thought that he would go to the smaller college. However, he decided to visit both schools himself for a day. He did not like what he saw at the private liberal arts college. Several people whom he met seemed cold and unpleasant; a professor he met with briefly seemed abrupt and uninterested in him; and he did not like the "feel" of the campus. He did like what he saw at the Ivy League university. Several of the people he met seemed like vital, enthusiastic, pleasant people, he met with two different professors who took a personal interest in him; and he came away with a very pleasant feeling about the campus. Please say which school you think David should go to and why.

Statistical Analysis

David just saw the Ivy League university for one day. His friends' reports are based on the whole year. So he should take his friends' word for it. Chances are that the liberal arts college is better.

Intermediate Analysis

If he went into the Ivy League with an optimistic attitude, eager to meet people and make friends, he will probably enjoy it. He should follow his own feelings but should visit both campuses again.

Deterministic Analysis

Because he is not his friends. Their feelings aren't necessarily his. After high school people tend to go on their own trails. David liked the Ivy [League] school, then that's where he belongs.

Problem 7 ("Fidelity")

Alvin said the following in a course on human sexuality: "I used to feel that fidelity was pretty important for relationships between men and women, but recently, my girlfriend walked out of a party with a tall blond guy she'd just met, and I found myself amazingly calm. She saw him twice, but we're back together, and our relationship is as good as it ever was. Now I feel that most people place too much importance on sexual fidelity — it's just not as important as they think." Do you agree with Alvin's reasoning? Why or why not?

Statistical Analysis

I personally agree with his point of view—however, I don't agree with his reasoning. He is making a generalization based on his own *single* experience. What if the girl had not stopped seeing the blond guy, and broken up with Alvin? He would not have the same view now, certainly. In addition, many people see fidelity as one of the most important things in a relationship, and it would take more than one guy's one experience to change their minds.

Intermediate Analysis

It is important. Alvin may have said nothing stirred him when she walked out with another guy. Maybe he is a calm person. Most people though wouldn't stand by and see their girl/boy friend walk out of a party with somebody else.

Deterministic Analysis

I disagree because it sounds as if Alvin is either trying to convince himself that it didn't matter, or he doesn't care about the girl as much as he thinks. No one who really cared about someone else would be calm as they walked out on them.

Problem 8 ("Job candidate")

The personnel manager of a large firm had to select a new head of the firm's accounting office. There were no people in the firm's accounting office who were qualified for the job, so an outside candidate had to be found. The job requirements were expertise and practical experience in accounting, organizational skills, and ability to get along with and to lead other people. There were two candidates for the job: a Mr. Simpson and a Mr. Barker. Each had worked for two small firms previously and the two men had had about the same amount of experience in accounting. Letters were available from both employers of both men. The personnel manager personally knew both previous employers of both men, and trusted the judgment of each of them. Both letters on Mr. Simpson indicated that he was an excellent accountant, and that his organizational skills (delegation of responsibility, regulation of paper flow, meeting deadlines) were fairly good. One letter said he was a fairly effective leader of his own staff, but that he did not get along well with several members of his staff and that some of his staff members actively disliked him. The other letter also expressed some fairly strong reservations about his ability to get along with the staff, but no questions about leadership ability otherwise. Both letters on Mr. Barker indicated that he, too, was an excellent accountant and indicated that his organizational skills were quite good. Both letters stressed that he was an excellent leader of his staff and got along extremely well with almost all staff members working under him. The personnel manager interviewed both men and introduced each of them to the twelve-member accounting staff at a half-hour get-acquainted session. Mr. Simpson seemed quite impressive, obviously intelligent, energetic and good humored. He made a very solid impression both on the personnel manager and on almost all of the staff members. Mr. Barker did not make such a good impression, either on the personnel manager or on the staff. He seemed intelligent enough, but somewhat ill-at-ease and awkward. Most of the staff wondered how easy he would be to get to know and to communicate with. Which candidate should the personnel manager pick and why? What are the most important things to take into consideration?

Statistical Analysis
Mr. Barker, because the people at the place he worked at knew him longer so they would know whether he was amiable. First impressions aren't too reliable.

Intermediate Analysis
Mr. Barker should be hired. First interview should not be heavily judged. Most people are nervous when openly judged by a committee. The letters should be taken heavily into account considering the personnel manager knew both former employers and respected them. How well each man gets along with his staff is one of the main points that should be considered for selection. If the man does not get along well with his staff then they will not work for him as well.

Deterministic Analysis
Mr. Simpson should be picked. People were impressed with him. Perhaps he was unhappy where he was and/or had personal problems which caused the personality reservations and dislikes. But people should be chosen on the way they personally present themselves and not what others have to say about them.

Problem 9 ("Class choice")
It is the first week of the Winter term. Henry has signed up for five classes, but plans to take only four. Three of these classes he knows he wants, so he must decide between the other two. Both are on subjects interesting to him. The student course evaluations indicate that Course A is better taught. However, he attended the first meeting of both classes this week, and found Class B's session more enjoyable. Which class should he take and why?

Statistical Analysis
You can't tell from only one time—thus a survey that is over a longer range is better. Although, Henry's idea of a good course could be different from most students.

Intermediate Analysis
Because, if he is interested in both classes, the teacher has a little less to do with it. He will probably perform better in the class he enjoys. However, the first meeting might not be an accurate assessment of what's to come. I think I would still go with B.

Deterministic Analysis
Other people's interests and what they consider enjoyable are different from our own. Follow your impressions and intuitions on matters of this sort. For me, a class that is enjoyable is taught well.

II TEACHING STATISTICAL RULES

5

The Effects of Statistical Training on Thinking about Everyday Problems

Geoffrey T. Fong
Northwestern University

Richard E. Nisbett
The University of Michigan

David H. Krantz
Columbia University

Do people solve inferential problems in everyday life by using abstract inferential rules or do they use only rules specific to the problem domain? The view that people possess abstract inferential rules and use them to solve even the most mundane problems can be traced back to Aristotle. In modern psychology, this view is associated with the theories of Piaget and Simon. They hold that, over the course of cognitive development, people acquire general and abstract rules and schemas for solving problems. For example, people acquire rules that correspond to the laws of formal logic and the formal rules of probability theory. Problems are solved by decomposing their features and relations into elements that are coded in such a way that they can make contact with these abstract rules.

This formalist view has been buffeted by findings showing that people violate the laws of formal logic and the rules of statistics. People make serious logical errors when reasoning about arbitrary symbols and relations (for a review, see Evans, 1982). The best known line of research is that initiated by Wason (1966) on his selection task. In that task, subjects are told that they will be shown cards having a letter on the front and a number on the back. They are then presented with cards having an A, a B, a 4, and a 7 and asked which they would have to turn over in order to verify the rule, "If a card has an A on one side, then it has a 4 on the other." This research showed that people do not reason in accordance with the simple laws of conditional logic, which would require turning over the A and the 7. Subsequent work showed that people do reason in accordance with the conditional for certain concrete and familiar problems. For example, when people are given envelopes and asked to verify the rule, "If the letter is sealed, then it has a 50-lire stamp on it," they have no trouble with the problem (Johnson-Laird, Legrenzi, & Sonino-Legrenzi, 1972). Many investigators have concluded from results of the latter sort that people do not use abstract rules of logic when solving concrete problems. Instead, people use only domain-specific rules (e.g., D'Andrade, 1982; Golding, 1981; Griggs & Cox, 1982; Johnson-Laird et al., 1972; Manktelow & Evans, 1979; Reich & Ruth, 1982). If people solve a problem correctly, it is because they are sufficiently familiar with the content domain to have induced a rule that allows them to solve problems in that domain.

Research on inductive reasoning has followed a similar history. Kahneman and Tversky (e.g., 1971, 1973; Tversky & Kahneman, 1974) demonstrated that people fall prey to a multitude of failures to employ statistical rules when reasoning about everyday life problems. In particular, people often fail to reason in accordance with the law of large numbers, the regression principle, or the base rate principle. (For reviews see Einhorn & Hogarth, 1981; Hogarth, 1980; Kahneman, Slovic, & Tversky, 1982; Nisbett & Ross, 1980).

We and our colleagues, however, have shown that people do use statistical concepts in solving particular kinds of problems in particular domains (Jepson, Krantz, & Nisbett, 1983; Nisbett, Krantz, Jepson, & Fong, 1982; Nisbett, Krantz, Jepson, & Kunda, 1983). For example, Jepson et al. (1983) presented subjects with a variety of problems drawn from three very broad domains. All of the problems dealt with events that are variable and, as such, can be analyzed in terms of statistical concepts such as sample size. One domain examined by Jepson et al. consisted of problems for which the random nature of the sample is obvious. In one problem, for example, the protagonist has to judge characteristics of a lottery. As expected, the great majority of the answers for these "probabilistic" problems were statistical answers, that is, they incorporated intuitive notions of the law of large numbers or the regression principle in their answer. At the other extreme, a different group of problems dealt with subjective judgments about the properties of some object or person. In one of these problems, for example, the protagonist has to decide which of two college courses he should take, either on the basis of one visit to each class or on the basis of the evaluations of students who took the courses the previous term. Statistical responses were relatively rare for these "subjective" problems, constituting only about a quarter of the total. In between these extremes, there were a number of problems that, while not containing broad hints as to the random nature of the events in question, dealt with events that are of a sufficiently objective nature that it is relatively easy to recognize that they are characterized by a degree of random variation. These problems dealt primarily with athletic events and academic achievements. For these "objective" problems, slightly more than half of the answers were statistical in nature.

Nisbett et al. (1983) interpreted these and similar results as reflecting the fact that people possess intuitive but abstract versions of statistical rules. They called these intuitive rules "statistical heuristics," and argued that people call on such heuristics to the degree that (a) problem features are readily coded in terms of statistical rules, that is, when the sample space and sampling process are clear, and when the events can be coded in common units (as is the case for athletic events and academic achievements, for example); (b) the presence of chance factors or random variation is signaled by the nature of the events or by other cues in the problem; and (c) the culture recognizes the events in question as being associated with random variation (for example, gambling games) and thus prescribes that an adequate explanation of such events should make reference to statistical principles.

This account presumes that statistical heuristics are abstract. It explains people's frequent failures to use abstract rules as being the result of difficulty in coding problem elements in terms that trigger the rules or as the result of the presence of competing heuristics. But the evidence to date does not rule out the view that statistical heuristics are not abstract at all, but rather are local, domain-bound rules that happen to overlap with formal statistical rules. These rules are better developed in some domains than in others, and it is for this reason that people are much more likely to give statistical answers for some problems than others.

If statistical heuristics are abstract, then it should be possible to improve people's statistical reasoning about everyday events by formal instruction in the rule system, without reference to any domain of everyday events. Such abstract instructional methods should help people apply the rules over a broad range of problem content. On the other hand, if such formal instruction fails to help people to solve concrete problems, despite the fact that people can be shown to have learned a substantive amount about the formal properties of the rules, this would be discouraging to the formal view. It would also be discouraging to the formal view if it were to turn out that abstract instruction affects only people's solution of probabilistic problems, where the relevance of statistical rules is obvious, and where competing rules have relatively little strength.

In order to test the view that formal training per se results in an increase in people's use of statistical principles across a variety of domains, we trained subjects, in brief but intensive laboratory sessions, on the concepts associated with the law of large numbers. We then presented them with a number of problems in each of three broad domains, dealing, respectively, with events generally construed as probabilistic, with objectively measurable events, and with events that are measurable only by subjective judgments.

We also tested the formal view in another way. Some subjects were not given formal instruction, but instead were shown how to apply the law of large numbers for three concrete example problems, all of which dealt with objectively measurable events. If subjects are capable of inducing generalized rules of some degree of abstraction from such training, then they might be expected to reason more statistically about problems in the other domains as well, even though they have not been presented with examples in those domains. Whereas the empirical view suggests that statistical training will be domain specific, with training in one domain failing to generalize to other domains, the formalist view predicts that statistical training in one domain should generalize readily to other domains.

All of the problems presented to subjects concerned everyday life events and were of a type that, in previous work, we have found at least some subjects answer in a statistical fashion. All questions were open ended, and we coded the written answers according to a system that distinguished among varying degrees of statistical thinking. This procedure provided us with a great deal of information about how people reason about events in everyday life and allowed us to determine whether training can enhance not only the likelihood of employing statistical concepts, but also the likelihood that those concepts will be employed properly.

EXPERIMENT 1

Testing Method

Subjects' intuitive use of statistical reasoning was tested by examining their answers to 15 problems to which the law of large numbers could be applied and 3 for which the law of large numbers was not relevant. In this section we describe the instructions that introduced the test problems, the design of the 18 problems, and the system of coding the open-ended answers. The actual text of the problems is given in Appendix A.

Instructions

The instructions for the control subjects read as follows:

We are interested in studying how people go about explaining and predicting events under conditions of very limited information about the events. It seems to us to be important to study how people explain and predict under these conditions because they occur very frequently in the real world. Indeed, we often have to make important decisions based on such explanations and predictions, either because there is too little time to get additional information or because it is simply unavailable.

On the pages that follow, there are a number of problems that we would like you to consider. As you will see, they represent a wide range of real-life situations. We would like you to think carefully about each problem, and then write down answers that are sensible to you.

For groups that received training, the first paragraph of the above instructions was presented as part of the introduction to the training materials. After the training, the test booklet was introduced by the second paragraph, which ended with the sentence, "In many of the problems, you may find that the Law of Large Numbers is helpful."

Problem Types and Problem Structure

The 18 problems were divided into three major types as follows:

Type 1. Probabilistic. In these six problems, subjects had to draw conclusions about the characteristics of a population from sample data generated in a way that clearly incorporated random variation. Randomness was made clear in various ways: by the explicitly stated variation in sample outcomes (for example, the number of perfect welds out of 900 made by a welding machine ranged from 680 to 740), by including in the problem a random generating device (for example, shaking a jar of pennies before drawing out a sample), or by simply stating that a sample was "random."

Type 2. Objective. In these six problems, subjects had to draw conclusions about characteristics of a population on the basis of "objective" sample data but with no explicit cue about randomness of the data. One problem, for example, asked subjects to decide which of two makes of car was more likely to be free of troublesome repairs, on the basis of various facts about the repair records. Other problems dealt with the outcomes of athletic events and with academic accomplishments.

Type 3. Subjective. In these six problems, subjects had to draw conclusions about subjective characteristics of a population from "subjective" sample data. In one problem, for example, a high school senior had to choose between two colleges. The underlying subjective characteristic in this problem was liking for the two schools and the data consisted of his own and his friends' reactions to the schools.

In order to systematize the kinds of problems we presented to subjects across the three domains, we selected six different underlying problem structures and for each structure we wrote one problem of each of the above three types. The structures varied in types of samples drawn, type of decision required, and type of competing information.

Structure 1 problems required subjects to draw conclusions about a population from a single small sample. Structure 2 problems pitted a small sample against a large sample. Structure 3 problems required subjects to explain why an outcome selected because of its extreme deviation was not maintained in a subsequent sample (i.e., regression). Structure 4 problems were similar to those in Structure 2, except that the large sample was drawn from a population that was related to, although not identical to, the target population. Structure 5 problems pitted a large sample against a plausible theory that was not founded on data. Structure 6 (false alarm) problems involved conclusions drawn from a sample that was large, but also highly biased. As such, criticism or arguments in these problems should be based on the sample *bias,* but not on sample size. We included these problems to determine whether subjects who received training on the law of large numbers would then proceed to invoke it indiscriminately, or if they would apply it only to the problems of Structures 1–5, for which it was genuinely relevant.

In short, the 18 test problems followed a 3 × 6 design, with problem type crossed with problem structure. The order of the 18 test problems was randomized for each subject, with the constraint that no 2 problems with the same structure appeared successively.

Coding System

To study the use of statistical reasoning, a simple 3-point coding system was developed for the 15 problems for which the law of large numbers was applicable (Structures 1–5). To illustrate this coding system, we present examples of responses to the "slot machine problem," the probabilistic version of Structure 2 (small sample vs large sample). The protagonist of the story, Keith, was in a Nevada gas station where he played two slot machines for a couple of minutes each day. He lost money on the left slot machine and won money on the right slot machine. Keith's result, however, ran counter to the judgment of an old man sitting in the gas station, who said to Keith, "The one on the left gives you about an even chance of winning, but the one on the right is fixed so that you'll lose much more often than you'll win. Take it from me — I've played them for years." Keith's conclusion after playing the slot machines was that the old man was wrong about the chances of winning on the two slot machines. Subjects were asked to comment on Keith's conclusion. Every response to the test problems was classified into one of three categories:

1 = an entirely deterministic response, that is, one in which the subject made no use of statistical concepts. In responses of this type, there was no mention of sample size, randomness, or variance. The following was coded as a deterministic response to the slot machine problem: "Keith's reasoning was poor, provided the information given by the man was accurate. The man, however, may have been deceiving Keith."

2 = a poor statistical response. Responses given this score contained some mention of statistical concepts, but were incomplete or incorrect. These responses contained one or more of the following characteristics: (1) the subject used both deterministic and statistical reasoning, but the deterministic reasoning was judged by the coder to have been preferred by the subject; (2) the subject used incorrect statistical reasoning, such as the gambler's fallacy; (3) the subject mentioned luck or chance or the law of large numbers but was not explicit about how the statistical concept was relevant. The following is an example of a poor statistical response to the slot machine problem:

> I think that Keith's conclusion is wrong because the old man had better luck on the left one, so he thought it was better. Keith had better luck on the right one so he thought it was better. I don't think you could have a better chance on either one.

3 = a good statistical response. Responses given this score made correct use of a statistical concept. Some form of the law of large numbers was used, and the sampling elements were correctly identified. If the subject used both deterministic and statistical reasoning, the statistical reasoning was judged by the coder to have been preferred by the subject. In general, the subject was judged to have clearly demonstrated how the law of large numbers could be applied to the problem. The following was coded as a good statistical response to the slot machine problem:

> Keith's conclusion is weak. He is wrong in making the assumptions against the old man. Keith is judging the machines on only a handful of trials and not with the sample number the old man has developed over the years. Therefore, Keith's margin of error is much more great than the old man's.

The coding system thus distinguished each response on the basis of whether or not a statistical concept had been used and, within the class of statistical responses, whether or not it was a "good" statistical response, that is, one that showed a correct use of the law of large numbers.

Such coding obviously runs into borderline cases. A coding guidebook was created which documented the principal types of borderline cases and the recommended treatment of them, for each problem. Reliability was tested by having four coders code a sample of 20 test booklets (300 law of large numbers problems). There was exact agreement among all four coders on 86% of these responses. Having achieved a high level of reliability, the primary coder (who had been one of the four coders), coded all of the responses, blind to conditions. His coding comprised the data we present here and in Experiment 2.

The coding of the three Structure 6 (false alarm) problems is described in a separate section below.

Training Procedures

All training procedures began with an introductory paragraph about decisions with limited information (quoted in full above as the first paragraph in the testing instructions for the control subjects).[1] Next followed a paragraph introducing the law of large numbers. This always began as follows:

> Experts who study human inference have found that principles of probability are helpful in explaining and predicting a great many events, especially under conditions of limited information. One such principle of probability that is particularly helpful is called the *Law of Large Numbers*.

Rule Training Condition

Subjects read a four-page description of the concept of sampling and the law of large numbers. This description introduced the important concepts associated with the law of large numbers and illustrated them by using the classic problem of estimating the true proportion of blue and red gumballs in an urn from a sample of the urn. Thus, the gumballs in the urn constituted the *population,* the proportion of blue and red gumballs in the urn formed the *population distribution* (in the example, the population distribution of gumballs was set at 70% blue and 30% red), and a selection of gumballs from the urn constituted a *sample.*

The concept of sampling was then presented by explaining that since it is often impractical or impossible to examine the entire population to determine the population distribution ("Imagine counting a million gumballs!"), it is necessary to rely instead on samples to *estimate* the population distribution. *Sample distributions,* subjects were told, vary in their closeness to the population distribution, and that the only factor determining the closeness of a *random* sample to the population is *sample size.* Finally, the law of large numbers was presented in the following way:

As the size of a random sample increases, the sample distribution is more likely to get closer and closer to the population distribution. In other words, the larger the sample, the better it is as an estimate of the population.

When subjects had finished reading this description, the experimenter performed a live demonstration of the law of large numbers, using a large glass urn filled with blue and red gumballs. In order to maximize subjects' understanding of the concepts they had just read, the demonstration was designed to adhere closely to the description. Each of the concepts introduced in the description was illustrated in the demonstration. For example, the population distribution of the urn was 70% blue and 30% red, just as it had been in the description.

After reintroducing all of the concepts, the experimenter drew four samples of size 1, then four of size 4, and finally, four of size 25. (The gumballs were returned to the urn after each sample.) The experimenter summarized each sample on a blackboard, keeping track of the deviation between each sample and the population. Subjects were told that the average deviation of a sample from the population would decrease as the sample size increased, in accordance with the law of large numbers. Thus, for example, samples of size 25 would, on the average, deviate less from the population than would samples of size 4 or 1. (By good luck, these expected results were obtained in all the training sessions.)

Examples Training Condition

Subjects in the examples training condition read a packet of three example problems with an answer following each problem that provided an analysis of it in terms of the law of large numbers. The three example problems were drawn from Structure 1 (generalizing from a small sample), Structure 3 (regression), and Structure 5 (large sample vs theory without supporting data), and were presented in that order. The three examples were all drawn from the domain of objective problems. After the paragraph that introduced the law of large numbers, there followed a single sentence describing one example of the principle (a public opinion poll based on a large sample is more likely to be accurate than one based on a small sample). The example problems were then introduced in the following way:

> The basic principles involved in the law of large numbers apply whenever you make a generalization or an inference from observing a sample of object, actions, or behaviors. To give you an idea of how broad the law of large numbers is, we have, in this packet, presented three situations in which the law of large numbers applies. Each situation is analyzed in terms of the law of large numbers.

For each example in turn, subjects read the problem and were asked to consider it for a few moments before turning the page to read the law of large numbers answer. The answers to the example problems were constructed so that subjects could learn how the law of large numbers might be applied to a variety of real-life situations. The format of the answers was constant across training domain and structure and included the following characteristics:

1. A statement about the goal of the problem;
2. Identification of the sample or samples and their distributions in the problem;
3. Explanation of how the law of large numbers could be applied to the problem. This identified the population distribution(s) and explained the relationship between the sample(s) and the population(s).
4. The conclusion that could be drawn from the application of the law of large numbers. The three example problems are presented in Appendix B.

Full Training Condition

Subjects received rule training, followed by examples training, except that the first sentence of the passage introducing the examples was replaced by the following sentence: "One reason that the law of large numbers is important to learn is that it applies *not only* to urns and gumballs."

Demand Condition

Subjects received only the one-sentence definition of the law of large numbers that introduced the examples training, along with the brief example. We included this condition in order to assess whether training effects might be due to experimenter demand or to simply making statistical rules salient to subjects. If performance of the demand group turned out not to be higher than that of the control group, these alternative explanations would be ruled out.

In addition, there was a *control* condition, which received no training before answering the test problems.

In summary, there were five conditions in Experiment 1, as shown in Fig. 5.1. They were defined by crossing the presence or absence of rule training with presence or absence of examples training. Note that the bottom-left cell of Fig. 5.1, where neither type of training was given, contains both the control and demand conditions.

Subjects and Procedure

The 347 subjects were adults (229) and high school students (118) from various New Jersey suburban communities. They were paid to participate in

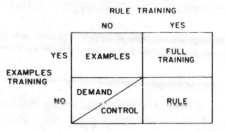

FIG. 5.1   Design of Experiment 1.

the experiment. The adult subjects varied widely in age and education, but almost all were females who were not employed fulltime outside the home. Most of them had participated previously in psychology experiments at Bell Laboratories. Because adults and high school students showed the same pattern of results, their responses were combined in the analyses we present.

Subjects were scheduled in groups of 4–6, with the same training condition presented to the entire group. Training condition was randomly determined. Subjects were told the general nature of the experiment, given the appropriate training, and then given the 18-problem test booklet. They were given 80 min to complete the problems.

Results

Overview of Data Analysis

Recall that subjects' responses were coded using a 3-point system: A code of "1" was given for responses that contained no mention of statistical concepts such as variability or sample size, whereas a "2" or "3" was given for responses that incorporated statistical notions. Within the class of statistical responses, a "2" was given for "poor" statistical responses, and a "3" was given for "good" statistical responses.

We analyzed the data in terms of two dichotomies. The first one asks whether the response was deterministic (code = 1) or statistical, regardless of quality (code = 2 or 3). We refer to analyses based on this dichotomy as analyses of *frequency* of statistical responses. The second dichotomy asks, for statistical responses only, whether the response was poor (code = 2) or good (code = 3). We refer to analyses based on this dichotomy as analyses of *quality*. The quality dichotomy is conditional: it is defined only for statistical responses and is undefined (missing) for deterministic responses.

These two analyses allowed us to separate the questions of whether training increased the incidence of any kind of statistical reasoning from whether it increased the *proper* use of statistical principles. If we found that training led to an increase in frequency but a decrease in quality, this would lead to the pessimistic conclusion that training merely serves to make statistical concepts salient to subjects without conveying any real sense about how such concepts should be used properly. On the other hand, if training was found to increase *both* frequency and quality, then this would support the optimistic notion that training not only makes salient the usefulness of statistical principles in analyzing inferential problems, but also improves the ability to use those principles correctly.

Because our basic variables were dichotomous, we used a log-linear modeling approach (e.g., Bishop, Fienberg, & Holland, 1975), in which we modeled frequency and quality as a function of (1) training differences, (2) individual differences within training groups, (3) problem differences, and (4) problem × training interaction. This approach closely parallels a three-factor ANOVA model, in which training is a between-subjects variable and problems are crossed with subjects (i.e., problems are treated as repeated measures).

Effect of Training on Frequency of Statistical Reasoning

Column 3 of Table 5.1 shows the overall frequency of statistical responses for each of the five experimental groups.[2] It is clear that training increased the frequency of statistical responses, as predicted. Specifically, there resulted a three-level ordering of the conditions. At the lowest level, subjects who received no training (the control and demand conditions) were least likely to employ statistical principles in their answers (42 and 44%, respectively, across all 15 problems). At the middle level, subjects who received only rule training or only examples training were more likely to reason statistically (56 and 54%, respectively). And at the highest level, subjects in the full training condition (those who received both rule and examples training) were most likely to use statistical reasoning in their answers (64%).

The statistical reliability of these proportions cannot be directly assessed

TABLE 5.1
Frequency and Quality of Statistical Answers in Experiment 1

| Condition | n | Frequency | | Quality | |
		Overall proportion	Log-linear effect	Overall proportion	Log-linear effect
Control	68	.421	−0.515	.542	−0.501
Demand	73	.440	−0.420	.577	−0.316
Rule	69	.557	0.188	.666	0.165
Examples	69	.535	0.074	.659	0.181
Full training	68	.643	0.673	.708	0.471

from the binomial, since they involve repeated measures over subjects. An alternative strategy would be to employ an analysis of variance on subject means. Such an approach, although quite feasible, would ignore problems as a source of variance, and thus would be inappropriate for our purposes.

Instead, we assessed the reliability of group differences by log-linear analysis. The log-linear effects of training groups, subjects within groups, and problems were all large and highly reliable; the training group × problem interaction was small and only marginally significant.

The simplest way to assess the effects of training is given by the effect sizes for an additive log-linear model based only on training group and problems as factors.[3] These effects are shown in Table 5.1, Column 4. The standard error of each pairwise difference was 0.19, which we obtained from jackknifing.[4] Hence, the difference between the control and the demand conditions and between the rule and examples conditions were not statistically reliable, whereas all of the other pairwise differences were highly reliable ($p < .01$). Thus *both* formal training and training by "guided induction" over examples were effective in increasing the use of statistical heuristics. In addition, training effects were not due to mere experimenter demand or mere salience of statistical rules, since the demand condition was significantly lower than any of the training conditions. In fact, there was no evidence that the demand instructions had any effect whatsoever, compared to controls.

Effect of Training on Quality of Statistical Reasoning

But does training have a beneficial effect on people's ability to use statistical principles *appropriately?* The right-most columns in Table 5.1 show the overall quality proportions and corresponding effects.[5] The jackknifed estimate of the standard error of the differences in quality between any two conditions was 0.18.

The effect of training on the quality of statistical responses was strikingly similar to the effects of training on frequency, though somewhat smaller in magnitude. As degree of training increased, the ability to utilize statistical concepts properly increased. This resulted in a similar three-level ordering of the conditions. However, the log-linear analysis indicated that the differences between the full training condition and the rule and examples conditions were significant only at the .10 level.

The effects of training on frequency and quality can be seen clearly in Figure 5.2, where the five conditions in Experiment 1 are represented by the filled points. (The open points are from Experiment 2, which are added to demonstrate the stability of training effects across experiments and across different subject populations.) Each training group is represented by one

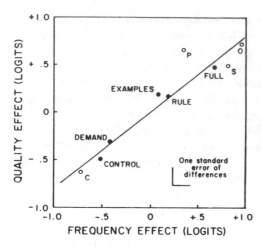

FIG. 5.2 Effects of training on frequency and quality of statistical answers in Experiment 1 and Experiment 2. Closed points (●) = Experiment 1; open points (○) = Experiment 2: P = probabilistic examples training; O = objective examples training; S = subjective examples training; C = control.

point, with the log-linear frequency effect on the abscissa, and log-linear quality effect on the ordinate. The standard errors of differences for frequency and for quality are shown by a horizontal and vertical bar, respectively.

The diagonal line in Fig. 5.2 is the least-squares regression line for the five conditions in Experiment 1. It is clear that there is a very stable relationship between the training effect on frequency and on quality, $r(3) = .98$, $p < .005$. The slope of the line is 0.80, which corresponds to the finding that the effect of training on quality was slightly less than the effect on frequency. (Equal effects would be indicated by a slope of 1.00.) This slope is an interesting way to characterize the nature of training procedures. One can imagine procedures that would lead to a much lower slope (for example, emphasizing the identification of chance processes without much concern for explaining the principles underlying them), or a much higher slope (for example, emphasizing the principles of mathematical statistics, with advice to use great caution in applying such principles broadly).

To summarize, training on the law of large numbers increased the likelihood that people will employ statistical concepts in analyzing everyday inferential problems. Moreover, there appears to be a three-level ordering such that either rule or examples training alone improves performance and that training on both has an additional effect. Training also serves to increase the proper application of statistical concepts in the same way, although this effect is somewhat weaker.

The Effect of Problem Type on the Use of Statistical Principles

Collapsing across training condition, subjects were most likely to employ statistical reasoning for probabilistic problems (75%), less likely to do so for objective problems (48%), and least likely for subjective problems (33%).[6] This result is consistent with the findings of Nisbett et al. (1983) that the use of statistical reasoning is associated with features of the inferential problem that relate to the clarity of the sampling elements and sample space, the salience of the presence of chance factors, and the cultural prescriptions concerning whether causal explanations should include statistical concepts.

Analysis of the quality proportions for the three problem types showed a quite different pattern. There was no significant differences. (The overall proportions for probabilistic, objective, and subjective problems were .63, .53, and .55, respectively.) This suggests that the source of the differences among problem types in statistical reasoning is in the likelihood that a person will notice the relevance of statistical principles to begin with. Given that a person has done so, the three problem types do not differ significantly in whether the person will be able to generate a *good* statistical response.

Thus, frequency of statistical answers was strongly associated with problem type while quality was only weakly associated with problem type. This result is consistent with the notion that people solve problems by use of abstract rules rather than by use of domain-dependent rules: different domains differ with respect to the likelihood that people will recognize the relevance of statistical rules, but once the relevance is recognized, the same abstract rules are applied across domains with approximately the same degree of success.

Relationship between Training and Problem Type

Are the effects of statistical training limited to the more obvious probabilistic problems, or do they extend to the objective and subjective problems? Figure 5.3 presents the frequency of probabilistic answers by training condition and problem type. The profiles are nearly parallel, which suggests that there is no interaction between training and problem type.

The log-linear analysis verifies this: Although the interaction between training condition and the 15 problems was significant ($\chi^2(56) = 80$, $p < .05$), the pattern of residuals from the additive model indicates very clearly that the source of the interaction was due to variation of problems *within* problem type and not at all to systematic differences *between* problem types. Thus, training increased statistical reasoning for subjective events just as much as it did for objective and probabilistic events.

Figure 5.4 presents the quality of probabilistic answers by training condition and problem type. Note that the three profiles are much closer to each other than are the profiles in Fig. 5.3: this reflects the fact that frequency was strongly related to problem type, whereas quality was

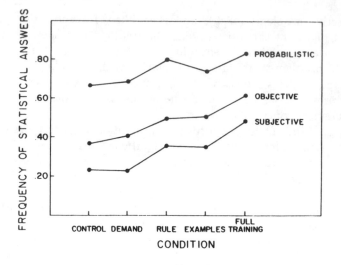

FIG. 5.3   Frequency of statistical answers as a function of condition and problem type in Experiment 1.

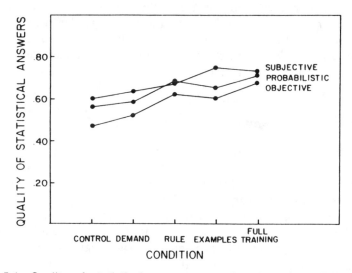

FIG. 5.4   Quality of statistical answers as a function of condition and problem type in Experiment 1.

unrelated. We used the same analytic approach to test whether the effect of training on quality of statistical reasoning interacted with problem type. The training × problem interaction was not significant, $\chi^2(54) = 60$, $p > .20$. Thus, as with frequency, training effects on quality did not interact with problem type.

These results are consistent with a strong version of the formalist view.

Formal rule training improves statistical reasoning and enhances the quality of such reasoning for all kinds of events, not just for probabilistic problems for which there are few plausible alternative kinds of solutions. This finding suggests that operations directly on the abstract rules themselves may be sufficient to produce change in subjects' analysis of essentially the full range of problems they might confront.

These results support the formalist view in a second way. The examples training consisted of example problems only in the domain of objective events. The empirical view predicts domain specificity of training: examples training should lead to greater use of the law of large numbers for the objective test problems but should have less effect for probabilistic and subjective problems. The formalist view, in contrast, predicts domain independence of training. In this view, examples training, insofar as it makes contact with people's relatively abstract rule system of statistical principles, should generalize to other domains as well.

As shown in Figs. 5.3 and 5.4, the results are much more consistent with the formalist view. Training on objective example problems improved performance on both probabilistic and subjective problems essentially as much as it improved performance on the objective problems. There was no residual advantage for problems in the domain on which training took place.

False Alarms

Since subjects can only learn so much in a 25-min training session, and since a little learning is a dangerous thing, we should be concerned that our training session may be dangerous in some way. One danger is false alarms, that is, the use of the law of large numbers in situations where it is inappropriate. For example, subjects might claim that the sample size is too small even for problems in which the sample size is quite large. It should be clear that the overuse of the law of large numbers as well as the failure to use it can lead to erroneous conclusions. We explored the possibility that our training may have promoted the indiscriminate use of the law of large numbers by including false-alarm problems in our test package.

There were seven problems for which false-alarm data could be examined. In the three Structure 5 (large sample vs theory without supporting data) problems, the conclusion based on a large sample was contradicted by an opposing argument that was plausible but which was unsupported by data. An answer was given a false-alarm code if it stated that the sample was too small to combat the argument. The three Structure 6 (false alarm) problems involved conclusions drawn from large but biased samples. A false-alarm code was given if a subject accepted the criticism that the sample size was too small. And the objective version of Structure 1 (which we will refer to as O1) asked subjects to comment on two conclusions—one based on a large sample (part a), and one based on a very small sample (part b). Part a was used to assess subjects' tendency to false alarm; part b was used to assess the subjects' ability to use the law of large numbers correctly.

Of the seven false-alarm problems, three of them (O5, S5, and S6) elicited virtually no false alarms (less than 2%). For a fourth problem (P6), the false-alarm rate was about 10%, with the false alarms distributed approximately equally among the five conditions. The results for these four problems suggest that trained subjects do indeed increase their use of the law of large numbers in a discriminating fashion.

For the other three problems, the false-alarm rates were only somewhat higher for the three trained groups (about 16%) than for the two untrained groups (about 10%). And it is interesting that the specific pattern of false alarms across the three trained groups varied depending on whether subjects had received examples training. In P5 (the probabilistic version of Structure 5), for instance, subjects exposed to examples training (the examples and full training conditions) were less likely to false alarm than those exposed to rule training only. This is probably because the examples training package included a Structure 5 problem. These subjects had thus been alerted to the possibility that large samples were indeed "large enough" to make confident conclusions and were therefore less likely to false alarm on P5. In contrast, subjects receiving only rule training were not given any information about when a sample was large enough. It is not surprising, then, that these subjects were more likely to false alarm to this problem.

There is also evidence from problem O1 that the tendency to false alarm was negatively related to the proper use of the law of large numbers. For this problem, there was a strong negative relationship between false alarms to part a and the quality of statistical responses to part b. Of the subjects who false alarmed on part a, none gave a good statistical answer to part b, that is, quality was equal to .00. In contrast, for those subjects who had not false alarmed, quality was equal to .16. This analysis suggests that a little learning can be somewhat dangerous, but that subjects who absorb the training more thoroughly are able to use it in a discriminating fashion.

In summary, our 25 min training session did *not* lead to widespread overuse of the law of large numbers.[7] Instead, subjects were surprisingly sophisticated in avoiding the improper use of the law of large numbers, sometimes citing intuitive versions of statistical concepts such as power and confidence intervals in their answers. Moreover, subjects who did false alarm were also less likely to use the law of large numbers correctly when it was appropriate.

EXPERIMENT 2

The results of Experiment 1 indicate very clearly that people can be taught to reason more statistically about everyday inferential problems. They can be taught through example problems showing how statistical principles can be applied, and they can also be taught through illustrating the formal aspects of the law of large numbers. These results are consistent with the formalist view that people possess abstract inferential rules and that these can be improved both by guided induction through examples and by direct manipulation.

One of the important results in Experiment 1 was the absence of an interaction between training and problem type. Examples training had an equal effect in enhancing statistical reasoning across all three problem types. Thus, training on objective problems increased the use of statistical thinking no more for objective events than for subjective events, such as choosing a college or explaining a person's compassionateness, or for probabilistic events, such as those involving lotteries or slot machines. That training effects were entirely domain independent is quite remarkable when contrasted with the strong domain specificity of subjects' spontaneous *use* of statistical reasoning. Subjects were much more likely to use statistical principles for probabilistic problems than for objective problems and much more likely to use them for objective problems than for subjective problems.

Experiment 2 was designed to explore more fully whether training effects might vary as a function of the training domain. In Experiment 1, all subjects who received examples training were given example problems only in the objective domain. In Experiment 2, subjects were taught how to apply the law of large numbers in one of the three problem domains: probabilistic, objective, or subjective. All subjects were then tested on all three problem domains. This design makes it possible to see whether there are domain-specific effects of training. The empirical view suggests that subjects would be expected to show more improvement for problems in the domain in which they were trained than for other problems. The formal view, on the other hand, predicts that there will be no such interaction between training domain and testing domain.

Method

Subjects

The subjects were 166 undergraduates at the University of Michigan who were enrolled in introductory psychology classes. They participated in the 2-h experiment in small groups.

Design and Procedure

Subjects were randomly assigned to one of four conditions. The *control* condition was identical to that in Experiment 1. In the other three conditions, subjects were given training identical to the full training condition in Experiment 1, except that the type of example problems varied. Subjects in the *probabilistic training* condition read three probabilistic example problems and were shown how each could be analyzed by the application of the law of large numbers. Subjects in the *objective training* condition were given the same three objective example problems that were used in Experiment 1. And subjects in the *subjective training* condition were given three subjective example problems. The probabilistic and subjective examples matched the objective examples in structure: they were drawn from Structures 1, 3, and 5.

All subjects then answered the same set of 18 test problems (15 law of large numbers problems and 3 false-alarm problems) used in Experiment 1.

The subjects' responses to the open-ended questions were coded by two raters under the same coding system used in Experiment 1. The reliability of the coding was high—there were exact matches by the two coders on 88% of the responses.

Results

The data analytic procedures we used in Experiment 1 were employed here. From the 3-point coding system, we derived frequency and quality dichotomies and then used log-linear models to estimate the effects of training, test problem, and training × test problem interaction. The jackknifed estimate of the standard error of the difference between any two conditions for frequency and quality were 0.20 and 0.18 on the log-linear scale, respectively. These standard errors correspond very closely to those found in Experiment 1.

Effects of Training

As in Experiment 1, training significantly enhanced the frequency of statistical responses. Subjects in the control conditions were least likely to use statistical concepts for the 15 test problems (53% of responses were statistical). The three training groups were significantly more likely than controls to give statistical answers (72, 81, and 79% for the probabilistic, objective, and subjective training groups, respectively. All comparisons with the control condition were significant at the .001 level). In addition, subjects trained on probabilistic examples were less likely than subjects trained on objective or subjective examples to reason statistically ($p < .01$ and .05, respectively); the objective and subjective example conditions did not differ from each other.

Training also increased the quality of statistical answers. The quality proportions were .47 for the control group and .70, .70, and .66 for the probabilistic, objective, and subjective groups, respectively. Once again, training significantly enhanced the quality of statistical responses (all comparisons with the control condition were significant at the .001 level). But, in contrast to the frequency data, no training domain was more effective than any other in enhancing the quality of statistical answers.

The relationship between the training effects on frequency and on quality was very consistent with Experiment 1, as can be seen by looking back to Fig. 5.2, where the open points represent the frequency and quality effects of the three training conditions and the control condition for Experiment 2.

Effect of Problem Type

The strong effect of problem type found in Experiment 1 was replicated here. Collapsing across conditions, subjects were most likely to reason statistically for probabilistic problems (91%), less likely to do so for objective problems (68%), and least likely for subjective problems (56%).[8]

As in Experiment 1, the quality of statistical answers varied only slightly across the three problem types. The quality proportions were .69, .65, and .60 for the probabilistic, objective, and subjective problems, respectively. These differences were not statistically significant.

Relationship between Training Domain and Test Domain

The primary goal of this experiment was to examine the relationship between training domain and test domain. Figures 5.5 and 5.6 present the frequency and quality of statistical answers as a function of training domain and test domain. If training effects were domain specific, we should find that frequency and quality for problems in a given domain will be highest

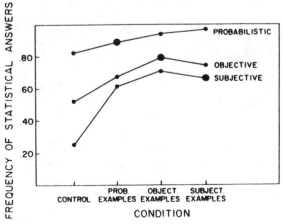

FIG. 5.5 Frequency of statistical answers as a function of condition and problem type in Experiment 2.

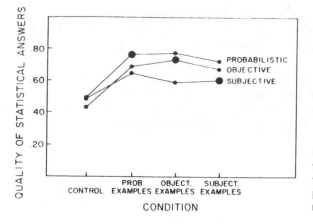

FIG. 5.6 Quality of sta-
tistical answers as a
function of condition and
problem type in Experi-
ment 2.

for those subjects who were trained on that domain. These domain-
specificity data points are represented as larger data points in the two
figures. Figures 5.5 and 5.6 make it clear that this was not the case: the
domain-specific data points are not consistently higher than the other data
points. For example, subjects who were trained on problems in the
probabilistic domain were actually *less* likely to think statistically on the
probabilistic test problems than were subjects trained on objective or
subjective problems. In short, training significantly increased statistical
reasoning; the domain of training had no differential effect.

The log-linear analysis confirms the absence of domain specificity of
training. There was no significant interaction between training domain and
test domain, either for frequency, $\chi^2(42) = 55$, $p = .10$, or for quality,
$\chi^2(42) = 49$, $p > .15$.

Finally, the false-alarm rates for Experiment 2 were generally higher than
they were for Experiment 1, for the control group as well as for the trained
groups. The difference may be due to the fact that the subjects in
Experiment 2 were college students, but this is only speculation.

Discussion

The results of Experiments 1 and 2 show that instruction in statistics can
have a marked effect on the way people reason about a broad range of
everyday problems. Such training affects not only their reasoning about
transparently probabilistic events such as lotteries, but also their reasoning
about events that most people analyze using only deterministic rules.

Both formal training, restricted to descriptions of the formal aspects of
the law of large numbers, and "guided induction," that is, teaching the rule
by means of examples, were effective in improving both the frequency and
the quality of statistical reasoning. The former finding suggests that the

more abstract aspects of academic training in statistics may, by themselves, be sufficient to produce significant improvement in the way people reason. We test this hypothesis in Experiments 3 and 4. The latter finding indicates that the use of examples adds greatly to people's ability to use their abstract rule systems.

The two types of training were approximately additive on the log-linear scale, that is, examples training plus rule training added as much improvement, both in frequency and quality, as would be expected from the sum of the effects of each type of training in isolation. It is important to note that, in the present experiments at least, the effect of examples training does not appear to be in the form of rules about how to "map" the law of large numbers onto the content of particular domains. This is because there was no domain specificity of training effects. In general, subjects taught examples in one domain learned no more about how to solve problems in that domain than they did about how to solve problems in other domains. There are two hypotheses that may account for this domain independence of examples training. What subjects learn from examples training may be an abstracted version of the law of large numbers. Alternatively, or perhaps in addition, they may learn an abstracted version of how to apply the principle to problems in general.

The domain independence of training effects we found should not be presumed to be highly general, however. Every teacher knows that students sometimes apply a rule beautifully in a domain in which they have been taught the rule and yet fail to apply it in another domain in which it is just as applicable. Two aspects of the present work probably contributed to the domain independence of statistical training that we found. First, the domains we used were very broad, constituting three haphazard samples of problems, one sample united only by the fact that some obvious randomizing device was present, another consisting of problems where a protagonist had to make a judgment about some objectively measurable aspect of a person or object, and another consisting of problems where a protagonist had to make a judgment about some subjective aspect of a person or object. Had we studied substantially narrower domains — the domain of sports, for example, or the domain of judgments about personality traits — and had we taught subjects specific tools for coding events in those domains and for thinking about their variability, we might well have found some domain specificity of training effects.

A second factor that almost surely contributed to the lack of domain specificity of training effects was the fact that testing immediately followed training. Thus subjects could be expected to have their newly improved statistical rules in "active memory" at the time they were asked to solve the new problems. This fact could be expected to reduce domain-specificity effects to a minimum.

It may have occurred to the reader to suspect that the temporal relation between testing and training might not only reduce domain-specificity effects of training but might be essential in order to produce any effects of training at all. In fact, it could be argued that all our "training" did was to increase the salience of subjects' statistical heuristics and did not teach them anything new at all. As we have known since Socrates' demonstration with the slave boy, it is always hard to prove whether we have taught someone something they did not know before or whether we have merely reminded them of something they already knew.

We have two main lines of defense, however, against the suggestion that our training effects in Experiments 1 and 2 were due simply to making the law of large numbers more salient to subjects. First, *reminding* subjects about the law of large numbers and encouraging them to use it had no effect either on the frequency or the quality of their answers. This is shown clearly by the fact that subjects in the demand condition were no higher than subjects in the control condition on either measure. Second, our training manipulations improved not only the frequency of statistical answers, which would be expected on the basis of a mere increase in salience, but the *quality* of answers, which would not be expected on the basis of a mere increase in salience.

The most effective response to the artifactual possibility of salience, however, would be to separate the time and context of training from the time and context of testing. We did this in two different experiments. In Experiment 3, we examined the effect of differing amounts of formal course training in statistics on subjects' tendencies to give statistical answers to problems. In Experiment 4, we examined the effect of course training in statistics, and we also disguised the context of testing as an opinion survey. In addition to helping rule out the salience and testing context alternatives, these experiments speak to practical questions about the effects of statistical training in formal courses on everyday inferential problems.

EXPERIMENT 3

In Experiment 3 we examined the effect of varying amounts of formal course training on the way people reasoned about two different versions of a problem from everyday life. The two versions were very similar, except that one had a powerful probabilistic cue. The study thus allows a comparison of the effects of training on both the likelihood of using statistical reasoning and the quality of statistical reasoning for both a problem for which statistical reasoning is relatively common and a problem for which it is relatively rare.

Subjects and Method

Four groups of subjects participated. These groups were chosen for their background, or lack of background, in formal statistical training. The *no statistics* group were 42 college undergraduates who were attending a lecture on attitudes; none had taken college level statistics. The *statistics* group were 56 students attending the same lecture who had taken an introductory statistics course. The *graduate* group were 72 graduate students in psychology, who were attending the first session of a course on statistical methods; all had taken at least one statistics course, and many had taken more than one. And the *tech* group were 33 technical staff members at a research laboratory who were attending a colloquium on probabilistic reasoning. Nearly all were Ph.D. level scientists who had taken many statistics courses.

Subjects were presented with a problem about restaurant quality. There were two versions. In the *no randomness cue* version, a traveling business-woman often returns to restaurants where she had an excellent meal on her first visit. However, she is usually disappointed because subsequent meals are rarely as good as the first. Subjects were asked to explain, in writing, why this happened.

The *randomness cue* version included a random mechanism for selection from the menu. In this version, the protagonist was a businessman in Japan who did not know how to read the language. When eating at a restaurant, he selected a meal by blindly dropping a pencil on the totally unreadable menu and ordering the dish closest to it. As in the other version, he is usually disappointed with his subsequent meals at restaurants he originally thought were superb. Why is this?

Answers were classified as "statistical" if they suggested that meal quality on any single visit might not be a reliable indicator of the restaurant's overall quality (e.g., "Very few restaurants have only excellent meals; odds are she was just lucky the first time"). "Non-statistical" answers assumed that the initial good experience was a reliable indicator that the restaurant was truly outstanding, and attributed the later disappointment to a definite cause such as a permanent or temporary change in the restaurant (e.g., "Maybe the chef quit") or a change in the protagonist's expectation or mood (e.g., "Maybe her expectations were so high on the basis of her first visit that subsequent meals could never match them"). Explanations that were statistical were coded as to whether they merely referred vaguely to chance factors ("poor statistical") or whether they also articulated the notion that a single visit may be regarded as a small sample, and hence as unreliable ("good statistical"). Thus, the coding system was essentially the same as the one used in Experiments 1 and 2.

Results

Figure 5.7 shows the frequency and quality of answers as a function of training and type of problem. The left side of Fig. 5.7 demonstrates clearly that the frequency of statistical answers increased dramatically with level of statistical training, $\chi^2(6) = 35.5$, $p < .001$. Almost none of the college students without statistical training gave a statistical answer to the version without the randomness cue, whereas 80% of Ph.D. level scientists did so.

Inclusion of the randomness cue markedly increased the frequency of statistical answers, $\chi^2(4) = 27.1$, $p < .001$. For the untrained college students, for example, the presence of the randomness cue increased frequency from 5 to 50%. The randomness cue thus apparently encourages the subject to code restaurant experiences as units that can be sampled from a population.

The right side of the figure indicates that degree of statistical training was also associated with *quality* of statistical answers, $\chi^2(3) = 12.3$, $p < .001$. Only 10% of the statistical answers by untrained college students were rated as good, whereas almost 80% of the statistical answers by Ph.D level scientists were rated as good.

Although the presence of the randomness cue was very important in determining whether subjects would think statistically at all, it did not affect the *quality* of statistical answers for subjects at any level of training. This duplicates the findings of Experiments 1 and 2, showing that problem difficulty does not affect the quality of answers, given that the answers are statistical. Apparently cues about randomness can trigger the use of statistical rules, but they do not necessarily produce good statistical answers. Such cues can only trigger rules at whatever level of sophistication the subject happens to possess them. This correlational study thus buttresses our assertion that, whatever plausibility the salience alternative has for the frequency results, it has very little plausibility for the quality results.

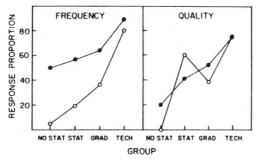

FIG. 5.7 Frequency and quality of statistical answers as a function of group and problem version in Experiment 3. Closed points (●) represent responses to the Randomness Cue version. Open points (○) represent responses to the No Randomness Cue version.

Discussion

These data indicate that, when one examines people who represent a broad range of statistical expertise, one can find very marked differences in the tendency to approach certain kinds of problems statistically. The data also indicate that, even when statistical approaches are preferred by untutored subjects, as for the version of the problem having the randomness cue, the quality of answers given by such subjects will be markedly inferior to that which more expert subjects can give.

But, while suggestive, the data do not show to precisely what degree formal rule training per se is effective. First, statistical training was undoubtedly confounded with intellectual ability, and perhaps even with experiences in superb restaurants. Second, more extensive training in statistics is normally associated with more extensive training in content disciplines that teach the use of statistical and methodological rules in at least an informal way, across a variety of domains. Thus statistical training is also confounded with other types of potentially relevant training.

In Experiment 4, we removed these sources of confounding and also provided a testing context that would not be expected to cue subjects into using statistical rules. We conducted Experiment 4 in order to examine the effects of formal statistical training in a setting completely outside of the context of training. Students enrolled in an introductory statistics course were contacted at home and were asked to participate in a telephone survey on "students' opinions on sports." Some of the questions could be analyzed with reference to statistical concepts such as the law of large numbers and the regression principle. None of the students was aware that the survey was related to the statistics class they were enrolled in. If training has an effect in this situation, this would provide very strong evidence for the formal view that statistical heuristics are represented at a highly abstract level and that statistical training provides inferential tools that are quite domain and context independent.

EXPERIMENT 4

Subjects

The subjects were 193 randomly selected males at the University of Michigan who were enrolled in an introductory statistics course. The course had a total enrollment of over 600 students.

Method

We obtained the class list from the instructor and randomly selected half of the males to be contacted during the first week of the semester, and the other half to be contacted during the last week of the semester.

The protocol we used was designed to convince subjects that we were conducting a genuine opinion survey. The interviewer introduced herself in the following way:

> I am calling from the Research Center for Group Dynamics at the University of Michigan. We're conducting a campus survey about students' opinions on sports. Some of the questions in this survey ask for opinions on current events in professional and collegiate sports; other questions ask for general opinions about sports. The whole survey takes only about 10 to 15 min. Would you have time now to answer our questions?

After asking for some demographic information[9], the interviewer went on to the questions. To enhance the idea that this was a legitimate opinion survey, the first two questions indeed asked subjects to give their real opinions about certain sports controversies (e.g., what colleges should do about recruiting violations). Respondents were quite unaware that the survey was really designed to test their statistical knowledge—none voiced any suspicion.

Following the filler items, subjects were asked a series of questions that could be answered with reference to statistical concepts. This was the first such question:

> In general, the major league baseball player who wins Rookie of the Year does not perform as well in his second year. This is clear in major league baseball in the past 10 years. In the American League, eight Rookies of the Year have done worse in their second year; only two have done better. In the National League, the Rookie of the Year has done worse the second year 9 times out of 10. Why do you suppose the Rookie of the Year tends not to do as well his second year?

Responses to this regression question were tape-recorded and coded for the presence of statistical reasoning and for whether a statistical response was a good one. A typical non-statistical response for this question would be, "The Rookie of the Year doesn't do as well because he's resting on his laurels; he's not trying as hard in his second year." A good statistical response would be, "A player's performance varies from year to year. Sometimes you have good years and sometimes you have bad years. The player who won the Rookie-of-the-Year award had an exceptional year.

He'll probably do better than average in his second year, but not as well as he did when he was a rookie."

Results and Discussion

Results indicated that training in a standard statistics course had a significant effect in enhancing the use of statistical explanations for this question. For those contacted at the beginning of the term, 16% gave statistical answers. For those contacted at the end of the term, over twice as many (37%) gave answers that utilized statistical thinking. This increase in frequency was significant, $z = 3.23$, $p < .005$. In addition, the statistics course also enhanced the quality of statistical responses, from .12 to .38, though this was only marginally significant, $z = 1.77$, $p < .10$.

Similar results were obtained on another problem, which asked subjects to explain why the top batting average after 2 weeks of the season is around .450, when such a high average has never been obtained over an entire season. Frequency increased from .50 to .70, $z = 2.87$, $p < .01$, and quality increased from .24 to .50, $z = 2.74$, $p < .01$.

The statistics course did not have any effect on two other problems that we included in the sports survey. One problem asked whether a more talented squash player should choose a five-point or a one-point tie breaker. The other asked subjects to critique a large sample study about whether marriage has an adverse effect on a professional athlete's performance. We have no explanation for why a statistics course failed to enhance statistical reasoning for these two problems.

This study indicates clearly that statistical training can enhance the use of statistical rules in reasoning about everyday life and can do so completely outside the context of training.

GENERAL DISCUSSION

The experiments presented here demonstrate that statistical training serves to enhance the use of statistical principles in reasoning. The effects of training are impressive in their generality across method, context, type of subject, and event domain. Statistical training conferred benefits whether the training consisted of several statistics courses, a single semester-long course, or even a 25-min training session. Training effects occurred not only when the testing context was identical to the training context, but also when the testing context was completely different from the training context in time and situation. Training enhanced statistical thinking not only for college students enrolled in introductory psychology, but also for high school students and adults. Training enhanced both the frequency and quality of statistical thinking not only for events commonly associated with uncertainty and probability, but also, to the same extent, for events rarely associated with such concepts.

A qualification that must be placed on the present results is that the effects at least of relatively brief training sessions may be limited to problems for which some untrained subjects are able to give a statistical answer. Many previous demonstrations of people's difficulties with statistical principles are based on problems to which no subjects, or almost no subjects, apply statistical reasoning (e.g., Hamill, Wilson, & Nisbett, 1980; Kahneman & Tversky, 1972, 1973; Tversky & Kahneman, 1983). Quite deliberately, we avoided such difficult problems in the present investigations. Even for the subjective problems in Experiment 1 and 2, the average rate of statistical answers for untrained subjects was slightly in excess of 20%.

It is indeed striking that statistical training enhances statistical thinking for subjective judgments, such as those made about the social world. Social judgments such as attributions of success or failure, or judgments of a person's traits based on a first impression, are those that, by their very nature, have a critical impact on our lives. At the same time, social judgments are those for which unexplained variation plays a major role.

But because social events are difficult to code, and because the sample space for such events is typically difficult to define, social judgments are also those that are least likely to be made with reference to statistical considerations. This is shown by the domain-specificity effects found in the experiments presented here and by Jepson et al., (1983) on the use of statistical thinking for probabilistic, objective, and subjective events. It is a disturbing state of affairs that the domain where statistical thinking is most necessary on an everyday basis is the one where it is least likely.

Our training studies, however, suggest that people are able to understand and accept the applicability of statistical principles for social events as well as for nonsocial events. The lack of an interaction between training and problem domain indicates that statistical training enhances statistical thinking for social events just as much as it does for nonsocial events. This domain independence of statistical training makes us optimistic that people can indeed be taught to understand the role of uncertainty and sample size in making social judgments.

More generally, the studies reported here make an important point concerning pedagogy in statistics. In the early 1800s, Laplace wrote, "the theory of probabilities is at bottom nothing but common sense reduced to calculus." It seems to us that courses in statistics and probability theory today concentrate almost entirely on the calculus, while often ignoring its commonsense roots. Experiments 3 and 4 clearly demonstrate how classroom training in statistics can potentially have a significant effect on how people make judgments. If introductory statistics courses were to incorporate examples of how statistical principles such as the law of large numbers can be applied to judgments in everyday life, we have no doubt that such courses would have a more far-reaching effect on the extent to which people think statistically about the world.

These studies suggest very strongly that people make use of abstract inferential rules in the form of statistical heuristics. We also know this because training on the purely formal aspects of the law of large numbers improves statistical thinking over a broad range of content, and because showing subjects how to use the rule in a given content domain generalizes completely to quite different content domains. We are aware of no more convincing evidence, in fact, for the existence of abstract rules of reasoning than the present work.

What is the origin of abstract inferential rules about the law of large numbers? Why do people develop such high-level representations of the law of large numbers? We suspect the answer comes, in large measure, from the ubiquity of the principle. The basic notion that large samples are more reliable than small samples underlies concept formation and generalization. It can be argued that during cognitive development, the child learns, through repeated exposure to the law of large numbers across many domains, a highly abstract representation of the principle.

The experiments presented here demonstrate the dual usefulness of inferential training studies. Such studies are important for pragmatic reasons because they provide information about how everyday reasoning might be improved. It is heartening to discover that a 25-min session on the law of large numbers can serve to significantly enhance people's use of statistical thinking, and that a formal course in introductory statistics can lead to a greater appreciation of variability in judgments, even those made outside the context of the classroom or laboratory. In addition, such studies are important for theoretical reasons not only because of what they tell us about how inferential rules are utilized, but also about how they are represented and how they can be modified.

FOOTNOTES

[1]All training materials can be obtained from the authors.

[2]Each of the frequency means represents the proportion of problems for which subjects in that condition utilized some kind of statistical concept. Thus, the frequency mean of .42 for the control condition is based on 1007 responses (68 subjects × 15 problem each, minus 13 unanswered problems).

[3]The additive log-linear model can be expressed as: $\log p_{ijk} - \log(1 - p_{ijk}) = \mu + \alpha_i + \beta_j + \epsilon_{ijk}$, where p_{ijk} is the probability of a statistical response by the kth subject in the jth training group for the ith problem. The parameters were estimated by maximizing the

likelihood of the 15 × 347 (problem × subject) matrix of zeroes and ones, subject to the identifying constraints that the sum of the problem effects, $;gS\alpha_j$, and the sum of the training group effects, $\Sigma\beta_j$, are zero. The estimation was accomplished by the Loglin function of the statistical package S (a product of AT&T Bell Laboratories). The Loglin function uses an algorithm developed by Haberman (1972). The entries in Table 5.1, column 4, are the estimated values of β_j. The fit was barely improved by including the problem × training interaction parameters, γ_{ij}, to the model. The fit was considerably improved by including subject parameters, δ_{jk}, to the model, but this created difficulties in identifying β_j, because a few of the subject parameter estimates were $+\infty$ or $-\infty$, corresponding to 15 out of 15 or 0 out of 15 statistical answers. Therefore, we stuck with the simple additive model when we tested for differences among training conditions. The β_js from the above model are good descriptive statistics for assessing the effects of training condition, and their sampling properties can be estimated by jackknifing (see Footnote 4).

[4]Jackknifing was performed with 10 subsamples, each formed by randomly dropping 10% of the subjects. The estimated standard error of the pairwise differences (that is, differences between any two β_js) varied only slightly from one pair of groups to another.

[5]The quality data were analyzed using the same models as for the frequency data (see Footnote 3). The corresponding parameter estimates, β_j, are shown in the right-most column of Table 5.1. The 15 × 347 data matrix of zeros and ones for quality had nearly half missing data, since quality was defined only for statistical answers. The nonlinearity of the log-linear model leads to some minor differences between the quality proportions and their corresponding log-linear effects. For example, note that although the rule proportion is greater than the examples proportion, the rule log-linear effect is actually less than the examples log-linear effect.

[6]The predicted ordering of the three problem types with respect to frequency of statistical answers (probabilistic > objective > subjective) resulted for each of the five problem structures for which the law of large numbers was relevant (Structures 1–5). The probability of this occurring by chance is extremely low, $p = (1/6)^5 < .001$.

[7]Complete details of the false-alarm analyses for Experiments 1 and 2 can be obtained from the authors.

[8]Although the pattern of these proportions are similar to those in Experiment 1, their magnitude is substantially greater. One reason is that whereas the five conditions in Experiment 1 varied considerably in the degree of training, three of the four conditions in Experiment 2 were essentially full training conditions (all were given rule training). When averaging across conditions, the proportions for Experiment 2 will reflect this more extensive training.

[9]In order to ensure that subjects had enough knowledge of sports to be able to understand the survey questions, they were asked to rate their knowledge about sports. Those who rated themselves as having little or no knowledge of sports were not used in this experiment.

REFERENCES

Bishop, Y. M. M., Fienberg, S. E., & Holland, P. W. (1975). *Discrete multivariate analysis: Theory and practice.* Cambridge, MA: MIT Press.

D'Andrade, R. (1982, April). *Reason versus logic.* Paper presented at the Symposium on the Ecology of Cognition: Biological, Cultural and Historical Perspectives, Greensboro, North Carolina.

Einhorn, H. J., & Hogarth, R. M. (1981). Behavioral decision theory: Processes of judgment and choice. *Annual Review of Psychology, 32,* 53–88.

Evans, J. St. B. T. (1982). *The psychology of deductive reasoning.* London: Routledge & Kegan Paul.

Golding, E. (1981). *The effect of past experience on problem solving.* Paper presented at the Annual Conference of the British Psychological Society, Surrey University.

Griggs, R. A., & Cox, J. R. (1982). The elusive thematic-materials effect in Wason's selection task. *British Journal of Psychology, 73,* 407–420.

Hamill, R., Wilson, T. D., & Nisbett, R. F. (1980). Insensitivity to sample bias: Generalizing from atypical cases. *Journal of Personality and Social Psychology, 39,* 578–389.

Haberman, S. J. (1972). Log-linear fit for contingency tables—Algorithm AS51. *Applied Statistics, 21,* 218–225.

Hogarth, R. M. (1980). *Judgment and choice: The psychology of decision.* New York: Wiley.

Jepson, C., Krantz, D. H., & Nisbett, R. E. (1983). Inductive reasoning: Competence or skill? *Behavioral and Brain Sciences, 6,* 494–501.

Johnson-Laird, P. N., Legrenzi, P., & Sonino-Legrenzi, M. (1972). Reasoning and a sense of reality. *British Journal of Psychology, 63,* 395–400.

Kahneman, D., Slovic, P., & Tversky, A. (Eds.). (1982). *Judgment under uncertainty: Heuristics and biases.* New York: Cambridge Univ. Press.

Kahneman, D., & Tversky, A. (1971). Subjective probability: A judgment of representativeness. *Cognitive Psychology, 3,* 430–454.

Kahneman, D., & Tversky, A. (1973). On the psychology of prediction. *Psychological Review, 80,* 237–251.

Manktelow, K. I., & Evans, J. St. B. T. (1979). Facilitation of reasoning by realism: Effect or non-effect? *British Journal of Psychology, 70,* 477–488.

Nisbett, R. E., Krantz, D. H., Jepson, C., & Fong, G. T. (1982). Improving inductive inference. In D. Kahneman, P. Slovic, & A. Tversky (Eds.), *Judgment under uncertainty: Heuristics and biases.* New York: Cambridge Univ. Press.

Nisbett, R. E., Krantz, D. H., Jepson, C., & Kunda, Z. (1983). The use of statistical heuristics in everyday inductive reasoning. *Psychological Review, 90,* 339–363.

Nisbett, R. E., & Ross, L. (1980). *Human inference: Strategies and shortcomings of social judgment.* Englewood Cliffs, NJ: Prentice-Hall.

Reich, S. S., & Ruth, P. (1982). Wason's selection task: Verification, falsification and matching. *British Journal of Psychology, 73,* 395–405.

Tversky, A., & Kahneman, D. (1974). Judgment under uncertainty: Heuristics and biases. *Science, 185,* 1124–1131.

Tversky, A., & Kahneman, D. (1983). Extensional versus intuitive reasoning: The conjunction fallacy in probability judgment. *Psychological Review, 90,* 293–315.

Wason, P. C. (1966). Reasoning. In B. M. Foss (Ed.). *New horizons in psychology. I.* Harmondsworth, England: Penguin.

APPENDIX A

The Eighteen Test Problems Used in Experiments 1 and 2

Probabilistic—Structure 1

At Stanbrook University, the Housing Office determines which of the 10,000 students enrolled will be allowed to live on campus the following year. At Stanbrook, the dormitory facilities are excellent, so there is always great demand for on-campus housing. Unfortunately, there are only enough on-campus spaces for 5000 students. The Housing Office determines who will get to live on campus by having a Housing Draw every year: every student picks a number out of a box over a 3-day period. These numbers range from 1 to 10,000. If the number is 5000 or under, the student gets to live on campus. If the number is over 5000, the student will not be able to live on campus.

On the first day of the draw, Joe talks to five people who have picked a number. Of these, four people got low numbers. Because of this, Joe suspects that the numbers in the box were not properly mixed, and that the early numbers are more favorable. He rushes over to the Housing Draw and picks a number. He gets a low number. He later talks to four people who drew their numbers on the second or third day of the draw. Three got high numbers. Joe says to himself, "I'm glad that I picked when I did, because it looks like I was right that the numbers were not properly mixed."

What do you think of Joe's reasoning? Explain.

Probabilistic—Structure 2

For his vacation, Keith decided to drive from his home in Michigan to California to visit some of his relatives and friends. Shortly after crossing the border into Nevada, Keith pulled into a gas station and went inside to buy a state map. There, in a corner of the gas station, were two slot machines. Keith had heard about slot machines before, but had never actually seen one. He went over to the slot machines and looked at them, trying to figure out how they worked. An old man who was sitting close to the machines spoke to Keith. "There ain't no winning system for slot machines. It's all luck. You just put in a coin, pull the lever, and hope that you'll win. But let me tell you this: some machines are easier to lose on than others. That's because the owners can change the mechanism of the slots so that some of them will be more likely to make you lose. See those two slot machines there? The one on the left gives you about an even chance of winning, but the one on the right is fixed so that you'll lose much more often than you'll win. Take it from me—I've played them for years." The old man then got up and walked out of the gas station.

Keith was by now very intrigued by the two slot machines, so he played the machine on the left for a couple of minutes. He lost almost twice as often as he won. "Humph," Keith said to himself. "The man said that there was an even chance of winning at that machine on the left. He's obviously wrong." Keith then tried the machine on the right for a couple of minutes and ended up winning more often than he lost. Keith concluded that the man was wrong about the chances of winning on the two slot machines. He concluded that the opposite was true—that the slot machine on the right was more favorable to the player than the machine on the left.

Comment on Keith's conclusion and his reasoning. Do you agree? Explain your answer.

Probabilistic—Structure 3

Bert H. has a job checking the results of an X-ray scanner of pipeline welds in a pipe factory. Overall, the X-ray scanner shows that the welding machine makes a perfect weld about 80% of the time. Of 900 welds each day, usually about 680 to 740 welds are perfect. Bert has noticed that on some days, all of the first 10 welds were perfect. However, Bert has also noticed that on such days, the overall number of perfect welds is usually not much better for the day as a whole than on days when the first 10 welds show some imperfections.

Why do you suppose the number of perfect welds is usually not much better on days where the first batch of welds was perfect than on other days?

Probabilistic—Structure 4

Joanna has a large collection of pennies with dates in the 1970s. Donny admires her collection and decides to start his own collection of pennies, but decides to collect only 1976 pennies because he wants to commemorate the Bicentennial. Looking through his pockets, he discovers he has only a dime. Examining it carefully, he finds that it is a 1971 dime, with a "D" (Denver) mint mark. Donny thinks it would be fun to collect 1976 pennies with the same initial as his name and asks Joanna what proportion of the 1976 pennies in her collection have a "D" mint mark on them. She doesn't know, but they decide to find out. They take the huge jar of her pennies out. Since the jar has thousands of pennies in it, Donny shakes the jar and then reaches into it and picks out a handful from the middle of the jar. Donny finds all the 1976 pennies that he scooped out (four of them) and finds that two of them have "D" mint marks. Because of this, he estimates that around 50% of all Joanna's 1976 pennies have the "D" mint mark. But Joanna looks through the other 36 pennies they have scooped out (dated 1970–1975 and 1977–1979) and discovers that only 2 of them have the "D" mint mark. She argues that only 4 of 40 pennies altogether have the "D" mark, and estimates that around 10% of the 1976 pennies in her collection are "D" pennies.

Comment on the validity of Joanna's and Donny's reasoning. Whose conclusion about the 1976 pennies in Joanna's collection is more likely to be correct? Explain.

Probabilistic — Structure 5

An auditor for the Internal Revenue Service wants to study the nature of arithmetic errors on income tax returns. She selects 4000 Social Security numbers by using random digits generated by an "Electronic Mastermind" calculator. And for each selected social security number she checks the 1978 Federal Income Tax return thoroughly for arithmetic errors. She finds errors on a large percentage of the tax returns, often 2 to 6 errors on a single tax return. Tabulating the effect of each error separately, she finds that there are virtually the same number of errors in favor of the taxpayer as in favor of the government. Her boss objects vigorously to her assertions, saying that it is fairly obvious that people will notice and correct errors in favor of the government, but will "overlook" errors in their own favor. Even if her figures are correct, he says, looking at a lot more returns will bear out his point.

Comment on the auditor's reasoning and her boss's contrary stand.

Probabilistic — Structure 6

A brewery buys nearly all of its reusable glass bottles from a local glass manufacturer. One summer, however, the local company is unable to deliver enough bottles, and the brewery orders a shipment from a large glass manufacturer that distributes its products nationwide. On the first day that these new bottles are used, however, the bottle-filling machinery has to be stopped four times because of jamming, and, as a result, production for the day is unusually low. (Ordinarily the brewery does not experience more than one jamming stoppage per day and frequently there are none at all.) The foreman is worried about the new bottles. He decides to test the new bottles produced by the national manufacturer carefully. He randomly selects 300 cases of these new bottles and instructs the bottle-filler operators to record carefully each jamming incident. Meanwhile, company mechanics carefully lubricate and check adjustments on the bottle-filling machinery. When they are finished, the bottle-filling machinery is running more smoothly than it has for years. During the next 2 days, the 300 cases of new bottles are fed to the machine. There are only two jamming incidents, one each day. The foreman concludes that there is in fact little or no real disadvantage of the new bottles with respect to jamming of the bottle-filling machinery.

Comment on the foreman's reasoning. Is it basically sound? Can his procedure be criticized?

Objective — Structure 1

A talent scout for a professional basketball team attends two college games with the intention of observing carefully the talent and skill of a particular player. The player looks generally excellent. He repeatedly makes plays worthy of the best professional players. However, in one of the games, with his team behind by 2 points, the player is fouled while shooting and has the opportunity to tie the game by making both free throws. The player misses both free throws and then tries too hard for the rebound from the second one, committing a foul in the process. The other team then makes two free throws, for a 4-point lead, and goes on to win by 2 points.

The scout reports that the player in question "has excellent skills, and should be recruited. He has a tendency to misplay under extreme pressure, but this will probably disappear with more experience and better coaching."

Comment on the thinking embodied in the scout's opinion that the player (a) "has excellent skills" and that the player has (b) "a tendency to misplay under extreme pressure." Does the thinking behind either conclusion have any weaknesses?

Objective—Structure 2

The Caldwells had long ago decided that when it was time to replace their car they would get what they called "one of those solid, safety-conscious, built-to-last Swedish cars"—either a Volvo or a Saab. As luck would have it, their old car gave up the ghost on the last day of the closeout sale for the model year both for the Volvo and for the Saab. The model year was changing for both cars and the dollar had recently dropped substantially against European currencies; therefore, if they waited to buy either a Volvo or a Saab, it would cost them substantially more—about $1200. They quickly got out their *Consumer Reports* where they found that the consensus of the experts was that both cars were very sound mechanically, although the Volvo was felt to be slightly superior on some dimensions. They also found that the readers of *Consumer Reports* who owned a Volvo reported having somewhat fewer mechanical problems than owners of Saabs. They were about to go and strike a bargain with the Volvo dealer when Mr. Caldwell remembered that they had two friends who owned a Saab and one who owned a Volvo. Mr. Caldwell called up the friends. Both Saab owners reported having had a few mechanical problems but nothing major. The Volvo owner exploded when asked how he liked his car. "First that fancy fuel injection computer thing went out: $250 bucks. Next I started having trouble with the rear end. Had to replace it. Then the transmission and the clutch. I finally sold it after 3 years for junk."

Given that the Caldwells are going to buy either a Volvo or a Saab today, in order to save $1200, which do you think they should buy? Why?

Objective—Structure 3

Howard was a teacher in a junior high school in a community known for truancy and delinquency problems among its youth. Howard says of his experiences: "Usually, in a class of 35 or so kids, 2 or 3 will pull some pretty bad stunts in the first week—they'll skip a day of class, get into a scuffle with another kid, or some such thing. When that kind of thing happens, I play it down and try to avoid calling the class' attention to it. Usually, these kids turn out to be no worse than the others. By the end of the term you'll find they haven't pulled any more stunts than the others have." Howard reasons as follows: "Some of these kids are headed toward a delinquent pattern of behavior. When they find out nobody is very impressed, they tend to settle down."

Comment on Howard's reasoning:

(a) Do you agree that it is likely that the students who pull a "pretty bad stunt in the first week" are "headed toward a delinquent pattern of behavior?"

(b) Do you agree that it is likely that the students who initially pull a "pretty bad stunt" turn out to be no worse than the others because they find no one is impressed with their behavior?

Objective—Structure 4

The psychology department of the University of Michigan keeps records on the performance of all its graduate students and relates this performance score to all kinds of background information about the students. Recently there was a debate on the admissions committee about whether to admit a particular student from Horace Maynard College. The student's scores on the GRE and his GPA were marginal—that is, almost all students actually admitted to the department have scores as high or higher, while most rejected students have lower scores. The student's letters of recommendation were quite good, but none of the writers of the letters were personally known to any of the Michigan faculty.

One member of the admissions committee argued against admission, pointing out that department records show that students who graduate from small, nonselective colleges like Maynard perform at a level substantially below the median of all Michigan graduate students. This argument was countered by a committee member who noted that 2 years ago Michigan had admitted a student from Maynard who was now among the three highest ranked students in the department.

Comment on the arguments put forward by these two committee members. What are their strengths and weaknesses?

Objective—Structure 5

The superintendent of schools was urging the school board to make an expensive curriculum shift to a "back-to-basics" stress on fundamental learning skills and away from the electives and intensive immersion in specialized arts and social studies topics that had recently characterized the secondary schools in the district. He cited a study of 120 school systems that had recently begun to emphasize the basics and 120 school systems that had a curriculum similar to the district's current one. The "back-to-basics" school systems, he said, were producing students who scored half-a-year ahead of the students in the other systems on objective tests of reading, mathematics, and science. Of the 120 "back-to-basics" school systems, 85 had shown improved skills for students in the system vs only 40 with improved skills in the 120 systems which had not changed. One of the school board members took the floor to argue against the change. In her opinion, she said, there was no compelling reason to attribute the improved student skills in the "back-to-basics" systems to the specific curriculum change, for two reasons: (1) school systems that make curriculum changes probably have more energetic, adventurous administrators and faculty and thus the students would learn more in those schools system no matter what the curriculum was. (2) *Any* change in curriculum could be expected to produce improvement in student performance because of increased faculty interest and commitment.

Comment on the reasoning of both the superintendent and the board member. On the basis of the evidence and arguments offered, do you think it is likely that the "back-to-basics" curriculum is intrinsically superior to the district's current curriculum?

Objective — Structure 6

An economist was arguing in favor of a guaranteed minimum income for everyone. He cited a recent study of several hundred people in the United States with inherited wealth. Nearly 92% of those people, he said, worked at some job that provided earned income sufficient to provide at least a middle-class life style. The study showed, he said, that contrary to popular opinion, people will work in preference to being idle. Thus a guaranteed income policy would result in little or no increase in the number of people unwilling to work.

Comment on the economist's reasoning. Is it basically sound? Does it have weaknesses?

Subjective — Structure 1

Gerald M. had a 3-year-old son, Timmy. He told a friend: "You know, I've never been much for sports, and I think Timmy will turn out the same. A couple of weeks ago, an older neighbor boy was tossing a ball to him, and he could catch it and throw it all right, but he just didn't seem interested in it. Then the other day, some kids his age were kicking a little soccer ball around. Timmy could do it as well as the others, but he lost interest very quickly and started playing with some toy cars while the other kids went on kicking the ball around for another 20 or 30 min."

Do you agree with Gerald's reasoning that Timmy is likely not to care much for sports? Why or why not?

Subjective — Structure 2

David L. was a senior in high school on the East Coast who was planning to go to college. He had compiled an excellent record in high school and had been admitted to his two top choices: a small liberal arts college and an Ivy League university. The two schools were about equal in prestige and were equally costly. Both were located in attractive East coast cities, about equally distant from his home town. David had several older friends who were attending the liberal arts college and several who were attending the Ivy League university. They were all excellent students like himself and had interests that were similar to his. His friends at the liberal arts college all reported that they liked the place very much and that they found it very stimulating. The friends at the Ivy League university reported that they had many complaints on both personal and social grounds and on educational grounds. David initially thought that he would go to the liberal arts college. However, he decided to visit both schools himself for a day. He did not like what he saw at the private liberal arts college: several people whom he met seemed cold and unpleasant; a professor he met with briefly seemed abrupt and uninterested in him; and he did not like the "feel" of the campus. He did like what he saw at the Ivy League university: several of the people he met seemed like vital, enthusiastic, pleasant people; he met with two different professors who took a personal interest in him; and he came away with a very pleasant feeling about the campus.

Which school should David L. choose, and why? Try to analyze the arguments on both sides, and explain which side is stronger.

Subjective — Structure 3

Janice is head nurse in a home for the aged. She says the following of her experiences: "There is a big turnover of the nursing staff here, and each year we hire 15–20 new nurses. Some of these people show themselves to be unusually warm and compassionate in the first few days. One might stay on past quitting time with a patient who's having a difficult night. Another might be obviously shaken by the distress of a patient who has just lost a spouse. I find though that, over the long haul, these women turn out to be not much more concerned and caring than the others. What happens to them, I think, is that they can't remain open and vulnerable without paying a heavy emotional price. They usually continue to be considerate and effective but they build up a shell."

Comment on Janice's reasoning. Do you think it is likely that she correctly identifies the nurses who are unusually warm and compassionate? Do you agree it is likely that most of the ones who are unusually warm at first later build up a shell to protect themselves emotionally?

Subjective — Structure 4

The director of a Broadway production of Shakespeare's *As You Like It* had just finished auditions for the female lead in the show. Two of the candidates gave readings for the part he liked a great deal. Another was an actress whom the director had worked with before in three Shakespeare comedies. The director thought she had been superb in each. Unfortunately, of her three readings for the lead in this play, one had been fairly good, but two had been quite flat. This third actress had to know immediately whether she was going to be chosen for the part. If not, she would take a minor role in a movie that would keep her on the West Coast for the next 6 months.

What should the director do — hire the third actress or hire one of the two whose readings he liked better? Why?

Subjective — Structure 5

Two New Yorkers were discussing restaurants. Jane said to Ellen, "You know, most people seem to be crazy about Chinese food, but I'm not. I've been to about 20 different Chinese restaurants, across the whole price range, and everything from bland Cantonese to spicy Szechwan and I'm really not very fond of any of it." "Oh," said Ellen, "don't jump to conclusions. I'll bet you've usually gone with a crowd of people, right?" "Yes," admitted Jane, "that's true. I usually go with half a dozen people or more from work." "Well, that may be it," said Ellen. "People usually go to Chinese restaurants with a crowd of people they hardly know. I know you, you're often tense and a little shy, and you're not likely to be able to relax and savor the food under those circumstances. Try going to a Chinese restaurant with just one good friend. I'll bet you'll like the food."

Comment on Ellen's reasoning. Do you think there is a good chance that if Jane went to a Chinese restaurant with one friend, she'd like the food? Why or why not?

Subjective — Structure 6

Martha was talking to a fellow passenger on an airplane. The fellow passenger was on his way to Hawaii for a month's vacation. "I don't like vacations myself," Martha said. "I've always worked. I put myself through college and law school and now I have a full-time legal practice. Frequently, of course, I've had slow periods when I wasn't working at all, but I never liked those times. For example, there would usually be a week or two between the end of school and the beginning of a summer job and another week or two of enforced idleness at the end of the summer. And there were many occasions when I was getting started in my career when I had no real work to do for fairly long periods. But I never enjoyed the leisure. I know there are some people who talk about using vacations to "recharge" themselves. But I suspect many of these people don't really enjoy their work or don't have a very high energy level. I do have a lot of energy, and I do enjoy my work, and I guess that's why I don't really like vacations."

Analyze Martha's reasoning. Do you think she had good evidence for feeling she doesn't like vacations?

APPENDIX B

The Three Objective Example Problems Used in Experiment 1, Also Used in the Objective Examples Training Condition of Experiment 2

Example 1 (Structure 1)

A major New York law firm had a history of hiring only graduates of large, prestigious law schools. One of the senior partners decided to try hiring some graduates of smaller, less prestigious law schools. Two such people were hired. Their grades and general record were similar to those of people from the prestigious schools hired by the firm. Although their manners and "style" were not as polished and sophisticated as those of the predominantly Ivy League junior members of the firm, their objective performance was excellent. At the end of 3 years, both of them were well above average in the number of cases won and in the volume of law business handled. The senior partner who had hired them argued to colleagues in the firm that, "This experience indicates that graduates of less prestigious schools are at least as ambitious and talented as graduates of the major law schools. The chief difference between the two types of graduates is in their social class background, not in their legal ability, which is what counts."

Comment on the thinking that went into this senior partner's conclusion. Is the argument basically sound? Does it have weaknesses? (Disregard your own initial opinion, if you had one, about graduates of nonprestigious law schools, and concentrate on the thinking that the senior partner used.)

Please consider this problem for a few moments. After you have considered the problem and analyzed it for a minute or two, turn the page for our analysis.

The senior partner is trying to draw a conclusion about a certain population. We can think of the members of this *population* as newly graduated lawyers, from nonprestigious law schools, who otherwise meet the law firm's hiring standards. If we divide the members of this population into *two categories,* "excellent" and "mediocre or worse," we can think of the *population distribution* as the percentage in each category. The senior partner has concluded that the percentage in the "excellent" category is very high, or anyway, just as high as in another population, involving graduates of prestigious law schools. This conclusion was based on observing a *sample* of *size* = 2, in which the *sample distribution* was 100% "excellent," 0% "mediocre or worse."

Apart from any other considerations, however, the *sample distribution* for size 2 is apt to be quite different from the *population distribution:* the latter could be only 60 or 50% or even perhaps as low as 40% "excellent," and a 2–0 sample split would not be so unusual; just as one would not be at all amazed to draw two out of two red gumballs from an urn with only 40% reds. So the senior partner's attitude is quite unwarranted: a larger sample is needed.

Example 2 (Structure 3)

Susan is the artistic director for a ballet company. One of her jobs is auditioning and selecting new members of the company. She says the following of her experience: "Every year we hire 10–20 young people on a 1-year contract on the basis of their performance at the audition. Usually we're extremely excited about the potential of 2 or 3 of these young people — a young woman who does a brilliant series of turns or a young man who does several leaps that make you hold your breath. Unfortunately, most of these young people turn out to be only somewhat better than the rest. I believe many of these extraordinarily talented young people are frightened of success. They get into the company and see the tremendous effort and anxiety involved in becoming a star, and they get cold feet. They'd rather lead a less demanding life as an ordinary member of the corps de ballet."

Comment on Susan's reasoning. Why do you suppose that Susan usually has to revise downward her opinion of dancers that she initially thought were brilliant?

Please consider this problem for a few moments. After you have considered the problem and analyzed it for a minute or two, turn the page for our analysis.

We can analyze this problem using the law of large numbers by thinking of each ballet dancer as possessing a *population* of ballet movements. Susan is interested in excellence, so we can divide the members of each population into two categories: "brilliant movements" and "nonbrilliant, or other movements." We can think of the *population distribution* as the percentage or proportion in each category. For many dancers, the population distribution is actually 0% brilliant and 100% other: these dancers simply lack the talent to perform a brilliant movement. For many other dancers, there is a small or moderate percentage of "brilliant movement" gumballs in their urn. A true ballet star would therefore have a population distribution with a greater percentage of "brilliant" movements than an ordinary member of the corps de ballet.

By conducting auditions, Susan is observing *samples* of each dancer's population distribution. An audition, however, is a very small sample of a dancer's movements. We know from the law of large numbers that small samples are very unreliable estimates of the population. When a dancer performs some brilliant moves during an audition, it is often because the dancer has happened to draw a couple of the "lucky gumballs" that day: it does not prove that the population distribution for that dancer consists of a large percentage of "brilliant movements." It is reasonable to think that there are really very few dancers that have population distributions with a large percentage of brilliant movements; and so when Susan sees a dancer performing brilliantly at audition, the chances are it is just a lucky draw from a dancer who is capable of performing some, but not necessarily a great number of "brilliant movements." Therefore, when Susan hires such dancers and evaluates them after seeing a much larger sample of their movements, it is not surprising that she finds that many of these dancers that were brilliant at audition turn out to be only somewhat better than the rest.

Example 3 (Structure 5)

Kevin, a graduate student in sociology, decided to do a research project on "factors affecting performance of major league baseball players" in which he gathered a great amount of demographic data on birthplace, education, marital status, etc., to see if any demographic factors were related to the performance of major league baseball players (e.g., batting average, pitching victories). Kevin was unable to use data for all the major league teams because information for some of the players was unavailable, but he was able to obtain data for some 200 players in the major leagues.

One finding that interested Kevin concerned the 110 married players. About 68% of these players improved their performance after getting married, while the remainder had equal or poorer performance. He concluded that marriage is beneficial to a baseball player's performance. At a social hour sponsored by the Office of the Commissioner of Major League Baseball, he happened to mention his finding to a staff member of the office. The staff member listened to Kevin's results and then said, "Your study is interesting but I don't believe it. I'm sure that baseball performance is worse after a marriage because the ball player suddenly has to take on enormous responsibilities: taking care of his spouse and children. Plus the factor of being stressed by having to be on the road so much of the time and therefore away from the family. The player will no longer be able to devote as much time to baseball as before he was married. Because of this he will lose that competitive quality that is necessary for good performance in baseball.

What do you think of the staff member's argument? Is it a sound one or not? Explain your reasoning.

Please consider this problem for a few moments. After you have considered the problem and analyzed it for a minute or two, turn the page for our analysis.

Kevin is trying to find out how performance in major league baseball is affected by being married. To do this, he obtained data for 200 players in the major leagues and discovered that out of the 110 that had gotten married, 68% had improved performance after the wedding (and 32% had equal or poorer performance). According to the law of large numbers, which states that the larger the sample, the better it is in estimating the population, there is substantial evidence that marriage is beneficial to baseball players' performance. Recall that in the gumball demonstration, samples of size 25 were very good estimates of the population: these samples did not differ much from population. Extending the argument, samples of size 110 are extremely accurate estimates of the population. Thus, it can be concluded that, in general, marriage is beneficial to baseball players' performance.

What about the staff member's theory that baseball performance is worse after a marriage because the ball player assumes enormous responsibilities and will no longer be able to devote as much time to baseball as before? Although this argument may have some intuitive appeal, it should be discounted because it is not supported by any data and is, in fact, contradicted by Kevin's large sample of 110 players.

6

Immediate and Delayed Transfer of Training Effects in Statistical Reasoning

Geoffrey T. Fong
University of Waterloo, Canada

Richard E. Nisbett
University of Michigan

Two central questions about the nature of reasoning have been addressed since Plato's time: At what level of generality and abstraction do rules for reasoning exist? and Is it possible to improve people's reasoning abilities? These two questions are intimately related. Plato, and most subsequent thinkers up until the late nineteenth century, believed that people possess very abstract rules and that, as a consequence, it is relatively easy to improve reasoning. According to this perspective, known as *formal discipline,* rules can be taught in the abstract, in the form of mathematics or logic, and they will then be applied across the concrete domains of everyday life. Psychologists and educators through the nineteenth century explained the process by drawing an analogy between physical and mental training: Just as one could exercise the muscles to obtain stronger muscles, so too could one exercise the reasoning faculties to strengthen them.

Twentieth-century psychology has been much less sanguine about the effects of training, partly because there has been substantial resistance to believing that inferential rules exist at a very general or abstract level. In his early studies, which suggested that practice in memorizing poetry did not serve to improve the faculty of memory more generally, William James (1890) called the analogy into question. So, too, did the extensive research program of Thorndike (1906; Thorndike & Woodworth, 1901). Thorndike concluded, on the basis of a number of experiments, that transfer of training was a will-o'-the-wisp that was dependent entirely on whether the target task shared "identical elements" with the task on which subjects had been trained. Thorndike's position was thus characterized by extreme concreteness and domain specificity of training, as is conveyed by the following quotation:

Training the mind means the development of thousands of particular independent capacities, the formation of countless particular habits, for the working of any mental capacity depends upon the concrete data with which it works. Improvement of any one mental function or activity will improve others only insofar as they possess elements common to it also. The amount of identical elements in different mental functions and the amount of general influence from special training are much less than common opinion supposes. (Thorndike, 1906, p. 246)

Thorndike's (1906) view finds its counterpart today in the positions of such theorists as D'Andrade (1982), Griggs and Cox (1982), Manktelow and Evans (1979), and Reich and Ruth (1982). These theorists hold that deductive reasoning occurs not by virtue of the application of abstract rules of logic but by virtue of local, concrete rules tied to the domain in question.

In contrast to Thorndike's (1906) antiformalist position, Piaget (e.g., Inhelder & Piaget, 1958) and modern theorists in the Piagetian tradition (e.g., Braine, 1978; Braine, Reiser, & Rumain, 1984) hold that extreme concreteness is characteristic only of the young child. By the beginning of adolescence, when the child reaches the stage of formal operations, reasoning is governed by the use of abstract inferential rules that are essentially identical to formal statistical and logical rules. Even Piaget and his followers, however, have been pessimistic about whether these abstract rules can be improved through instruction. Piaget believed that the acquisition of abstract inferential rules was almost entirely dependent on spontaneous cognitive development resulting from active self-discovery and that formal instruction could not accelerate the process to any great extent.

The possibility that reasoning ability might be improved through instruction has thus been met with considerable pessimism throughout the history of modern psychology. It should be noted that although Thorndike's research on transfer of training provided some of the early pessimism for the effects of instruction on reasoning, the studies actually had little to do with reasoning as it would be defined today. Instead, they examined transfer from tasks such as canceling parts of speech and estimation of areas of rectangles. Nevertheless, more recent research on transfer of training for problem-solving tasks has hardly been more encouraging. Strong positive transfer effects seem to be difficult to obtain (see Gick & Holyoak, 1987, for a review of the literature on transfer effects). For example, exposure to the Tower-of-Hanoi problem does not readily transfer to other, formally identical problems (Hayes & Simon, 1977).

Other researchers have attempted to improve intelligence, critical thinking skills, and other skills through formal training (see Nickerson, Perkins, & Smith, 1985, and Resnick, 1987, for reviews). Some of these attempts have been shown to be effective in improving higher order reasoning skills, at least within the classroom. Whether such training generalizes to contexts outside the classroom, however, has not been rigorously examined.

In contrast, a recent set of experiments conducted by Fong, Krantz, and Nisbett (1986) showed that training in statistics strongly influences the way people reason about events involving uncertainty in everyday life and that such training readily transfers to domains outside of the domain of training. For example, Fong et al. presented subjects who had varying degrees of statistical training with a problem about a manufacturer's representative who travels a great deal and tries to maximize the quality of her dining experiences by returning to restaurants where she had an excellent meal on her first visit. She finds, however, that subsequent meals are rarely as good as the first. Subjects were asked to explain why this occurs. Subjects without training in statistics almost invariably gave a purely "deterministic" answer that stressed possible causal explanations. For example, they suggested that "the chefs may change a lot" or "her expectations were so high that she could only be disappointed." Subjects with some training in statistics were more likely to give "statistical" answers, that is, those that made at least some mention of the variability of meal quality at a restaurant over time. These statistically sophisticated subjects were more likely to state that "maybe it was just by chance that she got such a good meal the first time." Finally, subjects with substantial training in statistics were quite likely not only to refer to statistical considerations but also to structure the problem as one involving sample values and population parameters. For example, "there are probably more restaurants where you might get an occasional excellent meal than restaurants that serve only excellent meals; chances are that when she got such a good meal the first time, it was just because she happened to hit it lucky at an inconsistent restaurant."

Fong et al. (1986) argued that statistical training is effective because people possess rudimentary but abstract intuitive versions of the law of large numbers and other statistical principles, or *statistical heuristics* (Nisbett, Krantz, Jepson, & Kunda, 1983). These rules exist in people's cognitive repertoire as the statistical counterpart to the nonstatistical heuristics, such as representativeness and availability, which have been identified by Kahneman and Tversky (1972, 1973; Tversky & Kahneman, 1974). Because people possess some statistical intuitions, it is possible to improve the rule system by relatively formal training procedures that work directly on the abstract rules themselves.

In support of the view that statistical heuristics exist in abstract form rather than simply in the form of concrete, domain-specific rules, Fong et al. (1986) presented two studies using two different training procedures. In the *rule training* condition, subjects were taught about the formal properties of the law of large numbers in a brief training session. The session began with formal definitions of sample, population, and sampling, and ended with a demonstration of the law of large numbers involving the classic gumball-urn model. This formal training increased both the frequency and the quality of statistical reasoning about a wide variety of everyday life problems, from probabilistic problems involving randomizing devices, for which even most untrained control subjects usually answered with reference to the law of large numbers, to objective problems involving events such as sports, which are readily codable in terms that allow application of the principle and for which many control subjects invoked the principle; to subjective problems about interpersonal relations and other judgments, for which only very few control subjects invoked the principle. Formal training enhanced statistical thinking about equally for these three problem domains.

In a second type of training procedure, *examples training,* subjects were presented with three concrete example problems that illustrated how the law of large numbers could be applied to make inferences about everyday life events. In one study, subjects were presented with example problems and the law of large numbers solutions in one of the three problem domains (probabilistic, objective, and subjective) and then were asked to solve problems in all three domains. Consistent with the formal view, subjects readily extrapolated from the examples: The training effect for problems in the untrained domain was just as great as it was for problems in the trained domain. Training effects were thus domain independent.

Fong et al. (1986) suggested that subjects readily induced abstract rules pertaining to the law of large numbers from the three example problems and thus were capable of applying the principle across domains. There are, however, alternative explanations for the very marked interdomain transfer found in the Fong et al. studies.

One alternative is that the domains used by Fong et al. (1986) were extremely broad. It is possible that the domain independence of training effects was due precisely to the breadth and looseness of the domains. The "domain" of all objectively codable events and the "domain" of all subjective events involving interpersonal relations and other social judgments may be congeries that are too broad to be domains in any meaningful sense. The similarities among problems within a domain may have been so slight that there was no greater ability to apply the rule to problems within the domain than to problems outside it. Research in classification learning (e.g., Fried & Holyoak, 1984; Medin & Schaffer, 1978) has shown that such learning is facilitated by both the similarity of a particular example to members of the target category and its dissimilarity to members of alternative categories. Thus, to the extent that the three example problems were so variable as to not be well-differentiated from problems in the untrained domain, one would not expect domain specificity effects.

In Experiment 1, we presented subjects with three example problems within more tightly defined domains, sports and ability testing, to explore whether training on more circumscribed content domains would result in reduced transfer effects, as the empirical, antiformalist position would argue. The formalist position, in contrast, would suggest that to the extent that examples training works directly on people's abstract rule system, training on more tightly defined domains would not serve to reduce the transfer to the untrained domain, at least not when testing followed immediately after training.

Our second goal was to address the alternative explanation that training effects were due largely to the use of direct analogies. In the direct analogies account, people map features of a base problem onto those of a target problem, and solution of the target problem is accomplished by direct analogy. As applied to the Fong et al. (1986) results, subjects given examples training may have solved the test problems simply by drawing direct analogies to the example problems. This alternative explanation requires, of course, that subjects remember the example problems at the time they attempt to solve the test problems. In the original Fong et al. studies, testing followed shortly after training, and thus memory for the example problems would have been very great. Because of this, the explanation based on drawing analogies from specific examples cannot be ruled out.

Recent approaches to analogical reasoning have explored the processes by which general principles can be induced from examples (e.g., Dellarosa, 1985; Gentner, 1983; Gick & Holyoak, 1983; Ross & Kennedy, 1990). Gick and Holyoak (1983), for instance, suggested that individuals given two examples abstract a schema based on the similarity and dissimilarity between the elements of the two examples, or base analogs, a process that enhances analogical transfer. Ross and Kennedy (1990) have found that explicit cuing of a prior problem with different content promotes generalizations about how a principle can be applied. They found that such cuing serves to enhance both the access to and the correct use of the principle.

In these studies and others, the details of the prior examples are available and readily accessible in memory because the testing typically occurs very shortly, if not immediately, after training. In the present studies, we wanted to test whether generalization occurred even when details of the examples would be much less accessible and hence more difficult to use in analogical mapping. We did this in Experiment 1 by testing some subjects after a delay of 2 weeks. This delay was intended to degrade memory for the example problems. If training was not maintained at all over the 2-week period, this would be a serious blow to the formalist position, implying that statistical training had no long-lasting effect on improving people's statistical heuristics and that so-called training effects in the immediate testing condition were merely exercises in drawing direct analogies from example problems that were easily accessible. If, on the other hand, there was significant retention of training effects even for the untrained domain, this would suggest that training had its effect through the induction of domain-independent rules. This suggestion would be strengthened by showing that memory for examples was poor after a delay and that individual differences in performance on test problems could not be predicted by individual differences in memory for the details of the example problems.

EXPERIMENT 1

Method

Overview of Design and Procedure

In a 2 × 2 factorial design, subjects were trained on the law of large numbers either in the domain of sports or in the domain of ability testing. They were then tested on problems in both domains either immediately after receiving training or after a delay of 2 weeks. In addition, there was a nonfactorial control condition in which subjects received no training before answering the test problems.

Subjects in the training conditions first read the law-of-large-numbers training booklet, which included three example problems. Subjects in the *sports training* condition were given example problems that all dealt with sports in some way. Subjects in the *ability testing training* condition were given example problems that involved sampling a person's mental abilities or intellectual achievements by means of a test or work sample. Each booklet took approximately 15 min to read.

Subjects in the *immediate* condition then answered 10 test problems, 5 in each domain. They were given 45 min to complete the problems. Subjects in the *delay* condition were told that they would return for a second session of the experiment 2 weeks later. They were not told the reason for the second session. The overwhelming majority returned for the second session after exactly 2 weeks, and more than 90% participated within 4 days after that. When delay subjects returned for the second session, they were given the test problems under the same instructions given to subjects in the immediate condition.

Subjects

Subjects were 231 undergraduates at the University of Michigan who participated in partial fulfillment of requirements for their introductory psychology classes. They participated in small groups.

Materials[1]

Training materials. The training booklet began with a one-page introduction to the law of large numbers. The introduction explained that the law of large numbers was a principle of probability that was helpful in understanding and predicting events, especially under conditions of limited information. The introduction then described how the law of large numbers could be used to understand events in one of two domains. In the sports training condition, subjects read the following:

> It is easy to see the application of the principle in the domain of sports. For example, when assessing an athlete's ability, the more games you see him or her play (the larger the sample), the better the idea you get of the athlete's true ability.

In the ability testing training condition, subjects were told the following:

> It is easy to see the application of the principle in the domain of ability testing. For example, when trying to determine whether a person is skillful on a certain task, the more information you have about that person's performance on that task (the larger the sample), the better the idea you get of that person's true ability.

The second part of the training booklet consisted of three example problems. Following each problem was an analysis of it in terms of the law of large numbers. Subjects read each problem and were asked to consider it for a few moments before turning the page to read the law-of-large-numbers answer.

The answers to the example problems were constructed so that subjects could learn how the law of large numbers could be applied to problems in one of the two domains. The example problems and their answers were designed to be structurally identical for both domains. In the sports training condition, the booklet presented three sports example problems. One of these concerned a professional football team that decided to test its policy concerning drafting only players from large colleges. One year, they tried drafting two players from small schools. Both did quite well, and at the end of the year the conclusion was drawn that there was no difference between players from smaller schools and players from bigger schools. The law-of-large-numbers analysis applied to this problem stressed that two players constituted a very small sample of the population. A second problem asked subjects to explain the following phenomenon: After the first 2 weeks of the major league baseball season the leading hitter typically has a batting average as high as .450, yet no batter has ever had an average that high over an entire season. The law-of-large-numbers analysis pointed out that 2 weeks provides a relatively small sample of a batter's ability and that batting averages that are highly discrepant from the average should therefore be more common than they are with a large sample. The third example problem pitted a plausible theory about the deleterious effects of marriage on professional athletes' performance against the conclusions of a controlled study with a large sample that argued against the theory. The law-of-large-numbers analysis emphasized the low probability that the theory could be correct in view of the very large sample of married and unmarried players whose performance was compared, thus illustrating the stability of parameter estimates based on large samples.

In the ability testing training condition, the booklet also presented three example problems. The first described a personnel director who hires flight attendants and who wishes to hire applicants with some knowledge of Spanish. She asks applicants to translate five English words into Spanish. Applicants who do this correctly for four or more words are given priority in hiring. The law-of-large-numbers analysis emphasized that a sample of five words is very small. A second problem described a math teacher who is puzzled about the fact that although he always has two or three students in his calculus class who have averages of 95 or more on the first few weekly tests he gives, no one ever finishes the term with such a high average. The law-of-large-numbers analysis emphasized that extreme scores, both high and low, are to be expected in small samples, because of the high variability associated with such samples. A third problem pitted a plausible theory about the effects of caffeine on intelligence test scores against the conclusions of a well-designed study of the question that used a large number of subjects. The law-of-large-numbers analysis emphasized the stability of large samples.

Testing materials. The testing problem booklet consisted of 10 open-ended problems: 5 sports problems and 5 ability testing problems. The instructions asked subjects to "think carefully about each problem, and then write down answers that are sensible to you. In many of the problems, you may find that the law of large numbers is helpful."

To systematize the kinds of test problems we presented to subjects across the two domains, we constructed the test problems so that each belonged to one of five problem structures (see Fong et al., 1986). Structure 1 problems asked subjects to judge whether a generalization from a small sample was appropriate. Structure 2 problems pitted a small sample against a large sample. Structure 3 problems were regression problems, requiring subjects to explain why an extreme outcome in a small sample was not maintained in a subsequent sample. Structure 4 problems were similar to Structure 2 problems except that the large sample was drawn from a population that was related to, rather than identical to, the target population. Structure 5 problems pitted a large sample against a plausible theory that was offered without any supporting data.

In summary, the 10 test problems followed a 5 × 2 design, with problem structure crossed with problem domain (sports or ability testing). Half of the subjects answered the 5 sports problems first; half answered the 5 ability testing problems first. The order of the problems was randomized within each domain.

Coding System

We developed a coding system similar to that used by Fong et al. (1986) to score the open-ended responses to the 10 test problems. This 3-point coding system was designed to measure the degree to which subjects used statistical concepts such as variability and sample size and whether they correctly invoked statistical principles such as the law of large numbers.

We illustrate the coding system with responses to a test problem used in Experiment 1. In this sports problem, a hockey coach had to decide which of two players, LaBrecque or Stephens, would fill the last spot on his roster. His scouting reports, which were based on five or six games, suggested that Stephens was better than LaBrecque on every dimension. But when the coach watched them for the first time at that afternoon's practice session, LaBrecque played better than Stephens. Subjects were asked which player the coach should choose and why.

Responses to this problem were coded as one of the following three categories:

1 = an entirely deterministic response. Responses in this category included those in which the subject made no use of statistical concepts such as sample size, randomness, or variability. The following was a deterministic response to the hockey problem: "The coach should choose LaBrecque because he played better than Stephens during the practice. Probably the scouts weren't very good judges of ability."

2 = a poor statistical response. Responses in this category included some mention of statistical concepts, but the explanation was incomplete or incorrect. These responses contained one or more of the following characteristics: (a) the subject used both deterministic and statistical reasoning, but was judged by the coder to have preferred the deterministic reasoning; (b) the subject used an incorrect statistical principle, such as Gambler's Fallacy; and (c) the subject mentioned some statistical concept, such as luck or chance, but was not clear about how it was relevant. The following was a poor statistical response: "One practice session is definitely not enough to base a decision on. If only one were allowed, I would choose LaBrecque, because the reports were made by two different people and probably not consistent."

3 = a good statistical response. Responses in this category made correct use of a statistical concept. Some form of the law of large numbers was used, and the sampling elements were correctly identified. In general, the subject was judged to have clearly demonstrated how the law of large numbers could be applied to the problem. The following was coded as a good statistical response: "He should select Stephens The coach had only seen the players once. During that one session, LaBrecque could have had an unusual day, or perhaps Stephens was ill. The scouts saw the players over a larger number of games, and Stephens was the better player."

Because the coding system was designed to identify answers that were statistical in nature, it was possible that a poorly reasoned answer (coded as 2) would be given a higher score because it mentioned some statistical principle than would a well-reasoned answer that nonetheless failed to incorporate any statistical or probabilistic principle.

Two coders achieved a high degree of reliability: There was exact agreement on 85% of subjects' responses. The statistical reasoning score was computed for each subject, for each of the two problem domains. This was the average score for each subject for the five problems in that domain.

Results

We analyzed the statistical reasoning scores with a modified three-way analysis of variance (ANOVA), using orthogonal contrasts so that the nonfactorial control group could be included. For example, the main effect of the three training conditions was partitioned into the effects of training (average of sports training and ability testing training vs. control) and the effects of training domain (sports training vs. ability testing training).[2]

Figure 6.1 presents mean statistical reasoning score as a function of testing domain, training domain, and timing of the test problems. Figure 16.1 also presents, within parentheses, two summary statistics. The first is the *frequency* of statistical reasoning, defined as the proportion of all responses that were coded as statistical, that is, $p(code = 2$ or $3)$. The second is the *quality* of statistical reasoning, defined as the proportion of all statistical responses that were coded as reflecting a good understanding of the principle, that is, $p(code = 3|code = 2$ or $3)$.

Analyses revealed that there was no effect of the domain of testing; that is, subjects were no more likely to reason statistically for the sports problems than for the ability testing problems, $F(1, 226) < 1.$[3] Apparently, problems in the two domains were approximately equal in the extent to which events could be coded by subjects in terms amenable to intuitive statistical reasoning.

It may be seen that statistical training had a strong effect on the likelihood that subjects would incorporate statistical concepts in their

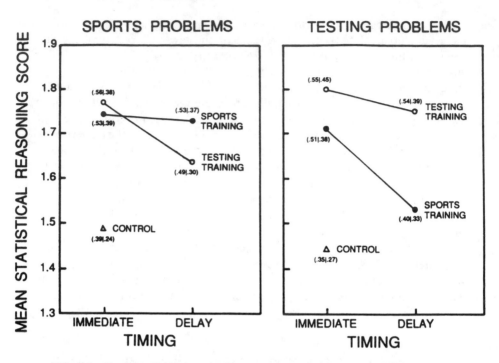

FIG. 6.1 Mean statistical reasoning score as a function of testing domain, training domain, and time of testing (immediate vs. 2-week delay) in Experiment 1. (Within the parentheses is the *frequency* of statistical answers, defined as the proportion of all answers that were statistical in nature [i.e., those answers given a code of 2 or 3], and the *quality* of statistical answers, defined as the proportion of all statistical answers that demonstrated proper use of the statistical principles [i.e., a code of 3|2 or 3] for each group. Frequency is the proportion to the left of the bar.)

answers to the test problems ($F = 19.34$, $p < .001$). This replicates the training effects found in Fong et al. (1986). It may also be seen that there was an interaction between training domain and testing domain ($F = 8.90$, $p < .005$). This interaction was dependent on timing. When subjects were tested immediately after training, there was no evidence for domain specificity: The Training Domain × Testing Domain interaction for subjects in the immediate condition was far from statistically significant ($F < 1$). The results thus replicate, for much tighter and more coherent domains, the Fong et al. finding that training effects for the law of large numbers are fully domain-independent when testing is immediate.

It should be noted that the higher statistical reasoning scores for the trained subjects in the immediate condition do not simply reflect a tendency to use the law of large numbers without regard to its correct usage. If that were the case, one would expect that although the frequency of statistical responses would increase, the quality would decrease. That did not occur. In fact, quality, as well as frequency, was higher for the trained subjects.

When subjects were tested 2 weeks after training, domain specificity of training was found, as shown by the significant Training Domain × Testing Domain interaction for subjects in the delay condition ($F = 13.38, p <$ .005).[4] The three-way interaction (Training Domain × Testing Domain × Timing) was not significant. Thus, the same basic pattern of results — greater loss of training effects over the 2-week delay in the untrained domain — was found for both the sports problems and the ability testing problems.

It is interesting to note that even after a delay of 2 weeks, both frequency and quality of statistical responses were still higher in the trained condition, which is again consistent with the view that subjects induced quite general principles from the examples.

Figure 6.2 presents (a) the effects of training and timing as a function of whether the testing domain was the same as the training domain or whether it was different and (b) the frequency and quality proportions for each group within parentheses. Figure 6.2, which simply averages over the specific domains in Figure 6.1, clearly shows that whereas the effect of training is domain-independent when testing immediately follows training, it is domain-specific after a 2-week delay. As can be seen in Figure 6.2, performance in the trained domain was unimpaired by a delay of 2 weeks ($F < 1$). In contrast, performance in the untrained domain was significantly lower after the 2-week delay ($F = 12.11, p < .001$).

Finally, it should be noted that although there was a significant decline in the retention of training effects in the untrained domain after 2 weeks, there still remained a greater ability to apply the law of large numbers for problems in the untrained domain compared with untrained controls ($F = 4.90, p < .05$). This was not a trivial effect. The effect size associated with this contrast, as defined by the standardized mean difference (see Cohen, 1988; Glass, 1976; and Hedges & Olkin, 1985) was 0.44, which is closer to Cohen's (1988) definition of a medium effect size (i.e., 0.50) than it is to a small effect size (i.e., 0.20).[5]

Discussion

The results of Experiment 1 make it clear that statistical training effects do not depend on presenting subjects with test problems immediately after training problems. Even when test problems are in a different domain than training problems, there is significant retention of training effects over a 2-week period. We believe that this is due to improvement of a rule system that transcends any given domain in its generality.

How can we account for the very strong retention of training effects in

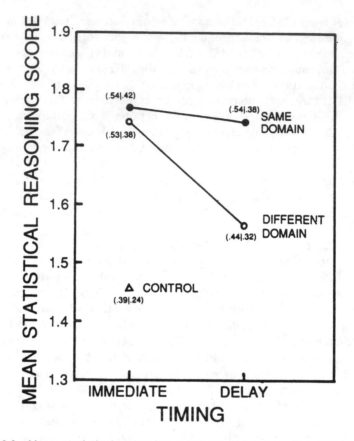

FIG. 6.2 Mean statistical reasoning score as a function of training and testing domain (closed points [●] = performance when testing domain was the same as the training domain; open points [○] = performance when testing domain was different than the training domain) and time of testing (immediate vs. 2-week delay) in Experiment 1. (The frequency and quality of statistical answers are within parentheses.)

the trained domain? One possibility is that examples training serves not only to enhance the inferential rule system itself, but also to provide subjects with ideas of how to code events within the trained domain in terms of the law of large numbers. These concepts or procedures may be called *coding rules*. For example, subjects given sports examples may learn to view baseball at-bats in terms of samples of a player's ability. Similarly, the intuition that "any team can beat any other team on a given day" can be linked, through examples training, to the formal statistical principle that relates sampling variability to sample size. These coding rules serve to link inferential rules to the content domains in which they are encountered. After a 2-week delay, when memory for the specific examples has decreased, subjects have at their disposal not only the general rules pertaining to the law of large numbers, but also more specific coding rules that aid their performance on the trained domain. These coding rules thus enhance the likelihood that the appropriate inferential rule will be accessed and considered by the individual for application to a given test problem.

This account shares some characteristics with Ross's (e.g., Ross, 1989; Ross & Kennedy, 1990) notion of reminding, in that exposure to earlier examples leads to the induction of general principles that are then invoked when solving new problems. The results of Experiment 1, however, go beyond previous studies in demonstrating that training effects can persevere when subjects are not explicitly cued to the principle and when testing takes place long after training.

Note also that subjects in Experiment 1 were not simply applying the law of large numbers without regard to its correct usage. If that were the case, one would expect that the increase in statistical reasoning scores would be due solely to an increase in the number of poor statistical responses (a code of 2) and not at all to an increase in the number of good statistical responses (a code of 3). No such pattern of results was found. Both frequency and quality of statistical responses were higher in trained subjects than in controls.

In addition, there is considerable evidence from Fong et al. (1986, Experiments 1 and 2) that statistical training of the kind used in the present studies did not lead to widespread overuse of the law of large numbers. Fong et al. included in their test package seven false-alarm problems, that is, problems in which application of the law of large numbers was inappropriate for their solution. Fong et al. found that subjects who were given statistical training of the kind used in the present studies were not significantly more likely to invoke the law of large numbers for these false-alarm problems.

Taken together, the results of Experiment 1 suggest that whatever the role of reminding, examples training created a strong and lasting improvement of the rule system itself.

The fact that statistical training effects were maintained with the domain of training over a considerable delay has important implications. It suggests that improvements to reasoning, at least within a fairly broad domain of events, can be very long-standing. This implication is consistent with our view that inferential rules can be abstracted to a high degree from the examples over which they were learned.

EXPERIMENTS 2 AND 3

Our interpretation of the effects of statistical training focuses on the abstraction of statistical inferential rules and coding rules. In this account, statistical training through examples serves both to enhance the abstract rule system corresponding to intuitions about statistical principles and to induce rules about how to code events in the domain represented by the example problems. There is one possible alternative to our theoretical account that suggests that retention of training after a delay results from memory for the example problems themselves and solution of the new problems by analogy. In this view, subjects remember the example problems in sufficient detail that they are able to map the elements of the example problems onto the elements of the test problems they encounter 2 weeks later. Greater retention of training effects in the same domain after a 2-week delay occurs because test problems from the same domain are more likely to remind subjects of the example problems than are test problems from a different domain.

Experiments 2 and 3 were designed to test whether this analogy explanation was plausible by assessing subjects' memory for the details of the example problems after 2 weeks. If memory for the example problems was fairly good, the analogy explanation could not be ruled out. But if memory was poor, then the analogy explanation would be weakened.

The analogy explanation suggests that memory for the example problems should be greater when the test domain is the same as the training domain. In other words, the domain specificity results found for statistical reasoning in Experiment 1 should be manifested in the same pattern for memory of the example problems.

In addition, if, on the one hand, retention of training effects is due to the construction of direct analogies from the example problems, there should be a correlation between statistical reasoning and memory for the details of the example problems. If, on the other hand, it is the memory for the general principle of the law of large numbers that is responsible, there should be a correlation between statistical reasoning and memory for the law of large numbers.

In Experiments 2 and 3, subjects were given examples training in the law of large numbers in either the sports or the ability testing domain. After a delay of 2 weeks, they received either sports or ability testing problems to solve. A third group received no test problems at all. All subjects were then given a questionnaire that assessed their memory for the specific details of the example problems and their memory for the general principle of the law of large numbers. In Experiment 3, there was an additional set of questions that asked subjects who received test problems after the 2-week delay whether the example problems had been helpful in solving the test problems.

Method

Subjects

Subjects in Experiment 2 were 60 members of the University of Michigan subject pool who participated in the experiment in small groups for payment. Subjects in Experiment 3 were 60 introductory psychology students at Northwestern University. There were no differences in the two subject groups; thus, we combined the two groups in the analyses reported here for those measures that were common to both experiments.

Procedure

Subjects were given the same instructions and materials as in Experiment 1. They were given the law-of-large-numbers training materials, which consisted of three example problems, each illustrating the use of the law of large numbers within a certain content domain. These examples were drawn either from the domain of sports or from the domain of ability testing and were identical to those used in Experiment 1. After reading the training materials, subjects were excused and were scheduled to return for the second session 2 weeks later. In other words, the first session was identical in every way to Experiment 1.

During the second session, subjects were assigned to one of three conditions. In two conditions, subjects were given three test problems to solve in which the law of large numbers was relevant. Subjects were given problems in either the sports domain or the ability testing domain. In the third condition, the no test condition, subjects were not given any test problems during the second session.

There were six conditions in all, crossing training domain (sports or ability testing) with testing domain (sports, ability testing, or no test problems).

All subjects then completed a questionnaire assessing their memory for the example problems they had read during the first session. The questionnaire consisted of three pages, each with instructions designed to elicit memory for both the example problems and the law of large numbers.

The instructions on the first page read as follows: "In the space below, we would like you to recall anything you can from the *first* session of this experiment. Provide as much detail as you can."

The instructions on the second page were as follows: "During the first session you read a packet of materials that described some principle. Tell us all you can about the training you received, other than what you already told us on the first page. What was the principle, and what did you read?"

The instructions on the third page were as follows: "In the training materials, you read some example problems. Tell us all you can about the problems, other than what you have already told us on the first two pages. What were the problems about?"

In Experiment 3, the memory questionnaire was lengthened to include a fourth page, which read as follows: "If you have not already done so, please describe how the examples illustrated the use of the principle." In addition, subjects in Experiment 3 were asked whether they had considered the example problems in solving the test problems. For each of the three example problems, they were asked to indicate which of four statements best described their use of the example problem: (a) I didn't think about this example problem in solving today's problems; (b) I thought about this problem, but didn't think it was relevant in solving today's problems; (c) I thought about this problem and tried to use it in solving today's problems; and (d) I definitely used this problem to guide my answers to today's problems.

A coding system was created to assess subjects' memory for the example problems and for the law of large numbers. Codes for each of the three example problems were assigned according to a 4-point scale, on which *1* = the example problem was not remembered at all or nothing was written; *2* = some details about the problem were recalled (e.g., "something about batting averages"), but there was no mention about how the law of large numbers or any other statistical concept was relevant to the problem; *3* = some mention about how the law of large numbers was used in the problem, but the explanation was sketchy, vague, or partly wrong; and *4* = a clear account of how the law of large numbers was used in the problem, that is, how the elements of the problem were relevant to the principle.

This coding for each of the three example problems was performed for each of the three pages of the memory questionnaire in Experiment 2 and for each of the four pages of the memory questionnaire in Experiment 3. In addition, subjects' memory for the law of large numbers or other statistical concepts presented in the training package was coded for each of the three (or four) pages according to a 4-point scale, on which *1* = no description of the law of large numbers, no mention of even its name; *2* = the law of large numbers was mentioned, but without further explanation; *3* = some explanation of the law of large numbers, but sketchy or vague; and *4* = clear explanation of the law of large numbers.

The overall reliability of the coding system was very high: There were exact matches on 88% of the codes assigned by two coders on a subset of the data in Experiment 2 and on 89% of the codes assigned in Experiment 3.

Results and Discussion

Statistical Reasoning

Responses to the open-ended test problems were scored in accordance with the 3-point coding system described in Experiment 1. Table 6.1 presents the mean statistical reasoning scores as a function of training domain and test domain (omitting, of course, those subjects who received no test problems after the 2-week delay). As can be seen, the domain specificity effects found after a 2-week delay in Experiment 1 were

TABLE 6.1
Mean Statistical Reasoning Scores by Training Domain and Test Domain:
Experiments 2 and 3

Training domain	Testing domain	
	Sports	Ability testing
Sports		
M	1.90	1.63
SD	0.49	0.51
Ability testing		
M	1.58	1.83
SD	0.36	0.44

Note. Higher scores indicate greater use of statistical reasoning. Maximum score = 3.0. In each condition, $n = 20$.

replicated here: The Training Domain × Testing Domain interaction was significant after a 2-week delay, $F(1, 76) = 6.58, p < .05$.

Memory for Example Problems

Did memory for the example problems also follow a domain-specific pattern? We analyzed responses to the memory questionnaire by using the highest code achieved across the first three pages of the questionnaire for each of the example problems. In this way, subjects would get credit for remembering the details of an example problem whether or not they had done so immediately or after three increasingly detailed prompts (i.e., the questions on each of the three pages of the questionnaire, presented earlier). It should be clear that this procedure was designed to produce the strongest possible memories for the example problems, and the data presented here undoubtedly overestimate subjects' actual spontaneous memory for the details of the example problems.

Having said this, the data show that subjects' memory for the example problems was very poor. Overall, only about one third (35.9%) of subjects recalled any of the three example problems, after all three prompts, with a good understanding of how the problem illustrated the use of the law of large numbers (that is, a code of 4). Of these, 18.5% recalled one problem, 11.9% recalled two problems, and 5.5% recalled all three.

The mean number of example problems (out of a possible three) that were recalled with a good understanding of the law of large numbers was less than one half of one problem (0.44).

Table 6.2 presents the mean number of problems recalled with a good understanding of the law of large numbers by training domain and testing domain. A two-way ANOVA demonstrated that there was a significant main effect for testing domain, $F(2, 114) = 3.14, p < .05$. Those subjects

TABLE 6.2
Mean Number of Example Problems Recalled With a Good Understanding of
the Law of Large Numbers by Training Domain and Testing Domain:
Experiments 2 and 3

Training domain	Testing domain		
	Sports	Ability testing	No training
Sports			
M	0.25	0.25	0.60
SD	0.72	0.55	0.88
Ability testing			
M	0.30	0.45	0.80
SD	0.66	0.76	1.15

Note. Scores are the average number of problems recalled (out of three). In each condition, $n = 20$.

who were not given test problems after the 2-week delay had a better memory for the example problems that did those who received test problems. Thus, answering test problems after a 2-week delay did not serve to enhance memory for the original example problems, as might be expected if subjects had drawn analogies from the example problems to solve the test problems.[6] In addition, there was no evidence for domain specificity of memory for the example problems, $F(2, 114) < 1$, for the Training Domain × Testing Domain interaction. Thus, when subjects answered test problems from the same domain as the example problems they had read, this did not enhance their memory for the example problems, as would be suggested by the analogical explanation.[7] Finally, there was no difference in memory between sports and ability testing example problems, $F(1, 114) = 1.03$, ns.

Memory for the Law of Large Numbers

In contrast to the poor memory for the example problems, memory for the law of large numbers was extremely good. More than three quarters (78.5%) of subjects recalled the law of large numbers in sufficient detail and clarity to be given the highest code in our 4-point coding system for law of large numbers memory. If we include subjects who gave at least a fair account of the law of large numbers (code of 3 or 4), then the percentage goes up to 89.0%. It is clear from these data that subjects remembered the general principle being illustrated in the example problems far better than they remembered the specific example problems themselves.

Table 6.3 presents the memory for the law of large numbers by training domain and test domain. In contrast to the memory for the example problems, we found a pattern of domain specificity for memory for the law of large numbers. The only significant effect was the Training Domain ×

TABLE 6.3
Mean Recall Scores for the Law of Large Numbers by Training Domain and
Testing Domain: Experiments 2 and 3

Training domain	Testing domain		
	Sports	Ability testing	No training
Sports			
M	3.80	3.35	2.85
SD	0.52	1.14	1.46
Ability testing			
M	3.15	3.75	3.65
SD	1.27	0.64	0.75

Note. Higher scores indicate better memory for the law of large numbers. Maximum memory score = 4.0. In each condition, $n = 20$.

Test Domain interaction, $F(2, 114) = 5.37$, $p < .05$. Specifically, memory for the law of large numbers was greatest when subjects received test problems that were from the same domain as they had been trained on 2 weeks previously (the contrast testing this specific effect was significant at the .05 level). This result supports the idea that retention of statistical training effects within the domain of training is partly due to exposure to problems within the same domain; such exposure serves to remind subjects of the general principle of the law of large numbers better than when they are exposed to problems in some other domain.

Relationship Between Statistical Reasoning and Memory

So far, the results presented demonstrate that the domain specificity pattern for statistical reasoning is mirrored by memory for the law of large numbers, but not by memory for the details of the example problems. This suggests that retention of training effects is due to memory for the inferential rule rather than to memory for the specific examples. However, it still might be the case that those subjects who retained some of the details of the example problems were more likely to use those details to solve the test problems. Thus, a correlation between memory for the example problems and performance on the test problems would support the direct analogy view.

An investigation of the correlations between statistical reasoning and memory, however, discounts this possibility. There was no evidence that memory for the details of the example problems was related to statistical reasoning. The correlation between statistical reasoning and memory for the details of the example problems was only +.06. In contrast, the correlation between statistical reasoning and memory for the law of large numbers was +.31 ($p < .05$).

*Reported Use of the Example Problems to Solve the
Test Problems*

In Experiment 3, subjects were asked whether they had used the example problems in solving the test problems. The most stringent criterion was agreement with the statement, "I definitely used this example problem in solving the test problems." Only 15.6% of subjects agreed with this statement for any of the three example problems. Of these, 9.4% agreed for only one problem, 6.3% agreed for two problems, and none of the 40 subjects who received test problems after the 2-week delay agreed for all three of the example problems. The mean number of example problems used by subjects was only 0.22 (out of a possible 3), and there was no evidence for domain specificity of example problem use, $F(1, 36) < 1$. For instance, subjects receiving sports examples were just as likely to report using the examples to solve ability testing problems as they were to report using them in solving sports problems.

In summary, the data from Experiments 2 and 3 show that (a) subjects had very poor memory for the details of the example problems and how the example problems illustrated the use of the law of large numbers, (b) subjects had very good memory for the general principle of the law of large numbers, (c) the domain specificity pattern for statistical reasoning was echoed in the memory for the law of large numbers but not in the memory for the example problems themselves, and (d) there was a significant correlation between statistical reasoning and memory for the law of large numbers but not between statistical reasoning and memory for the details of the example problems. This pattern of results supports our contention that examples training works by teaching subjects more about the inferential rule system rather than by merely giving them examples to which they can draw analogies when given the test problems. The results also suggest that high retention of training effects is due in part to a greater ability to access the inferential rule system within the trained domain through the use of a rather general set of coding rules linking events in the domain to the inferential rule system.

GENERAL DISCUSSION

The results of the experiments reported here are consistent with our view that people make use of abstract inferential rules in reasoning about everyday events and that improvements to these rules can be induced from reasoning about particular examples. In this way, our results are consistent with current views of analogical reasoning that emphasize the induction of general principles from examples (e.g., Dellarosa, 1985; Gentner, 1983;

Gick & Holyoak, 1983; Ross & Kennedy, 1990). In contrast, the results are not consistent with the alternative view that people solve such problems exclusively by use of direct analogy.

We found independence of training effects when subjects were tested immediately after training. In this case, reminding certainly played a major role in the effects of training. The example problems were readily accessible in the immediate condition, and analogies were easily constructed. But this same account cannot be readily applied to the results obtained in the delay condition. When subjects were tested 2 weeks after training we found significant retention of training effects even in the domain in which subjects had not been trained. It is highly unlikely that this improvement was produced by direct analogies or remindings of the specific content of the example problems because subjects could recall few details of the examples by that point. In addition, performance was not related to memory for example problems, whereas it was related to the ability to state the abstract rule. Finally, for problems in the trained domain, subjects performed just as well after 2 weeks as they did immediately. If performance was significantly mediated by analogical processes, there should have been some decrement over 2 weeks because of a decline in memory for the example problems.

We suspect that performance on problems within the domain of training was better after 2 weeks than was performance on problems in the untrained domain for two reasons. First, reminding effects (although not for the details of the example problems) were probably at least somewhat responsible: Most subjects would have remembered that they had been told to use the rule for problems in the domain for which they had been trained. However, subjects were more likely not only to use the rule, but also to use it correctly. We believe that they did so by virtue of having learned what we call *coding rules,* which serve to connect the inferential rule system to the domain of training. These rules probably exist at a fairly abstract level, because the test problems differed from the example problems in the kinds of specific content used. Thus, the statistical rules could not have been used to develop answers to the test problems unless the coding rules were represented at a sufficient level of abstraction to accommodate the many dissimilarities between the example problems and the test problems while still being used by subjects.

In prior studies of inferential rule training, it has not been possible to properly test the alternative explanation that training effects are due to using direct analogies with the actual example problems. By assessing subjects' performance after a delay — when memory for the example problems was greatly reduced, as shown in Experiments 2 and 3 — we were able to demonstrate that an explanation based on direct mapping of the example problems onto the test problems is not tenable.

The results are consistent with the assertion that people reason using rules at a high degree of generality and abstraction. A great many scholars today are solidly in the concrete, empirical, domain-specific camp established by Thorndike and Woodworth (1901), arguing that people reason without the aid of abstract inferential rules that are independent of content domain. The present findings—along with those of Fong et al. (1986); Lehman, Lempert, and Nisbett (1988); Nisbett, Fong, Lehman, and Cheng (1987); and Nisbett et al. (1983)—suggest strongly that people do possess abstract rules and that the rules can be improved by methods such as formal instruction (Fong et al., 1986; Fong, Lurigio, & Stalans, 1990; Lehman et al., 1988).

One important implication of our view of inferential rules, and one that is supported in the present studies, is that the effects of inferential rule training need not decay, at least over time periods of days or weeks. When context and content were reinstated, subjects' performances showed the same training increment after a delay of 2 weeks that they showed immediately after training, when the training domain was sufficiently well-defined and codable in terms of the rule system. Indeed, the effect size of training after a 2-week delay was still very large (1.04). Even when the content of the test problems was not the same as that of the training examples, the effect of training was significant after 2 weeks, and the effect size was close to moderate (0.44), as defined by Cohen (1988).

An important task for future research would be to delimit the types of rules and the breadth and nature of the content domains over which such marked retention effects may be found. We note here our strong expectation that such effects will turn out to be more likely for rules that are relatively intuitive and that have counterparts in people's natural intuitive repertoires, such as the law of large numbers (Nisbett et al., 1987). Holyoak, Nisbett, and their colleagues (Cheng & Holyoak, 1985; Cheng, Holyoak, Nisbett, & Oliver, 1986; Holland, Holyoak, Nisbett, & Thagard, 1986) have argued that the laws of formal logic are not included in this category. They have argued that people solve problems, which the logician might solve by applying logical rules, by instead using "pragmatic reasoning schemas." Such schemas are based on the recurrence of certain high regular patterns, for instance, of causal relations, or on the recurrence of contractual relations such as obligations and permissions. These schemas are highly general and abstract, but not so abstract as the purely syntactic rules of formal logic. Consistent with this view, abstract instruction in formal logic was found not to have an effect on the solution of problems involving deductive logic, whereas abstract instruction in pragmatic reasoning schemas did have an effect.

The notion that there is a close relationship between the inferential rule systems that people possess and the extent to which training will succeed helps us to understand why our very optimistic results seem to run counter to the general pessimism of other researchers in the area of transfer of training. Most other transfer studies of problem solving have attempted to teach entirely novel concepts or algorithms, such as the Tower-of-Hanoi problem (e.g., Hayes & Simon, 1977), the missionary-cannibals problem (e.g., Reed, Ernst, & Banerji, 1974), or mathematical rules of probability (e.g., Ross, 1984). When subjects are taught such rules *de novo,* it is likely that it is very difficult for them to induce the appropriate rules at a level of abstraction required for substantial transfer. It is not surprising, therefore, that transfer of training in problem solving leads to a rather pessimistic picture. Although some researchers have demonstrated that teaching completely novel principles can serve to create some degree of generalization (e.g., Ross & Kennedy, 1990), it is an open question whether the effects of training on such novel concepts would be maintained over a long delay, as they were in the present studies.

In the present studies we taught concepts that were already part of subjects' inferential repertoire, and thus the example problems served in part to improve understanding of preexisting inferential rules and in part to provide a set of coding rules that linked the inferential rule system more tightly to events in the trained domain. We believe that such learning should result in potentially better performance in any domain, but especially in those for which coding rules have been formed.

In general, the results of the present studies are more in tune with Plato's abstract view than with the concretism of many twentieth-century views (Nisbett et al., 1987). Rules taught in one domain can transfer to a new domain. And as long as a domain is reasonably tightly defined and coding rules for the domain can be induced, it is possible for the effects of inferential rule training to be retained for a considerable period of time. The results suggest, in fact, that inferential rule training may be the educational gift that keeps on giving.

FOOTNOTES

[1]All training and test materials may be obtained from Geoffrey T. Fong.

[2]There was no main effect for order and no interactions of order with any of the other factors. Thus, order is disregarded in the analyses presented.

[3]The degrees of freedom for all F statistics in Experiment 1 are (1, 226). They are omitted here for the sake of brevity. All p levels reported are based on two-tailed tests.

[4]We also conducted analyses on the frequency of statistical answers (see text for the definition of *frequency*). The analyses of frequency were consistent with the analyses reported here.

[5]It should be noted that the difference in statistical reasoning between controls and the condition in which the testing domain was the same as the training domain after the 2-week

delay was very strong. The effect size was 1.04, which is well above Cohen's (1988) definition of a large effect size (i.e., 0.80).

[6]In Experiment 3, a fourth prompt was added that asked subjects to describe how the example problems illustrated the use of the law of large numbers. This prompt elevated the overall average number of example problems recalled with a good understanding of the law of large numbers to only 0.70 (out of a possible 3.0); it did not change the particular pattern of recall by example domain or by test domain.

[7]These data used the most stringent criterion for memory, that is, when subjects were able to remember how the law of large numbers could be used to answer an example problem. If we relax the criterion so that we include subjects whose recall of the example problems with reference to the law of large numbers was only fair to poor (a code of *3* or *4*), the mean number of problems recalled increases to only 0.85 (out of a possible 3.0). Once again, there is no advantage in memory accorded by answering test problems from the same domain as the example problems.

REFERENCES

Braine, M. D. S. (1978). On the relation between the natural logic of reasoning and standard logic. *Psychological Review, 85,* 1–21.

Braine, M. D. S., Reiser, B. J., & Rumain, B. (1984). Some empirical justification for a theory of natural propositional logic. In G. H. Bower (Ed.), *The psychology of learning and motivation* (Vol. 18, pp. 313–371). San Diego, CA: Academic Press.

Cheng, P. W., & Holyoak, K. J. (1985). Pragmatic reasoning schemas. *Cognitive Psychology, 17,* 391–416.

Cheng, P. W., Holyoak, K. J., Nisbett, R. E., & Oliver, L. M. (1986). Pragmatic versus syntactic approaches to training deductive reasoning. *Cognitive Psychology, 18,* 293–328.

Cohen, J. (1988). *Statistical power analysis for the behavioral sciences (2nd ed.).* San Diego, CA: Academic Press.

D'Andrade, R. (1982, April). *Reason versus logic.* Paper presented at the Symposium on the Ecology of Cognition: Biological, Cultural, and Historical Perspectives, Greensboro, NC.

Dellarosa, D. (1985). *Abstraction of problem-type schemata through problem comparison* (Report No. 146). Boulder: University of Colorado, Institute of Cognitive Science.

Fong, G. T., Krantz, D. H., & Nisbett, R. E. (1986). The effects of statistical training on thinking about everyday problems. *Cognitive Psychology, 18,* 253–292.

Fong, G. T., Lurigio, A. J., & Stalans, L. J. (1990). Improving probation decisions through statistical training. *Criminal Justice and Behavior, 17,* 370–388.

Fried, L. S., & Holyoak, K. J. (1984). Induction of category distributions: A framework for classification learning. *Journal of Experimental Psychology: Learning, Memory, and Cognition, 10,* 234–257.

Gentner, D. (1983). Structure-mapping: A theoretical framework for analogy. *Cognitive Science, 7,* 155–170.

Gick, M. L., & Holyoak, K. J. (1983). Schema induction and analogical transfer. *Cognitive Psychology, 15,* 1–38.

Gick, M. L., & Holyoak, K. J. (1987). The cognitive basis of knowledge transfer. In S. M. Cormier & J. D. Hagman (Eds.), *Transfer of learning: Contemporary research and applications* (pp. 9–46). San Diego, CA: Academic Press.

Glass, G. V. (1976). Primary, secondary, and meta-analysis of research. *Educational Researcher, 5,* 3–8.

Griggs, R. A., & Cox, J. R. (1982). The elusive thematic-materials effect in Wason's selection task. *British Journal of Psychology, 73,* 407–420.

Hayes, J. R., & Simon, H. A. (1977). Psychological differences among problem isomorphs. In N. J. Castellan, Jr., D. B. Pisoni, & G. R. Potts (Eds.), *Cognitive theory* (Vol. 2, pp. 21–41). Hillsdale, NJ: Erlbaum.

Hedges, L. V., & Olkin, I. (1985). *Statistical methods for meta-analysis.* San Diego, CA: Academic Press.

Holland, J., Holyoak, K. J., Nisbett, R. E., & Thagard, P. (1986). *Induction: Processes of inference, learning, and discovery.* Cambridge, MA: Bradford Books/MIT Press.

Inhelder, B., & Piaget, J. (1958). *The growth of logical thinking from childhood to adolescence.* New York: Basic Books.

James, W. (1890). *Principles of psychology.* New York: Holt.

Kahneman, D., & Tversky, A. (1972). Subjective probability: A judgment of representativeness. *Cognitive Psychology, 3,* 430–454.

Kahneman, D., & Tversky, A. (1973). On the psychology of prediction. *Psychological Review, 80,* 237–251.

Lehman, D. R., Lempert, R. O., & Nisbett, R. E. (1988). The effects of graduate training on reasoning: Formal discipline and thinking about everyday-life events. *American Psychologist, 43,* 431–442.

Manktelow, K. I., & Evans, J. St. B. T. (1979). Facilitation of reasoning by realism: Effect or non-effect? *British Journal of Psychology, 70,* 477–488.

Medin, D. C., & Schaffer, M. M. (1978). Context theory of classification learning. *Psychological Review, 85,* 207–238.

Nickerson, R. S., Perkins, D., & Smith, E. E. (1985). *The teaching of thinking.* Hillsdale, NJ: Erlbaum.

Nisbett, R. E., Fong, G. T., Lehman, D. R., & Cheng, P. W. (1987). Teaching reasoning. *Science, 238,* 625–631.

Nisbett, R. E., Krantz, D. H., Jepson, C., & Kunda, Z. (1983). The use of statistical heuristics in everyday inductive reasoning. *Psychological Review, 90,* 339–363.

Reed, S., Ernst, G., & Banerji, R. (1974). The role of analogy in transfer between similar problem states. *Cognitive Psychology, 6,* 436–456.

Reich, S. S., & Ruth, P. (1982). Wason's selection task: Verification, falsification and matching. *British Journal of Psychology, 73,* 395–405.

Resnick, L. B. (1987). *Education and learning to think.* Washington, DC: National Academy Press.

Ross, B. H. (1984). Remindings and their effects in learning a cognitive skill. *Cognitive Psychology, 16,* 371–416.

Ross, B. H. (1989). Distinguishing types of superficial similarities: Different effects on the access and use of earlier problems. *Journal of Experimental Psychology: Learning, Memory, and Cognition, 13,* 629–639.

Ross, B. H., & Kennedy, P. T. (1990). Generalizing from the use of earlier examples in problem solving. *Journal of Experimental Psychology: Learning, Memory, and Cognition, 16,* 42–55.

Thorndike, E. L. (1906). *Principles of teaching.* New York: A. G. Seiler.

Thorndike, E. L., & Woodworth, R. S. (1901). The influence of improvement in one mental function upon the efficiency of other functions. *Psychological Review, 8,* 247–261, 384–395, 553–564.

Tversky, A., & Kahneman, D. (1974). Judgment under uncertainty: Heuristics and biases. *Science, 185,* 1124–1131.

III RULES FOR CONDITIONAL REASONING

7 Pragmatic versus Syntactic Approaches to Training Deductive Reasoning

Patricia W. Cheng
Carnegie-Mellon University

Keith J. Holyoak
University of Michigan

Richard E. Nisbett
Lindsay M. Oliver
University of Michigan

How do people reason about problems in everyday life? Two views have dominated theories of deductive reasoning. According to one view people use syntactic, domain-independent rules of logic. Some philosophers (e.g., Goodman, 1965) and psychologists (including Piaget and his followers) who are sympathetic to this view believe that these rules correspond closely to those in standard logic. Substantial evidence shows, however, that typical college students often do not reason in accord with the rules of standard logic (see Evans, 1982, for a review). Partly in response to this evidence, other proponents of the syntactic view have proposed that people use a *natural* logic which consists of a repertory of syntactic rules that people untutored in standard logic naturally use (e.g., Braine, 1978; Braine, Reiser, & Rumain, 1984; Rips, 1983). The empirical adequacy of the natural-logic approach has also been challenged, however (Johnson-Laird, 1983, chap. 2).

Partly in response to the empirical difficulties encountered by the syntactic view, an opposing view has developed that holds that people do not use syntactic rules at all but instead develop much narrower rules tied to particular content domains in which people have actual experience. Such specific rules, or perhaps simple memory of examples and counterexamples, are used to evaluate the validity of propositions (e.g., Griggs & Cox, 1982; Manktelow & Evans, 1979; Reich & Ruth, 1982).

In contrast to both the extreme syntactic view and the specific-experience view, Cheng and Holyoak (1985) proposed that people often reason using *pragmatic reasoning schemas:* clusters of rules that are highly generalized and abstracted but nonetheless defined with respect to classes of goals and types of relationships. An example of a pragmatic reasoning schema is the set of abstracted rules for situations involving "permission," that is, situations in which some action A may be taken only if some precondition B is satisfied. If the semantic aspects of a problem suggest to people that they are dealing with a permission situation, then all of the rules about permissions in general can be called on, including "If action A is to be taken, then precondition B must be satisfied," "Action A is to be taken only if precondition B is satisfied," "If precondition B is not satisfied, then action A must not be taken," and so on. A related example is the schema for situations involving "obligation," that is, situations in which the occurrence of some condition A incurs the necessity of taking some action B. Rules about obligations are similar to but not identical with rules about permissions. For instance, the rule "If condition A occurs, then obligation B arises" implies "If obligation B does not arise, then condition A must not have occurred," but not "Condition A occurs only if obligation B arises."

The rules composing these schemas are the ones that people call on when solving problems of various kinds. Since the rules of some of the schemas lead to the same solution as do the rules of standard logic, people's answers to problems will often appear consistent with those of standard logic. This consistency does not mean that their answers have been produced by the application of syntactic logical rules, since the same people will at other times produce answers that violate those same rules of logic. This occurs when the rules of the schema used lead to conclusions that differ from those that follow from standard logic. By manipulating the semantic features of the problems to evoke different reasoning schemas, one should be able to manipulate whether or not people's answers are correct according to standard logic.

Cheng and Holyoak obtained several empirical results that speak strongly for the existence of reasoning schemas. Two of these findings involve Wason's (1966) selection task. In one version of the Wason task subjects are presented with four cards, which show an "A", a "B", a "4", and a "7". They are informed that the cards have letters on one side and numbers on the other, and are then given the rule, "If a card has an 'A' on one side, then it has a '4' on the other." The task is to indicate all and only those cards that *must* be turned over to determine whether the rule is violated. Interpreting the *if-then* connective as the material conditional in standard logic, the correct answer in this example is to turn over the cards showing "A" and "7". More generally, the rule used in such problems is a conditional statement, *if p then q,* and the relevant cases are p (because if p is the case it must be established that q is also the case) and *not-q* (because if it is not the case that q it must be established that it is also not the case that p).

When the selection problem is presented in an arbitrary form, as in the above example, fewer than 10% of college students typically produce the correct answer. A frequently chosen pattern is "A and 4." One of the errors in such an answer is omission of the card showing "7", indicating a failure to see the equivalence of a conditional statement and its contrapositive (i.e., "If a card does not have a '4' on one side, then it does not have an 'A' on the other"). Other errors include the fallacy of affirming the consequent (which corresponds to insistence on examining "4", which is unnecessary because the rule does not specify anything about the obverse of cards with a "4" on one side), and denying the antecedent (which corresponds to insistence on examining "B", which also is unnecessary because the rule does not specify anything about cards that do not have an "A" on one side).

Cheng and Holyoak pointed out that the schema for "permission" should be particularly useful in performing the selection task because the rules that comprise it lead to the same responses as follow from the material conditional. In one of their experiments subjects were presented with a selection problem based on an abstract description of a permission situation: "If one is to take action 'A', then one must first satisfy precondition 'P'." Subjects were also given an arbitrary card version that is syntactically identical to the permission problem. About 60% of subjects solved the abstract permission problem correctly, versus only about 20% who correctly solved the card problem. The fact that a purely abstract description of a permission situation produces facilitation supports the schema hypothesis over proposals based on either purely syntactic rules or specific experiences.

In another experiment, Cheng and Holyoak demonstrated that providing an explicit purpose for a rule that would otherwise seem arbitrary could serve to cue the permission schema and hence facilitate performance. For example, the rule "If a passenger's form says 'Entering' on one side, then the other side must include 'cholera,' " was rationalized by explaining that it involved a regulation requiring that travelers show proof of cholera vaccination in order to enter a country. The benefit conveyed by provision of a purpose is inexplicable according to either the specific-experience view or the syntactic view. Since subjects had no experience with the specific content in question and hence no memory for counterexamples to the rule, improvement due to provision of a purpose could not be attributed to processes consistent with the specific-experience view. On the other hand, improvement could not be attributed plausibly to manipulation of the syntactic properties of the problems either, since the added purpose did not affect the logical structure of the problems.

The notion of pragmatic reasoning schemas, represented as sets of inferential rules (Holland, Holyoak, Nisbett, & Thagard, 1986), is essentially a generalization of similar ideas that have been proposed to explain people's causal and inductive reasoning. Kelley (1972, 1973) suggested that people make causal attributions in part by relying on "causal schemas." These are highly generalized, domain-independent, but not purely syntactic rule systems for analyzing causality. People may have, for example, a schema for multiple sufficient causes, where a given effect could be produced solely by operation of a single cause, but a number of different causes could play that role. People's search for causal candidates and their degree of certainty about the effects of a given causal candidate are influenced by the particular causal schema they bring to the analysis of a situation.

Pragmatic reasoning schemas are also related to Johnson-Laird's concept of "mental models." For example, Johnson-Laird (1983, p. 416) discusses a representation of "ownership" in terms of such inferences as, "If I own something then it is permissible for me to use it." In our terms, the concept of ownership is a pragmatic schema based in part on the yet more general permission and obligation schemas. However, the focus of Johnson-Laird's theory of mental models is not on the role of pragmatic inference rules in reasoning, but rather on a domain-independent scheme for manipulating sets that are represented in terms of tokens for their individual members. The theory has been developed in most detail as an account of reasoning with syllogisms in which the premises specify arbitrary set relations (e.g., "All of the beekeepers are artists"). The theory attributes reasoning errors in this domain largely to limitations on memory capacity. In contrast, the present theory explains errors (as defined by the dictates of standard logic) in terms of the ease of mapping concrete situations into pragmatic schemas, as well as the degree to which the evoked schemas generate inferences that in fact conform to standard logic.

People not only have deductive reasoning schemas, but also inductive reasoning schemas. Nisbett, Krantz, Jepson, and Kunda (1983) and Fong, Krantz, and Nisbett (1986) have proposed that people often reason about events using sets of heuristics or intuitive rules of thumb that are informal equivalents of statistical rules such as the law of large numbers (LLN), the regression principle, and so on. Like causal schemas, these are clusters of inferential rules for predicting and explaining events. They are invoked for reasoning about events that are perceived to be subject to random variations.

Just as Cheng and Holyoak showed that people can solve selection problems if they are given cues that serve to trigger the permission schema, Nisbett et al. (1983) (as well as Jepson, Krantz, & Nisbett, 1983, and Fong et al., 1986) showed that people can produce solutions that are in accord with statistical requirements when the problem contains cues about variability or chance that encourage the use of statistical heuristics. For example, Fong et al. gave subjects a problem about a businesswoman who eats out frequently when she travels to different cities. She returns often to restaurants where she got an excellent meal on her first trip, but is usually disappointed. Most statistically untrained subjects give a causal explanation such as "her hopes were too high" or "the chefs change a lot." But if a cue as to the variability characteristic of restaurant meals is presented, many more subjects give a statistical explanation, such as "maybe it was just by chance that she got such a good meal the first time; there are probably more restaurants than can turn out an occasional excellent meal than restaurants that consistently do that."

Subjects are not only easily cued to use statistical heuristics, but they can also readily be taught to use, and to improve, their statistical heuristics. For example, subjects with no statistical education only rarely give a statistical answer for the uncued version of the restaurant problem above, but increasing amounts of statistical training increase the likelihood of a statistical answer. The great majority of subjects with postgraduate training in statistics gave a statistical answer to the problem.

Even more dramatically, very brief training session in LLN were helpful in encouraging subjects to apply LLN to problems such as the restaurant problem (Fong et al., 1986). This was true even for completely abstract training, in which the concepts of "sample" and "population" were defined formally and illustrated using problems involving balls in an urn. Fong et al. argued that such abstract training could be effective because subjects already had an informal, approximate grasp of LLN and an ability to apply it to actual events. Thus, they could take immediate advantage of formal improvements to their intuitive understanding. Consistent with this view, Fong et al. found that brief instruction showing subjects how to model example problems in terms of LLN, *without* any additional instruction in the abstract nature of LLN, was also effective in encouraging subjects to use LLN. Fong et al. argued that this could only be true if subjects already had an intuitive version of LLN and could readily generalize from the examples to improvements in this intuitive version. The present investigations are modeled on those we have just described. We test several hypotheses.

First, if people have pragmatic reasoning schemas corresponding to the "permission schema," the "obligation schema," and so on, then it should be easy to encourage them to use these schemas by presenting them with semantic cues designed to trigger them. Triggering a schema that produces the same solution to an *if-then* problem as does the material conditional, such as the permission schema, should help subjects to solve it. Conversely, triggering a schema that does not produce the same solution as the material conditional should be less helpful.

Second, unlike abstract training in LLN, which produces a marked improvement in peoples' ability to apply LLN to concrete problems, abstract training in the material conditional should produce little improvement in people's ability to apply the rule system to concrete problems. Since in our view the rule system is not used in natural contexts, people lack the requisite skills to interpret problems in terms of the material conditional, and hence would profit little from instruction in it. Similarly, simply providing subjects with a few example problems solved by the application of the material conditional would likewise produce little benefit, since few subjects would be able to spontaneously induce the abstract rules from the examples. Thus, if people are to be able to use the rule system at all they must be given training both on abstract rules and on how to apply the rule system to specific examples.

Third, abstract training in pragmatic reasoning schemas, like abstract training in LLN, and unlike abstract training in the material conditional, should produce improvement in ability to use the schemas. Since rules for interpreting concrete problems in terms of the abstract rules of reasoning schemas already exist, improvement on the abstract rules should carry over to improved ability to solve concrete problems.

EXPERIMENT 1

Experiment 1 was designed to assess the influence of reasoning schemas on performance on the selection task, as well as to assess the usefulness of different training procedures.

If people interpret *if-then* in terms of reasoning schemas, selection problems that evoke different pragmatic reasoning schemas might lead systematically to different response patterns. We tested this prediction by measuring the effect of three types of selection problems on reasoning performance. The problems described relations that we thought would be suggestive of permission situations, relations with a causal flavor that we thought would invite a converse assumption (i.e., assuming *if q then p* when given *if p then q*), and relations that were purely arbitrary. The pragmatic schema hypothesis leads us to expect that performance would be better for permission problems than for problems with a converse bias or arbitrary problems. Performance on converse-bias problems should be no worse than for arbitrary problems, because the latter do not evoke any useful schema. In addition to the above three types of problems, all of which involve conditional rules, we included problems that explicitly stated biconditional rules.

We also assessed the effect of different training procedures. The design with respect to training was the same as that employed by Fong et al. (1986). Subjects received either abstract rule training in the conditional, training in how to apply the conditional to concrete example problems, both, or neither. Consistent with the view that subjects already possessed an intuitive version of LLN, Fong et al. found that abstract rule training was effective by itself, as was example training. In contrast, we anticipated that since people do not possess rules corresponding to the conditional, neither type of training would be effective by itself. Abstract rule training should not be effective because subjects have no means of interpreting problems so that the rules can be applied. Example training, showing how to apply the conditional, should also not be effective by itself, because subjects have no intuitive version of the conditional to begin with.

Method

Subjects

Eighty students at the University of Michigan were randomly assigned in equal numbers to each of four training conditions. (1) Rule training, (2) Examples training, (3) Rule plus Examples training, and (4) No training. None of the subjects had previously received any formal training in logic.

Training Materials

Rule training. Subjects receiving rule training read a seven-page booklet consisting of an exposition on conditional statements, followed by an inference exercise. These materials are presented in Appendix A. The exposition consisted of an explanation of the equivalence between a conditional statement and its contrapositive, as well as an explanation of the two common fallacies of affirming the consequent and denying the antecedent. The contrapositive was explained in part by the use of a truth table, in part by Euler diagrams that used concentric circles to show the relations between a conditional statement and its contrapositive, and in part by an illustrative conditional statement. The illustrative statement expressed a realistic causal relation. Similarly, the fallacies were explained in part by diagrams and in part by alternative possible causes related to the illustrative statement.

At the end of rule training, subjects were given an *inference* exercise in which they were to select statement(s) that can be validly inferred from each of three given conditional statements. The statements were all in the form of *if p then q*. The randomly ordered possible inferences were in the following forms: *if not-p then not-q* (invalid), *if not-q then not-p* (valid), and *if q then p* (invalid). Subjects were given immediate feedback on correctness, followed by a brief explanation of the correct answer.

Examples training. Subjects receiving examples training were requested to attempt to solve two selection problems. They were given immediate feedback about their performance. One example was the "department store" problem used by D'Andrade (1982), and the other was a problem in which a catalog of paintings had to be checked to determine whether "all the Cubist paintings are by Picasso." Neither example bore any obvious similarities to the later test problems. The correct answer to each example was explained in terms specific to the particular problem.

Rule plus example training consisted of the materials for the rule condition followed by those for the examples condition. The only further addition was that for these subjects the explanation of the correct answer for each example was couched in terms of the abstract rules they had just learned.

Test Problems

Eight selection problems were used, consisting of two of each of three types of problems involving a conditional rule and two problems involving a biconditional rule. The problems are presented in Table 7.1. Arbitrary problems (the Wason "card" problem and the "bird" problem) bore little relationship to the prior knowledge subjects were likely to have. Converse-bias problems were more realistic; however, subjects' prior knowledge was expected to encourage assumption of the converse (i.e., *if q then p*). The "washing labels" problem involved a regulation for which causal knowledge would suggest an "if and only if" interpretation, and the "electrical charges" problem involved a causal regularity in which only a single cause was likely to be considered, also leading to an "if and only if" reading. The permission problems ("cholera" and "drinking age") are readily interpreted as permissions, which should not encourage assumption of the converse, but instead should yield the same responses as follow from the conditional of standard logic. Finally, the biconditional problems stated explicitly that the converse of a conditional rule was also true. The content of the biconditional problems was relatively arbitrary. The anticipation was that this arbitrary content would block application of any pragmatic reasoning schema and that performance on these problems would be poor.

Each problem described a brief scenario. Within each scenario was embedded a conditional or biconditional rule, a question asking the subject to determine the correctness of the rule, and a list of the four possible cases (*p, not-p, q,* and *not-q*) from which the subject was to select. These cases were randomly ordered.

In order to provide a second measure of the effectiveness of abstract training, subjects were asked to judge which of a series of transformations of a conditional rule retained the basic meaning of the rule itself. The conditional rules in this *equivalence judgment* task were directly excerpted from the selection problems that preceded them. The six equivalence judgment problems consisted of conditional rules excerpted from the six corresponding selection problems, each followed by a randomly ordered list of four transformations of each of these rules. The rules were always in the form *if p then q*. The forms used as transformations were a simple syntactic

TABLE 7.1
If-Then Rules of Various Types and Corresponding Choices in the Selection
Problems (Experiments 1 and 2)

Problem type	Rule	Choices (p, not-p, q, not-q)
Arbitrary	If a card has an "A" on one side, then it has a "4" on the other side	A B 4 7
	If a bird on this island has a purple spot underneath each wing, then it builds nests on the ground	Bird A has a purple spot underneath each wing Bird B does not have any purple spots Bird C builds nests on the ground Bird D builds nests in trees
Converse bias	If a washing label has "silk" on one side, then it has "dry clean only" on the other side	Silk Cotton Dry clean only Machine wash in warm water
	If two objects carry like electrical charges, then they will repel each other	Two objects that carry like electrical charges Two objects that carry opposite charges Two repelling objects Two objects that do not repel
Permission	If a passenger wishes to enter the country, then he or she must have had an inoculation against cholera	Entering Transit Inoculated against cholera and hepatitis Inoculated against typhoid
	If a customer is drinking an alcoholic beverage, then he or she must be over twenty-one	Customer A is drinking a beer Customer B is drinking tea Customer C is certainly over 50 Customer D looks less than 18
Biconditional	If a card has a circle on one side, then it has the word "red" on the other, and conversely, if it has the word "red" on one side, then it has a circle on the other	(Picture of a circle) (Picture of a triangle) Red Purple
	If a turtle crosses a road, then the flag by the palace flies, and conversely, if the flag by the palace flies, then a turtle crosses a road	A turtle is crossing a road No turtle is crossing any road The flag by the palace is flying The flag by the palace is not flying

variation, *q if p* (valid); the contrapositive, *if not-q then not-p* (valid); the converse, *if q then p* (invalid); and the inverse, *if not-p then not-q* (invalid). Subjects were to judge which of the transformations retained the basic meaning of the corresponding rules. This test was similar to the inference exercise included in the rule and rule plus examples training conditions. Biconditional rules were not included in this test.

Results and Discussions

Results on the selection task were analyzed using analysis of variance with problem type as a within-subject variable and training condition as a between-subject variable. Two measures of performance were analyzed: Whether a subject made at least one error on a problem (i.e., failed to solve the problem perfectly) and whether he or she made each of the four possible kinds of errors. For conditional problems, the four kinds of errors in the selection task were failing to select p, failing to select *not-q*, selecting q, and selecting *not-p*. These errors correspond, respectively, to errors on modus ponens, modus tollens, affirming the consequent, and denying the antecedent. For biconditional problems the correct response was to select all four alternatives.

Since the two dependent measures of overall performance on a problem — whether a subject made at least one error and the number of errors — reflected the same pattern of results, statistics for only the former measure are reported as an indicator of overall performance on a problem. Performance on conditional and biconditional problems were analyzed separately. For conditional problems, type of problem and training condition did not interact according to either measure of performance ($F < 1$). Accordingly, results for type of problem and training condition are reported separately, each collapsed over the other variable. Table 7.2 presents the percentages of subjects (collapsed over training conditions) who made errors of various types on each of the four kinds of selection problems. Table 7.3 presents the percentage of subjects in each training condition (collapsed over conditional selection problems) who made errors

TABLE 7.2
Percentage Errors in Selection Task as a Function of Problem Type
(Experiment 1)

Problem type	Type of error				At least one error
	p	not-q	q	not-p	
Conditional					
Arbitrary	15 ± 5	62	65	12	81 ± 6
Converse bias	16 ± 5	42	34	17	66 ± 6
Permission	5 ± 5	24	8	2	34 ± 6
Biconditional	14 ± 7	48	14	54	80 ± 9

Note. Error margins indicated in the table are half-widths of 95% confidence intervals for the respective conditions. Numbers in the three center columns have the same half-widths as the left-most numbers in the corresponding rows. The half-width of a 95% confidence interval for pairwise comparisons between mean frequencies of particular errors on the three types of conditional problems is 7. The corresponding half-width for comparisons between the percentages of subjects who made at least one error on various types of problems is 8.

of various types on the same task. Half-widths of 95% confidence intervals for various pairwise differences between means are indicated at the bottom of each table of results.

Effects of Problem Type

Consistent with our reasoning schema hypothesis, performance differed markedly across types of conditional problems, $F(2, 152) = 64.7, p < .001$, for the percentage of subjects making at least one error. Fewest subjects made at least one error on permission problems ($34 \pm 6\%$), more subjects did so on converse-bias problems ($66 \pm 6\%$), and still more subjects did so on arbitrary problems ($81 \pm 6\%$). Moreover, type of error interacted strongly with type of problem, $F(6, 456) = 20.7, p < .001$. In particular, frequency of erroneously selecting q was highest for arbitrary problems ($65 \pm 5\%$), next highest for converse-bias problems ($34 \pm 5\%$), and lowest for permission problems ($8 \pm 5\%$), confirming our prediction that permission problems have a lower tendency to invite assumption of the converse than the other two types of problems. Interestingly, the frequency of selecting q was much higher for arbitrary than for converse-bias problems. Because arbitrary problems do not evoke any pragmatic schemas, subjects would have to fall back on whatever syntactic logical rules are available or on nonlogical strategies such as "matching" (Manktelow & Evans, 1979). A matching strategy would produce apparent converse errors for our arbitrary problems. Frequency of failure to select *not-q* similarly depended on type of problem, being highest for arbitrary problems ($62 \pm 5\%$), next highest for converse-bias problems ($42 \pm 5\%$), and lowest for permission problems ($24 \pm 5\%$).

Many fewer subjects ($17 \pm 5\%$) made the other two types of errors (i.e., failure to select p or erroneous selection of *not-p*) for all three types of conditional problems. Permission problems again produced fewer errors than either arbitrary or converse-bias problems, which produced comparable percentages of errors for these two cases. It is particularly noteworthy that the permission problems yielded more accurate performance even for the choice of p, which corresponds to modus ponens, perhaps the most plausibly psychological of all the syntactic inference rules in standard logic and in Braine's (1978) natural logic.[1]

The two permission problems can be used to test the domain specificity hypothesis, which claims that only rules with which subjects have prior familiarity will yield good performance. For most subjects the "drinking age" rule was presumably much more familiar than the "cholera inoculation" rule. Although the percentage of subjects making at least one error was marginally lower for the more familiar rule ($29 \pm 7\%$ versus $39 \pm 7\%$, $p = .05$), even the relatively unfamiliar rule produced a much lower error rate than any converse-bias or arbitrary problem ($p < .002$). Thus subjects were able to reason in accord with standard logic even for a relatively unfamiliar rule if it evoked a permission schema. These results indicate that while specific experiences may play a role in reasoning, they cannot account for the large effect of type of problem on performance.

Performance on biconditional problems was poor: $80 \pm 9\%$ of the subjects (averaged over training conditions) made at least one error on such problems. Because all four cases should be selected, the four types of errors for biconditional problems all indicate failure to select. As Table 7.2 indicates, the most frequent errors were failure to select the two negated cases. Biconditional problems, unlike permission problems, cannot be solved by application of the permission schema. Furthermore, the arbitrary formulation of the particular biconditionals used presumably discouraged application of any pragmatic schema, so that subjects' performance on these problems was poor.

Training Effects

It may be seen in Table 7.3 that the percentage of subjects who make at least one error on conditional problems varied significantly across training conditions, $F(3, 76) = 6.04$, $p < .01$. Neither rule training by itself nor examples training by itself was effective. In contrast, rule training coupled with examples training significantly decreased the frequencies of three types of errors — failure to select p, failure to select $not\text{-}q$, and erroneous selection of q. These effects are reflected in a substantial decrease in the mean percentage of subjects who made at least one error on a problem, from $75 \pm 12\%$ to $39 \pm 12\%$.[2]

TABLE 7.3
Percentage Errors in Selection Task as a Function of Training Condition
(Experiment 1)

Training condition	Type of error				At least one error
	p	$not\text{-}q$	q	$not\text{-}p$	
Rules & examples	5 ± 9	27	28	8	39 ± 12
Rules only	14 ± 9	48	33	7	65 ± 12
Examples only	10 ± 9	45	37	12	62 ± 12
Control	18 ± 9	51	44	14	75 ± 12

Note. Error margins indicated in the table are half-widths of 95% confidence intervals for the respective conditions. Numbers in the three center columns have the same half-widths as the left-most numbers in the corresponding rows. The half-width of a 95% confidence interval for pairwise comparisons between mean frequencies of particular errors for the three training groups is 12. The corresponding half-width for comparisons between the percentages of subjects who made at least one error for various training conditions is 17.

The above pattern is quite different from that observed by Fong et al. (1986) for the effects of training on use of LLN. They found both rule training and examples training to be effective in isolation, and the effects of both were approximately additive. The present pattern of results supports our contention that the material conditional is not a rule system that subjects use naturally. Thus rule training is ineffective because subjects have no ability to apply it to concrete problems and examples training is ineffective because subjects have no intuitive grasp of the rule they are being shown how to apply. Because the confidence intervals for pairwise differences between means are quite wide, however, the null hypothesis that neither rule nor examples training alone yielded any benefit cannot be accepted with confidence. In Experiment 2 we examine the effects of a greatly augmented rule-training procedure, namely, exposure to an entire course in logic.

Training did not affect the percentage of subjects who made at least one error on biconditional problems, $F < 1$. Training and type of error did not interact, $F < 1$. These results indicate that training on conditional reasoning did not transfer to solution of biconditional problems. If subjects had an intuitive appreciation of the material conditional, then it might be expected that any advantage gained by training on the conditional would result in some degree of improved understanding of biconditional problems.

In sum, the semantic content of problems significantly influenced reasoning performance. In particular, permission problems yielded better performance than either converse-bias or arbitrary problems, confirming our reasoning schema hypothesis. Training on the conditional in standard logic, when coupled with examples of conditional selection problems, clearly improved performance on subsequent conditional selection problems, though training effects did not transfer to biconditional problems. Training on either standard logic, by itself, or on examples of selection problems, by itself, failed to produce significant improvements, but firm conclusions cannot be drawn from the latter results.

EXPERIMENT 2

The results of Experiment 1 indicated that training in standard logic, when coupled with training on examples of selection problems, leads to improved performance on subsequent selection problems. In contrast, training on rules of logic without such examples failed to significantly improve performance. This is consistent with our view that the material conditional is not part of people's intuitive reasoning repertoire, and hence they lack any ability to put abstract rule training to use. An obvious possibility, however, is that our experimental "micro-course" on the logic of the conditional was simply too minimal to convey much benefit. To assess this possibility, Experiment 2 examined the impact of a much broader and more prolonged abstract training condition: a one-semester undergraduate course in standard logic.

Method

Course Content

Two introductory logic classes provided subjects for Experiment 2. One class was held at the Ann Arbor campus of the University of Michigan and one at the branch campus at Dearborn. Both classes involved about 40 h of lectures and covered topics in propositional logic, including modus ponens, modus tollens, affirming the consequent, and denying the antecedent, and the distinction between the conditional and the biconditional. The textbook in one class was *Elementary Logic* (Simco & James, 1982), and in the other it was *Introduction to Logic* (Copi, 1982). In both classes the treatment of the valid and invalid inference patterns was primarily formal. While meaningful conditional sentences were introduced in lectures to illustrate the inference rules and fallacies, emphasis was placed on formal logical analyses (i.e., truth-table analyses and construction of proofs). Neither class provided any exposure to the selection task or other psychological research on deductive reasoning.

Procedure and Subjects

A pretest and post-test were administered to each class. The pretest was given in the first week of class before any discussion of the conditional had taken place; the post-test was given in the final week of the semester. To generate matched test materials, the eight selection problems used in Experiment 1 were divided into two sets of four. Each set consisted of one of each of the four problem types (arbitrary, converse bias, permission, and biconditional). The assignment of the two resulting sets of test materials to the pretest and post-test was counterbalanced across subjects.

The test sessions took place during regular class meetings; however, they were introduced to the students as a psychology experiment rather than as part of the course. In each session subjects were asked simply to complete booklets with four selection problems. No feedback of any kind was provided until after completion of the post-test. Only data from students who completed both the pretest and the post-test were analyzed, so that the effect of logic training could be treated as a within-subjects variable. Across the two classes a total of 53 students completed the study.

Results and Discussion

The pattern of results did not differ across the two classes that provided subjects; accordingly, all results are reported using the combined data from both classes. The percentages of subjects who made errors of various types on conditional selection problems (collapsing over arbitrary, converse-bias, and permission types) on the pretest and post-test are presented in Table 7.4. No significant improvement was obtained in percentage of problems on which at least one error was made. The mean improvement was a bare 3 ± 7%, $t < 1$. T tests performed on each error type separately revealed that the only type of error for which the improvement was individually significant was erroneous selection of the q alternative, an error that decreased by 10 ± 8% from pretest to post-test.

No interactions involving training and type of conditional problem approached significance. Performance on biconditional problems showed no sign of improvement between the pretest and post-test. The percentage of subjects making at least one error on the biconditional problem was 81 ± 8% on the pretest and 87 ± 8% on the post-test, a nonsignificant *increase* in error rate, $t < 1$. No significant changes in the frequency of individual error types were obtained for the biconditional problems. Overall, then, the only apparent influence of a one-semester logic course was small decrease in the tendency to make the error corresponding to affirming the consequent (i.e., selecting the q alternative) for conditional selection problems.

The weak effect of a semester's training in logic contrasts dramatically with the effects of semantic variations in description of the selection problem. Table 7.5 presents the percentages of subjects who made the various types of errors for each of the four problem types, collapsing over the pretest and post-test (since no interactions between logic training and

TABLE 7.4
Percentage Errors as a Function of Logic Training for Conditional Selection Problems (Experiment 2)

| | Type of error | | | | At least one error |
	p	not-q	q	not-p	
Pretest	20 ± 6	55	41	18	75 ± 5
Post-test	14 ± 6	58	31	12	72 ± 5

Note. Error margins indicated in the table are half-widths of 95% confidence intervals for the respective conditions. Numbers in the three center columns have the same half-widths as the left-most numbers in the corresponding rows. The half-width of a 95% confidence interval for pairwise comparisons between mean frequencies of particular errors on the pretest and the post-test is 8. The corresponding half-width for comparisons between the percentages of subjects who made at least one error on the pretest and the post-test is 7.

TABLE 7.5
Percentage Errors as a Function of Problem Type (Experiment 2)

Problem type	Type of error				At least one error
	p	*not-q*	*q*	*not-p*	
Conditional					
Arbitrary	23 ± 7	71	58	21	91 ± 6
Converse bias	19 ± 7	69	37	19	87 ± 6
Permission	10 ± 7	30	12	6	40 ± 6
Biconditional	24 ± 8	64	25	61	84 ± 9

Note. Error margins indicated in the table are half-widths of 95% confidence intervals for the respective conditions. Numbers in the three center columns have the same half-widths as the left-most numbers in the corresponding rows. The half-width of a 95% confidence interval for pairwise comparisons between mean frequencies of particular errors on the three types of conditional problems is 10. The corresponding half-width for comparisons between the percentages of subjects who made at least one error on various types of problems is 9.

problem type approached significance). The impact of problem type was very similar to that observed in Experiment 1. The three types of conditional problems differed in both percentage of subjects making at least one error and percentage of errors on individual alternatives, $F(2,104) = 63.1$, $p < .001$, for the latter analysis. Performance was much more accurate for the permission type than for the other two conditional types. The interaction between conditional problem type and type of error was also significant, $F(6,312) = 6.90$, $p < .001$. As the data in Table 7.5 indicate, fewer errors of all types were made for permission problems than for the other problem types. The patterns of errors for the arbitrary and converse-bias types were similar except that fewer erroneous selections of the q alternative were made for the latter type. For all three conditional problems, the most common error was failure to select the *not-q* case.

The pattern of errors for biconditional problems was also similar to that observed in Experiment 1. Most subjects (84 ± 9%) made at least one error per biconditional problem, and the bulk of the individual errors involved failures to select the two negative cases, *not-q* and *not-p*.

EXPERIMENT 3

We have found that abstract training in the logic of the conditional does not by itself have much effect on the way people reason about problems that could potentially be solved by its use. In contrast, problems that lend themselves to interpretation in terms of pragmatic reasoning schemas are solved by a large fraction of subjects. If this is because people normally solve problems using such schemas, and if Fong et al. (1986) are correct in their assertion that even purely abstract training in naturally occurring rule systems can be effective in encouraging people to use them, then it ought to be possible to improve people's deductive reasoning by training on pragmatic reasoning schemas.

In Experiment 3 we tested this possibility. We provided subjects with an abstract statement of the notion of "obligations," together with a description of the procedures necessary to check whether an obligation has been carried out. The anticipation was that this training would facilitate subjects' solution of problems that are in fact semantically interpretable in terms of the obligation notion. We predicted that subjects would not need training on how to map the abstract rules of obligations onto examples of particular problems. Since, as in the case of the schema for LLN, some form of an obligation schema is naturally induced, mapping rules must already exist. Schema training could nonetheless improve performance in at least three ways: (1) by providing subjects with more general mapping rules for interpreting situations in terms of the obligation schema; (2) by ensuring that the inferential rules attached to the schema are valid; and (3) by simply providing checking procedures consistent with the conditional that can be applied to even arbitrary problems.

It was important to establish that it is not merely the latter checking procedure training which is effective, however. Griggs (1983) has argued that facilitation can be obtained merely by virtue of orienting subjects toward detecting violations of a rule. Thus, in a separate, "contingency" training condition, we trained subjects in the use of checking procedures for so-called contingencies involving the relation between one event or its absence and another event or its absence. It was anticipated that the latter procedure would have little effect on subjects' solution of semantically interpretable problems, since such problems would be understood either in terms of a reasoning schema that maps onto the conditional, in which case the checking procedures would be redundant, or in terms of a reasoning schema that does not map onto the conditional, but which would entail its own checking procedures that would override any purely arbitrary procedures.

On the other hand, we anticipated that it might be useful for subjects' solutions of arbitrary problems to teach them correct checking procedures in the abstract. So long as subjects are able to map the events in a problem onto the checking procedures, their mechanical application would result in correct solution. Thus, training in an obligation schema was expected to improve both problems that are normally interpreted in terms of such reasoning schemas and problems that are not (because the checking-procedure drill contained in schema training should be effective for arbitrary problems as well as for semantically interpretable ones.) In contrast, the simple checking-procedure training of the "contingency" condition was expected to be useful, if at all, primarily for arbitrary problems.

Method

Subjects and Procedures

Seventy-two University of Michigan undergraduates served as paid subjects. Subjects were randomly assigned in equal numbers to one of three conditions: a control condition in which no training was given, the obligation-training condition, and the contingency-training condition. Subjects in the two training conditions were given the appropriate training materials to read for 10 min and were then asked to complete the test problems. The control subjects were simply given the test problems and asked to complete them.

Training Materials

Obligation training. Subjects in the obligation-training condition received a two-page booklet detailing the nature of obligations and the procedures necessary for checking if a violation of the obligation has occurred. An example of an obligation statement presented in the *if-then* conditional form was given. The procedures for assessing obligations were described in terms of four rules, one for each of the four possible situations that might arise (situations that can be mapped onto *p, not-p, q,* and *not-q*). The full training materials are presented in Appendix B.

Contingency training. The contingency-training materials, also presented in Appendix B, were closely matched to the obligation-training materials, except that the checking procedures were described in terms of assessment of "contingencies" rather than "obligations." Two examples were provided, one of which was the same as that used in the obligation-training materials, and one of which described a contingency between properties associated with a category. The contingency-training materials thus provided one more example than did the obligation-training materials. Checking procedures were again described in terms of four rules that mapped onto the conditional.

Test Problems

The test-problem booklet consisted of eight selection problems, presented in Table 7.6. Four of the problems are readily interpretable as obligation situations, and four are relatively arbitrary. Subjects always received the obligation problems as a block and the arbitrary problems as a block. Order of the blocks was counterbalanced across subjects within each training condition.

TABLE 7.6

If-Then Rules of Various Types and Corresponding Choices in the Selection Problems (Experiment 3)

Problem type	Rule	Choices (p, not-p, q, not-q)
Arbitrary	If a card has an "A" on one side, then it has a "4" on the other side	A B 4 7
	If a bird on this island has a purple spot underneath each wing, then it builds nests on the ground	Bird A has a purple spot underneath each wing Bird B does not have any purple spots Bird C builds nests on the ground Bird D builds nests in trees
	If a bolt of cloth has any red threads in it, then it must be stamped with a triangle	Bolt A has red threads in it Bolt B has no red threads in it Bolt C is stamped with a triangle Bolt D is not stamped with a triangle
	If a house was built before 1979, then it has a fireplace	House A was built before 1979 House B was built after 1979 House C has a fireplace House D does not have a fireplace
Obligation	If a steel support is intended for the roof, then it must be rustproof	Support A is intended for the roof Support B is intended for the foundation Support C is rustproof Support D is not rustproof
	If any urithium miner gets lung cancer, then the company will pay the miner a sickness pension	Urithium miner A has lung cancer Urithium miner B does not have lung cancer Urithium miner C is receiving a company sickness pension Urithium miner D is not receiving a company sickness pension
	If any of you wins an athletic award, then that person will have to treat the others to a round of drinks at Sam's	Person A won a letter in basketball Person B never played any sport Person C treated everyone to a round of drinks several times Person D has never bought a round of drinks
	If one works for the Armed Forces, then one must vote in the elections	Person A works for the Armed Forces Person B does not work for the Armed Forces Person C voted Person D did not vote

Results and Discussion

Table 7.7 presents the percentage errors for the two problem types as a function of training condition. These results are based on the percentage of subjects making at least one error on a problem (i.e., failing to give the correct choice, p and not-q). An analysis of variance was performed with the three training conditions as a between-subject factor and the two problem types (artibrary and obligation) as a within-subject factor. Both main effects were highly significant. Subjects made significantly fewer errors on obligation problems than on arbitrary problems, $F(1, 69) = 63.0$, $p < .001$. Thus, conditional problems that trigger the obligation schema, like those that trigger the permission schema, result in higher solution rates. Training effects were also highly significant. As anticipated, obligation training produced the best performance, followed by contingency training, followed by the control condition that received no training, $F(2, 69) = 5.71$, $p < .005$. Analyses of individual types of errors yielded a similar pattern, with both the error of selecting q and of omitting not-q being decreased by obligation training and by obligation content.

The trends apparent in Table 7.7 indicate that the benefit conveyed by obligation training was in part specific to problems interpretable as obligations. Individual t tests revealed that for obligation problems, training in obligations produced performance superior either to contingency training or to the no-training control condition, and, as anticipated, the mere checking procedure instruction of the contingency-training condition produced no detectable improvement for these semantically meaningful problems. For the arbitrary problems, on the other hand, the effects of obligation and contingency training did not differ from each other (although only the former produced significantly fewer errors than the control condition). A more fine-grained analysis of the response patterns for the four arbitrary problems provided further evidence that the effect of

TABLE 7.7
Percentage Errors as a Function of Problem Type and Training Condition
(Experiment 3)

Problem type	Training condition Control	Contingency	Obligation	X
Arbitrary	73	55	45	58 ± 6
Obligation	36	34	8	26 ± 6
X	54 ± 12	45 ± 12	27 ± 12	

Note. Error margins indicated in the table are half-widths of 95% confidence intervals for the row and column means. The half-width of a 95% confidence interval for pairwise comparisons between row means is 8. The corresponding half-width for pairwise comparisons between column means is 17.

obligation training varied across problems. For two of the problems ("red threads" and "fireplace"; see Table 7.6) the average percentages of errors were 60, 50, and 27 for the control, contingency-, and obligation-training conditions, respectively. This pattern resembles that for the obligation problems in that only the difference between obligation training and the other two conditions was significant. It seems possible that some subjects might have been able to interpret these two problems as obligation situations, once they had received training in obligations. In contrast, for the two remaining arbitrary problems ("card" and "bird"), which were the most difficult of all, obligation training reduced errors no more than did contingency training. Percentages of errors were 85, 60, and 58 for control, contingency, and obligation conditions, respectively.

These results contrast in a very clear way with those of the effects of purely abstract training observed in Experiments 1 and 2, in which we found that neither a brief rule-training session in the logic of the conditional nor an entire course in logic had any substantial effect on the way subjects dealt with selection problems. In contrast, the two brief procedures used in Experiment 3 both had substantial effects. First, and most importantly, obligation schema training improved subjects' performance on problems that were readily interpretable in terms of the appropriate obligation schema. The selective benefit of obligation training extended to two of the relatively arbitrary problems which were interpretable in terms of the obligation schema. These results support our reasoning schema hypothesis. Training in a pragmatic reasoning schema encourages use of that schema for problems that compel a semantic interpretation consistent with the schema and, in addition, may refine subjects' understanding of situations that are potentially interpretable in terms of the schema.

Second, both schema-based training and training in a simple checking procedure improved subjects' performance on the most arbitrary problems. Unlike other studies in which orientation toward violation checking provided no benefit for arbitrary problems (Griggs, 1984; Yachanin, 1985), the present training procedure provided subjects with information as to which cases in fact constituted violations as well as simply orienting them toward checking violations. It is noteworthy that this brief procedure was effective for at least the arbitrary problems, whereas the formal logic instruction in Experiments 1 and 2 was not.

GENERAL DISCUSSION

Summary

The present results provide support for the view that people typically reason using abstract knowledge structures organized pragmatically, rather than in terms of purely syntactic rules of the sort that comprise standard logic. Subjects reasoned in closer accord with standard logic when thinking about problems intended to evoke permission or obligation schemas than when thinking about purely arbitrary relations. This pattern is rather ironic, since standard propositional logic does not capture the deontic content of permissions and obligations, whereas it could represent relations of the sort described in our arbitrary problems. These results on problem types are incompatible with the domain specificity view because experience with the precise rules referred to in the permission and obligation problems was not necessary for successful performance (Experiments 1 and 3). The results are also incompatible with the syntactic view, because all problem types were stated in syntactically equivalent forms.

Our training results provide further evidence favoring the pragmatic over the syntactic view. An entire course in standard logic had no effect on the avoidance of any error save a slight reduction in the fallacy of affirming the consequent. A brief training session in formal logic, of a type shown to produce substantial effects on people's ability to reason in accord with the law of large numbers (Fong et al., 1986), had no significant effect on subjects' ability to use modus ponens or modus tollens or to avoid the errors of affirming the consequent or denying the antecedent. This was not simply because the rule training was inherently useless, since, when it was combined with examples training, subjects were able to make substantial use of it.

The near total ineffectiveness of purely abstract training in logic contrasts dramatically with the ready ease with which people seem able to apply a naturally acquired pragmatic reasoning schema. After one semester's training in standard logic, the students in Experiment 2 solved only 11% of the arbitrary problems correctly, whereas the same students, prior to receiving any formal training, solved 62% of the permission problems correctly. Moreover, subjects who received a brief training session on the obligation schema improved markedly on selection problems interpretable in terms of that schema.

The generality of the benefit apparently conveyed by evocation of a pragmatic schema is also striking. The permission problems yielded significantly fewer errors of all types, including not only the common error of failing to select *not-q* (equivalent to modus tollens), but also the much less frequent error of failing to select *p* (equivalent to modus ponens). In contrast to the benefit conveyed by the evocation of a permission schema, a course in logic produced no significant reduction in either of these errors. The failure to reduce the frequency of errors for modus ponens cannot be attributed to a floor effect, since evocation of the permission schema did reduce the frequency of errors for the *p* alternative. This failure of abstract training to facilitate use of modus ponens suggests that even this rule may not be a general rule of logic for at least some subjects. The evidence that modus ponens can be overridden by a matching strategy (Manktelow & Evans, 1979; Reich & Ruth, 1982) also supports this hypothesis. If modus ponens is not a universal rule of natural logic, as our results suggest, it is difficult to imagine any formal deductive rule that is general across the adult population. In fact, some logicians (e.g., Anderson & Belnap, 1975; Nelson, 1933) have objected to indiscriminate use of modus ponens to draw inferences across irrelevant propositions. Since pragmatic deductive schemas place semantic restrictions on the antecedent and the consequent, inferences involving irrelevant propositions do not occur.

Possible Criticisms of the Schema Hypothesis

A critic might argue that to explain performance on the selection task, one could simply consider the biconditional or converse bias of various *if-then* statements. (Biconditional bias refers to the tendency to invoke a *p if and only if q* interpretation of a given statement *if p then q;* converse bias refers to the tendency to invoke the *if q then p* assumption without entailing the contrapositive of either the given *if p then q* statement or the assumed *if q then p* statement.) Both permission and obligation problems tend not to invite the biconditional or converse assumption, and one might thus argue that their conditional bias is sufficient to explain facilitation. Henle (1962) has suggested that if invited assumptions are taken into consideration, adults if fact reason in accord with standard logic. Others have pointed out that certain contexts invite the biconditional interpretation of *if-then,* whereas other contexts do not (Fillenbaum, 1975, 1976; Geis & Zwicky, 1971). What, then, warrants an emphasis on the notion of reasoning schemas?

First, an account in terms of invitation of the biconditional cannot in fact explain selection performance. As many investigators have pointed out, most patterns of selection are irreconcilable with either the conditional or the biconditional interpretation of *if-then.* Moreover, our own results show that error rate is high even when the problem in fact requires treatment as a biconditional (Experiments 1 and 2). Thus, no interpretation in terms of standard logic can explain our results. Neither can an interpretation in terms of any natural logic. In particular, no natural-logic interpretation can explain why the *not-q* case was selected more often for permission and obligation problems than for converse-bias and arbitrary problems. Decision on the *not-q* case is not logically dependent on the converse or biconditional assumption, and although a natural logic such as Braine's (1978; Braine et al., 1984) can explain omission of the *not-q* case by some subjects, it cannot explain both the inclusion of the *not-q* case for some problems and its omission in other problems by the same subjects.

Second, *if-then* statements that have a conditional bias differ in regard to the appropriateness of inferring *p only if q* from *if p then q*. Cheng and Holyoak (1985) showed that when subjects were asked to rephrase *if-then* statements into a logically equivalent form, permission statements such as "If you are to enter this country, then you must have an inoculation against cholera" were often rephrased into "You are to enter this country only if you have an inoculation against cholera." Now consider an obligation statement such as, "If an employee is injured at work, then the company must pay for medical expenses." Applying the same syntactic transformation as in the above permission statement, we get "An employee is injured at work only if the company pays for medical expenses." This rephrasing sounds anomalous, because it suggests that the company's payment is a precondition for an employee getting injured. More generally, from an obligation statement of the form, "If situation *P* obtains, then one must fulfill obligation *Q*," one would not want to infer, "Situation *P* obtains only if one fulfills obligation *Q*." In contrast, from a permission statement of the form "If one is to take action *P*, then one must satisfy precondition *Q*," one can quite appropriately infer, "One is to take action *P* only if one satisfies precondition *Q*." Thus, an inference from *if p then q* into *p only if q* depends crucially on the reasoning schema onto which an *if-then* statement is mapped, even among statements that have a conditional bias (also see Wason & Johnson-Laird, 1972, pp. 73–75). This state of affairs is inexplicable in terms of either standard logic or natural-logic models.

Another potential criticism of our schema hypothesis might be based on the fact that the schemas that produced the most facilitation in our experiments (permission and obligation) all involved checking for violations of established rules, rather than testing whether rules were true or false. Is there any need to invoke the schema notion rather than simply to suppose that violation checking is easier than hypothesis testing?

We believe the latter alternative is inadequate for the following reasons. As we pointed out in discussing the results of Experiment 3, it appears that orientation toward violation checking does not improve performance unless it is made clear what cases would in fact constitute violations. This, of course, is information that regulation schemas of the sort we have discussed are able to provide. Moreover, obligation training was more effective than contingency training, even though both procedures were concerned with violation checking. Therefore, improved violation checking cannot account for our results. In addition, the schema hypothesis predicts that if rules are mapped onto a schema that corresponds closely to standard logic, performance in hypothesis testing as well as violation checking can be improved. In particular, if a rule is mapped onto a causal schema that suggests the presence of multiple deterministic causes, people should select relevant evidence in accord with the dictates of standard logic (i.e., judging the q case to be irrelevant to the truth of the rule, and the *not-q* case to be potentially falsifying). We would predict, for example, that such a pattern would be observed in evaluating a hypothesis such as, "If Peter has thrown a vase at Paul, then the vase is broken." In contrast, if the rules in an evoked schema do not correspond closely to those in standard logic, then little facilitation will result even if the rules check for violations (see Cheng & Holyoak, 1985).

Relations between Pragmatic Schemas and Other Modes of Deductive Reasoning

Our results speak strongly for the existence of pragmatic schemas, since the findings are inexplicable in terms of either the domain specificity view or the domain independence view. It is nonetheless conceivable that multiple types of knowledge relevant to deductive reasoning coexist within a population and even within an individual. Our results do not rule out this interpretation. First, as in other reasoning studies, most of our subjects were correct on modus ponens, even in arbitrary problems, whereas very few were correct on modus tollens. Although modus ponens may not be universal, as discussed above, our results do not exclude the possibility that *some* people may in fact reason with this syntactic rule. (See Rips & Conrad, 1983, for evidence of individual differences in the use of deductive rules.) Moreover, the same individuals who use ponens as a syntactic rule may use tollens only within the context of certain pragmatic schemas. Second, familiarity with a rule may facilitate performance to some extent, as suggested by the marginal difference in selection performance between the two permission problems in Experiment 1. The presumably more familiar "drinking age" rule yielded slightly better performance than the "cholera inoculation" rule. Since familiarity with counterexamples has been shown to be insufficient by itself for facilitation (Manktelow & Evans, 1979), the effect of remembered counterexamples must be indirect. It seems that familiarity might produce facilitation by ensuring that a counterexample was experienced as such in the context of a reasoning schema, so that when it is remembered, the schema is indirectly evoked.

If pragmatic schemas and syntactic rules coexist, within a population as well as within an individual, what determines when alternative types of knowledge will be used? We propose that if a rule is interpretable in terms of a pragmatic reasoning schema, then a subject will apply the schema. If the rule is not interpretable in terms of a reasoning schema, however, the subject might fall back on whatever syntactic rules are available, or on nonlogical strategies such as "matching".

Why Formal Deductive Rules are Difficult to Induce

In view of our negative conclusion regarding the prevalence of a natural logic based on syntactic rules, an obvious question arises: Why are such rules apparently difficult to induce? Many logicians throughout the centuries have assumed the existence of a natural repertoire of purely syntactic logical rules, as have psychologists such as Piaget. Yet apparently Piaget may have been wrong about people having formal operations of deductive logic, but right about them having a schema corresponding to the inductive rule system embodied in the law of large numbers.

The difficulty of inducing deductive rules may appear paradoxical, since one typically thinks of deductive rules as being more trustworthy than inductive rules. The difficulty is probably not due to greater complexity of the deductive rules, since there is no a priori reason to think that a rule such as modus tollens is more complex than a rough version of LLN. Moreover, people are able to apply the equivalent of modus tollens in some contexts such as permissions.

We believe that the contrast between induction of an intuitive version of LLN and failure to induce the material conditional reflects the relatively narrow range of applicability of the material conditional. A rule such as, "The information from a random sample is likely to be more reliable when the sample is large than when it is small," is virtually context independent. The sample can consist of a collection of any stochastic events specifying any kind of relationship in any domain. In contrast, *reliable, useful* constancies in deductive rules do not hold at a context-independent level. In particular, the abstract concept of the material conditional — i.e., the formal type of contingency situation invented by logicians — does not have universal pragmatic value. It has been pointed out that the "fallacies" of denying the antecedent and affirming the consequent often lead to pragmatically useful inferences in many contexts (Fillenbaum, 1975, 1976; Geis & Zwicky, 1971). Moreover, the "valid" inferences are not applicable or useful under some conditions. An obligation statement in the form *if p then q* seems anomalous when transformed into *p only if q,* a transformation based on a rule in standard logic. More generally, statements that can correspond to the symbols *p* and *q* in the rule *if p then q* are restricted to those that can be true or false (e.g., Quine, 1974). Imperative and interrogative statements are obviously ruled out. (For example, it makes no sense to apply the contrapositive transformation to the sentence, "If John cooks dinner, will Susan do the dishes?") For the same reason, rules associated with the material conditional do not apply to counterfactual, probabilistic, future contingent, or deontic statements. For example, since a deontic statement such as, "If a burglar breaks into your house, then you should call the police," is right or wrong rather than true or false, it is outside the scope of standard logic (although extended logics may describe such cases).

Application of rules associated with the material conditional to statements that are not truth functional may lead to anomalous or useless inferences. For example, the contrapositive transformation of the above deontic statement gives us: "If it is not the case that you should call the police, then a burglar does not break into your house"—an inference that is useless at best. Similarly, the contrapositive transformation of the future contingent sentence, "If the bomb explodes, then everyone will die," gives us, "If not everyone will die, then the bomb does not explode." Whereas the original sentence, although not truth functional, is a meaningful causal prediction, the contrapositive reverses the cause and the effect, yielding an anomalous statement (Cheng & Holyoak, 1985).

Not only are rules associated with the material conditional restricted in their range of applicability, they are never applied in a natural context to antecedents and consequents that are irrelevant to each other, as the syntactic form of the rules ought to allow. For example, according to standard logic the following statements are all true: (1) If France is in Europe, then the sea is salt; (2) If France is in Australia, then the sea is salt; (3) If France is in Australia, then the sea is sweet (Quine, 1974, p. 21). However, even though the formulation of the material conditional was motivated by a desire to represent mathematics in a rigorous way, it is not applied irrelevantly even in the realm of mathematics.[3]

Given the above restrictions on applicability, it should not be surprising if people typically do not induce some of the syntactic deductive rules associated with the material conditional. Unlike inductive rules such as the LLN, deductive rules are not context independent. But since deductive rules such as those associated with the material conditional do hold some of the time, one might still ask, do people induce syntactic "probabilistic deductive rules" (a concept that might seem inherently contradictory), just as they apparently induce some syntactic probabilistic inductive rules? Our results do not rule out the possibility, any more than they rule out the possibility that people may have some "deterministic" syntactic deductive rules; however, they suggest that regardless of the exact form of the syntactic rules induced, such rules are overridden most of the time by reasoning schemas that pragmatically separate conditions under which the rules hold from conditions under which they do not.

Implications for Education

Our results have clear educational implications. We have shown that deductive reasoning is not likely to be improved by training on standard logic. It seems that since there are many conditions under which the formal rules do not apply, clarifying when the rules do and do not apply is important if students are not to be confused. Unfortunately, the concept of truth functionality seems to be extremely difficult to teach, as a small sample of logicians we asked concurred. And, although the material conditional is useful under certain conditions, people seem to lack the knowledge required to map particular situations onto the syntactic rules. The only comfort given by the present results to the possibility that the conditional may be trainable, in a way that renders it useful for some novel problems, is that in Experiment 1 we found that when examples training was combined with abstract training, there was some improvement on the selection task. The most obvious implication of this result is that, if logic instructors wish to influence their students' inferential behavior in the face of novel problems, they must do much more than they currently do to show how to apply logical rules to concrete problems.

But in our view, the material conditional is a largely artificial reasoning tool that does not capture and purify natural reasoning. Rather, it offers an alternative to it that has pragmatic utility perhaps only for very specialized problems of a kind that do not occur frequently in everyday life. As an approach to improving everyday reasoning, training on pragmatic reasoning schemas seems to us to be more promising. An advantage of training based on naturally induced reasoning schemas lies in the prior existence of interpretative rules for mapping specific situations onto schemas. Moreover, the schemas specify the conditions under which certain clusters of rules would apply. Education in reasoning is most likely to be effective when it serves to refine pragmatically useful rules that most people will have naturally induced in at least a rudimentary form from everyday experiences.

APPENDIX A: TRAINING MATERIALS USED IN EXPERIMENT 1

Abstract and Abstract Plus Examples Conditions

In this study we are interested in how people interpret and reason about a very important type of logical statement, called the *conditional.* Even though conditional statements are really very simple, people often make errors in dealing with them. These instructions are intended to help you understand conditional statements. Read through these instructions carefully; they should help you solve some reasoning problems you will receive afterward.

A conditional statement consists of two component statements which are often joined by the conjunctions "if . . . then." The conditional statement can be expressed in the standard form.

If p, then q (a)

where it is understood that the letters *"p"* and *"q"* each represent a statement. Statement (a) means "if statement *p* is true, then statement *q* is also true." For example, let *p* stand for "It is raining," and let *q* stand for "The pavement is wet." Then (a) says "If it is raining, then the pavement is wet."

Statement (a) can be expressed in a variety of ways. We will use a horizontal bar above a letter to indicate that a statement is not true. For example, *"p̄"* means "not *p̄*." One way of reformulating (a), then, is

If q̄, then p̄. (b)

This means "if statement *q* is false, then statement *p* is also false." Rephrasing the above example into form (b) gives, "If the pavement is *not* wet, then it is *not* raining."

People often don't realize at first that statements (a) and (b) are equivalent (identical to each other). To understand the equivalence of statements (a) and (b), consider the circumstances under which (a) is true. The truth of *"If p, then q"* depends on the truth of *p* and *q*. The table below lists the truth values of various statements. Reading across and down the table, we see that when *p* is true and *q* is also true, then (a) is true (first line). When *p* is true and *q* is false, then (a) is false (second line), since (a) says that *p* implies *q*. So, in order for (a) to be true when *q* is false, *p* cannot be true (comparing the second and third lines). In other words, (a) implies *"If q̄, then p̄."*

p	*q*	(a): *If p, then q*
T	T	T
T	F	F
F	F	T

Another way of understanding the equivalence of (a) and (b) is through the concept of *sets*. In the following diagrams,[4] we will use circles to represent a set, or class of things. We will put circles within circles to represent the inclusion of one class within another. For example, consider Fig. 7.1 below:

Figure 7.1 represents the fact that oranges are a subset of citrus fruit, which in turn are a subset of things containing vitamin C.

Now, let *p* stand for the statement *"x is an element in the set P,"* and let *q* stand for the statement *"x is an element in the set Q."* That is, *"If p, then q"* means "If *x* is an element in the set *P*, then *x* is also an element in the set *Q*." For what set relation would this statement be true? If *p* is a subset of *Q*, as illustrated in Fig. 7.2a, then every element in *P* would be an element in Q.

From the same inclusion relation, we can see that if an element x is *not* in the set Q, it cannot be in the set P (see Fig. 7.2b). Thus, again we see that (a) is equivalent to (b) (i.e., *"If p, then q"* is equivalent to *"If $\bar{q}$, then $\bar{p}$"*).

To check your understanding of the conditional statement, please answer the question below.

Statement (a), *"If p, then q,"* can be rephrased without changing its basic meaning. Which of the following is a correct rephrasing of (a)? Put a check next to the correct rephrasing(s) before checking the answer on the next page.

( )1. *If q, then p.*
( )2. *If $\bar{p}$, then $\bar{q}$.*
( )3. *If $\bar{q}$, then $\bar{p}$.*

Only 3 is a correct rephrasing. You should note that statement (a) *"If p, then q,"* does *not* imply

    If q, then p.   (c)

It is a common error to assume that (a) implies (c). Rephrasing the example on Page 1 into form (c) gives "If the pavement is wet, then it is raining," which does *not* logically follow from "If it is raining, then the pavement is wet." The pavement may get wet from lawn sprinklers nearby, for instance. In terms of set relations, statement (c) would be true only if the set P includes the set Q, as in Fig. 7.3:

So it should be clear that *"If p, then q"* does *not* imply *"If q, then p."*

It is also a common error to assume that *"If p, then q"* implies

    If $\bar{p}$, then $\bar{q}$.   (d)

Rephrasing the example on Page 1 into form (d) gives "If it is *not* raining, then the pavement is *not* wet," which again does not follow from "If it is raining, then the pavement is wet," for the same reason we mentioned earlier (e.g., a lawn sprinkler might have made the pavement wet even though it isn't raining).

To sum up, these are the most important facts you need to know about the conditional statement. First, statement (a) is equivalent to statement (b): *"If p, then q"* implies *"If $\bar{q}$, then $\bar{p}$."* Second, statement (a) is *not* equivalent to either statement (c) or statement (d): *"If p, then q"* does *not* imply either *"If q, then p"* or *"If $\bar{p}$, then $\bar{q}$."*

Rephrasing Exercise

This exercise will check your understanding of the conditional statement. Which of the statement(s) below follow logically from the statement, "If the tablecloth is brown, then the wall is white?" Please put a check next to the correct statement(s) below before checking the answer on the next page.

( )1. If the tablecloth is *not* brown, then the wall is *not* white.
( )2. If the wall is *not* white, then the tablecloth is *not* brown.
( )3. If the wall is white, then the tablecloth is brown.

Only 2 is correct. To see this, we can reformulate the statement into the form *"If p, then q"* by substituting *p* for "the tablecloth is brown" and *q* for "the wall is white." Then we see that 2 is in the form *"If q̄, then p̄,"* which we saw earlier is equivalent to *"If p, then q."* But 1 is in the form *"If p̄, then q̄,"* which does *not* follow from *"If p, then q "* And 3 is in the form *"If q, then p,"* which likewise does *not* follow from *"If p, then q."*

Below are two more rephrasing problems. When you are done, check the answer on the next page. Statement: If the cube is plastic, then the sphere is metallic. Rephrasings:

( )1. If the sphere is metallic, then the cube is plastic.
( )2. If the cube is *not* plastic, then the sphere is *not* metallic.
( )3. If the sphere is *not* metallic, then the cube is *not* plastic.

Statement: If the beach is white, then the music is slow. Rephrasings:

( )1. If the beach is *not* white, then the music is *not* slow.
( )2. If the music is slow, then the beach is white.
( )3. If the music is *not* slow, then the beach is *not* white.

Answer to rephrasing problems: Only 3 is correct in the above two problems.

Examples and Abstract plus Examples Conditions

The two examples below illustrate how the conditional statement is used to solve problems.

Example 1

As part of your job as an assistant at Sears, you have the task of going through customers' checks to make sure that any check $30 or over has been approved by the section manager. The amount is written on the front of the check, while the section manager's approval is initialed on the back of the check. Which of the checks below would you have to turn over to make sure that the sales clerk has followed the rule? Turn over only those which you need to check the rule. Mark an x below the check(s) you would have to turn over.

Please think carefully and solve the problem before checking the answer on the next page.

Answer to Example 1

Conditional statement: If the check is $30 or over, then it has to be approved by the section manager. The correct answer is (a) and (c). Check (a) obviously needs to be turned over. Check (c) also needs to be turned over, because the rule would be violated if the check is over $30. If the check is less than $30, as in (b) and (e), we do not care whether or not it is approved. And if the check is already approved, as in (d), it doesn't matter whether or not it's over $30.

NEXT PARAGRAPH, ABSTRACT PLUS EXAMPLES CONDITION

To reformulate the rule into the form *"If p, then q,"* we substitute *p* for "the check is $30 or over," and *q* for "it has to be approved by the section manager." Since alternative (a) corresponds to *p,* we clearly have to check whether *q* follows. Since (c) corresponds to *q̄,* and *"If q̄, then p̄"* is equivalent to *"If p, then q,"* we have to check whether *p̄* follows. But we need not turn over checks (b) and (e), since they correspond to *p̄,* and, as we said earlier, *"If p, then q"* does not imply *"If p̄, then q̄."* Nor do we need to turn over check (d), which translated into *q.* As you learned earlier, *"If p, then q"* is *not* equivalent to *"If q, then p";* accordingly, the other side of check (d) is irrelevant to the truth of the rule.

Example 2

You are helping to compile illustrations for a book on modern painting. The editor's intention is to illustrate each style with works of several painters, rather than a single painter. She suspects, however, that she might have made a slip. She is certain of having included several Picasso cubist paintings, but is not sure whether she has illustrated cubism by any painter other than Picasso. To check this possibility, she asks you to go through a card catalog which you've kept for the list of illustrations. On one side of each card is written the name of the painter, and on the other side is written the style and title of a painting. Which of the four cards below would you need to turn over in order to check her suspicion that all the cubist paintings are by Picasso? In other words, you need to find out whether it is the case that if the painting is cubist, then it is a Picasso.

When you are done, check the answer on the next page.

Answer to Exercise 2

Conditional statement: If the painting is cubist, then it is a Picasso. The correct answer is to turn over cards (c), (d), and (e). Card (c) should obviously be checked. Cards (d) and (e) should also be checked, since Metzinger and Leger might be cubist painters, in which case the conditional statement would be violated. Card (a) need *not* be checked since it won't help if the Picasso painting is cubist and it is irrelevant if the Picasso painting is not cubist. The surrealist card is obviously irrelevant.

Next Paragraph, Abstract Plus Examples Condition

To reformulate the above conditional statement into the form *"If p, then q,"* we substitute p for "the painting is cubist," and q for "the painting is a Picasso." Since card (c) translates into p, we clearly have to check whether q follows. And since cards (d) and (e) translate into $\bar{q}$, and *"If $\bar{q}$, then $\bar{p}$"* is equivalent to *"If p, then q,"* we have to check whether $\bar{p}$ follows. But we need not turn over card (a), since it corresponds to q, and *"If q, then p"* does not follow from *"If p, then q."* Accordingly, the backside of card (a) is irrelevant to the truth of *"If p, then q."* Similarly, we need not turn over card (b), which corresponds to $\bar{p}$, a condition whose implications are irrelevant to the truth of *"If p, then q."*

APPENDIX B: TRAINING MATERIALS USED IN EXPERIMENT 3

Obligation Condition

In this experiment you will be asked to solve a series of problems involving decisions about what needs to be checked in various situations in order to see whether specified regularities hold. In particular, you will need to apply what you know about regulations involving *obligations* of various sorts. In order to help you with the problems that will follow, please study the following description of the rules required to properly enforce obligations. Obligations are deceptively simple. Thus, although you probably already know what obligations are, these rules will help you think about such situations.

Obligations

As you know, an obligation arises whenever it is the case that certain circumstances or situations create an obligation to perform some action. Obligations can often be stated in an *"If . . . then"* form. For example, the following regulation specifies an obligation: "If a student is a psychology major, then the student must take an introductory psychology course." More generally, if we call the initial situation *I* and the action *C,* an obligation has the form, "If *I* arises, then *C* must be done." In our first example, *I* is "being a psychology major," and *C* is "taking an introductory psychology course."

In order to assess whether an obligation is being satisfied, we need to consider the four possible situations that might arise. These are:

1. *I* occurs.
2. *I* doesn't occur.
3. *C* is done.
4. *C* is not done.

Corresponding to each of these possible situations is a rule related to the fulfillment of the obligation. These rules are the following:

1. If *I* occurs, then it is obligatory to do *C*. Clearly, if *I* arises then failure to take the required action would constitute a violation of the obligation. To use our example, if a student is a psychology major, then that student must take an introductory psychology course.
2. If *I* does not occur, then the obligation does not arise. Consequently, *C* need not be done, although the person may do *C* anyway. For example, if a student is not a psychology major the student is not obliged to take an introductory psychology course. It may be permissible, however, for an English major to take an introductory psychology course. But in any case, the basic obligation is simply irrelevant if the student is not a psychology major.
3. If *C* is done, then the obligation is certainly not violated, regardless of whether or not *I* has occurred. If *I* did occur, then the obligation is satisfied. If *I* didn't occur, then the obligation didn't even arise (Rule 2). For example, if we know a student has taken an introductory psychology course, we can be sure the obligation has not been violated: Either the student was a psychology major, and hence fulfilled the obligation, or the student was not a psychology major, in which case the obligation didn't arise.

4. If *C* has not been done, then *I* must not have occurred. This is because if *I had* occurred, then the failure to do *C* would constitute a violation of the obligation. Thus, if a student has not taken an introductory psychology course, the student must not be a psychology major, or else the obligation will have been violated.

If you understand the above four rules, you should find it very easy to assess whether or not an obligation is being met. Note that there are only two situations in which it is possible for an obligation to be violated: When *I* occurs (and *C* is not done) (Rule 1), and when *C* is not done (and *I* occurs) (Rule 4). In the other two situations the obligation can't be violated. These are the cases in which *I* doesn't occur (in which case the obligation doesn't arise) (Rule 2), and in which *C* is done (in which case the obligation will have been met if it arose) (Rule 3).

You may wish to reread these instructions carefully in order to be sure you understand the rules for evaluating obligations. You will then be able to apply what you learned to the test problems. The test problems will include both obligations and other similar types of regularities. You will find it easy to solve these problems if you carefully apply Rules 1–4.

Contingency Condition

In this experiment you will be asked to solve a series of problems involving decisions about what needs to be checked in various situations in order to see whether specified regularities hold. In particular, you will need to apply what you know about situations involving *contingencies* of a certain sort. In order to help you with the problems that will follow, please study the following description of the rules required to properly evaluate contingencies. Contingencies are deceptively simple. Thus, although you probably already know what contingencies are, these rules will help you think about such situations more systematically.

Contingencies

A *contingency* arises whenever it is the case that a certain condition implies some necessary consequence. Contingencies can be stated in an *"If . . . then"* form. For example, the following statement specifies a contingency: "If a mushroom is red, then it is edible." Another example would be "If a student is a psychology major, then the student must take an introductory psychology course." More generally, if we call the initial condition *I* and the consequence *C*, a universal contingency has the form, *"If I, then C."* In our first example, *I* is "red mushroom" and *C* is "edible." In the second example, *I* is "being a psychology major," and *C* is "taking an introductory psychology course."

In order to assess whether a contingency in fact holds, we need to consider the four possible situations that might arise. These are:

1. *I* is obtained.
2. *I* is not obtained.
3. *C* is obtained.
4. *C* is not obtained.

Corresponding to each of these possible situations is a rule related to the truth of the contingency. These rules are the following:

1. If *I* is obtained, then *C* must be obtained. Clearly, if *I* is obtained then for *C* not to obtain would show that the contingency doesn't hold. To use our examples, if a mushroom is red, then it must be edible or else the contingency is false: and if a student is a psychology major, then the student must take an introductory psychology course.
2. If *I* is not obtained, then the contingency is not tested. *C* need not obtain, although it may. For example, if a mushroom is not red, it need not be edible, although it may be (perhaps brown mushrooms are also edible). Similarly, if a student is not a psychology major the student need not take an introductory psychology course. It may be possible, however, for an English major to take an introductory psychology course. But in any case, the basic contingency is simply irrelevant if the student is not a psychology major.
3. If *C* is obtained, then the contingency is certainly not falsified, regardless of whether or not *I* obtains. If *I* did occur, then the contingency is satisfied. If *I* is not obtained, then the contingency wasn't even tested (Rule 2). For example, if we know a certain mushroom is edible, we can be sure the contingency was not falsified regardless of the mushroom's color: Either the mushroom is red, and the contingency is satisfied, or it is not red, in which case the contingency was not tested. Similarly, if we know a student has taken an introductory psychology course, we can be sure the contingency has not been falsified: Either the student was a psychology major, and hence satisfied the contingency, or the student was not a psychology major, in which case the contingency wasn't tested.
4. If *C* is not obtained, then *I* must not obtain or else the contingency is falsified. This is because if *I had* occurred, then the failure to obtain *C* would falsify the contingency. Thus, if a mushroom is not

edible, it must not be red or else the contingency is false. And if a student has not taken an introductory psychology course, the student must not be a psychology major, or else again the contingency will be falsified.

If you understand the above four rules, you should find it easy to assess whether or not a contingency is being satisfied. Note that there are only two situations in which it is possible for a contingency to be falsified: When I is obtained (and C is not obtained) (Rule 1), and when C is not obtained (and I is obtained) (Rule 4). In the other two situations the contingency can't be falsified. These are the cases in which I does not obtain (in which case the contingency is not tested) (Rule 2), and in which C is obtained (in which case the contingency will have been satisfied if it was tested) (Rule 3).

You may wish to reread these instruction carefully in order to be sure you understand the rules for evaluating contingencies. You will then be able to apply what you learned to the test problems, which will include a variety of types of such contingencies. You will find it easy to solve these problems if you carefully apply Rules 1–4.

FOOTNOTES

[1]Problem type did not strongly influence errors in the equivalence judgment task. Over all types, the error rate was 33 ± 3% for failing to select the syntactic variation, 48 ± 3% for failing to select the contrapositive, 6 ± 3% for selecting the converse, and 4% for selecting the inverse. Contrary to our expectations, the frequency of converse errors was low even for the converse-bias problems (10 ± 4%), and the frequency of the contrapositive error was not lower for permission problems (46 ± 4%), than for other types. We have no confident explanation for the differences between the effects of problem type observed for equivalence judgments versus selection task performance.

[2]For the equivalence judgment task, training interacted strongly with type of error, $F(9, 228)$ = 14.0, $p < .001$. None of the training procedures had any significant effects on the converse and inverse. However, rule training, either alone or coupled with examples, reduced errors on the contrapositive by large and significant amounts, from 73 ± 11% for the control group, to 19 ± 11% for the subjects who received rule training alone, and 28 ± 11% for subjects who received both rule and examples training. Surprisingly, rule training, either alone or together with examples, greatly *increased* errors on the syntactic variation, from 17 ± 11% for the control group, to 55 ± 11% for subjects who received abstract training alone, and 49 ± 11% for subjects who received both rule and examples training. This negative effect of rule training may have resulted from the fact that the inference exercise included as part of the rule training did not include examples of the syntactic variation. It may be that by alerting subjects to fallacies of which they were previously unaware, rule training instilled a general reluctance to accept unfamiliar transformations, leading to the detrimental effect observed. In any case, the fact that rule training affected performance on both the contrapositive and the syntactic variation indicates that the lack of an effect of rule training alone in the selection task was not

due to subjects' simply learning nothing from our training protocol. Rule training by itself did alter subjects' performance on a direct inference task, even though what was learned could not be readily applied in the selection task.

[3]Anderson and Belnap (1975, pp. 17–18) relate the following hypothetical anecdote: "A mathematician writes a paper on Banach spaces, and . . . concludes with a conjecture. As a footnote to the conjecture, he writes: 'In addition to its intrinsic interest, this conjecture has connections with other parts of mathematics which might not immediately occur to the reader. For example, if the conjecture is true, then the first order functional calculus is complete; whereas if it is false, then it implies that Fermat's last conjecture is correct.' . . . The editor counters . . . 'In spite of what most logicians say about us, the standards maintained by this journal require that the antecedent of an 'if . . . then' statement must be *relevant* to the conclusion drawn.' " Anderson and Belnap (1975) have argued that relevance is critical to one's intuitive sense of what it is for an argument to be valid.

[4]The materials actually presented are omitted to conserve space.

REFERENCES

Anderson, A. R., & Belnap, N. D., Jr. (1975). *Entailment* (Vol. 1). Princeton, NJ: Princeton Univ. Press.

Braine, M. D. S. (1978). On the relation between the natural logic of reasoning and standard logic. *Psychological Review, 85,* 1–21.

Braine, M. D. S., Reiser, B. J., & Rumain, B. (1984). Some empirical justification for a theory of natural propositional logic. In G. H. Bower (Ed.), *The psychology of learning and motivation* (Vol. 18, pp. 313–371). New York: Academic Press.

Cheng, P. W., & Holyoak, K. J. (1985). Pragmatic reasoning schemas. *Cognitive Psychology, 17,* 391–416.

Copi, I. M. (1982). *Introduction to logic* (6th ed.). New York: Macmillian Co.

D'Andrade, R. (1982, April). *Reason versus logic.* Paper presented at the Symposium on the Ecology of Cognition: Biological, Cultural, and Historical Perspectives. Greensboro, NC.

Evans, J. St. B. T. (1982). *The psychology of deductive reasoning.* London: Routledge & Kegan Paul.

Fillenbaum, S. (1975). If: Some uses. *Psychological Research, 37,* 245–260.

Fillenbaum, S. (1976). Inducements: On phrasing and logic of conditional promises, threats and warnings. *Psychological Research, 38,* 231–250.

Fong, G. T., Krantz, D. H., & Nisbett, R. E. (1986). The effects of statistical training on thinking about everyday problems. *Cognitive Psychology, 18,* 253–292.

Geis, M. C., & Zwicky, A. M. (1971). On invited inferences. *Linguistic Inquiry, 2,* 561–566.

Golding, E. (1981). *The effect of past experience on problem solving.* Paper presented at the Annual Conference of the British Psychological Society, Surrey University.

Goodman, N. (1965). *Fact, fiction, and forecast.* Indianapolis: Bobbs-Merrill.

Griggs, R. A. (1983). The role of problem content in the selection task and in the THOG problem. In J. St. B. T. Evans (Ed.), *Thinking and reasoning: Psychological approaches.* London: Routledge & Kegan Paul.

Griggs, R. A. (1984). Memory cueing and instructional effects on Wason's selection task. *Current Psychological Research and Reviews, 3,* 3–10.

Griggs, R. A., & Cox, J. R. (1982). The elusive thematic-materials effect in Wason's selection task. *British Journal of Psychology, 73,* 407–420.

Hempel, C. G. (1965). *Aspects of scientific explanation, and other essays in the philosophy of science.* New York: Free Press.

Henle, M. (1962). On the relation between logic and thinking. *Psychological Review, 69,* 366–378.

Holland, J., Holyoak, K. J., Nisbett, R. E., & Thagard, P. (1986). *Induction: Processes of inference, learning, and discovery.* Cambridge, MA: Bradford Books/MIT Press.

Jepson, C., Krantz, D. H., & Nisbett, R. E. (1983). Inductive reasoning: Competence or skill? *Behavioral and Brain Sciences, 6,* 494–501.

Johnson-Laird, P. N. (1983). *Mental models.* Cambridge, MA: Harvard Univ. Press.

Johnson-Laird, P. N., Legrenzi, P., & Legrenzi, M. S. (1972). Reasoning and a sense of reality. *British Journal of Psychology, 63,* 395–400.

Kelley, H. H. (1972). Casual schemata and the attribution process. In E. E. Jones et al. (Eds.), *Attribution: Perceiving the causes of behavior.* Morristown, NJ: General Learning Press.

Kelly, H. H. (1973). The process of casual attribution. *American Psychologist, 78,* 107–128.

Manktelow, K. I., & Evans, J. St. B. T. (1979). Facilitation of reasoning by realism: Effect or non-effect? *British Journal of Psychology, 70,* 477–488.

Nelson, E. J. (1933). On three logical principles in intension. *Monist, 43,* 268–289.

Nisbett, R. E., Krantz, D. H., Jepson, C., & Kunda, Z. (1983) The use of statistical heuristics in everyday inductive reasoning. *Psychological Review, 90,* 339–363.

Piaget, J., & Inhelder, B. (1975). *The origin of the idea of chance in children.* New York: Norton. (Original work published in 1951)

Quine, W. V. O. (1974). *Methods of logic* (3rd ed.). London: Routledge & Kegan Paul.

Reich, S. S., & Ruth, P. (1982). Wason's selection task: Verification, falsification and matching. *British Journal of Psychology, 73,* 395–405.

Rips, L. J. (1983). Cognitive processes in propositional reasoning. *Psychological Review, 90,* 38–71.

Rips, L. J., & Conrad, F. G. (1983). Individual differences in deduction. *Cognition and Brain Theory, 6,* 259–285.

Simco, N. D., & James, G. G. (1982). *Elementary logic* (2nd ed.). Belmont, CA: Wadsworth.

Wason, P. C. (1966). Reasoning. In B. M. Foss (Ed.), *New horizons in psychology I.* Harmondsworth: Penguin.

Wason, P. C., & Johnson-Laird, P. N. (1972). *Psychology of reasoning.* Cambridge, MA: Havard Univ. Press.

Wason, P. C., & Shapiro, D. (1971). Natural and contrived experience in a reasoning problem. *Quarterly Journal of Experimental Psychology, 23,* 63–71.

Yachanin, S. A. (1985). *Facilitation in Wason's selection task: Content and instruction.* Unpublished manuscript, Lake Erie College.

IV RULES FOR CAUSAL REASONING

8 Pragmatic Constraints on Causal Deduction

Patricia W. Cheng
University of California, Los Angeles

Richard E. Nisbett
University of Michigan

INTRODUCTION

The notion of cause pervades everyday discourse. Statements about causality are often expressed as conditionals, in the form, "if *<cause>*, then *<effect>*." For example, a mother explaining to her son why he should not throw stones at windows might say, "If a stone hits a window, then the glass will break." Or, an advocate of stricter gun control might argue, "If there is stricter gun control, then the homicide rate will be lowered." Conditional statements are not, however, all causal. For example, the conditional statement, "If today is Monday, then tomorrow is Tuesday," does not involve causality. Neither do the statements, "If a triangle has a right angle, then the square of its hypotenuse is equal to the sum of the squares of the other two sides," or "If a person is to drink alcohol, then he or she must be over 21."

Given the common expression of causal relations in *if-then* form, a question that arises is whether causal deductive reasoning is governed by the set of inferential rules associated with *if*—a connective that has been called "the heart of logic" (Anderson & Belnap, 1975, p. 1). A number of psychologists have proposed that there are *natural logics* consisting of repertoires of inferential rules specified in terms of connectives such as *if* (e.g., Braine, 1978; Braine & O'Brien, 1991; Johnson-Laird, 1975; Osherson, 1975; Rips, 1983). These rules, which are modeled after those in *natural deduction* systems of logic formulated by logicians such as Fitch (1952), operate independently of both the content of the propositions linked by a connective and the context in which a statement is embedded. These rules are assumed to be naturally used by people untutored in logic.

207

A related proposal is that causal relations can be represented in terms of whether a potential causal factor is a necessary and/or sufficient condition for the occurrence of the effect. J. S. Mill (1843/1973), for example, proposed that his "method of agreement" identifies factors necessary for the occurrence of a target effect among a set of factors assumed to be potentially necessary, whereas his "method of difference" identifies factors sufficient for the occurrence of a target effect among a set of factors assumed to be potentially sufficient (see von Wright, 1960). These concepts frequently appear in discussions of causality in textbooks on logic (e.g., Copi, 1961; Salmon, 1984), and are sometimes, among other concepts such as functional relations, proposed to supplant the term "cause" (see von Wright, 1975; Skyrms, 1986). Causality as defined by condition relations has been proposed to underlie both deductive and inductive everyday reasoning about causality (e.g., Bindra, Clarke, & Shultz, 1980; Kelley, 1967, 1973; Piaget, 1974; Shultz & Butkowsky, 1977). For example, Bindra et al. (1980, p. 423) argued that necessity and sufficiency each supports deductive causal inference: "effects can be validly inferred from known determining conditions . . . when the latter are sufficient conditions, whereas determining conditions can be legitimately inferred from known effects . . . when the determining conditions are necessary. . . ." Kelley (1967, p. 194) hypothesized that one induces a factor that is both necessary and sufficient to produce an effect to be the cause of the effect: "The effect is attributed to that condition which is present when the effect is present and which is absent when the effect is absent." He also hypothesized schemas for reasoning about "multiple sufficient causes" and "multiple necessary causes" (Kelley, 1967, 1973).

In the present paper, we will argue against both of the above positions. We think that, despite the common expression of causal relations in *if-then* form, and despite the ready classification of causal relations in terms of sufficiency and necessity, causal deduction cannot be subsumed under rules of natural logic associated either with the connective *if* or with the condition relations of necessity and sufficiency. We take an alternative approach that results from considering the usefulness of inferences for everyday goals (Cheng & Holyoak, 1985, 1989; Cheng, Holyoak, Nisbett, & Oliver, 1986; Holland, Holyoak, Nisbett, & Thagard, 1986; Nisbett, Fong, Lehman, & Cheng, 1987).

Cheng and Holyoak (1985) and Cheng et al. (1986) reported evidence showing that a much larger percentage of college students appeared to use an inferential rule that corresponds to *modus tollens* (i.e., "if p then q" and "*not-q*" imply "*not-p*") in a permission context or an obligation context than in an arbitrary context (i.e., a context that is not interpretable in terms of typical life experiences). They explained this and other results indicating context dependence by positing that people make use of *pragmatic rea-*

soning schemas, which are clusters of abstract inferential rules that are specialized for certain classes of goal-directed relationships. To explain context dependence, Cheng and Holyoak (1985, p. 395) noted, "Although a syntactically based reasoning system tells us which inferences are valid, it does not tell us which inferences are useful among the potentially many that are valid." They gave an example involving the *contrapositive* of a conditional remedy. The statement "If a burglar breaks into a house, then the police should be called" implies "If it is not the case that the police should be called, then a burglar is not breaking into a house." This contrapositive inference—though valid—seems hardly ever useful. Although it is not impossible to construct scenarios in which such an inference is useful, knowledge about a burglar not breaking into a house is typically not inferred from the impropriety of calling the police. The relatively low utility of inferential rules such as modus tollens and the contrapositive in some contexts may explain why they do not appear to be general rules of natural logic.

The variability of the application of modus tollens across different contexts cannot be explained by natural-logic rules associated with *if*. One move is to simply omit modus tollens from the repertoire of rules. This can explain why subjects often fail to apply it in an arbitrary context, but cannot explain why the same subjects who fail to apply it in one context do so in other contexts. As we (Cheng & Holyoak, 1985, p. 410; Cheng et al., 1986, p. 317) noted, however, our evidence for the existence of pragmatic schemas does not rule out the existence of natural-logic rules. We agree that convincing arguments and evidence for the use of natural-logic rules have been presented by many researchers (e.g., Braine, 1978; Braine & O'Brien, 1991; Braine, Reiser, & Rumain, 1984; Johnson-Laird, 1975; Macnarama, 1986; Osherson, 1975; Rips, 1983). Cheng et al. proposed a priority relation between the two coexisting types of rules: If a rule is interpretable in terms of a pragmatic reasoning schema, then a subject will apply the schema; otherwise, the subject would fall back on natural-logic rules. This proposal entails that if rules from the two systems conflict, then pragmatic rules will override natural-logic rules. Otherwise, the two types of rules will complement each other. Such a relationship between the two types of rules is consistent with the priority of more specific over more general information, a principle commonly adopted in knowledge-representation systems (e.g., Anderson, 1983; Holland et al., 1986; also see Neches, Langley, & Klahr, 1987).

Braine and O'Brien (1991) proposed an alternative integration of the natural-logic and pragmatic views whereby a set of natural-logic rules associated with a connective, which they call the *lexical entry* of the connective, may be supplemented by pragmatic inferential rules. They assume that supplementary pragmatic rules apply when a connective is embedded in a context that elicits such rules. Braine and O'Brien proposed that the representation of a sentence that elicits pragmatic rules "includes, but is richer than, the representation that could be gotten from the lexical entry alone" (p. 184). Their proposal assumes a strictly complementary relationship between natural-logic rules and pragmatic inferential rules (or at least does not consider the possibility of conflict). We will discuss this issue of the integration of the two views with respect to reasoning about causality in a later section.

The pervasiveness of the notion of causality in everyday reasoning would suggest a causal schema (or set of such schemas) as a likely candidate to be among the pragmatic reasoning schemas that people use instead of, or to supplement, natural-logic rules (Kelley, 1967, 1973; Tversky & Kahneman, 1980). Evidence for a causal schema would further generalize the concept of pragmatic schemas, which has so far been applied in detail only to conditional regulations such as permission and obligation.

Candidate General Inferential Rules

If

Let us examine in more detail some possible proposals for formal inferential rules that might underlie judgments about causality. We will first consider the set of propositional rules associated with the connective *if*. An example of such a rule is *modus ponens*. When given the premises "If p then q" and "p", virtually everyone agrees that "q" follows, regardless of the propositions that are represented by the symbols p and q (e.g., Braine et al., 1984; Rips & Marcus, 1977; Smith, Langston, & Nisbett, 1992; Wason & Johnson-Laird, 1972). A second rule of natural logic that has been proposed (e.g., Braine, 1978; Braine & O'Brien, 1991; Johnson-Laird, 1975; Osherson, 1975; Rips, 1983) is one that corresponds to, or is analogous to, the *schema for conditional proof* (sometimes called the schema for implication introduction) in natural-deduction systems. Braine and O'Brien (in press, p. 5 in ms), for example, state this schema as follows: "To derive or evaluate *If p then* . . . , first suppose *p;* for any proposition, *q,* that follows from the supposition of p taken together with other information assumed, one may assert *If p then q*." An example of a rule associated with *if* that is generally omitted from natural-logic theories is modus tollens (e.g., Braine, 1978; Rips, 1983). The use of this rule is far from universal—about half of college-student subjects fail to give an answer consistent with this rule (Rips & Marcus, 1977; Rumain, Connell, & Braine, 1983; Wason & Johnson-Laird, 1972). Even in cases in which the correct answer was given, it appeared to have been derived using *reductio ad absurdum* rather than obtained directly by modus tollens (Wason & Johnson-Laird, 1972).

One proposal about the use of *if* for causality would be that "p causes q"

means nothing other than "if p then q," perhaps with the stipulation that modus ponens and the schema for conditional proof, but not modus tollens, apply as rules of natural logic. Two problems might appear to confront this account. First, many causal relations do not have the properties of the above natural-logic connective *if*. In particular, modus ponens applies only to causal relations in which the cause always produces the effect. Consider the statement "smoking causes lung cancer." When rephrased as "if one smokes, then one will have lung cancer," modus ponens clearly does not apply, because the antecedent is not interpreted as a deterministic cause of the consequent (Cummins, Lubart, Alksnis, & Rist, 1991). However, the fact that there are causal relations that do not correspond to the conditional does not in itself rule out the conditional as the representation of causal relations altogether, as long as there exists *some* type of deterministic causal relation that does correspond to the conditional.

A second apparent problem is that *if-then* statements may invite assumptions. The above conditional statement regarding "lung cancer," for example, might potentially be interpreted as a biconditional ("one will have lung cancer if and only if one smokes"). However, invited assumptions do not present an intrinsic problem for the conditional as a representation of causal relations, because the interpretation of a statement can be separated from inferences based on the interpretation (Henle, 1962). That is, the hypothesis that the conditional is the underlying representation for causal relations, at least for some type of causal relation, remains plausible when one considers the disambiguated psychological interpretation of a conditional statement rather than the explicit statement itself. We will show in our experiments, however, that even for the type of causal relation that is most likely to correspond to the conditional, and even when ambiguities in interpretation are removed, inferences regarding this type of relation still cannot be adequately described by propositional natural-logic rules associated with the conditional.

Condition Relations

To characterize the full range of causal relations, psychological and philosophical discussions of causality have often described causal relations in terms of the condition relations of necessity and sufficiency. Condition relations and the connective *if* are obviously related. Statements of the form "if p then q" in ordinary language contain two ambiguities. First, they may mean either "p is sufficient for q" or "if p then sometimes q." Natural-logic theories adopt the default meaning "p is sufficient for q," the interpretation to which modus ponens does apply. Second, although the statement "if p then q" implies the necessity of q for p (if *not-q* then *not-p*), it does not specify the necessity of p for q. The latter is left undetermined. Characterizing a causal relation in terms of necessity and sufficiency removes both of the above ambiguities. In other words, the connective *if* with its ambiguities removed may be treated as a special type of condition relation—the type in which the antecedent is sufficient but not necessary for the consequent. In a causal context, this is the type in which the cause is sufficient but not necessary to produce the effect.

It has been noted that the concepts of necessity and sufficiency cannot account for the asymmetry between causes and effects (e.g., Mackie, 1974; von Wright, 1975). To say that p is sufficient for q (i.e., if p then q) implies that *not-q* is sufficient for *not-p* (i.e., if *not-q* then *not-p*). However, to say that p is a cause of q is not the same as to say that *not-q* is a cause of *not-p*. For example, heavy rainfall may be the cause of flooding, but the absence of flooding cannot be the cause of the absence of heavy rainfall. Similarly, given certain background conditions such as the position of the sun and the angle at which a pole is stuck to the ground, the length of the pole is a necessary and sufficient condition for the length of its shadow, and vice versa. Yet, although the length of the pole is the cause of the length of the shadow, the length of the shadow is *not* the cause of the length of the pole. To overcome this shortcoming, von Wright proposed that the concept of *manipulation* by an agent be included, in addition to condition concepts, in the definition of causation. That is, causes are sufficient and/or necessary conditions that can be manipulated, whereas effects cannot be manipulated (other than by manipulating the cause). The length of the pole in the above example can be manipulated and is sufficient to produce a shadow of a certain length, whereas the length of the shadow cannot be manipulated other than by manipulating the pole (given the background assumptions). It is thus clear that condition relations would have to be amended (though it seems to us that they *can* be amended) to deal with the asymmetry between causes and effects. We will, however, raise other arguments against characterizing causal relations in terms of condition relations.

A Pragmatic Constraint on Causal Inferences: Informative Prediction

To develop a pragmatic approach to understanding causal deduction, we need to consider the goals of causal reasoning. We assume that two basic goals are explanation and the effective prediction of events. We will focus on the latter in the present paper.

It has been argued that the concepts of necessity and sufficiency are useful for prediction (Bindra et al., 1980). If p is known to be a sufficient condition for q, then q can be predicted to occur whenever p occurs. Similarly, if p is known to be necessary for q, then the absence of q can be predicted whenever p is absent. Although we agree that these concepts support predictions, it seems to us that they are not necessarily *informative* for making predictions, because the concepts of necessity and sufficiency individually do not specify any *contingency* between a cause and an effect. By contingency, we mean

$$P(e|c) - P(e|\bar{c}) \neq O, \tag{1}$$

where $P(e|c)$ is the probability of the effect e given the presence of the potential causal factor c, and $P(e|\bar{c})$ is the probability of e given the absence of c.[1] It has been proposed that this concept of contingency underlies normative causal induction (e.g., Alloy & Abramson, 1979; Jenkins & Ward, 1965; Rescorla, 1968; Salmon, 1984; Skyrms, 1986), human causal induction (Alloy & Tabachnik, 1984; Cheng & Novick, 1990, 1991, 1992), and classical conditioning (Alloy & Tabachnik, 1984; Rescorla, 1968).

Although the concept of contingency has been proposed as a component of inductive causal reasoning, we think that it is also important in deductive causal reasoning.[2] Deductions based on a causal conditional will elicit assumptions about contingency, which cannot be represented in propositional logic. If so, deductive reasoning regarding causal conditionals will be governed by rules in addition to, or instead of, propositional rules associated with *if* or with condition relations.

To see why necessity and sufficiency individually do not support informative prediction, consider the case in which a potential cause c is a sufficient condition for an effect e (i.e., when c occurs, e always occurs). If e inevitably occurs, in the absence of c as well as in the presence of c (i.e., there is no contingency between c and e), then the status of c is not informative for predicting e. For example, in the context of the atmosphere of the Earth, oxygen is present *(e)*, regardless of whether Willy robbed the bank *(c)*. Knowing whether Willy robbed the bank therefore would not add any useful information for predicting the presence of oxygen in the atmosphere. To allow informative prediction, understanding c as a cause of e should carry the assumption of contingency; that is, when there is no contingency between c and e, c will not be a cause of e, even when it is sufficient for e. Willy robbing the bank, clearly, is not a cause of oxygen being in the atmosphere, despite the fact that it is sufficient for the presence of oxygen in the atmosphere and that it involves "manipulation" by an agent (Willy). An analogous problem plagues the characterization of a causal relation in terms of necessity: because necessity does not specify any contingency between a cause and an effect, it is not necessarily informative for prediction.

We have argued above that it is contingency rather than sufficiency or necessity that is informative for making predictions. Contingency can be defined deterministically, but we have adopted a probabilistic definition. We did so because a further problem with the characterization of causal relations in terms of condition relations is the probabilistic nature of many,

if not most, causal relations. Because causal relations are typically probabilistic, prediction requires probabilistic rules in which necessity and sufficiency are only special cases. Consider tobacco-smoking as a cause of lung
cancer. Although tobacco-smoking may be characterized as a cause that is
neither necessary nor sufficient to produce lung cancer, this causal relation
cannot possibly be fully specified in terms of necessity and sufficiency (or
rather the lack thereof): Many factors that are neither necessary nor sufficient for producing an effect are simply causally irrelevant. Robbing a bank,
for example, is not necessary nor sufficient to produce a fire, and is causally
irrelevant to it. It may be hypothesized that the understanding of probabilistic and deterministic causes involve distinct psychological mechanisms,
and that deterministic causes are specified in terms of necessity and sufficiency. Such an account, however, lacks parsimony. A probabilistic model
with deterministic relations as extreme cases would seem preferable.

Some philosophers of science have argued that only in the case in which
a condition is both necessary and sufficient for an effect is there a causal
relationship (e.g., Nagel, 1961). This deterministic condition relation does
specify a contingency between a cause and an effect. Regardless of the
philosophical debate on the issue, however, this definition of causality does
not seem to be psychologically descriptive. Since Kelley's (1967) proposal of
a deterministic inductive rule, evidence has accumulated showing that
people's concept of causality is not limited to situations in which a factor is
both necessary and sufficient to produce an effect. In McArthur's (1972)
study, for example, systematic causal attributions were obtained with
materials specifying insufficient relations (e.g., "Ralph has almost always
tripped over Joan's feet"). More recently, Cheng and Novick (1990b) found
that, when presented with materials that specified conditions that are *not*
necessary and sufficient to produce an effect, a large majority of college
subjects nonetheless believed that the materials described causal relations—
the same percentage, in fact, as when the materials did specify necessary
and sufficient conditions. Using deductive inference tasks, Cummins et al.
(1991) found that conditional statements judged to describe strong causal
relations include those for which subjects perceived alternative causes and
disabling conditions (i.e., conditions that prevent a cause from yielding its
effect). Their subjects clearly did not interpret causal relations exclusively as
deterministic relations.

The issue of informative prediction is also relevant to probabilistic causal
relations. Consider the case in which the effect e is present with a
probability of .8 when cause c is present. The effect e can therefore be
predicted with a probability of .8 given the presence of c. However, if e
occurs with the same probability given the absence of c, then the status of
c, just as in the deterministic case, is not informative for predicting the
status of e.

The same issue of contingency versus conditional probability was raised by Rescorla (1968) in his work on classical conditioning. Rescorla demonstrated that classical conditioning is a function of contingency rather than of conditional probability. When the probability of the reinforcer was the same in the absence of the conditioned stimulus as in its presence, little or no conditioning resulted. Our argument regarding contingency versus condition relations may be regarded as an application of Rescorla's distinction to human deductive causal reasoning. Contingency predicts that "A is a sufficient cause of B" implies not only "if A occurs then B always occurs," but also "if A does not occur then B is less likely to occur." We will test this implication in our experiments.

It might be argued that such a difference could be due to a greater tendency of assuming a biconditional interpretation for causal than for non-explanatory conditionals. That is, perhaps subjects are more likely to assume for causal than for arbitrary conditionals that the consequent is true if and only if the antecedent is true. We will show, however, that even when people are not assuming a biconditional interpretation, they still think that the set of cases in which the consequent is true is relevant for testing the truth of a causal conditional.

To summarize, our consideration of the usefulness of inferences has led us to predict that reasoning about causal and non-causal relations should differ, even when the causal and non-causal situations are formally identical in terms of condition relations. Because the concept of causality involves the concept of contingency—a difference between the probabilities of the effect given the presence versus the absence of the cause—we assume that asserting a causal relation, unlike asserting an arbitrary conditional, elicits the assumption expressed by Equation 1, and deriving a causal relation, unlike deriving an arbitrary conditional, requires the same assumption. In contrast, the formal rules associated with the connective *if* and the conditions of sufficiency and necessity are not contingency-based.

EXPERIMENT: AN IMPLICATION OF THE GOAL OF INFORMATIVE PREDICTION FOR CAUSAL DEDUCTION

Overview

In this experiment we tested our prediction contrasting causal and non-causal deduction based on the goal of informative prediction for causal reasoning. We created two conditions, one with a cover story involving a *causal* conditional relation and another with a cover story involving an *arbitrary*, non-causal, conditional relation. To be sure that any differences in deductive reasoning between our causal and arbitrary control conditions are due to distinctive characteristics of causal reasoning rather than to the specific content of our control condition, we used in the control condition an arbitrary relation that does not have any ready interpretation in terms of meaningful everyday situations. Cheng et al. (1986) proposed that in such situations, because no pragmatic representation of the conditional is available, people may fall back on a formal representation of the conditional. The causal situation was specified in abstract terms to avoid the possibility that inferences about the causal situation, in contrast to those about the arbitrary situation, might be produced by concrete knowledge about a particular domain of events.

We have argued that a causal relation "c is a sufficient cause of e" implies not only that c is sufficient for the effect e, but also that e is contingent on c (i.e., the effect is more likely in the presence of the cause than in its absence). In contrast, an arbitrary conditional relation "if c then always e" need not imply any contingency. We predicted that "A is a cause of B" will not be interpreted as equivalent to "If A, then B" *even* when the condition relations assumed by the subject are equated across the statements. To test this prediction, we explicitly specified a strictly conditional relation (one in which the antecedent is sufficient but not necessary for the consequent) in a causal as well as an arbitrary context.

In the causal version of this question, we asked subjects to evaluate the statement "A is a cause of B" in a situation in which an event B always occurs when a potential causal factor A occurs, but B always occurs also when A does not occur. (Subjects were to assume that events other than A and B remained constant.) A formally equivalent question was cast in terms of an arbitrary conditional. If contingency is more likely to be relevant for the causal than for the arbitrary relation, then subjects should be more likely to answer "no" to the "contingency" question in the causal than in the arbitrary condition.

To check whether subjects had interpreted the condition relations in the rule as we specified, we included an inference task in which subjects were asked to state what conclusion follows from the given rule together with each of several additional statements. Our prediction — a difference between the causal and the arbitrary conditions on the contingency evaluation question that are not accompanied by corresponding differences in the inference task across the two conditions — cannot be explained by other current theories of reasoning.

Method

Subjects

The subjects were 62 students at the University of California, Los Angeles (UCLA), participating to fulfill a requirement for an introductory-psychology course.

Design, Materials, and Procedure

Subjects were randomly assigned to the causal version ($N = 33$) and the arbitrary version ($N = 29$) of the materials. They were tested in groups of six or fewer. Because the experiment required less than 15 minutes, the subjects were tested either before another experiment or in the middle of another experiment as a distracting task. When subjects were tested in the middle of another experiment, that other experiment involved an unrelated memory task.

Causal and Arbitrary Cover Stories.   The causal cover story specified an abstract causal relation between two events. It stated:

Suppose a scientist believes she has discovered a law governing the relation between two events, A and B. She believes she has discovered that **A is a cause of B.** Here is the law:

Proposed law: **If Cause A occurs, then it always produces Event B.**

She understands, however, that when Event B occurs, Cause A has not always occurred.

The arbitrary version of the cover story specified a relation involving letters on an imaginary blackboard (adapted from Osherson, 1975). It stated:

Suppose there is an imaginary blackboard on which letters appear. A person observing the blackboard believes she has discovered a law governing the relation between two letters, A and B. She believes she has discovered that **A is a condition for B.** Here is the law:

Proposed law: **If there is an A, then there is always a B.**

She understands, however, that when there is a B, there is not always an A.

Contingency evaluation question.   The contingency question was aimed at assessing whether subjects assumed contingency. In the causal condition, this question stated, "Consider occasions on which events other than A and B remain constant. Suppose that on all such occasions Event B always occurs when Cause A occurs. Now, Event B always occurs also when Cause A does not occur. Can the scientist's proposal, 'A is a cause of B,' be true?" In the arbitrary condition, this question stated, "Consider occasions on which letters other than A and B remain constant. Suppose that on all such occasions there is always a B when there is an A. Now, there is always a B also when there is not an A. Can the observer's proposal, 'If there is an A, then there is a B,' be true?"

Inference task. There were four inference questions for checking whether subjects interpreted the condition relations in the rule as we specified.

In the causal condition, the causal law described in the evaluation task was repeated. Subjects were reminded that when Event B occurs, Cause A has not always occurred, and were asked to assume that the law holds. They were then asked to state what conclusion, if any, follows from each of four statements. These statements were:

1. Cause A occurs. (affirmed antecedent)
2. Event B occurs. (affirmed consequent)
3. Event B does not occur. (negated consequent)
4. Cause A does not occur. (negated antecedent)

If Cause A is assumed to be sufficient for Event B (as we specified) then Statement 1 should lead to the conclusion that Event B occurs. Likewise, Statement 3 should lead to the conclusion that Cause A has not occurred. If Cause A is assumed to be unnecessary for Event B (as we specified), then Statement 2 should not lead to any definite conclusion about whether Cause A occurred (it may or may not have occurred). Likewise, Statement 4 should not lead to any definite conclusion about whether Event B occurs (it may or may not occur).

The arbitrary version of this task was formally identical to the one described above, except that the content concerned the arbitrary law about letters on the imaginary blackboard. The four premises (in addition to the conditional premise) were:

1. There is an A.
2. There is a B.
3. There is not a B.
4. There is not an A.

At the end of the questionnaire, subjects were asked to indicate whether they (a) had ever taken a logic class, (b) had ever taken a course that included a discussion of causality, and (c) were a native speaker of English.[3]

Results

Based on the goal of informative prediction in causal reasoning, we anticipated that subjects in the causal condition would be more likely than those in the arbitrary control condition to answer "no" to the question asking whether a conditional relation can be true when the antecedent is sufficient for the consequent but there is no contingency between the two.

We predicted that this difference would *not* be due to the greater propensity of subjects in the causal condition to assume a biconditional interpretation, as measured by the inference tasks. The results supported the above predictions.

Contingency

Recall that after specifying a disambiguated conditional relation in both the causal and the arbitrary versions, we asked subjects to consider a situation in which the consequent always occurs, regardless of whether the antecedent occurs (i.e., the antecedent is sufficient for the consequent, but there is no contingency between the two events). In the causal version, we asked subjects to evaluate whether the causal statement, "A is a cause of B," can be true in such a situation. In the arbitrary version, we asked subjects to evaluate whether the statement regarding letters on the blackboard, "If there is an A, then there is a B," can be true in such a situation. We predicted that subjects would be more likely to answer "no" in the causal than in the arbitrary condition. Supporting our prediction, whereas more than half of the subjects in the causal condition (58%) answered "no", less than a tenth of the subjects in the arbitrary condition (7%) did so, $\chi^2(1, N = 62) = 17.7, p < .001$.

Inference Questions

Subjects' responses to the inference questions demonstrate that the above differences could not have resulted from subjects in the causal and arbitrary conditions interpreting differently the condition relations that we specified. Table 8.1 lists the percentage of correct responses to each of the inference questions in the two conditions. A large majority of the subjects in both conditions gave correct answers to all of the inference questions. This is not surprising, given that our materials explicitly specified that the antecedent was sufficient but not necessary for the consequent. These results thus confirm that subjects interpreted the condition relations as we specified. Differences between the causal and the arbitrary conditions were small, and

TABLE 8.1

Percentage of Correct Responses on Inference Questions with a Conditional Statement as the First Premise

	Second Premise			
Condition	affirmed antecedent	negated antecedent	affirmed consequent	negated consequent
Causal (N = 33)	94	82	97	91
Arbitrary (N = 29)	100	86	86	83

none of them approached statistical significance. These results indicate that neither the assumptions about condition relations nor the inferential rules applied in answer to these questions differed across the two conditions.

In sum, as we predicted, even for subjects who held the *same* assumptions regarding condition relations between two events A and B, "A is a cause of B" was not interpreted as equivalent to "If A, then B." No alternative current theory of deductive reasoning explains this pattern of results, which support our view that the goal of informative prediction has led to a rule of deductive inference particular to causal reasoning.

DISCUSSION

We have proposed that due to the goal of informative prediction, a schema for causal deduction includes the contingency constraint expressed by Equation 1. Asserting a causal relation elicits the assumptions expressed by this equation, and deriving a causal relation requires the same assumptions. This constraint implies that a causal relation involving the same assumptions of necessity and sufficiency as an arbitrary conditional will be less likely than the arbitrary conditional to be considered true when the relation involves sufficiency but not contingency. The results of our experiment support our prediction.

Goal-Directed Inferential Rules

Equation 1 is substantially different from rules in the regulation schemas proposed by Cheng and Holyoak (1985) and Cheng et al. (1986). For comparison, an example of a rule in the permission schema is, "If the precondition is satisfied, then the action may be taken" (Cheng & Holyoak, 1985, p. 397). Although rules in both domains are often stated in *if-then* form, we think the differing goals in these domains should lead to different inferential rules. Whereas the goals of hypothesizing causal relations are explanation and informative prediction, the goals of establishing permissions consist of the reasons for satisfying a particular precondition (e.g., protecting an individual's health in the case of a health regulation) and the freedom of choice for an individual within the constraints of those reasons (e.g., once the precondition is satisfied, the individual may choose to take, or not take, the relevant action).

The goals of the above two types of relations require inferential rules that go beyond the purview of classical propositional logic. In the case of regulation situations, the need for satisfying particular requirements led us (Cheng & Holyoak, 1985; Cheng et al., 1986) to hypothesize that permission and obligation schemas contain rules involving the modal term "must".

Similarly, the freedom of choice once the reason for the regulation is satisfied led us to hypothesize rules involving the modal term "may".[4] In the case of causal relations, the goal of informatively predicting probabilistic relations has led us to adopt a probabilistic rule that provides information on how much more likely the effect is to occur given the presence rather than absence of a potential causal factor.

We do not imply that contingency is the only constraint in a causal schema. A number of researchers (e.g., Bullock, Gelman, & Baillargeon, 1982; Tversky and Kahnemann, 1980) for example, have presented evidence for temporal directionality in causal reasoning.

Questioning Pragmatic Reasoning Schemas

A number of researchers have raised questions about the concept of pragmatic reasoning schemas. Some have proposed that the concept is superfluous (Jackson & Griggs, 1990; Thompson, 1989); others have proposed that pragmatic rules complement natural-logic rules but do not override them (Braine & O'Brien, 1991). We will briefly discuss these claims, especially in relation to the results of the present experiment.

Are Differences in Conditional-Reasoning Performance Due Solely to Assumptions Regarding Condition Relations?

Henle (1962) has argued that reasoning errors may be due to subjects' interpretations of given premises, rather than to the use of fallacious inferential rules. Applying this argument to conditional statements, Thompson (1989) argues that conditional reasoning in various domains may appear to differ due to differences across domains in the assumptions regarding the sufficiency and necessity of the antecedent for the consequent, rather than due to the use of context-specific inferential rules.

Although we agree with Thompson that invited assumptions are likely to differ across domains, we think that such assumptions cannot satisfactorily explain reasoning performance and the effects of context. With respect to Wason's selection task (see Evans, 1982, 1989 for reviews), a widely reported finding regarding arbitrary versions of the task is that although subjects virtually always select the case representing the positive antecedent (indicating the use of modus ponens), they seldom select the case representing the negated consequent (indicating the failure to use modus tollens). A similar result has been obtained for inference-evaluation tasks (Rips & Marcus, 1977; Rumain et al., 1983; Wason & Johnson-Laird, 1972). But ponens and tollens are valid under the *same* assumption of the sufficiency of the antecedent for the consequent. The consistent difference in reasoning performance corresponding to the use of ponens and tollens in arbitrary conditionals therefore contradicts an account of reasoning based purely on assumptions regarding sufficiency and necessity.

It might be argued, however, that a potential amendment of Thompson's hypothesis is that only ponens is associated with the condition relation of sufficiency. But this amendment fails to salvage her hypothesis for the same reason that it fails to salvage the natural-logic rules associated with the connective *if:* Although this amendment can explain why subjects often fail to select the negated consequent in an arbitrary selection task, it cannot explain why the same subjects who fail to select it in one context do select it in other contexts. For versions of the selection task cast in terms of permissions, for example, the selection of the negated consequent is much more common (e.g., Cheng & Holyoak, 1985; Johnson-Laird, Legrenzi, & Legrenzi, 1972).

The present results further undermine Thompson's hypothesis. The causal and arbitrary materials in our experiment were explicitly equated for necessity and sufficiency. Moreover, our instructions specifying these condition relations were found to be equally effective for the two conditions. Nonetheless, reasoning judgments differed across the conditions in the goal-directed manner as we predicted.

Similarly, Kroger, Cheng and Holyoak (in preparation) explicitly equated for necessity and sufficiency across an arbitrary selection task and an abstract-permission version of the task, and they found that subjects nonetheless selected the "correct" pattern (the positive antecedent and the negated consequent) much more often for the abstract-permission version than for the arbitrary version. The explicit specification of a condition relation in which the antecedent is sufficient but unnecessary for the consequent yielded little enhancement of performance on the arbitrary task. In sum, although assumptions on condition relations partially explain differences in reasoning judgments across some contexts, they clearly fail to explain many findings in the literature.

Are Context Effects Due Solely to the Combination of Explicitly Negative Labels and a Violation-Checking Context?

A different objection to positing pragmatic reasoning schemas has been raised by Jackson and Griggs (1990). They argue that the enhancement of reasoning performance in the abstract-permission selection task reported in Experiment II of Cheng and Holyoak (1985) is due to the interaction of (a) labelling the negated antecedent and consequent with the explicitly negative term "not" and (b) using a violation-checking "detective set" (Van Duyne, 1974). In that experiment, Cheng and Holyoak (1985, p. 403) respectively labeled the two negated cases in the abstract-permission task "has not taken action A" and "has not fulfilled precondition P" (for the rule "If one is to take action 'A', then one must first satisfy precondition 'P' "). To match these explicit negatives, they labelled the analogous cases in the arbitrary version "B (i.e., not A)" and "7 (i.e., not 4)" (for the rule "If a card has an 'A' on one side, then it must have a '4' on the other side"). ("B" and "7" in the above labels are in the implicitly negative form used in all selection problems previous to Cheng & Holyoak's study.) Jackson and Griggs (1990) presented evidence to show that without either of the two proposed components, selection performance was not enhanced.

We will not discuss in any detail Jackson and Grigg's findings and their critique of Cheng and Holyoak (see Kroger, Cheng, & Holyoak, in preparation). We will only note the following prediction from their argument: if enhancement in performance is due to the interaction of a violation-checking context and the use of explicitly negative labels, rather than to the use of pragmatic inferential rules, then embedding an arbitrary selection task in a detective-set context and labelling the relevant cases using explicit negatives should lead to an enhancement in performance. To our knowledge, results supporting this prediction have never been reported. To the contrary, experiments that may be considered approximations of such a test, reported in Jackson and Griggs (1990, Experiment III) and Cheng and Holyoak (1985, Experiment II), have failed to find any enhancement for an arbitrary task that carried explicit negative labels and required violation checking.

The present results further undercut Jackson and Griggs' objection to the thesis of pragmatic reasoning schemas. Our causal and arbitrary materials in the three experiments reported above uniformly used explicitly negative labels (both versions used only such labels for the negated antecedent and consequent) and a hypothesis-testing (rather than violation-checking) context. Nonetheless, reasoning judgments differed across the two conditions.

Do Pragmatic Rules Complement Natural-Logic Rules, but Not Override Them?

As mentioned earlier, Braine and O'Brien (1991) have proposed a strictly complementary relation between natural-logic rules and pragmatic inferential rules. In contrast, Cheng et al. (1986) proposed a priority relation between the two kinds of rules, with pragmatic rules taking precedence in case of conflict. The present results support a priority relation, with the pragmatic causal rules apparently overriding one of the natural rules proposed for *if*—the schema for conditional proof (e.g., Braine, 1978; Braine & O'Brien, 1991; Johnson-Laird, 1975; Rips, 1983). This schema implies one of the classical paradoxes of implication: For any propositions *p* and *q,* given *q,* one can infer *if p then q.* In other words, a true proposition is implied by anything.

Recall that in the contingency question of our experiment subjects were asked to consider a situation in which the consequent of a strictly conditional law is always true, regardless of the status of the antecedent. For such a situation, the schema for conditional proof predicts that the conditional can be asserted (regardless of context). Under the context of evaluating the causal law, "If Cause A occurs, then it always produces Event B", subjects were asked whether "A is a cause of B" can be true in the above situation. Most subjects answered "no". In the corresponding arbitrary condition, subjects rarely answered "no" when asked whether "If there is an A, then there is a B" can be true under the analogous situation. Our contingency question was constructed as a test of the hypothesis that "A is a cause of B" is interpreted as equivalent to "If A then B" when the condition relations underlying the two statements are equated. Even though that question was not a direct test of the relation between context and form, responses to that question suggest that the above paradox of implication would be considered anomalous when cast in a causal context, under which causal inferential rules appear to override the schema for conditional proof. Thus, in addition to providing evidence for a pragmatic constraint for causal relations, our results also shed light on the relation between natural-logic rules and pragmatic rules.

FOOTNOTES

[1]The concept of contingency can be generalized to causes that involve multiple factors (e.g., see Cheng & Novick, 1990, 1992).

[2]By noting the importance of the concept of contingency in causal reasoning, we do not wish to imply that we think contingency per se defines causality. Our argument does not require such an assumption; it only requires that contingency is an essential component of the concept of causality.

[3]Three subjects in the causal condition had taken a logic course, 2 had taken a course that included a discussion of causality, and 2 were not native speakers of English. The corresponding numbers in the arbitrary condition were 2, 3, and 1. No subjects were excluded from the reported analyses because the pattern of results did not change when the above subjects were excluded.

[4]It might be argued that the context effects explained by the permission and obligation schemas could be alternatively explained by rules in modal logics, which extend classical propositional logic by including the notions of possibility and necessity. For two reasons we think this is unlikely. First, the materials in all three experiments reported in Cheng and Holyoak (1985) matched the modal terms across their permission and arbitrary materials. Yet, a consistent difference in reasoning performance between the two versions was found. Second, we (Cheng & Holyoak, 1985; Cheng et al., 1986) found that the primary effect of the schema-evoking materials in their experiments was to increase the use of a rule that corresponds to modus tollens. Because modus tollens is part of classical propositional logic rather than part of a modal-logic extension, context effects on the use of tollens is not readily explained by the extension.

REFERENCES

Alloy, L. B., & Abramson, L. Y. (1979). Judgment of contingency in depressed and nondepressed students: Sadder but wiser? *Journal of Experimental Psychology: General, 108,* 441–485.

Alloy, L. B., & Tabachnik, N. (1984). Assessment of covariation by humans and animals: The joint influence of prior expectations and current situational information. *Psychological Review, 91,* 112–149.

Anderson, A. R., & Belnap, N. D., Jr. (1975). *Entailment* (Vol. 1). Princeton, NJ: Princeton University Press.

Anderson, J. R. (1983). *The architecture of cognition.* Cambridge, MA: Harvard University Press.

Bindra, D., Clarke, A. K., & Shultz, T. R. (1980). Understanding predictive relations of necessity and sufficiency in formally equivalent "causal" and "logical" problems. *Journal of Experimental Psychology: General, 109,* 422–443.

Braine, M. D. S. (1978). On the relation between the natural logic of reasoning and standard logic. *Psychological Review, 85,* 1–21.

Braine, M. D. S., & O'Brien, D. P. (1991). A theory of *if:* A lexical entry, reasoning program, and pragmatic principles. *Psychological Review, 98,* 182–203.

Braine, M. D. S., Reiser, B. J., & Rumain, B. (1984). Some empirical justification for a theory of natural propositional logic. In G. H. Bower (Ed.), *The psychology of learning and motivation* (Vol. 18, pp. 313–371). New York: Academic Press.

Bullock, M., Gelman, R., & Baillargeon, R. (1982). The development of causal reasoning. In W. J. Friedman (Ed.), *The developmental psychology of time* (pp. 209–254). Orlando, FL: Academic Press.

Cheng, P. W., & Holyoak, K. J. (1985). Pragmatic reasoning schemas. *Cognitive Psychology, 17,* 391–416.

Cheng, P. W., Holyoak, K. J., Nisbett, R. E., & Oliver, L. M. (1986). Pragmatic versus syntactic approaches to training deductive reasoning. *Cognitive Psychology, 18,* 293–328.

Cheng, P. W., & Holyoak, K. J. (1989). On the natural selection of reasoning theories. *Cognition, 33,* 285–313.

Cheng, P. W., & Novick, L. R. (1990). A probabilistic contrast model of causal induction. *Journal of Personality and Social Psychology, 58,* 545–567.

Cheng, P. W., & Novick, L. R. (1991). Causes versus enabling conditions. *Cognition, 40,* 83–120.

Cheng, P. W., & Novick, L. R. (1992). Covariation in natural causal induction. *Psychological Review, 99.*

Copi, I. M. (1961). *Introduction to logic.* New York: Macmillan.

Cummins, D., Lubart, T., Alksnis, O., & Rist, R. (1991). Conditional reasoning and causation. *Memory & Cognition, 19,* 274–282.

Evans, J. St. B. T. (1982). *The psychology of deductive reasoning.* London: Routledge and Kegan Paul.

Evans, J. St. B. T. (1989). *Bias in human reasoning: Causes and consequences.* Hillsdale, NJ: Lawrence Erlbaum Associates.

Fitch, F. B. (1952). *Symbolic logic: An introduction.* New York: Ronald.

Henle, M. (1962). On the relation between logic and thinking. *Psychological Review, 69,* 366–378.

Holland, J., Holyoak, K. J., Nisbett, R. E., & Thagard, P. (1986). *Induction: Processes of inference, learning, and discovery.* Cambridge, MA: Bradford Books/MIT Press.

Humphreys, W. (1968). *Anomalies and Scientific Theories.* San Francisco: Cooper, Freeman.

Jackson, S., & Griggs, R. (1990). The elusive pragmatic reasoning schemas effect. *Quarterly Journal of Experimental Psychology, 42A,* 353–373.

Jenkins, H., & Ward, W. (1965). Judgment of contingency between responses and outcomes. *Psychological Monographs, 79,* 1–17.

Johnson-Laird, P. N. (1975). Models of deduction. In Falmagne, R. J. (Ed.), *Reasoning: Representation and process in children and adults.* Hillsdale, NJ: Erlbaum.

Johnson-Laird, P. N., Legrenzi, P., & Legrenzi, M. S. (1972). Reasoning and a sense of reality. *British Journal of Psychology, 63,* 395–400.

Kelley, H. H. (1967). Attribution theory in social psychology. In D. Levine (Ed.), *Nebraska symposium on motivation, 15,* (pp. 192–238). Lincoln: University of Nebraska Press.

Kelley, H. H. (1973). The processes of causal attribution. *American Psychologist, 28,* 107–128.

Klayman, J., & Ha, Y. (1987). Confirmation, disconfirmation, and information in hypothesis testing. *Psychological Review, 94,* 211–228.

Kroger, J., Cheng, P. W., & Holyoak, K. J. (in preparation). Are there really pragmatic reasoning schemas? University of California, Los Angeles.

Mackie, J. L. (1974). *The cement of the universe: A study of causation.* Oxford, England: Clarendon Press.

Macnamara, J. (1986). *A border dispute: The place of logic in psychology.* Cambridge, MA: Bradford Books, MIT Press.

McArthur, L. (1972). The how and what of why: Some determinants and consequences of causal attribution. *Journal of Personality and Social Psychology, 22,* 171–193.

Mill, J. S. (1973). A system of logic ratiocinative and inductive (8th ed.). In J. M. Robson (Ed.), *Collected works of John Stuart Mill* (Vols. 7 & 8). Toronto, Canada: University of Toronto Press. (Original work published 1843).

Nagel, E. (1961). *The structure of science.* New York: Harcourt, Brace & World.

Neches, R., Langley, P., & Klahr, D. (1987). Learning, development, and production systems. In D. Klahr, P. Langley, & R. Neches (Eds.), *Production system models of learning and development.* Cambridge, MA: MIT Press.

Nisbett, R. E., Fong, Lehman, & Cheng, P. W. (1987). Teaching reasoning. *Science, 238,* 625–631.

Osherson, D. N. (1975). *Logical abilities in children* (Vol. 3). Hillsdale, NJ: Erlbaum.

Piaget, J. (1974). *Understanding causality.* New York: Norton.

Rescorla, R. A. (1968). Probability of shock in the presence and absence of CS in fear conditioning. *Journal of Comparative and Physiological Psychology, 66,* 1–5.

Rips, L. J. (1983). Cognitive processes in propositional reasoning. *Psychological Review, 90,* 38–71.

Rips, L. J., & Marcus, S. L. (1977). Suppositions and the analysis of conditional sentences. In M. A. Just & P. A. Carpenter (Eds.), *Cognitive processes in comprehension.* Hillsdale, NJ: Erlbaum.

Rumain, B., Connell, J., & Braine, M. D. S. (1983). Conversational comprehension processes are responsible for reasoning fallacies in children as well as adults: *If* is not the biconditional. *Developmental Psychology, 19,* 471–481.

Salmon, L. (1984). *An introduction to logic and critical thinking.* New York: Harcourt Brace Jovanovich.

Shultz, T. R., Butkowsky, I. (1977). Young children's use of the scheme for multiple sufficient causes in the attribution of real and hypothetical behavior. *Child Development, 48,* 464–469.

Skyrms, B. (1986). *Choice and chance: An introduction to inductive logic* (3rd Edition). Belmont: Wadsworth.

Smith, E. E., Langston, C., & Nisbett, R. E. (1992). The case for rules in reasoning. *Cognitive Science, 16,* 1–40.

Thompson, V. (1989). Conditional reasoning: The necessary and sufficient conditions. Unpublished manuscript, University of Western Ontario.

Tversky, A., & Kahneman, D. (1980). Causal schemas in judgments under uncertainty. In M.

Fishbein (Ed.), *Progress in social psychology*. Hillsdale, NJ: Erlbaum.

von Wright, G. H. (1975). On the logic and epistemology of the causal relation. In E. Sosa (Ed.), *Causation and conditionals*. London: Oxford University Press.

Wason, P. C. (1966). Reasoning. In B. M. Foss (Ed.), *New horizons in psychology*. Harmondsworth, England: Penguin.

Wason, P. C., & Johnson-Laird, P. N. (1972). *Psychology of reasoning*. Cambridge, MA: Harvard University Press.

9 Tools of the Trade: Deductive Schemas Taught in Psychology and Philosophy

Michael W. Morris
Stanford University

Richard E. Nisbett
University of Michigan

Since antiquity, educators have pondered the relationship between academic learning and everyday reasoning. Most educators have agreed that academic disciplines establish abstract, general rules for deducing new conclusions from established principles. Educators have disagreed on two questions: (1) Do similar general rules guide everyday, non-academic deduction? (2) Can everyday deduction be improved by training in academic disciplines?

THREE VIEWS OF DEDUCTION

Formal View

Plato's doctrine of formal discipline answered both of these questions in the affirmative. His curriculum for the philosophers who would rule the Republic prescribed years of academic training in geometry, arithmetic, astronomy, and music to train their minds for reasoning about ethical and practical problems. Despite his faith in abstract forms of knowledge over the concrete data of the senses, Plato also recognized the risks in applying abstract rules to concrete problems. In the *Republic*, he explains why "one who comes from the contemplation of divine things to the miseries of human life should appear awkward and ridiculous . . ." (1948, p. 231). In the *Theatetus,* he explains that the abstract reasoning philosophy teaches can bring one's downfall in the practical world:

> /T/he clever Thracian handmaid said . . . about Thales, when he fell into a well as he was looking up at the stars . . . /that/ he was so eager to know what was going on in heaven that he could not see what was before his feet. This is a jest which is equally applicable to all philosophers (1949, p. 38).

Plato's student, Aristotle, proposed the first logic–categorical syllogisms. His goal was to identify the valid forms of deduction in order to teach students to argue coherently. Until the 20th century, philosophers viewed syllogisms as the "rules of thought" (e.g., Boole, 1854), and they were central to standard curricula (Mann, 1979). In the 20th century, propositional logic has replaced Aristotle's as the system most widely used and studied, and its curricular role is marginal. Frege, Whitehead, and Russell developed this abstract, formally powerful system to describe the logical underpinning of mathematics (c.f., Haack, 1975). Yet Piaget adopted it as a model of deduction; he took the view that "reasoning is nothing more than the propositional calculus itself" (Inhelder & Piaget, 1958, p. 305).

Against this view, however, stand empirical findings that typical college students do not reason in accord with the rules of standard propositional logic (reviews by Evans, 1982, 1990). A crucial finding was Wason's (1966) demonstration of the great difficulty people face in solving problems requiring application of the material conditional. In Wason's task subjects have to check whether a conditional rule, such as "*If there is a vowel on one side of a card, then there is an even number on the other side,*" is violated in a set of four cards, which might show an "A," a "B," a "4," and a "7." Selecting the relevant cards requires recognizing four implications of the conditional: one must turn over the A card to check for an even number *(modus ponens),* one must turn over the 7 card to check that there is not a vowel *(modus tollens),* one need not turn over the 4 card (the fallacy of affirming the consequent), and one need not turn over the B card (the fallacy of denying the antecedent). The majority of subjects do apply *modus ponens;* however, only 10–20% of subjects apply *modus tollens.* Subjects show similar difficulty recognizing the implications of a biconditional rule, such as "*If and only if there is a vowel on one side of the card, then there is an even number on the other side,*" which requires turning over all four cards. Partly in response to this evidence, recent proponents of the syntactic view have proposed that deduction follows a *natural* logic, constituted of those syntactic rules that people untutored in standard propositional logic naturally use (e.g., Braine, 1978; Rips, 1983). Once again, however, empirical evidence has been raised to show that subjects' performance does not show the patterns predicted by proposed natural logics (Johnson-Laird, 1983, chap. 2).

Content View

Although subjects perform poorly on the original Wason problem, they perform quite well on a formally equivalent problem with content familiar to them from direct experience, such as the drinking-age law. Over 70% of subjects given the rule "*If a person is drinking a beer, then the person must be over 19"* correctly selected the "person drinking beer" card to check the person's age and correctly selected the "person 18 years old" card to check the person's drink (Griggs & Cox, 1982). Hence, some have proposed that everyday deduction is guided by domain-specific content rules or perhaps by simple memory of examples and counterexamples (e.g., Griggs & Cox, 1982; Manktelow & Evans, 1979).

Pragmatic View

Recent researchers have identified deduction rules at a level of generality in between formal and content rules. These psychologists (Cheng & Holyoak, 1985; Cheng, Holyoak, Nisbett, & Oliver, 1986) argue that *pragmatic reasoning schemas* guide much of people's everyday deduction. These researchers examined the Wason problems with everyday content on which subjects performed particularly well and noticed that the rules involved relationships of permission, obligation, and causation. They argued that the high performance on these problems comes not from a familiarity with the content domain but rather a familiarity with domain-independent pragmatic schemas. These schemas are structured around relationships of practical relevance to social and physical problem solving. Although pragmatic schemas can be applied across content domains, they are restricted in application to certain qualities of relationship (e.g., permission) between certain kinds of entities (e.g., actions). Proponents of the schema view of deduction grant that content knowledge may influence reasoning in familiar domains and that people may use propositional rules when no schema can be applied (c.f., Rips & Conrad, 1983), but maintain that for problems interpretable in terms of pragmatic schemas, deduction is primarily schema-based. Moreover, proponents claim that training in the use of schemas or training in academic disciplines based on these schemas improves deduction whereas training in formal, propositional rules does not (Cheng, Holyoak, Nisbett & Oliver, 1986).

Two systems of pragmatic reasoning schemas that can be compared to propositional logic are *contractual schemas* and *causal schemas*. Cheng and Holyoak (1985) identified contractual schemas that people use to solve deductive problems involving obligation and permission. Situations involving obligation are those in which some action A *must be taken if* some precondition B is satisfied. Situations involving permission are those in which some action A *may be taken only if* some precondition B is satisfied. Unlike logic which simply relates two propositions, contractual schemas relate a precondition with an action. The obligation schema allows inference from preconditions to actions (if precondition, then action) and the permission schema allows inference from actions to preconditions (if action, then precondition). Some contracts involve both permission and obligation (if and only if precondition then action).

Kelley (1972, 1973) proposed that people form attributions for behaviors based on causal schemas, which specify the implications of necessary or sufficient causes. We propose that deduction is guided by similar schemas for the implications of causal relationships, which differ depending on whether the cause-effect relationship is necessary, sufficient, both, or neither. Sufficiency allows inference from cause to effect, whereas necessity allows inference from effect to cause. However, causal schemas are more restricted than formal necessary and sufficient conditions; the effect has to temporally succeed and be contingent on the cause; hence, application of causal schemas is determined by temporality (Kahneman & Tversky, 1980) and contingency (Cheng & Nisbett, 1992).

Table 9.1 shows correspondences between three systems: propositional logic, contractual schemas, and causal schemas. At the strongest level of relationship (A ↔ B), the arrow of implication runs in both directions. This level is represented by the logical biconditional, by contracts of permission and obligation, and by causation that is necessary and sufficient. At the next level, the arrow of implication only runs in one direction. For obligation contracts and sufficient causation, this implication is from earlier to later events (A → B). For permission contracts and necessary causation, this implication runs from later events to preceding events (A ← B). The logical conditional applies without temporal restriction, so it encompasses both these possibilities. At the weakest level of relationship (A − B), no deterministic implications can be drawn. This is the level of non-necessary and non-sufficient causation.

The implicational structure of these three rule systems can be compared in greater detail. Recall the four implications of the material conditional that were required to successfully solve the selection task: *modus ponens,*

TABLE 9.1
Deductive Rule Systems

Relationship	Formal View	Pragmatic View	
	Propositional Logic	Contractual Schemas	Causal Schemas
if and only if A, then B (A ↔ B)	Biconditional	Permission and Obligation	Necessary and Sufficient
if A, then B (A → B)	Material Conditional	Obligation	Non-Necessary but Sufficient
if B, then A (A ← B)[a]	Material Conditional	Permission	Necessary but Non-Sufficient
A is associated with B (A − B)			Non-Necessary and Non-Sufficient

[a]Arrows represent the direction of deduction or implication. For pragmatic schemas, unlike logic, this arrow has a temporal interpretation. In schemas for obligation or sufficient causation, the arrow of implication runs with the arrow of time from present conditions to future events. In schemas for permission or necessary causation, the arrow of implication runs counter to the arrow of time, from present events to past conditions.

modus tollens, denial of antecedent fallacy, and affirmation of consequent fallacy. Table 9.2 expresses these implications (left column) and the parallel implications of the Permission Contract Schema (middle column) and the Sufficient Causation Schema (right column). The isomorphism between these three inference rules means that they would guide a person to check the same kind of evidence to test whether a material conditional rule, a permission-contract rule, or a sufficient-causation rule is violated. However, this does not mean the formal and pragmatic models of reasoning predict the same reasoning performance; the formal rule would govern a broader scope of problems. It would be activated by a conditional containing any sort of propositions (even arbitrary ones), whereas a pragmatic schema would be activated by only a small subset of conditionals—those that describe a particular pragmatic relationship.

The primary evidence for contractual schemas comes from experiments showing that subjects perform well on Wason problems based on contractual rules, even if abstract and unfamiliar. Cheng and Holyoak (1985)

TABLE 9.2
Mapping of Three Inference Rules and Their Implications for Evidence Checking

Material Conditional	Permission Contract	Sufficient Causation
If A, then B ($A \rightarrow B$)	If one takes action A, one must meet precondition B.	If cause A is present, then effect B always occurs.
modus ponens $A \rightarrow B$	If one takes Action A, one must meet precondition B.	If cause A is present, then effect B always occurs.
A	One takes action A.	Cause A is present.
—	—	—
B	One must meet precondition B	Effect B occurs.
modus tollens $A \rightarrow B$	If one takes action A, one must meet precondition B.	If cause A is present, then effect B always occurs.
~B	One fails to meet precondition B	Effect B does not occur.
—	—	—
~A	One must not take action A.	Cause A is not present.
denying antecedent $A \rightarrow B$	If one takes action A, one must meet precondition B.	If cause A is present, then effect B always occurs.
~A	One does not take action A.	Cause A is not present.
—	—	—
~~B~~	One may meet precondition B or may not meet precondition B.	Effect B may occur or may not occur.
affirming consequent $A \rightarrow B$	If one takes action A, one must meet precondition B.	If cause A is present, then effect B always occurs.
B	One meets precondition B.	Effect B does occur.
—	—	—
~~A~~	One may take action A or may not take action A.	Cause A may be present or may not be present.

demonstrated that subjects can solve contractual problems without relying on domain knowledge (thus ruling out the content-view interpretation for successful performance on the task). In one experiment subjects were presented the original arbitrary rule problem and also a problem based on an abstract permission rule: "*If one is to take action A, then one must first satisfy precondition P.*" About 60% of subjects solved the abstract permission problem correctly, versus only about 20% who correctly solved the arbitrary problem. This result cannot be explained by the formal view of deductive reasoning—which would predict successful performance in both conditions—nor by the content view—which would predict unsuccessful performance in both conditions. Further studies have shown that whereas training in formal logic has little effect on people's ability to solve either arbitrary or semantically meaningful versions of the Wason selection task, training in contractual schemas has a substantial effect. Cheng, Holyoak, Nisbett and Oliver (1986) found that neither an intensive training session on the nature of conditional rules nor even an entire semester-long college course in logic improved subjects' deductive performance. In contrast, Cheng *et al.* found that even brief instruction in the obligation schema improved performance.

Similar experiments have shown that performance on the Wason problem is facilitated by causal content, even when the causal rules are unfamiliar. Marcus and Rips (1979) found that subjects were much more successful at correctly solving a problem with an unfamiliar causal rule (e.g., "*If the ball rolls left, then the red light flashes*") than a problem with an unfamiliar arbitrary rule (e.g., "*If the fish is red, then it is striped*"). Again, this result cannot be explained by the formal view—which would predict successful performance in both conditions—nor by the content view—which would predict unsuccessful performance in both conditions. Rips (1983) tried to account for this result in terms of the formal view by adding specialized rules for causal conditionals to the propositional rules in his natural logic model, but, to the extent that he proposes specialized, restricted rules for important relationships, he departs from the formal view and takes the pragmatic view. To gather the same evidence for causal schemas as exists for contractual schemas, we would experimentally test whether performance is facilitated on problems with abstract causal rules and that performance is improved by training sessions in the implications of causal relationships.

However, training experiments are not the only way to investigate the effects of training in rules on reasoning. A more ecologically valid test would be to measure the deductive performance of students in actual academic programs. An ideal study would examine motivated people studying one discipline for a long period of time, not laboratory subjects put through a brief and artificial training session. Fortunately, the institution of graduate school provides an opportunity to observe just the ideal subjects. Graduate training emphasizes the discipline's methodology—its rules of inference—and, unlike undergraduate school, where subjects are exposed to many different disciplines, the narrow focus of graduate programs makes it possible to predict and measure unique patterns of improvement.

A comprehensive study of graduate education and reasoning skills was conducted by Lehman, Lempert, and Nisbett (1988), who studied the effects of two years of graduate education in several disciplines, including law, psychology, and medicine. They chose disciplines which train students in rule-based methods for thinking about particular pragmatic relationships. They hypothesized that students in a discipline would acquire pragmatic schemas based on its method and that these schemas would improve students' reasoning about problems involving the particular relationship, even in unfamiliar domains. One set of problems that they tested students on was conditional reasoning; they used Wason problems with causal, contractual, and arbitrary rules. Law students, who are drilled in the implications of legal contracts, were predicted to acquire permission and obligation schemas and, thereby, improve on these problems. Psychology students, who are taught how to reason about the implications of causal hypotheses, were predicted to acquire necessary and sufficient causation schemas and, thereby, improve on these problems. Lehman et al. found these patterns of performance gain in conditional reasoning, which provides some evidence that people acquire contractual and causal reasoning schemas.

Lehman et al. also predicted and found other distinct patterns of improved performance predicted from methods taught in various academic disciplines. For example, Lehman et al. predicted that medical students, who are trained to make diagnoses based on symptoms probabilistically related to diseases, would acquire statistical reasoning schemas. And, as predicted, they found that medical students improved in performance on statistical reasoning, even when the problems concerned domains like sports which are remotely distant from the content of medical education. In contrast, law students, who are not trained about probabilistic relationships, were predicted not to improve and did not. This pattern of findings— that students of different disciplines show distinct gains in reasoning performance—was replicated by Lehman et al. in both cross-sectional and longitudinal designs and at two different universities. This work suggests that graduate education can be treated as a natural experiment to test whether certain inference rules are acquired from education. The current studies used graduate education in this way for three purposes:

1. We provided a test comparing the pragmatic, formal, and content views of reasoning by administering conditional reasoning problems with

unfamiliar causal content to students of psychology and of philosophy. Psychology students should improve, according to the pragmatic view, due to acquisition of causal schemas. Philosophy students should improve, according to the formal view, due to acquisition of propositional rules such as *modus ponens* and *modus tollens*. According to the content view, neither group of students should improve on problems with unfamiliar content.

2. We conducted tests of various predictions about hypothesized causal reasoning schemas. We tested first- and third-year psychology students on the conditional reasoning problems used by Lehman *et al.*, as well as on causal problems with *unfamiliar* rules, and on causal problems with *abstract* rules. In short, we aimed to collect the same kinds of evidence for the use of causal schemas that exists for contractual schemas.

3. We tested the hypothesis that philosophy students acquire reasoning schemas for categorical relationships, like those governed by Aristotle's syllogisms.

STUDY 1

In our first study, we investigated whether training in the disciplines of psychology and philosophy imparts to students inference rules for conditional reasoning. Our prediction, from the pragmatic view of deduction, was that psychology students, who are trained to test causal hypotheses, would acquire abstract, domain-general rules about the implications of various causal relationships and hence would improve, whereas philosophy students would not acquire such inference rules and hence would not improve. A contrasting prediction, from the formal view of deduction, was that philosophy students, who are trained in propositional logic, would acquire propositional rules and hence improve, whereas psychology students would not acquire such rules and hence would not improve. We used Lehman *et al.*'s problem set as well as two new problem sets.

Lehman *et al.* combined causal, permission, and arbitrary problem results to look for a broad overall pattern of improvement in conditional reasoning. We wanted to replicate the overall psychologist improvement measured by Lehman *et al.*, who found a 30% improvement in their cross-sectional study and a 40% improvement in their longitudinal study. A more fine-grained pattern in the Lehman *et al.*, data (not reported in their paper) was that the psychologists' improvement occurred primarily for the causal rule problem rather than for the permission or arbitrary rule problems. We also predicted a replication of this result. Finally, because education in formal logic showed no effects in previous studies of deduction (Cheng *et al.*, 1986), we predicted that philosophy students would not improve on conditional reasoning.

The new set of problems was designed to test our hypothesis about why psychologists improve on causal reasoning—that they acquire domain-general, abstract inference rules about the implications of necessary and sufficient causation relationships. In other words, we designed tests to rule out several alternative explanations for deductive improvement. One alternative explanation for the predicted improvement of psychology students might be that they become familiar with the content of problems. Two kinds of selection problems were devised that could not be solved by drawing on familiar content knowledge: problems with rules referring to unfamiliar content (fictional chemicals, products, and diseases) and problems with rules in an abstract, contentless form.

An alternative explanation for the predicted non-improvement of philosophy students might be that they are taught not to believe in necessary or sufficient causation, so their putative errors may actually reflect a subtler, more sophisticated conception of causality than that used to score the test. To examine subjects' preconceptions about causality, the selection task procedure was altered. Instead of presenting a causal rule about unfamiliar events these problems merely presented a pair of events and asked subjects to state the causal relationship between them. Subjects were initially presented with a pair of unfamiliar events and asked to state the causal relationship between them. Their own causal hypothesis then became the rule to check against evidence in the selection task.

In sum, the new set of problems tested predictions that psychologists would improve and philosophers would not in (1) reasoning about causal relationships in unfamiliar domains, (2) reasoning about causal relationships stated with only abstract information about necessity and sufficiency, and (3) reasoning coherently from one's assumptions about a causal relationship.

Method

Subjects

Subjects were first- and third-year graduate students in psychology at the University of Michigan and students of philosophy at the University of Michigan, Brown University and the University of Chicago. All of these programs have a very low attrition rate in the first three years. In the Fall of 1987, 39 of 51 (77%) first year and 31 of 32 (97%) third year psychology students participated. Because of the relatively small size of philosophy programs, subjects were recruited at three universities for two seasons. In the Fall of 1987, the response rates were as follows: at Michigan, 6 of 7 first-year and 7 of 10 third-year students; at Brown, 5 of 6 first-year and 7 of 11 third-year students; at Chicago, 5 of 11 first-year and 9 of 20 third-year students (because the cohorts were so small, the 1987 third-year group at Brown and Chicago also included all available fourth-year students). In the Fall of 1988, the response rates were: at Michigan, 9 of 9 first-year and 5 of 7 third-year; at Brown, 5 of 5 first-year and 3 of 5 third-year; at Chicago, 6 of 8 first-year and 4 of 7 third-year students. Overall, philosophy response rates were 78% for first-year students and 58% for third-year students. These rates are lower than would be desirable. They are mainly attributable to the difficulty in scheduling convenient sessions for everyone during our short visits to the campuses. The overall response rates at Michigan, where we could schedule more sessions, were 94% for first year and 71% for third year students.

Stimulus Materials

Conditional Reasoning.   The first set of problems were Wason selection tasks, which varied in form and content, developed by Lehman et al. (1988). There were three problems that could be solved by application of the material conditional and two that could be solved by application of the biconditional. Of the conditional problems, one involved a causal relationship, one a permission relationship, and one an arbitrary relationship (like the original Wason problem). The arbitrary conditional problem, for example, presented the rule:

If a bird on this island has a purple spot underneath each wing, then it builds nests on the ground,

and then four cases pertaining to the rule:

Bird A has a purple spot underneath each wing
Bird B does not have any purple spots
Bird C nests in trees
Bird D builds nests on the ground.

Subjects were asked which cases must be checked to verify that the rule is not violated; the correct answer is the first and third.

Causal Reasoning.   The first part of this section was designed to test how well subjects could reason about causal rules concerning causal schemas to unfamiliar events. One problem was constructed corresponding to each of the four causal schemas. Each problem described a pair of unfamiliar events. The event pairs for necessary and sufficient, non-necessary but sufficient, necessary but non-sufficient, and non-necessary and non-sufficient causation, respectively, were:

A room rises in temperature to above 1500 degrees at standard pressure
A sample of the element Floridium, in the room, turns into gas

The electric current in a model toy plane falls below 5 volts
The plane stalls

The bite of the mila-mila bug
Catching Tropimydia, a newly discovered tropical disease

Inhaling paint fumes
Having a chronic respiratory disorder.

Subjects were instructed to form their best guess of the causal relationship that exists between the pair of events, based on their general knowledge of the world. They were asked to state this relationship as accurately as possible on the blank lines provided. After stating the relationship, subjects performed two tasks. The first task required that subjects consider four reliable cases of evidence and indicate whether or not they disprove the causal relationship. For example, in the necessary and non-sufficient problem, subjects were presented with these cases:

Eric was bitten by a mila-mila bug and caught tropimydia
Trent was bitten by a mila-mila bug and did not catch tropimydia
Betty was not bitten by a mila-mila bug and caught tropimydia
Keith was not bitten by a mila-mila bug and did not catch tropimydia.

The second task was similar. Subjects were presented half of the information about four cases pertinent to the relationship and asked to indicate whether or not each case could possibly disprove the relationship, were information about the other event provided. For example:

Matthew was bitten by a mila-mila bug,
Cindy was not bitten by a mila-mila bug
Danny has tropimydia
Carrie does not have tropimydia.

This second task is analogous to the original Wason card selection task, in which subjects only saw one side of each card; the first task is analogous to a card selection task in which subjects would see both sides of the card. For both tasks, the correct pattern of responses differed for each problem, since each causal schema has distinct implications.

After the four problems described above, subjects were explicitly queried about whether they assumed sufficient and/or necessary causation in the causal relationships they stated for each problem. For example, they were asked to indicate which of the following assumptions they made:

The bite of the mila-mila bug *always* causes tropimydia
The bite of the mila-mila bug *sometimes* causes tropimydia.

Then, which of these assumptions they made:

In order tó catch tropimydia, one must *necessarily* be bitten by the mila-mila bug

It is *possible* to catch tropimydia without being bitten by the mila-mila bug

Questions about assumptions were positioned after all four problems so as not to bias the way subjects stated their hypotheses. These questions allowed scoring of responses according to the subjects' interpretation of the causal relationship (i.e., an analysis of *coherence* in causal reasoning).

The final part of this section was designed to test reasoning about abstract, contentless causal rules. Again, four problems were constructed corresponding to hypothesized causal schemas. In these problems, however, causal rules were stated abstractly, without a content domain.

Event A is the only cause of event B, and event A always causes event B.
Event A is one of many causes of event B, and event A always causes event B.
Event A is the only cause of event B, and event A only sometimes causes event B.
Event A is one of many causes of event B, and event A only sometimes causes event B.

The tasks were isomorphic to those in the previous section. The first task asked subjects to indicate which of the following cases of evidence could disprove the hypothesis:

Event A occurred, and event B occurred
Event A occurred, and event B did not
Event A did not occur, and event B did
Event A did not occur, and event B did not occur.

The second task gave only partial information about the cases:

Event A occurred
Event A did not occur
Event B occurred
Event B did not occur.

There was no need to query about assumptions for these problems since the causal relationship was explicitly stated. Once again, the pattern of correct responses was different for each of the four problems. For necessary and sufficient causation, all four partial cases should be checked. For non-necessary but sufficient causation, only the first and the fourth ones should be checked. For necessary but non-sufficient causation, only the second and the third case should be checked. For non-necessary and non-sufficient causation, none of the partial cases should be checked.

Procedure.   First-year psychology students were given the test during a mass orientation meeting during the first week of graduate school. Third-year psychology students were given the test in group sessions at the Institute for Social Research. Philosophy students were given the test in group sessions held in philosophy department classrooms. Subjects were told to work at their own pace and to answer the questions in order. The test took between 40 and 60 minutes to complete. Third-year psychologists and philosophers were paid $20.00 for their participation. In the Fall of 1988, philosophy subjects completed the brief study 2 test first and then the study 1 test. They were paid $25.

Results

Cohort Differences and Initial Differences

In order to determine whether there were any cohort differences in general ability or initial differences between disciplines in general ability, we compared the admissions test scores of first-year and third-year students within each discipline. The mean GRE score (average of verbal, math, and analytic sections) was computed for first-year psychology (664), third-year psychology (660), first-year philosophy (721), third-year philosophy (671). The cohort difference in philosophy is significant, $F(1, 66) = 13.136, p < .001$[1], and the initial difference between disciplines is also significant, $F(1, 74) = 19.68, p < .001$. The initial difference is untroubling, since we compare disciplines by gains in performance, not absolute levels of performance. The import of the cohort difference is that our measurements may underestimate the performance of third year philosophers relative to first year philosophers. However, we performed analyses of covariance to correct for possible distortion due to correlation with GRE scores.

Conditional Reasoning

The conditional reasoning results for psychology students perfectly replicate those of Lehman et al. (1988). Third-year psychologists ($M = 3.52$) showed 33% better performance than first-year psychologists ($M = 2.64$), $t(68) = 2.12, p < .05$. Contrastingly, the performance of third-year philosophers ($M = 3.58$) showed no gain over first-year students ($M = 3.58$). To ensure that this effect reflects more than the cohort difference, we computed the correlation between performance and GRE, $r(133) = .39, p < .001$. When this correlation is controlled for in an analysis of covariance, the pattern of results remains unchanged.[2] Third-year psychologists ($M = 3.71$) showed significantly better performance than first-year students ($M = 2.96$), $t(68) = 2.01, p < .05$, and third-year philosophers ($M = 3.62$) did not show significantly better performance than first-year students ($M = 3.18$), $t(67) = .96$.

We also analyzed results at a more fine-grained level to test that psychologists' improvement came primarily on the conditional problem involving a causal rule rather than on problems involving permission or arbitrary rules. On the *causal* problem, third-year psychologists ($M = .77$) performed significantly better than first-year psychologists ($M = .49$), $t(68) = 2.53$, $p < .025$, whereas third-year philosophers ($M = .70$) did not perform better than first-year philosophers ($M = .75$). On the *permission* problem, third-year psychologists ($M = .68$) did not perform better than first-year psychologists ($M = .73$) and third-year philosophers ($M = .91$) did not significantly improve over first-year philosophers ($M = .88$), although this may reflect a ceiling effect. On the *arbitrary* problem, third-year psychologists ($M = .52$) showed non-significant improvement over first-year psychologists ($M = .38$), $t(68) = 1.32$, $p > .15$, whereas third-year philosophers ($M = .39$) showed *no* improvement over first-year philosophers ($M = .63$), a pattern not attributable to a ceiling effect. In sum, these results suggest (1) psychologists acquire rules for reasoning about causal conditionals, (2) philosophers do not acquire rules for conditionals.

Causal Reasoning

Table 9.3 presents mean performance on the causal reasoning problems by discipline and year, combining scores from both tasks (which showed identical patterns of results). As predicted, on the unfamiliar content problems psychologists' accuracy improved, $t(68) = 3.95$, $p < .01$, and philosophers did not, $t(68) = .297$, producing an interaction of discipline by year, $F(1, 140) = 10.63$, $p < .001$. Could it be merely that philosophers learn to make different assumptions than psychologists (i.e., more cautious

TABLE 9.3
Mean Percent Accuracy in Causal Reasoning

Discipline	Problem Type		
	Unfamiliar Content	*Coherence*	*Contentless*
Psychology			
Year 1	.274	.472	.692
	(.282)	(.508)	(.715)
Year 3	.473	.617	.871
	(.480)	(.641)	(.883)
Philosophy			
Year 1	.333	.614	.882
	(.318)	(.557)	(.856)
Year 3	.321	.629	.779
	(.327)	(.636)	(.781)

Note. Parenthesized values show mean percent accuracy adjusted for GRE scores.

or skeptical), but learn to reason coherently from these assumptions? However, the coherence results show that psychologists become more consistent in their causal reasoning, $t(68) = 2.61$, $p < .05$, and philosophers did not, $t(68) = .23$.

Results with the abstract, contentless problems provide even stronger evidence for the role of causal schemas in deduction. Psychologists showed improvement, $t(68) = 3.64$, $p < .01$, and philosophers a nonsignificant decline, $t(68) = 1.91$. This interaction of academic discipline and year was highly significant, $F(1, 137) = 14.86$, $< .0001$.

To ensure that effects do not merely reflect the cohort difference, we computed the correlations between mean GRE and performance. GRE was slightly correlated with performance on the unfamiliar, content problems, $r(130) = .11$, $p > .05$, the coherence measurement, $r(130) = .32$, $p < .01$, and performance on the abstract, contentless problems, $r(130) = .24$, $p < .05$. Analyses of covariance show that, when the cohort effect is removed, the year by discipline interactions remain significant for the unfamiliar content problems, $F(1, 134) = 7.90$, $p < .01$, and the abstract, contentless problems, $F(1, 131) = 10.57$, $p < .001$.

Figure 9.1 presents a graphical representation of changes in causal reasoning by area and discipline, controlling for initial differences and cohort differences in GRE scores. As these graphics show, a critic could possibly interpret results on contentless problems as partially due to a ceiling effect, but results on unfamiliar content problems cannot be plausibly interpreted as due to a ceiling effect. The best interpretation for our findings is that psychology students learn methods of hypothesis testing

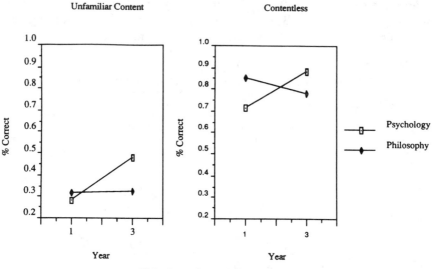

FIG. 9.1   Causal Reasoning.

that become schemas used to solve deductive problems involving causal relationships. The methods of research and analysis taught in philosophy rest on different principles and do not seem to transfer into useful rules for solving deductive problems involving causal relationships.

Discussion

We have argued that training in propositional logic does not improve the deductive performance of philosophy graduate students. Most students intuitively understand *modus ponens* prior to graduate training, hence improvement requires that they learn to use *modus tollens*, which few do. One explanation for the difficulty of *modus tollens* inferences is that they often result in knowledge that is useless because it is irrelevant to one's goals. The goal of conditional reasoning is to move from current knowledge to a goal; a typical rule might be *"If one has a headache, then one should take aspirin."* Given this rule, *modus ponens* generates the inference *"I should take aspirin"* from the premise *"I have a headache,"* which moves toward the goal of headache relief. *Modus tollens* generates the inference *"I do not have a headache"* from the premise *"It is not the case that I should take aspirin,"* which does not move toward a goal (c.f., Cheng & Holyoak, 1985).

Another explanation for the lack of deductive improvement from training in propositional logic may be its sheer abstractness. Research on both inductive and deductive reasoning (Nisbett, Fong, Lehman, & Cheng, 1987) has concluded that very abstract inferential rules can only be applied in problem solving when there are clear cues to when rules are applicable. For example, people can more easily apply inductive statistical rules, like the Law of Large Numbers, to domains in which randomness is salient, such as gambling, than to domains where it is not, such as scholastic achievement. *Modus ponens* and *modus tollens* apply to conditionals with propositional content. Although conditionals are cued by the words "if . . . then," there is no salient cue to distinguish conditionals with propositional content from conditionals with non-truth-functional content, such as probabilistic, deontic, alethic, or future-contingent statements. In short, philosophers do not acquire propositional inference rules because (1) *modus tollens* does not generate information useful in argument or problem-solving and (2) propositional rules are highly abstract and not well cued by the problems to which they apply.

Our pragmatic interpretation implies that people for whom *modus tollens* is useful would develop an inference rule for it. Consistent with this is Jackson and Griggs' (1986) finding that mathematics students correctly make this inference on Wason problems more than students of computer science or engineering. Mathematics students, who rely on proof by contradiction ("If p were the case, q would have to be the case . . . Not q, therefore not p") find *modus tollens* useful in moving toward the goal of proving a theorem. Computer scientists, who are trained to solve problems not prove theorems, find *modus tollens* provides unhelpful information.

Our interpretation also implies that philosophers would develop reasoning schemas for logical rules which are more useful, less abstract, and more clearly cued than propositional logic. According to our view, psychologists would not develop schemas for these logical rules because psychologists are not trained in logic. Our second study investigated this.

STUDY 2

Philosophers do not acquire general inference rules from their training in propositional logic, but propositional logic is not the only tool of the philosopher's trade. Do they acquire other inference rules? That philosophers acquire from their training a distinctive form of reasoning, a cast of mind, a *deformation professionelle*, is widely attested to both by philosophers and those around them. What inferential tool gives philosophers their ability to spontaneously draw valid conclusions from complicated premises, even when reasoning about domains other than philosophy? Perhaps, the logic of categorical syllogisms, which in the 20th century has fallen into the shadow of the more formally powerful propositional logic, is a logic from which philosophers do acquire schemas.

Categorical logic is based on statements with the quantifiers *some, all, no,* and *some-not* (e.g., "Some A are B," "All A are B," "No A are B," "Some A are not B"). Aristotle's syllogisms consist of two premises and a conclusion inter-relating categories from the two premises. Aristotle proposed a system of 64 syllogisms but wider systems have since been developed, and there are also general rules dictating the conclusions that can be derived from various kinds of premises, such as: (1) If both premises are *particular* (quantified by "some"), nothing can be derived, (2) If both premises are *negative* (quantified by "no" or "some-not"), nothing can be derived, (3) If one premise is *negative*, the conclusion cannot be *positive* (quantified by "all" or "some"), and so on. Recent research provides evidence that people use such rules. Galotti, Baron, and Sabini (1986) found that subjects' performance was facilitated on syllogism problems susceptible to these rules and that subjects stated intuitive versions of these rules when thinking aloud as they reasoned. In a second study they found that subjects who had taken a logic course showed enhanced accuracy and speed on problems governed by syllogistic rules; this result can be contrasted with the findings of Cheng *et al.* (1986) who found such subjects did not show improved performance on problems governed by propositional rules.

We would predict that philosophers develop reasoning schemas for categorical syllogisms because (1) syllogisms generate inferences which are very useful in philosophical argument, and (2) syllogistic inference rules are not exceedingly abstract and are saliently cued by the problems they govern. First, the pragmatic value of syllogistic reasoning in academics and everyday life has been convincingly argued (see Johnson Laird and Bara, 1984) but its value in philosophy, specifically, seems particularly clear. Unlike in science where victories are won by accounting for variance, in philosophy they are won by valid arguments to strong conclusions; the difference between the conclusions "All A are B" and "Some A are B" can make or break a thesis. Second, rules related to categorical syllogisms are not exceedingly abstract. One way to see that categorical rules are less abstract than propositional rules is that less is left to variables (c.f., Smith, Langston, & Nisbett, 1992): in propositional logic, variables (the A and B in "If A then B") are filled by entire sentences; in categorical logic, variables (the A and B in "All A are B") are filled by nouns. Moreover, there are clear lexical cues to whether a categorical statement is *particular* ("some"), *universal* ("all"), *negative* ("no" or "not"), so it is easy to apply syllogistic rules to problems.

Research on syllogistic reasoning has used problems in which subjects are given premises and asked to derive the conclusion. Generally, results show that some of the 64 classical syllogisms are solved by over 90% of subjects and others by fewer than 10%; there has been a long debate about how best to account for errors (Begg & Denny, 1969; Chapman & Chapman, 1959; Cesaro & Provitera, 1971; Henle, 1962; Wilkins, 1928; Woodworth & Sells, 1935). One major source of difficulty is the syllogism's *figure*, defined as the degree to which the order of terms in premises matches that in the conclusion (Johnson-Laird & Steedman, 1978). Subjects err on complex figures. Compare, for example, the ease of comprehending a simple figure ("Some A are B," "All B are C," "Thus, some A are C") and a complex figure ("No A are B," "All B are C," "Thus, some C are not A"). Another source of difficulty is content that "invites" invalid inferences (Bucci, 1975). Subjects tend to endorse conclusions that are true, believable, or connoted by premises even when not implied (c.f., Johnson-Laird & Oakhill, 1989). In order to measure possible improvement from graduate education we used syllogism problems with both of these sources of difficulty. We predicted that philosophy students, who are trained in logic and rely on categorical arguments, would acquire syllogistic schemas and hence improve.

An alternative to the rule-based view of deduction described so far would be a heuristic view. Deductive arguments can be evaluated by the simple criterion of whether or not there are any counterexamples. Everyday deduction may reflect efficient heuristics to guide the search for counter-examples rather than inference rules that yield correct conclusions. People who recognize the relevance of counterexamples, in principle, often fail to search for them correctly (Oakhill & Johnson-Laird, 1985). Deftness at raising counterexamples does not require extensive knowledge as much as skill at searching the implications of one's knowledge. For students of philosophy, the counterexample is the primary tool for casting doubt on rival arguments. Students of psychology, contrastingly, learn to critique experimental and statistical methods and rarely rely on counterexamples to disprove a thesis. Hence, with a second problem-set we investigated whether philosophers acquire heuristics that guide the search for counterexamples. We predict that psychologists would not develop such heuristics. As a test for counterexample heuristics in the second part of Study 2, we presented flawed-argument problems and requested subjects to generate counter-examples for them.

Method

Subjects

Subjects were first- and third-year graduate students in psychology at the University of Michigan and students of philosophy at the University of Michigan, Brown University, and the University of Chicago, in the Fall of 1988. 34 of 38 (89%) first-year psychology students participated and 18 of 25 (72%) third-year students participated. The overall response rates for philosophy students were (91%) for first-year and (63%) for third-year. Specifically, at Michigan, 9 of 9 first-year and 5 of 7 third-year students participated; at Brown, 5 of 5 first-year and 3 of 5 third-year students participated, at Chicago, 6 of 8 first-year and 4 of 7 third-year students participated.

Stimulus Materials

Syllogistic Reasoning.   The first section tested ability to complete syllogistic arguments. Subjects were instructed to draw the strongest valid inference to complete the conclusion, even if merely by re-stating a premise, and were given an example. Problems with difficult figures were adapted from Johnson-Laird & Bara (1982). For example, the most figurally complex problem was the following:

Some of the accountants are not chemists.
All of the beekeepers are artists.
None of the chemists are beekeepers.
_____

Some of the artists _____

The correct answer was that "Some of the artists are not chemists." Problems with invited inferences were adapted from Bucci (1975):

No oranges are apples.
No lemons are oranges.
_____

No lemons _____

The strongest implication for this problems was that "No lemons are oranges." There were three problems altogether. Interspersed with these were two filler problems not governed by syllogistic inference rules.

Raising Counterexamples.   These problems were designed to measure the ability to produce a counterexample to a flawed argument. Instructions explained that a counterexample "describes a state of affairs in which the *premises* of the argument are all true but the *conclusion* is false." The state of affairs should be "physically possible" and "plausible" but "need not be factual." Two of the four problems primarily required detecting the flaw in the logical structure. An example is the following argument:

If the incumbent is telling the truth, then the challenger is lying.
If the challenger is telling the truth, the incumbent is lying.
_____

We conclude that the incumbent is telling the truth.

The counterexample, here, was that both candidates could be lying. For the other two problems, the flaw in the argument could be discovered by thinking about relationships in the world. One of these problems was the following:

In the year 1995, the US president marries while in office.
_____

In the year 1995, the US gains a new First Lady.

Some acceptable counterexamples, here, were that the president is a woman, a male homosexual, a male re-marrying his ex-wife, or a male marrying the wife of the former president.

Procedure.   First-year psychology students were given the test during a mass orientation meeting during the first week of graduate school. Third-year psychology students were given the test in group sessions at the Institute for Social Research. Philosophy students were given the test in group sessions held in philosophy department classrooms. Subjects were told to work at their own pace and to answer the questions in order. First-year psychologists were paid $10.00 to complete the test booklet, which took between 10 and 30 minutes. Third-year psychologists and philosophers were paid $25.00 to complete a booklet containing these problems followed by problems from study 1, which took between 40 and 90 minutes. The philosophers who participated in this study also were subjects in study 1.

Results

Cohort and Initial Differences

In order to determine whether there were any cohort differences in general ability or initial differences between disciplines in general ability, we compared the admissions test scores of first-year and third-year students within each discipline. The mean GRE score (average of verbal, math, and analytic sections) were calculated for the first-year psychology (677), third-year psychology (660), first-year philosophy (722), third-year philosophy (687) samples. The cohort difference in philosophy is marginally significant, $F(1,30) = 3.98$, p < .06, and the initial difference between disciplines is significant, $F(1,52) = 8.28$, p < .01. Since we are comparing gains in performance, not absolute levels, the initial difference does not affect our scores. The cohort difference puts our measurements at risk of underestimating the performance of third-year philosophers to first-year philosophers. Importantly, this cohort difference works *against* the predicted effect in this study rather than working for it, as in Study 1.

Syllogistic Reasoning

Table 9.4 presents mean performance on the two types of problems by discipline and year. As predicted, philosophers improved on syllogistic inference problems, $t(30) = 1.97$, $p < .06$. Psychologists became trivially worse, $t(50) = 1.06$. There was a significant interaction of discipline and year, $F(1,80) = 4.83$, $p < .05$. Since scoring the counterexamples problems required adjudicating the acceptability of counterexamples, the first author and a philosopher independently scored the answer forms. The judges agreed on 93.6% of their ratings and reconciled all of the disagreements through discussion. Although effects for the counterexample problems were in the expected directions, they fell short of significance. Scores for syllogistic reasoning, $r(82) = .21$, $p < .05$, and for raising counterexamples, $r(82) = .26$, $p < .05$, were slightly correlated with GRE scores.

TABLE 9.4
Mean Percent Accuracy in Argument Reasoning

Discipline	Problem Type	
	Syllogism	Counterexample
Psychology		
Year 1	.569	.463
	(.576)	(.470)
Year 3	.481	.431
	(.533)	(.462)
Philosophy		
Year 1	.633	.688
	(.600)	(.656)
Year 3	.833	.750
	(.832)	(.748)

Note. Parenthesized values show mean percent accuracy adjusted for GRE scores.

Analyses of covariance still revealed a significant interaction of year and discipline for syllogistic reasoning, $F(1,79) = 4.64, p < .05$. The changes in performance by year and discipline, adjusted for GRE scores, are presented graphically in Figure 9.2. These results indicate that there are distinct gains in deductive performance between the first and third year of philosophy graduate programs that are not attained by students of psychology. The fact

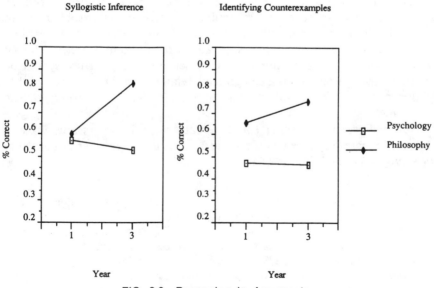

FIG. 9.2   Reasoning in Arguments.

that results in Study 1 and Study 2 are in opposite directions makes it difficult to attribute findings to anything but the differential academic training of psychologists and philosophers. Any other difference between the groups (e.g., attrition rates, motivation level, etc.) would produce the same pattern of results in both studies.

GENERAL DISCUSSION

The current studies compared the gains in reasoning performance shown by graduate students of psychology and philosophy. Our findings shed light on three issues about which we tested predictions. First, we tested contrasting predictions about whether psychologists or philosophers would improve in conditional reasoning. We found that psychologists improved on a variety of conditional reasoning problems (those involving causal relationships) and that philosophers do not improve. Thus, our results support a view of conditional reasoning as guided by schemas for pragmatic relationships, such as causal schemas, rather than a view of conditional reasoning as guided by the more abstract and general propositional rules. Second, we tested detailed predictions about causal reasoning to extend the evidence that people use causal schemas based on necessity and sufficiency. We found that psychologists' academic training about causality improved their ability to solve causal problems with unfamiliar rules and problems with abstract rules. It is hard to explain these effects other than in terms of an abstract, domain-general causal schema. Third, we have extended the evidence that people use syllogistic schemas to reason about categorical relationships by showing that philosophers' academic training improves their ability to solve syllogistic problems.

Our findings that training for different academic professions imparts distinctive reasoning schemas is remindful of Bruner's account of *deformation professionelle* in terms of inference rules:

> We propose that when one goes beyond the information given, one does so by virtue of being able to place the present given in a more generic coding system and that one essentially reads off from the coding system additional information . . . /B/y living in a certain kind of professional or social setting, our approach to new experience becomes constrained — we develop, if you will, a professional deformation with respect to coding events. The mathematician tends with time to code more and more events in terms of certain formal codes

that are the stock in trade of his profession. The historian has his particular deformations, and so too the psychologist (1956, p. 226)

A natural direction for the research on pragmatic reasoning schemas would be to identify the characteristic schemas of different professions. There are many popular intuitions about professional deformations which could be put to an empirical test, such as: Do lawyers learn to reason about every relationship as a contract? Do economists treat every problem as an investment? Do natural scientists think about causality differently than social scientists?

Natural Experiments and Alternative Interpretations

We used the method of a natural experiment or quasi-experiment for the sake of external validity. We can be much more confident than if we had run a laboratory study of training and reasoning that the differences we measured are phenomena that exist and have consequences in the real world. Notwithstanding this virtue, a *quasi-experimental* design has inherent limitations. Critics might contend that since we did not randomly assign students to academic disciplines, we cannot be sure that differences in training are the cause of differential improvement. A standard criticism is that differences which *pre-exist*, before the "treatment" of interest, may be the source of the differential effects. But it is hard to imagine what pre-existing differences might have caused the differential improvements in reasoning we measured. The most obvious pre-existing difference among psychology and philosophy graduate students is their undergraduate training, which would have its effects before their first year of graduate school, not between their first and third years (Lehman & Nisbett, 1990). The fact that first-year students were already well-steeped in their disciplines made our study a relatively conservative test of whether disciplines have differential effects on reasoning.

Another alternative explanation might be that the psychology and philosophy graduate programs differ in ways other than curriculum and hence differences *concurrent* with the "treatment" may be the source of the differential effects. For example, a critic might contend that psychology programs inculcate enthusiasm, and philosophy programs skepticism, about empirical studies like ours. This critic would argue that differential training is confounded with differential motivation to perform well, differential sensitivity to demand characteristics, differential attitudes toward the experimenter, etc.

Another line of criticism would be that *cross-sectional* studies suffer from other potential confounds. Cohort effects can create the illusion of improvement or the illusion of lack thereof. Selection effects due to attrition of poor students before their third year can create the illusion of improvement.

However, all these various alternative explanations are ruled out by the *opposing trends* across our studies (improvement by psychologists but not philosophers in Study 1, improvement by philosophers but not scientists in Study 2). This cross-over effect cannot be explained by the confounds affecting quasi-experimental designs, such as pre-existing or concurrent differences, or by the confounds affecting cross-sectional designs, such as cohort effects or selection effects, since any of these factors would have produced the same pattern of results in both studies.

Parallels between the Psychology of Logic and the Logic of "Psychologism"

An interesting souce of corroboration for our critique of propositional logic as a model of reasoning is the work of modern logicians sympathetic to *"psychologism,"* the view that logic's purpose is to describe the way people think (c.f., Haack, 1975). These logicians have reacted against *"mathematicism,"* the view that logic's purpose is to describe the underpinnings of mathematics, which motivated the development of modern logic. Their proposals are diverse, but they have the common effect of *restricting inferences from the material conditional*. Some logicians have argued that two truth-values are insufficient, and have proposed logics with a third value (c.f. Rosser & Turquette, 1952). In a three-valued logic, the conditional rule "If A then B" and knowledge that "A" is true would still warrant the *modus ponens* inference that "B" is true, but knowledge that "B" is false would not warrant the *modus tollens* inference that "A" is false (because "A" could have the third truth-value).

Other logicians have directly criticized the material conditional because of the paradoxes it generates. They have suggested different connectives to represent the *if-then* relationship. Lewis proposed a stricter relation of antecedent to a consequent, arguing that "a relation which does not indicate relevance of content is merely a connection of 'truthvalues', not what we mean by a 'logical' relation or 'inference'" (Lewis, 1917, p. 356). More radically, Anderson and Belnap proposed that the antecedent must be relevant to the consequent. They argued that "relevance was central to logic from the time of Aristotle until, beginning in the nineteenth century, logic fell increasingly into the hands of those with mathematical inclinations. The modern tradition, however, stemming from Frege and Whitehead-Russell, gave no consideration whatever to the classical notion of relevance" (Anderson & Belnap, 1975, p. 5).

Although his work is closer in spirit to natural logic models than to pragmatic models, Gentzen's proposals also have the effect of constraining conditional inferences. Gentzen proposed a revised formulation of propositional logic so that proofs would resemble "actual logical reasoning" (1935/1964, p. 291). The standard formulation — proposed by logicians concerned with "mathematicism," — presented only a few rules as primitive and left most to be derived. Gentzen's aim was to formulate propositional logic with a primitive rule for every elementary inference (i.e. every inference that people naturally make in a single step). Gentzen determined which inferences were elementary by studying people's reasoning in mathematical proofs. His formulation presented as primitive *modus ponens* (he observed people make this step) but not *modus tollen* (he did not observe people make this step).

No comparable revisions have been proposed for Aristotle's categorical logic because they are unneeded; Aristotle designed his system with the goal of psychologism not mathematicism. The fact that Aristotle's logic survived as a central part of the university curriculum for centuries provides some evidence that it makes contact with natural ways of reasoning. It is interesting that although the advent of propositional logic has brought great advances in the formal elegance and power, there has simultaneously been a great decline in logic's role in the university curriculum. Moreover, among undergraduates who do study propositional logic, it is common to hear complaints that it does not improve their thinking — that it is unnatural, inapplicable, or irrelevant. Our findings suggest that they may have a point.

FOOTNOTES

[1] All p values reported are based on two-tailed tests.

[2] An assumption of the analysis of covariance model — homogeneity of regression — was violated in our data; however, Pechman (1968) found that only very extreme departures from homogeneity significantly alter the analysis and that with heterogeneity the analysis becomes more conservative with respect to making a type 1 error. He also found the model to be robust in quasi-experimental settings in which the covariate differs by treatment group. Hence, we proceeded with the analyses.

REFERENCES

Anderson, A. R., & Belnap, N. D., Jr. (1975). *Entailment: The logic of relevance and necessity.* (Vol. 1). Princeton, NJ: Princeton University Press.

Begg, I., & Denny, J. P. (1969). Empirical reconciliation of atmosphere and conversion interpretations of syllogistic reasoning errors. *Journal of Experimental Psychology, 81,* 351–354.

Boole, G. (1854). *An investigation of the laws of thought, on which are founded the mathematical theories of logic and probabilities.* London: Walton G. Maberly.

Braine, M. D. S. (1978). On the relation between the natural logic of reasoning and standard logic. *Psychological Review, 85,* 1–21.

Bruner, J. S. (1957). Going beyond the information given. In J. S. Bruner, *et al., Contemporary Approaches to Cognition,* Cambridge: Harvard Press.

Bucci, W. S. (1975). The interpretation of universal alternative propositions: A developmental study. Disseration, New York University.

Cesaro, J., & Provitern, A. (1971). Sources of error in syllogistic reasoning. *Cognitive Psychology, 2,* 400–410.

Chapman, L. J., & Chapman, J. P. (1959). Atmosphere effect reexamined. *Journal of Experimental Psychology, 58,* 220–226.

Cheng, P. W., & Holyoak, K. J. (1985). Pragmatic reasoning schemas. *Cognitive Psychology, 17,* 391–416.

Cheng, P. W., Holyoak, K. J., Nisbett, R. E., & Oliver, L. M. (1986). Pragmatic versus syntactic approaches to training deductive reasoning. *Cognitive Psychology, 18,* 293–328.

Cheng, P. W. & Nisbett, R. E. (1992). Pragmatic constraints on causal deduction. [Summary]. Proceedings of the 1990 Convention of the Rocky Mountain Psychological Association. Los Angeles, CA: University of California.

Einhorn, H. J. & Hogarth, R. M. (1986). Judging probable cause. *Psychological Bulletin, 99,* 3–19.

Evans, J. St. B. T. (1990). *Bias in human reasoning: Causes and consequences.* Hillsdale, NJ: Erlbaum.

Evans, J. St. B. T. (1982). *The psychology of deductive reasoning.* London: Routledge & Kegan Paul.

D'Andrade, R. (1982). *Reason versus Logic.* Paper presented at the Symposium on the Ecology of Cognition: Biological, Cultural, and Historical Perspectives. Greensboro, NC.

Fillenbaum, S. (1975). If: Some uses. *Psychological Research, 37,* 245–260.

Fillenbaum, S. (1976). Inducements: On phrasing and logic of conditional promises, threats, and warnings. *Psychological Research, 38,* 231–250.

Fong, G. T., Krantz, D. H., & Nisbett, R. E. (1986). The effects of statistical training on thinking about everyday problems. *Cognitive Psychology, 18,* 253–292.

Galott, K., Baron, J., & Sabini, J. (1986). Individual differences in syllogistic reasoning: Deduction rules or mental models? *Journal of Experimental Psychology: General, 115.* 16–25.

Geis, M. C., & Zwicky, A. M. (1971). On invited inferences. *Linguistic Inquiry, 2,* 561–566.

Gentzen, G. (1935/1969). Investigations into logical deduction. In M. E. Szabo (Ed. and Trans.), *The collected papers of Gerhard Gentzen.* Amsterdam: North-Holland.

Goodman, N. (1965). *Fact, fiction, and forecast.* Indianapolis: Bobbs-Merill.

Grice, H. P. (1975). Logic and conversation. In P. Cole and J. L. Morgan (eds.), *Syntax and Semantics, Vol. 3: Speech Acts.* New York, Academic Press.

Griggs, R. A., & Cox, J. R. (1982). The elusive thematic-materials effect in Wason's selection task. *British Journal of Psychology, 73,* 407–420.

Haack, S. (1978). *Philosophy of logics.* Cambridge: Cambridge University Press.

Henle, M. (1962). On the relation between logic and thinking. *Psychological Review, 69,* 366–378.

Holland, J. H., Holyoak, K. J., Nisbett, R. E., & Thagard, P. (1986). *Induction: Processes of inference, learning, and discovery.* Cambridge, Mass.; Bradford Books/MIT Press.

Inhelder, B., & Piaget, J. (1958). *The growth of logical thinking from childhood to adolescence.* New York: Basic Books. (Original work published in 1955)

Jackson, S. L. & Griggs, R. A. (1988). Education and deductive reasoning. Unpublished manuscript, Department of Psychology, University of Florida, Gainesville.

Johnson-Laird, P. N. (1982). Thinking as a skill. *Quarterly Journal of Experimental Psychology, 34A,* 1–29.

Johnson-Laird, P. N. (1983). *Mental Models.* Cambridge, MA: Harvard University Press.

Johnson-Laird, P. N. and Bara, B. G. (1984). Syllogistic inference. *Cognition, 16,* 1–61.

Johnson-Laird, P. N. and Steedman, M. J. (1978). The psychology of syllogisms. *Cognitive Psychology, 10,* 64–99.

Kahneman, D. & Tversky, A. (1982). Causal schemas in judgment. In D. Kahneman, P. Slovic, & A. Tversky. (Eds.) *Judgment under uncertainty. Heuristics and biases.* New York: Cambridge University Press.

Kelley, H. H. (1972). Causal schemata and the attribution process. In E. E. Jones, D. E. Kanouse, H. H. Kelley, R. E. Nisbett, S. Valins, & B. Weiner (Eds.), *Attribution: Perceiving the causes of behavior.* Morristown, NJ: General Learning Press.

Kelley, H. H. (1973). The process of causal attribution. *American Psychologist, 28,* 107–128.

Lehman, D. R., Lempert, R. O., & Nisbett, R. E. (1987). The effects of graduate training on reasoning. *American Psychologist, 43,* 1–11.

Lehman, D. R. & Nisbett, R. E. (1990). A longitudinal study of the effects of undergraduate education on reasoning. *Developmental Psychology, 26,* 952–960.

Lewis, C. I. (1917). The issues concerning material implication. *Journal of Philosophy, 14.*

Manktelow, K. I., & Evans, J. St. B. T. (1979). Facilitation of reasoning by realism: Effect or non-effect? *British Journal of Psychology, 70,* 477–488.

Mann, L. (1979). *On the trail of process.* New York: Grune & Stratton.

Marcus, S. L., & Rips, L. J. (1979). Conditional reasoning. *Journal of Verbal Learning and Verbal Behavior, 18,* 199–223.

Nisbett, R. E., Fong, G. T., Lehman, D. R., & Cheng, P. W. (1987). Teaching reasoning. *Science, 238,* 625–631.

Oakhill, J. V. & Johnson-Laird, P. N. (1985). Rationality, memory and the search for counterexamples. *Cognition, 20,* 79–94.

Oakhill, J., Johnson-Laird, P. N., & Garham, A. (1989). *Cognition, 31,* 117–140.

Pechman, P. D. (1968). An investigation of the effects of non-homogeneity of regression slopes upon the F-test of analysis of covariance. Laboratory of Educational Research, Report No. 16. Boulder: University of Colorado.

Plato (1949). *Theaetetus.* Indianapolis: Bobbs-Merrill Company. (Transl. by B. Jowett)

Plato (1941). *The Republic.* New York: Oxford Press. (Transl. by F. M. Cornford)

Rips, L. J. (1983). Cognitive processes in propositional reasoning. *Psychological Review, 90,* 38–71.

Rips, L. J., & Conrad, F. G. (1983). Individual differences in deduction. *Cognition and Brain Theory, 6,* 259–285.

Rosser, J. B. & Turquette, A. R. (1952). *Many-valued logics.* Amsterdam: North-Holland.

Russell, B. (1960). *An Outline of Philosophy.* New York: Meridian.

Smith, E. E., Langston, C. & Nisbett, R. E. (1992). *Cognitive Science, 16,* 1–40.

Wason, P. C. (1966). Reasoning. In B. M. Ross (Ed.), *New horizons in psychology I,* Hammondsworth: Penguin.

Wilkins, M. C. (1978). The effect of changed material on the ability to do formal reasoning. *Archives of Psychology, 16,* 83.

Woodworth, R. J. & Sells, S. B. (1935). An atmosphere effect in formal syllogistic reasoning. *Journal of Experimental Psychology, 18,* 451–460.

V RULES FOR CHOICE

10 Teaching the Use of Cost-Benefit Reasoning in Everyday Life

Richard P. Larrick
James N. Morgan
Richard E. Nisbett
The University of Michigan

Do people think about leaving bad movies, taking losses on investments, and demolishing outdated buildings in the same way, relying on the same inferential rules? Are there general rules of choice that guide people's decisions across a broad range of domains? If so, can the nature of these rules be altered by instruction?

Economists have long assumed that a set of abstract rules of choice exists, and that people make choices according to those rules across the economic spectrum from consumer choices to decisions about time use (Becker, 1976). On the other hand, many psychologists share Thorndike's (1906) view that people's behavior is governed by domain-dependent rules that do not generalize across situations that are very different from one another. Even among psychologists who believe that people have domain-independent rules, a pervasive opinion originating with Piaget is that such rules can only be learned by self-discovery methods and cannot really be taught in a formal way (Brainerd, 1978; Newell, 1980).

In this paper, we examine whether people use abstract rules in making choices and whether these principles can be taught so that people will use them across a wide range of situations. We first sketch the cost-benefit model of choice and show that there is ample evidence that people depart from it in their everyday choices. We next present original evidence about differential rule usage, comparing people trained in the use of the normative rules with those who are less trained. Finally, we present evidence about the trainability of people by relatively brief interventions, about the degree of domain specificity of training, and about the durability of training.

COST-BENEFIT RULES OF CHOICE

The basic assumption underlying the microeconomic model of choice is that people choose actions that maximize their overall welfare. The model assumes people are confronted by a set of actions, each of which is associated with outcomes that will occur with some probability. Each of these outcomes has a value to the person that can be compared with the values of the other outcomes by converting the values to a single scale (for example, dollars). Three principles follow from this model. (a) The *greatest net benefit principle,* which states that the action with the greatest positive difference between the total benefit and total cost of its outcome should be chosen from the set of possible actions. (b) The *sunk cost principle,* which states that only future benefits and costs should be considered when making a choice. (c) The *opportunity cost principle,* which states that a cost of undertaking a given course of action is foregoing the expected net benefits associated with other courses of action.

These principles may seem incomplete to readers familiar with standard textbook cost-benefit analysis (Mishan, 1976; Morgan & Duncan, 1982). We eliminated certain principles from the list of inferential rules of choice because they were either derivable from the principles listed above, or because they were not sufficiently general to apply to all choice situations. Also, these cost-benefit rules certainly are not exhaustive of the principles that guide choice. Moral, esthetic, and social principles may compete with the cost-benefit rules, and humanistic values may be included as costs and benefits in the economic calculus. Thus, departures from economic reasoning could be due to people's favoring humanistic values or principles rather than ignorance of the normative rules. We will return to the question of whether noneconomically trained people know cost-benefit reasoning but are more likely to favor humanistic values, or whether they are actually less likely to know and use cost-benefit reasoning.

Lay Use of the Cost-Benefit Rules of Choice

A fundamental assumption of economics is that people make choices consistent with the cost-benefit rules (Friedman, 1953). There now exists, however, a good deal of research indicating that people violate the maximization rules of microeconomics. An early dissenting view introduced by Simon (1955) proposed that people do not attempt to maximize utility but simply attempt to attain some minimal level of satisfaction. In the past few decades, many empirical violations of expected utility theory have been documented, including violations of the independence axiom (Allais, 1953) and transitivity (Lichtenstein & Slovic, 1971; Tversky, 1969) and various violations of utility maximization (Kahneman & Tversky, 1979). These critiques have buttressed the psychologists' case against the view that a single, coherent set of abstract rules underlies choice behavior and have revealed serious shortcomings in choice behavior that produce nonoptimal outcomes. We shall focus on several economic traps that occur when people fail to use the sunk cost and opportunity cost principles.

Violations of the Sunk Cost Principle

A particularly clear case of an economic trap occurs when people consider past investments of money, effort, or time in their current decisions. For instance, imagine you have bought $15 tickets for a basketball game weeks in advance, but on the day of the game it is snowing and the star player you wanted to see is sick and will not play. The game is no longer of much interest to you. Do you decide to go to see the game or stay home and forget the money you have spent? (Adapted from Thaler, 1980.)

In these circumstances, some people will go to the game for the primary reason that they spent a large amount of money on it. What is wrong with this? Once the money is sunk, going to the game will not enable the person to get his or her "money's worth," but will simply inflict additional costs of a dangerous trip and a boring game. The sunk cost principle prescribes that a decision maker should consider only the benefits and costs that are going to be incurred from the time of the decision forward and ignore the past costs. To make it easier to ignore past costs, the person can do a thought experiment: Would I go to the game if someone called me on the day it was scheduled and offered me a free ticket? If not, then a sunk cost trap should be suspected.

The sunk cost effect has been demonstrated in studies by Arkes and Blumer (1985), who proposed that an important cause of the trap is peoples' ignorance of the normative sunk cost rule and their reliance on the generally effective rule of "waste not, want not." The "waste not, want not" rule is normative for economic choices that involve decisions about the future. People would be acting counternormatively if they deliberately chose to expend resources in pursuit of some benefit they intended to waste. But the rule is not normative for economic decisions involving irretrievable past costs. Note that this interpretation implies that people do operate with highly abstract rules of choice, but that these rules may differ from the normative ones.

A second type of economic dilemma that occurs when people fail to ignore sunk costs is a situation we call the extra cost trap. In this type of trap, people abandon an enjoyable activity because they are attending to past costs. For instance, imagine you are on your way to see one of your favorite plays for which you have bought a ticket in advance, but when you get to the theater, you discover you have lost the ticket. (Adapted from

Tversky & Kahneman, 1981.) Would you decide to buy a second ticket or to skip the play? Some people in this situation might skip the play because they feel that they have already spent $20 on a ticket and the play is not worth $40 (which is the total cost if the person buys a second ticket). They feel that it is a waste to spend twice as much on a play ticket as it is worth. The sunk cost principle, however, prescribes that you ignore the sunk $20 ticket, and decide whether the future benefits of seeing the play exceed the future cost, which is $20, the price of a second ticket. A thought experiment is also helpful here: Would you still go to the play if you had lost $20 in cash on the way to the theater? The answer is probably yes, because the value of the performance has not been affected.

Violations of the Opportunity Cost Principle

Another type of economic trap occurs when people ignore the opportunities they forego by choosing one course of action rather than another. For instance, imagine that you have paid off the mortgage on your home, and you are deciding whether to keep your house or move into an apartment. Many people compare the out-of-pocket costs of living in a house with those of living in an apartment and conclude that keeping the home is much cheaper than renting. However, by tying up wealth in a house, a person foregoes interest income, which is often more than enough to offset the difference in the out-of-pocket costs between owning and renting. The waste not, want not principle leads people to feel that it is a waste to "throw away" money on rent when they could live in their own home for "free."

Research on opportunity costs establishes that people often fail to calculate opportunity costs when they are unstated (Neumann & Friedman, 1980) and tend to underestimate them when they are explicitly stated but small (Hoskin, 1983). Additional evidence that people have poor understanding of opportunity costs is provided by research on buying and selling behavior in experimental markets, which shows that the lowest amount of money subjects are willing to accept for a good is higher than the highest amount they are willing to pay for the same good (Kahneman, Knetsch, & Thaler, in press). An analogous discrepancy occurs in people's use of time. People will often perform a service for themselves (for example, mowing the lawn) even though the amount they could earn performing some other activity would be higher than the amount they would have to pay for someone else to perform the service. An awareness of opportunity costs should lead people to pay more for the services of others and to invest in time-saving devices.

Evidence that People Use Inferential Rules

Taken as a whole, the evidence indicates that the economic model is wrong in assuming that people act as though they use the abstract normative rules.

Indeed, the findings are consistent with the view that people do not use abstract rules of any type but rely on highly concrete domain-dependent rules.

In a recent series of studies, however, Nisbett and his colleagues have found that people do use abstract, domain-independent inferential rules to reason about certain everyday problems, and that their reasoning can be improved by formal instruction (for a review see Nisbett, Fong, Lehman, & Cheng, 1987). The rules examined include statistical rules (Fong, Krantz, & Nisbett, 1986; Fong & Nisbett, in press; Kunda & Nisbett, 1986; Nisbett, Krantz, Jepson, & Kunda, 1983), as well as causal and contractual rules (Cheng & Holyoak, 1985; Cheng, Holyoak, Nisbett, & Oliver, 1986; Cheng & Nisbett, 1990; Morris & Nisbett, 1990). But these rules represent only a portion of the range of possible inferential rules that people use for everyday decisions. More importantly, judgmental rules affect behavior only indirectly. In the following work, we wanted to extend the inferential rules findings to the choice domain and examine whether knowledge of inferential rules affects actual behavior.

DISCIPLINE DIFFERENCES IN THE USE OF THE NORMATIVE RULES OF CHOICE

In the first study, we examined whether professional training in economics affects a wide range of behaviors governed by normative choice principles. We compared the self-reported decisions and behaviors of economics professors with those of biology and humanities professors.

Study 1

Subjects

The subjects were 126 professors from the departments of economics, biology, art history, and Romance languages at the University of Michigan. Telephone interviewers stated that "we are interested in finding out how faculty feel about some choices that may confront the university over the next few years, and we're also interested in some personal decisions faculty have made. In addition, we're interested in the relationship between the two." The overall volunteer rate was 88%.

Stimulus Materials

The survey contained two types of questions—reasoning questions and behavioral self-report questions. Six reasoning questions asked about University policy issues and two about international policy issues. The questions were designed to draw on the use of three normative principles: the sunk cost principle, the opportunity cost principle, and the net-benefit principle. Each problem presented subjects with two arguments — one that expressed a normative principle and one that contradicted it. The subjects were then asked which view they agreed with more. An example of each type of problem is given in Figure 10.1. (The scoring is indicated for each alternative on the extreme left, with higher numbers indicating more normative answers.)

For the sunk cost problem about replacing versus renovating the old hospital, the normative analysis indicates that the original cost of building the hospital is irrelevant to the current decision (sunk), and the only concern should be the future costs of renovation versus new construction. For the opportunity cost problem about scholarship aid, the normative analysis indicates that, as the opportunity costs of going to college increase for students, universities will have to increase their financial aid in order to maintain their attractiveness to students. And for the net-benefit problem involving purchasing blood, the net-benefit principle implies that both parties should choose their most preferred action, which for this problem is to engage in the transaction.

The behavioral section of the survey measured various consumer and financial decisions the professors had made in the past. The initial questions in this section were used to control for the opportunities professors had to display either normative behavior or trap behavior. These questions asked how often in the past year the subject had engaged in seven different consumer activities, such as going to movies. The remainder of the questions in this section assessed whether the subjects behaved in accordance with the normative principles. Subjects were asked the following four types of questions, each of which was scored as a 1, for a behavior consistent with the normative principles, or a 0, for a behavior that could indicate trap reasoning.

1. *Discontinuing activities after incurring a sunk cost.* "In the past five years have you ever started one of the following items and then not finished it?" There followed a list of seven consumer activities (e.g., a movie, a restaurant meal, a sports event).

2. *Foregoing activities after incurring a sunk cost.* "In the past five years have you ever bought one of the following items and then not used it?" There followed seven consumer activities.

3. *Personal decisions involving sunk costs or opportunity costs.* For example, "Have you ever dropped a research project because it was not proving worthwhile?" and "Have you ever had more income withheld from your paycheck than you actually owed in taxes in order to get a large refund?"

SUNK COST PROBLEM (UNIVERSITY POLICY)

As you may know, the university is currently planning the demolition of the old hospital. The argument has been made, however, that the building was extremely expensive to build for its time and that it is wasteful simply to destroy it. The counterargument is that renovation in the case of this building is more expensive than construction. Do you tend to favor:

(0.00)____renovation;

(1.00)____demolition; or

(0.50)____you do not have an opinion.

OPPORTUNITY COST PROBLEM (UNIVERSITY POLICY)

Some financial planners for the university anticipate that jobs for young people may soon be much more plentiful than in the recent past, for the simple reason that a much smaller fraction of the population is in the younger age group. One implication is that pay will increase for entry level jobs in all kinds of industries. The argument has been made that the university should respond to this situation by offering more money for scholarships in order to lure low income students away from starting work and toward continuing their education. Do you feel:

(1.00)____scholarships should be kept competitive with salaries;

(0.00)____scholarships should simply maintain pace with inflation and not respond to competitive inducements;

(0.50)____you do not have an opinion.

NET-BENEFIT PROBLEM (INTERNATIONAL POLICY)

As you may know, there are continuing problems with assuring that blood supplies for patients are free of all viruses. The suggestion has recently been made to purchase blood from Asians for use in the West, on the grounds that many of the most dangerous viruses, including AIDS, are less common there. Many citizens of relatively poor Asian countries would be happy to have the extra cash; however, others have argued that such a practice would be an inappropriate form of exploitation. Do you tend to:

(1.00)____favor the idea strongly;

(0.75)____favor it somewhat;

(0.50)____have no preference;

(0.25)____oppose the idea somewhat;

(0.00)____oppose it strongly.

265

4. *Opportunity costs of time use.* For example, "Do you do some of your own yard work?" and "Do you own a microwave?"

The survey also asked about a variety of demographic variables, including age. Information about salaries was obtained from published University records.

Results

The goal was to examine whether economics training is related to choice. Because there were no theoretical reasons to distinguish biologists and humanists, they were combined in the statistical analyses to form a single, noneconomist category. (The means for both biologists and humanists are reported to verify that this procedure was justifiable.) The survey responses were used to create one reasoning and four behavioral indices that were averages of individual questions. All of the indices were analyzed using multiple regression, which controlled for salary, age, and gender.[1] The unadjusted means for each group are reported in Table 1 along with the standardized coefficients and *p* levels for the discipline variable.

It may be seen in Table 1 that economists' reasoning on the university and international policy questions was more in line with cost-benefit rules than was that of biologists and humanists. This pattern was found for the net-benefit questions ($p < .05$), and for the opportunity cost questions ($p < .05$) and a trend was found for the sunk cost questions ($p < .15$).

It also may be seen in Table 10.1 that economists were more likely to behave in line with the cost-benefit rules. First, economists reported discontinuing a significantly greater percentage of the consumer activities than the biologists and the humanists. Second, economists tended to report foregoing a greater percentage of the consumer items than the biologists and the humanists, although this was not significant. Third, economists were more likely than biologists and humanists to report that they ignored sunk costs or attended to opportunity costs in their personal decisions. For instance, they were more likely to have dropped a research project because it was not proving worthwhile. (It is interesting to note that economists were not simply more likely to drop projects. All three disciplines gave the same answer on average to the question "have you ever dropped a research project because of a lack of funding?") Finally, economists participated in a greater number of time-saving activities.

Training in economics was strongly related to reasoning and behavior across a wide range of choices. Economics thus is a system of rules of choice that is practiced by its adherents as well as preached.[2] Additional analyses indicate that the discipline difference is not due to economists favoring cost-benefit rules over humanistic rules or values (Larrick et al., 1990).

TABLE 10.1
Economic Policy Preferences and Reported Behavior as a Function of Academic Discipline

Index	Discipline				
	Economics	Biology	Humanities	Regression Coefficient	p-value
Reasoning about policy	.73	.58	.54	(.27)	.01
Discontinuing activities	.42	.24	.22	(.35)	.001
Foregoing activities	.24	.16	.14	(.16)	.15
Personal decisions	.71	.57	.49	(.22)	.05
Time-saving activities	.61	.48	.52	(.28)	.01
Overall behavior	.50	.36	.34	(.41)	.001
Overall reasoning and behavior	.61	.47	.44	(.39)	.001

Note. Scores range from 0 to 1.0, with higher scores indicating more normative responses. Means are unadjusted. Biologists and humanists were included in a single, noneconomist category in the analyses. Regression coefficients are the standardized coefficients from the multiple regression analysis controlling for salary, age, and gender (the analyses for discontinuing and foregoing activities were also controlled for consumption opportunities). The *p*-values are from the multiple regression analyses. Because people rarely reported foregoing consumer activities, those activities that were skipped by less than ten percent of the subjects were excluded from the foregone activities index. The overall behavior index is an average of the four behavior indices. The overall reasoning and behavior index is an average of the policy index and overall behavior index.

When the questions on the survey were categorized according to whether there was a conflict between cost-benefit rules and humanistic rules (for example, the question about buying blood from poor Asians) or there was no conflict (for example, discontinuing a video), economists were more likely to give cost-benefit reasoning in both instances. Thus, noneconomists are not just applying other humanistic principles or values. Rather, noneconomists are less likely to apply the cost-benefit rules than are economists.

These results support our claim that training produces knowledge of the normative rules, but we cannot rule out the alternative explanation that economists are predisposed to behave and reason in accordance with the normative rules before they actually receive any training. In order to show that self-selection is not a necessary condition for acquisition of the normative rules, we brought naive undergraduates into the laboratory and trained them on the sunk cost principle.

TEACHING THE NORMATIVE RULES OF CHOICE

The first of two training studies examined the effects of instruction on answers to questions about choice. It also examined whether domain of training (financial problems or nonfinancial problems) affects how well people use the principles in a given domain. A finding that domain is not important would suggest that economic principles are readily generalized from examples to become abstract inferential systems. Subjects were brought into the laboratory and trained for half an hour on the sunk cost principle and the derivative extra-cost principle.

Study 2

Seventy-nine subjects from the University of Michigan's paid subject pool were assigned randomly to receive financial training, nonfinancial training, or no training. In the training sessions, materials employed either exclusively financial or nonfinancial examples and terminology. A typical training problem is the lost theater ticket question presented in the introduction (which is a financial, extra cost problem). Following training, subjects were given a test containing both financial and nonfinancial instances of sunk cost and extra cost problems. An example of a financial, sunk cost problem is the basketball question presented in the introduction. The nonfinancial problems were similar to financial problems in structure but the resource in question was time or effort rather than money.[3]

When they were tested, trained subjects were instructed, first, to use the reasoning of the economic principles to solve the problems for which they thought the principles were appropriate; and second, to indicate whether they agreed or disagreed with this reasoning. In the control sessions, subjects received no training materials. They were asked to complete a "decision-making" test. They were instructed to think carefully about the problems and to write down what they thought they would do.

Answers were coded for normativeness of choice, measuring the extent to which a subject's choice agreed with the choice prescribed by the appropriate economic principle, and for normativeness of reasoning, measuring the extent to which a subject's reasoning accurately employed the appropriate economic principle. In order for an answer to be normative, it had to state either that the past costs are irrelevant or that only future benefits and costs are relevant. For an answer to be counternormative, it had to state that the previous costs are a reason for choosing the counternormative action. Responses were coded as (a) counternormative, (b) mixed or unstated, or (c) normatively correct.[4] Note that the sunk cost and extra cost problems serve as catch trials for each other, because the normative choice in the former situation is to abandon the activity and the normative response in the latter situation is to persevere. Thus, in order to reason correctly, subjects had to go beyond stating that past costs are irrelevant to actually comparing future costs with future benefits. This prevented subjects from relying on a simple rule of thumb such as always quitting after a sunk cost.

The mean scores for subjects' own choice and reasoning measures for each cell are given in Table 10.2. A 3 × 2 × 2 (Training × Domain × Principle) ANOVA, with repeated measures on the last two factors, showed that trained subjects chose more normatively, $F(2, 76) = 9.26$, $p < .001$, and reasoned more normatively, $F(2, 76) = 24.55$, $p < .001$, than untrained subjects.[5]

Domain specificity of training would be indicated by an interaction such that financially trained subjects performed more normatively on financial problems than on nonfinancial problems, and nonfinancially trained subjects did the opposite. This pattern of means, however, was not obtained for either measure. Indeed, there appears to be complete domain independence of training effects.

The results show that training people only briefly on an economic principle significantly alters their solutions to hypothetical economic problems. Moreover, training effects generalize fully from a financial domain to a nonfinancial one and vice versa.

Study 3

The first training study could not assess whether subjects retained the principles they learned nor could it assess whether the subjects applied the principles outside the laboratory. These issues were addressed in Study 3, which had a laboratory phase and a follow-up phase. In the laboratory phase, a new group of subjects was trained on the sunk cost and extra cost principles. In the follow-up phase, subjects were contacted by phone one month after training, and, under the guise of a consumer survey, they were

TABLE 10.2
Mean Scores for Normativeness of Choice and Normativeness of Reasoning

Training Condition	n	Problem Type			
		Financial Sunk Cost	Financial Extra Cost	Nonfinancial Sunk Cost	Nonfinancial Extra Cost
Normativeness of Choice					
Financial	25	2.28	2.90	2.60	2.56
Nonfinancial	33	2.35	2.91	2.69	2.59
Control	21	1.90	2.31	2.43	2.26
Normativeness of Reasoning					
Financial	25	2.38	2.62	2.48	2.50
Nonfinancial	33	2.59	2.60	2.45	2.36
Control	21	1.90	2.09	2.00	2.00

Note. Scores range from 1 to 3. Higher scores represent choices that are more normative.

asked questions about their consumer decisions and their opinions on University policy. Because all of the questions tacitly involved sunk cost issues, the subjects' responses were an indication of the degree to which they behaved or reasoned according to the normative principles.

Another purpose of this second training study was to test the view that laypeople use what they take to be an economically correct principle, namely the "waste not, want not" rule. In the laboratory phase, all subjects were asked to indicate the response they thought economists would give as well as their personal response for each problem. We anticipated that subjects would misidentify the rule that economists would invoke.

Laboratory Methods and Results

Eighty-nine undergraduates from the University of Michigan's introductory psychology pool participated to receive credit toward a research requirement. Trained subjects received both financial and nonfinancial materials. Untrained subjects received a superficial description of cost-benefit analysis, which briefly stated that people should choose the action with the greatest positive difference between benefits and costs and should pay attention only to future benefits and costs when they are making a decision. The same test problems were used as before. The responses, however, were no longer open-ended but were restricted to four types of action-reasoning combinations, as shown in Figure 10.2 for the sunk cost problem concerning basketball tickets.

The subjects' understanding of the normative principle was measured by the question "Which response would an economist be most likely to choose?" Each subject was given a score corresponding to the percentage of the eight problems for which the subject chose a particular alternative as the economic response. These means are presented in Table 10.3. The 2×4 (Training by Alternative) ANOVA revealed that the two-way interaction was significant, $F(3, 261) = 122.18, p < .001$. The trained subjects were far more likely to choose the normative alternative as the economic response and far less likely to choose the trap response. These results indicate that untrained subjects overwhelmingly misidentify the economist's reasoning principles. Apparently they take the "waste not, want not" principle underlying the trap alternative to be normative.

The subjects' own reasoning was measured by the question "Which response would you choose?" The mean scores showing how often each alternative was chosen as a personal response are given in Table 3. The 2×4 (Training by Alternative) ANOVA revealed that the two-way interaction was significant, $F(3, 261) = 7.95, p < .001$. The trained subjects chose the normative alternative as their personal response for 44% of the problems compared to 28.6% for the untrained subjects, $t(87) = 4.77, p < .01$. The

1. Normative alternative (Normative action-normative reasoning). "I would skip the game because it's less interesting than when I bought the tickets and it's more difficult to get to. No matter what I do, I can't get my $30 back, so why should I make matters worse by going to the game? I'd forget the $30 and find something else to do."

2. Trap alternative (Trap action-trap reasoning). "I would go to the game because, even though it's less interesting and more difficult to get to, it would be wrong to waste the $30 I spent on the tickets. I probably wouldn't go if someone gave me the tickets, but since I have bought them, it's important not to waste money—if I didn't go to the game, I couldn't get my money's worth."

3. Mixed Trap alternative (Normative action-trap reasoning). "I would skip the game because, if I were in an accident, someone could be seriously hurt, and I'm sure that the damage to my car would add up to more than $30. The game is no longer interesting and the cost of being in an accident is far more than the cost of the tickets, so I would stay home."

4. Noneconomic alternative (Trap action-non-economic reasoning). "I would go to the game despite the fact that it's less interesting and more difficult to get to. When I bought the tickets, I should have realized that it might be snowing and that the other team might no longer be in contention for the playoffs. If it was worth going in the first place, it still is."

FIG. 10.2 Multiple choice responses for the basketball problem used in Study 3.

trained and untrained subjects did not differ in how often they chose the trap alternative as their own response (11.1% and 13.1%, respectively). The trained subjects, however, chose the mixed trap response significantly less often ($M = 30.1\%$) than the untrained subjects ($M = 38.6\%$), $t(87) = 2.26$, $p < .05$. Whereas the modal answer for the trained subjects was the normative alternative, the modal answer for the untrained subjects was the mixed trap alternative.

It is important to note that untrained subjects were more likely to prefer the normative answer for themselves than they were to pick it as the economist's answer, $Ms = 28.6\%$ vs. 16.9%, $t(44) = 3.30$, $p < .01$. This suggests the ironic conclusion that our subjects would feel that they were being uneconomical in choosing the answer actually preferred by economists.

Follow-up Methods and Results

A telephone survey was conducted four to six weeks after subjects participated in the laboratory training. Several steps were taken to reduce

TABLE 10.3

Mean Frequency with Which an Alternative was Chosen as an Economist's Response and as a Personal Response

Training Condition	Alternative Chosen			
	Normative	*Trap*	*Mixed Trap*	*Noneconomic*
Economist's Response				
Trained	75.6	5.9	12.2	5.9
Untrained	16.9	41.9	24.4	15.5
Personal Response				
Trained	44.0	11.1	30.1	14.2
Untrained	28.6	13.1	38.6	19.2

Note. The scores are the percentage of the eight problems for which a subject chose that particular alternative as an economist's response and as a personal response.

the possibility of suspicion.[6] Eighty subjects were interviewed, of which 40 were trained and 40 untrained. The follow-up survey asked a variety of behavioral and reasoning questions that were designed to detect the subject's use of the sunk cost principle. In the first section of the survey, subjects were asked questions about discontinuing and foregoing consumer activities, which were essentially the same as those asked of the faculty in Study 1. The means for both indices showed that trained subjects were ignoring sunk costs more than untrained subjects, but only the nine-item index based on the question "Have you bought one of the following items at some time and then not used it in the past month" approached significance. Trained subjects reported that they had paid for but not used 1.14 objects and activities compared to .84 for untrained subjects, $t(78) = 1.64$, $p = .10$.

The second section contained six questions about a range of University of Michigan issues. These questions described a particular University issue, and then asked subjects what their preferences or their actions would be. All of the questions tacitly involved sunk costs. For instance, one question asked how much rent they would need to save each month on a 10-month lease for a new apartment to forfeit a $50 application fee they paid on a similar apartment. To get credit for a correct answer, subjects had to realize that it would be reasonable to pay a modest amount of money less each month (credit was given for $5–10) for the second apartment to cover the second application fee and let the first apartment go.

An index was created by scoring one point for the normative response and no points for either the trap or indifference response. The trained subjects answered the policy questions more normatively ($M = 3.64$) than the untrained subjects ($M = 3.12$), $t(78) = 2.16$, $p < .05$. Five trained subjects expressed suspicion following the university policy section. Their average score for the reasoning questions was 3.4, which falls between the means of the trained and untrained groups. This suggests that demand characteristics, or subject "cooperativeness," was not responsible for the difference between trained and untrained subjects.

Discussion

Training on the normative principles substantially improved subjects' ability to identify normative reasoning. Untrained subjects thought that an economist's normative answer is the trap alternative—that is, to behave in a way that minimizes wasting resources. The untrained subjects tended personally to favor the mixed trap reasoning, which allowed them to choose the action that had the greatest net benefit (e.g., skipping the basketball game) but to rationalize it by saying that the net benefit outweighed the wasted resource (e.g., the cost of an accident far outweighed the cost of the tickets). This suggests that naive subjects do not know the sunk cost rule and instead adhere to the "waste not, want not" principle. Both in their assumptions about correct economic reasoning and in their own reasoning the untrained subjects preferred attending to past costs.

Subjects trained on the normative principles not only applied them immediately on similar problems but retained them for a full month, applying them to a different type of problem in a different context. Trained subjects also tended to differ from untrained ones in their actual behavior as well. The weak result for behavior could be due in part to the low rate at which subjects engaged in consumer activities over the brief time studied. Subjects were unlikely to have encountered a movie bad enough to leave because the average subject saw only one or two in the month following training. Recall that faculty subjects were asked about consumer behavior over a much longer time period.

GENERAL DISCUSSION

Our research shows that abstract rules are used to guide decisions about choices and that these can be altered. The reasoning of economically-naive subjects became more normative following a simple, brief training session. The fact that subjects did not require extensive direct experience with particular situations in order to give rule-consistent reasoning indicates that subjects are relying on an inferential rule and not on concrete knowledge limited to specific problems or domains. The generalization of training from one content domain to another indicates that rules are coded at a level above that of concrete domains: Performance was as good for the untrained domain as for the trained domain. Most importantly, training improved performance on novel judgments, having content and form very different from training examples, one month after the training in a context quite different from that in which the training took place.

Our research indicates that knowledge of the abstract rules affects actual decisions and behaviors. The economists' data indicate that the normative rules guide reasoning, and actual choices, about activities as diverse as recommended university policy, personal career decisions, consumer behavior, and even international relations.

At the same time, the present results also make it clear that lay choice theory is fundamentally different from the normative theory. The noneconomically trained faculty were less likely to use the cost-benefit principles even when the principles were not in conflict with other principles or values. Untrained subjects in Study 3 chose the normative action-trap reasoning combination more often than the other combinations. This means that subjects were selecting the normative action but for a counternormative reason. Such reasoning seems dangerous because it suggests that, as sunk costs are increased, there will come a point at which a person will no longer choose the normative action. For instance, if the cost of the basketball tickets were high enough, the person might go to the game because the past costs would outweigh the future costs. But no matter how much money has been spent, whether it be on a game, a house, or a bomber, if the outcome will not be beneficial, the investment should be abandoned.

Our research demonstrates that, although people ordinarily are not perfectly rational by economists' standards, they are capable of becoming more rational. Before calling for the widespread teaching of these rules, however, we must note that the economic conception of rationality has been challenged by many who have doubted the appropriateness of its self-interest assumptions. A complete set of prescriptive principles of choice should include both moral and economic principles, and rules to adjudicate between the two.

FOOTNOTES

[1]Analyses of the behavioral indices about discontinuing and foregoing consumer activities also controlled for consumption opportunities. An opportunity index was calculated by standardizing the number of times subjects reported engaging in each consumer activity and then averaging these scores for each subject.

[2]For all of the findings, the effect of training existed independent of the effect of salary, though it is interesting to note that salary also had an independent effect (Larrick, Nisbett, & Morgan, 1990). Answers to both policy and behavioral questions were more in line with cost-benefit principles for subjects with higher salaries ($\beta_s = .33$ and $.23$) and this was especially true for noneconomists ($\beta_s = .43$ and $.33$).

[3]For example, in one nonfinancial problem, the protagonists have driven a great distance to a Western park of little interest, thinking that it was another park of much more interest. The

question is whether they should stay and see the meager attractions of the park or drive on immediately to another park. The sunk cost lure is to stay and see the uninteresting park in order to justify the time spent getting there.

[4]Coders agreed on 92% of the answers. The disputed answers were coded through consensus.

[5]All significance levels are for two-tailed tests.

[6]The survey did not refer to the experiment or to the psychology department but was disguised as a consumer and opinion survey that was being conducted for local Ann Arbor merchants; the survey and the experiment were conducted by different people who were of opposite sex; and, when identifying themselves to the subjects, the experimenter affiliated himself with the University of Michigan psychology department whereas the interviewers affiliated themselves with the Research Center for Group Dynamics (RCGD).

REFERENCES

Allais, M. (1953). Le comportement de l'homme rationnel devant le risque: Critique des postulats et axiomes de l'Ecole americaine. *Econometrica, 21,* 503–546.

Arkes, H. R., & Blumer, C. (1985). The psychology of sunk cost. *Organizational Behavior and Human Decision Processes, 35,* 124–140.

Becker, G. (1976). *The economic approach to human behavior.* Chicago: University of Chicago Press.

Brainerd, C. (1978). *Piaget's theory of intelligence.* Englewood Cliffs, NJ: Prentice-Hall.

Cheng, P. W., & Holyoak, K. J. (1985). Pragmatic reasoning schemas. *Cognitive Psychology, 17,* 391–416.

Cheng, P. W., Holyoak, K. J., Nisbett, R. E., & Oliver, L. (1986). Pragmatic versus syntactic approaches to training deductive reasoning. *Cognitive Psychology, 18,* 293–328.

Cheng, P. W., & Nisbett, R. E. (1990). *A pragmatic schema for causal deduction.* Unpublished manuscript. University of California, Los Angeles.

Fong, G. T., Krantz, D. H., & Nisbett, R. E. (1986). The effects of statistical training on thinking about everyday problems. *Cognitive Psychology, 18,* 253–292.

Fong, G. T., & Nisbett, R. E. (In press). Immediate and delayed transfer of training effects in statistical reasoning. *Journal of Experimental Psychology: General.*

Friedman, M. (1953). *Essays in positive economics.* Chicago: University of Chicago Press.

Hoskin, R. E. (1983). Opportunity cost and behavior. *Journal of Accounting Research, 21,* 78–95.

Kahneman, D., Knetsch, J. L., & Thaler, R. H. (In press). Experimental tests of the endowment effect and the coase theorem. *Journal of Political Economy.*

Kahneman, D., & Tversky, A. (1979). Prospect theory: An analysis of decision under risk, *Econometrica, 47,* 263–291.

Kunda, Z., & Nisbett, R. E. (1986). Prediction and the partial understanding of the law of large numbers. *Journal of Experimental Social Psychology, 22,* 339–354.

Larrick, R. P., Nisbett, R. E., & Morgan, J. N. (1990). *Who uses cost-benefit reasoning?* Unpublished manuscript, University of Michigan, Ann Arbor.

Lichtenstein, S., & Slovic, P. (1971). Reversals of preference between bids and choices in gambling decisions. *Journal of Experimental Psychology, 89,* 46–55.

Mishan, E. J. (1976). *Cost-benefit analysis.* New York: Praeger.

Morgan, J. N., & Duncan, G. J. (1982). *Making your choices count: Economic principles for everyday decisions.* Ann Arbor: University of Michigan Press.

Morris, M. W., & Nisbett, R. E. (1990). *Deformation professionelle: Reasoning schemas taught in psychology and philosophy.* Unpublished manuscript, University of Michigan, Ann Arbor.

Neumann, B. R., & Friedman, L. A. (1980). The effects of opportunity costs on project investment decision: A replication and extension. *Journal of Accounting Research, 18,* 407–419.

Newell, A. (1980). One final word. In D. T. Tuma & F. Reif (Eds.), *Problem-solving and education: Issues in teaching and research.* Hillsdale, NJ: Erlbaum.

Nisbett, R. E., Fong, G. T., Lehman, D. R., & Cheng, P. W. (1987). Teaching reasoning. *Science, 238,* 625–631.

Nisbett, R. E., Krantz, D. H., Jepson, D., & Kunda, Z. (1983). The use of statistical heuristics in everyday inductive reasoning. *Psychological Review, 90,* 339–363.

Simon, H. (1955). A behavioral model of rational choice. *Quarterly Journal of Economics, 69,* 174–183.

Thaler, R. H. (1980). Toward a positive theory of consumer choice. *Journal of Economic Behavior and Organization, 1,* 39–60.

Thorndike, E. L. (1906). *Principles of teaching.* New York: A. G. Seiler.

Tversky, A. (1969). Intransitivity of preferences. *Psychological Review, 76,* 31–48.

Tversky, A., & Kahneman, D. (1981). The framing of decisions and the psychology of choice. *Science, 211,* 453–458.

11

Who Uses the Cost-Benefit Rules of Choice? Implications for the Normative Status of Microeconomic Theory

Richard P. Larrick
Richard E. Nisbett
James N. Morgan
University of Michigan

IMPLICATIONS FOR THE NORMATIVE STATUS OF MICROECONOMIC THEORY

A basic distinction is made in the field of decision-making between normative and descriptive models of choice behavior. A normative model is one that depicts how people ought to make decisions in order to maximize their personal outcomes and a descriptive model is one that depicts how people actually make decisions. The maximization model of microeconomic theory, a set of principles governing appropriate choice given the decision maker's assessment of costs and benefits (Mishan, 1976; Morgan & Duncan, 1982), has been advanced as both a normative and a descriptive model (Becker, 1976; see also Hirshleifer, 1985). But it has fared better as a normative model than as a descriptive one. A large accumulation of empirical evidence indicates that certain aspects of the microeconomic model do not describe people's ordinary decision processes (Arkes & Blumer, 1985; Hoskin, 1983; Tversky and Kahneman, 1986). The fact that the model often fails descriptively raises the question, If people do not commonly use cost-benefit reasoning, why should we believe that it is normative? Why should it guide our choices?

Different methods are typically used to evaluate the normative versus the descriptive strength of a model. Normative adequacy has usually been tested by formal, mathematical proof, whereas descriptive adequacy has been tested by empirical means. To defend the normative adequacy of microeconomic models of choice, economists have argued that the model is based on a few assumptions about consistency that most people agree are intuitively reasonable criteria for good decision-making. If one assents to the assumptions, economists argue, then one assents to the model because it is mathematically implied by the assumptions.

But there is also a tradition of justifying, and amending, normative models in response to empirical considerations. March (1978), for example, argues that the fact that clients are willing to purchase the services of experts with skills in the decision sciences speaks positively to the normativeness of the model employed by the experts. And Simon (1955) argued that "satisficing" due to time and energy constraints more nearly describes people's choice behavior than the optimizing posited by the normative model. Simon and others have reasoned that this suggests that a model is normative only if it is practicable.

Some people might be inclined to think that empirical arguments are not appropriately raised in connection with considerations of normativeness, viewing this as an instance of the *naturalistic fallacy,* or moving from an "is" to an "ought." But in fact there is a long-standing tradition in epistemology of treating pragmatic considerations as prior to purely reflective ones. Hume held that "reason is and ought to be the slave of passion," by which he meant that human needs and their most efficient means of solution dictate the mental procedures that underlie inference and choice. The modern inheritors of the Hume tradition in epistemology describe their position as *consequentialism,* by which they mean that the appropriate gauge of a putatively normative cognitive procedure is whether it produces consequences that are beneficial for the individual (Goldman, 1978, 1986; Stich, 1990; see also Stich and Nisbett, 1980; Thagard, 1982; Thagard and Nisbett, 1983).

A second respect in which empirical considerations affect normative assumptions concerns whether people's behavior is *corrigible* by a putatively normative model. Goldman (1978, 1986) has argued that a rule system cannot be held to be normative if people cannot actually use it, or be taught to use it. Applying these considerations to microeconomic, cost-benefit choice theory, we can generate three easily-tested predictions that would reflect on the normativeness of the theory.

First, it should be the case that the consequences of using putatively normative rules ought to be superior. Economists claim that using the cost-benefit rules of choice will maximize (or at least improve) outcomes and lead to greater life success. The argument is that use of the rules makes people more efficient in their use of scarce resources such as time and effort. As a result, one would expect that people who use cost-benefit rules would be more productive and thereby receive greater returns in school or work. We measured outcomes in two different ways—by grade point averages in the case of undergraduates, and by salaries and raises in the case of professional academics. Of course, other explanations for a positive relationship would be plausible. Perhaps productive people seek optimal rules to help them manage their time and energy; or a third factor, such as motivation, leads to both greater productivity and the use of economic reasoning. Whatever the explanation, the finding is relevant to questions of normativeness. If it were to turn out *not* to be the case that people who use the rules have better outcomes, this would throw doubt on the claims of the model to normativeness.

A second expectation from present considerations is that intelligent people would be more likely to use cost-benefit reasoning. Because intelligence is generally regarded as being the set of psychological properties that make for effectiveness across environments (Baron, 1985, p. 15; Sternberg, 1985, 1988), intelligent people should be more likely to use the most effective reasoning strategies than should less intelligent people. Evidence for a link between intelligence and use of normative inferential rules has been obtained by Jepson, Krantz, and Nisbett (1983) in the statistical reasoning domain. They found that, in a sample of untrained undergraduates, use of presumably normative statistical rules to solve problems drawn from everyday life was positively correlated with verbal and mathematical skills as measured by standardized test scores. In this paper, we examine the relationship between the use of economic reasoning and intelligence as measured by undergraduates' scores on the Scholastic Aptitude Test.

A third implication is that people ought to be trainable by the cost-benefit rules in the sense of coming to use them in everyday life choices once they have been exposed to them. If use of the rules leads to more desirable outcomes, people should be increasingly likely to use them both because they see the superiority of the rules in principle and because they experience improved outcomes when they use them. We have shown in a previous paper (Larrick, Morgan, and Nisbett, 1990) that professional training in economics is positively correlated with cost-benefit reasoning, and that naive subjects who have been given brief training in one of the cost-benefit rules (the sunk cost rule) subsequently use the rule outside the laboratory. In this paper we attempt to extend the finding by examining the relationship between taking university economics courses and the use of cost-benefit reasoning. Once again, of course, we cannot assess the causal relationship between training in economics and the use of cost-benefit rules. Nonetheless, if people who were well-versed in economics failed to employ their knowledge, it would undermine our confidence that the cost-benefit rules were normative.

Cost-Benefit Rules

We envision microeconomics as a set of rules that can be used to maximize the outcomes of choices. We depict the model as a set of rules because the rule-based approach to reasoning has been influential in cognitive psychology and has received substantial empirical support in a range of reasoning domains (Newell and Simon, 1972; Holland, Holyoak, Nisbett, and Thagard, 1986; Smith, Langston, & Nisbett, in press). The particular rules we consider serve as general guides for maximizing the benefits of a course of action (Mishan, 1976; Morgan and Duncan, 1982). When a person is confronted with a set of possible actions each of which can lead to some set of outcomes, the person should convert the benefits and costs of all possible outcomes to a single scale, and adjust them for the probabilities that the outcomes will occur. In this calculation, the following three rules apply.

1. *The net-benefit rule.* The action that has the greatest expected net-benefit should be chosen from a set of possible actions.
2. *The sunk cost rule.* Only future benefits and costs should be considered in current decisions. Past costs and benefits are not relevant, unless they predict future benefits and costs.
3. *The opportunity cost rule.* The cost of engaging in a given course of action is the loss of the benefits of the next-best course of action.

We will attempt to distinguish use of rules such as these from mere preference or value differences. The question of whether different kinds of people are using different rules or simply hold different values arises in several contexts. One has to do with alleged differences between men and women in their use of economic rules of choice. There is a well-established finding in the literature on the teaching of economics that men perform better than women in economics classes and on tests of economic knowledge (Heath, 1989; Watts and Lynch, 1989). The most common explanations refer to the well-documented differences in socialization between boys and girls with respect to mathematics ability. Boys are more likely to be encouraged to be interested in math in general and financial matters in particular, whereas girls may be actively discouraged from such interests, or at least made to doubt their abilities. We propose that the difference between men and women in their use of economic rules may not be entirely due to differences in math socialization. It may be due at least in part to differences in moral reasoning between the sexes. This topic has received attention in the literature on moral development, following Carol Gilligan's (1982) work, which holds that women tend to value compassion for others more than do men, whereas men tend to value justice more than do women. In the studies described below we examined subjects' use of microeconomic rules both when they conflicted with humanitarian values and when they did not. If women differ from men in their values rather than in their understanding of microeconomic rules of choice, their answers should differ from those of men primarily when the rules of choice conflict with a humanitarian value.

We also examined a second issue concerning values. It is sometimes contended that formal exposure to economics makes people more selfish or more concerned with money (Frank, 1988) or, alternatively, that more selfish people choose to make themselves familiar with economics. To examine this possibility, we measured the extent to which subjects were concerned with money, pleasure and other benefits.

We present two studies in which we examined correlates of cost-benefit reasoning. In the first study, we administered an economic reasoning survey to a random sample of University of Michigan seniors, and obtained information on economics training (number of economics classes), academic effectiveness (grade point average), intellectual skills (standardized aptitude test scores), and gender. In the second study, we surveyed University of Michigan faculty from three disciplines (economics, biology, and humanities), and obtained information on career effectiveness (salary and raises), gender, and age. Some of the discipline results from the second study have been reported previously in a paper on the effect of training (Larrick et al., 1990).

STUDY 1

In Study 1, we examined whether academic effectiveness, intellectual aptitude, economics training, and gender of college students are related to economic reasoning. We surveyed seniors because they have had a greater opportunity for their reasoning about everyday choices to affect their academic performance.

We constructed four types of questions—questions about people's own behavior and choices, questions reflecting a recognition of what rules are recommended by economics, questions about social policy that involved a conflict between cost-benefit rules and other values, and questions about the salience of money and pleasure. If cost-benefit rules are normative, we would expect academic effectiveness, intellectual ability, and economics training to be associated with use of the rules in subjects' personal choices. If economics training is effective, we would expect that it would be positively related to the recognition of cost-benefit reasoning. Because we argue that it is reasoning about costs and benefits and not the sheer pursuit of money or pleasure that underlies the use of cost-benefit reasoning, we expected that the predictor variables would not be related to salience of money and enjoyment.

Method

Subjects. One hundred students who were listed as seniors at the beginning of the 1989–1990 academic year were randomly selected from the student directory (56 men, 44 women). Near the end of the 1989–1990 academic year, they were contacted by mail and offered five dollars for filling out and returning a short questionnaire on decision-making. Three follow-up contacts were made to encourage people who had not returned it to complete the survey. Eighty-six subjects completed and returned the questionnaire (48 men, 38 women).

Materials.   Four measures were created by averaging the scores for each of several types of question. All questions were scored on a 0 to 1 scale, with 0 indicating reasoning counter to cost-benefit rules and 1 indicating reasoning in line with the rules. A lack of preference was assigned an intermediate score of .5. Questions were designed to cover a wide range of behaviors and opinions. The questions for each index were similar in that each contained a response that reflected the use of cost-benefit rules, though of course reasons for giving a particular response to a particular question may have been due in part to other considerations as well. Indices were constructed based on a priori, common-sense considerations about what sort of question was best regarded as a reflection of actual behavior, of recognizing economic principles, and so on. We took the precaution, however, of eliminating any items that were negatively correlated with the other items on the index.

1. Own behavior and decisions (6 items)

The first set of questions was about reasoning subjects used in their own decisions and behaviors. These questions were intended to measure the extent to which subjects ignored sunk costs and attended to opportunity costs in their day-to-day decisions. An example of a question about decisions they had actually made was "In the past 3 years, have you ever started one of the following but not finished it?" The question was followed by a list of activities, such as a restaurant meal, a movie at a theater or attendance at an athletic event. The item score consisted of the average across all of the questions.

Subjects were also asked open-ended questions about some common decisions they might make in their everyday lives. One question read, "You and a friend have each spent $5 to see a movie that is turning out to be pretty bad. What are good reasons for staying to see the end? What are good reasons for leaving?" Stating that the spent money was a good reason for staying was scored as a failure to ignore sunk costs. Stating that the movie was a waste of time was a good reason for leaving was scored as partial attendance to opportunity costs, and stating that there might be better things to do was scored as full attendance to opportunity costs. (All of the open-ended questions were coded by two coders who agreed on 90 percent of the classifications. The remaining 10 percent were coded through consensus.)

2. Recognition of economic reasoning (3 items)

The second set of questions measured whether subjects could correctly identify the sort of reasoning that would be endorsed by economists. An example of a sunk cost recognition problem is the following. The multiple choice responses represented different combinations of behavior (continuing vs. discontinuing an activity that involved a sunk cost) and rationale for the behavior (attending to sunk costs vs. ignoring sunk costs):

> Imagine that you have paid $5 for a movie that is turning out to be pretty bad. If the movie had been free, you probably wouldn't stay. What do you think an economist would recommend doing?
>
> (0.00) ___ Stay, even though it's bad, because you've spent the $5 on it. Otherwise, you're wasting your money. (Sunk cost trap behavior, sunk cost trap rationale.)
>
> (0.50) ___ Leave, because the boredom of a bad movie is worse than the $5 you lose by leaving. It's more costly to stay than to leave. (Cost-benefit behavior, sunk cost trap rationale.)
>
> (1.00) ___ Leave, because the movie is bad and $5 doesn't matter anymore. If you wouldn't stay for free, you shouldn't stay because it cost $5. (Cost-benefit behavior, cost-benefit rationale.)
>
> (0.50) ___ Stay, because the movie might get better. You should think of the $5 as a gamble that might pay off. (Sunk cost trap behavior, cost-benefit rationale.)

The cost-benefit combination was given the highest score, the trap combination the lowest score, and the mixed combinations were given the same intermediate score.

3. Value conflict (8 items)

The third set of questions was about university and government policy issues for which cost-benefit reasoning led to a conflict with a salient humanitarian consideration. The following is an example of a net-benefit problem in which the cost-benefit answer conflicts with values against exploitation of another's weakness.

> As you may know, there are continuing problems with assuring that blood supplies for patients are free of all viruses. The suggestion has recently been

made to purchase blood from Asians for use in the West, on the grounds that many of the most dangerous viruses, including AIDS, are less common there. Many citizens of relatively poor Asian countries would be happy to have the extra cash; however, others have argued that such a practice would be an inappropriate form of exploitation. Do you tend to:

(1.00) ___ favor the idea strongly

(0.75) ___ favor it somewhat

(0.50) ___ have no preference

(0.25) ___ oppose the idea somewhat

(0.00) ___ oppose it strongly (from Larrick et al., 1990)

The following is an example of an opportunity cost problem in which the economic answer conflicts with the knowledge of certain harm to individuals resulting from the choice.

The state of Michigan is anticipating a large budget deficit, and is trying to find budget items on which it can reduce spending. One program that has recently been mentioned is funding for road and bridge repair. Experts estimate that a $200 million cut in the highway fund would lead to only five to ten more people dying each year in automobile accidents than do at the present. Many legislators have argued that it is morally wrong to let people die due to the state's negligence. Others have argued that this large saving would keep more beneficial programs funded. Do you tend to favor:

(0.00) ___ spending the money to repair the state's highways and bridges.

(1.00) ___ spending the money on other programs

(0.50) ___ no preference

4. Salience of money or enjoyment (5 items)

The fourth set of questions was about the importance of money or enjoyment in the person's own decisions and behaviors. This index was used to measure the pursuit of self-interest. For example, an open-ended question asked "Of the careers that you have decided not to pursue, what is the career that you liked the best? Why did you decide not to pursue it?" and was coded for a) mention of pay or financial stability and b) mention of anticipated enjoyment.

Questions about gender and number of economics classes taken were included at the end of the questionnaire. In addition, subjects were asked for permission to contact the University for college grade point average (GPA) and standardized test scores, which were either Scholastic Aptitude

TABLE 11.1

Zero-Order Correlation Coefficients Between Measures of Economic Reasoning and Grade Point Average, Verbal Score, Number of Economics Classes, and Gender

Predictor Variables	Own Behavior and Decisions	Recognition of Economists' Position	Value Conflict	Salience of Money and Enjoyment
Grade Point Average	.40***	.20	.14	− .02
Verbal Score	.13	.39***	.36**	− .12
Economics Classes	.10	.27**	.33**	− .20
Gender	.25*	.14	.32**	− .24*

Note. *p < .05, **p < .01, ***p < .001, two-tailed.

Test (SAT) or American College Test (ACT) verbal and mathematics aptitude scores.

Results and Discussion

The four cost-benefit reasoning measures were correlated with GPA, SAT Verbal score, SAT Math score, number of economics classes, and gender, which was coded as a dummy variable with males as 1 and females as 0. In these analyses, American College Test (ACT) scores were converted to SAT score form for subjects who had not taken the SAT.[1] SAT Verbal and SAT Math scores had zero-order correlations with the economic reasoning measures that were similar except that in every case the Verbal scores were more highly positively correlated with the reasoning measures than were the Math scores, in most cases substantially so. The same relationship held when the analyses were repeated using ordinary least squares multiple regression. The zero-order correlations are reported in Table 11.1 and the standardized regression coefficients are reported in Table 11.2 for all the predictor variables except SAT Math score. It may be seen that the two analyses yield very similar results.

TABLE 11.2

Standardized Regression Coefficients for Measures of Economic Reasoning Regressed on Grade Point Average, Verbal Score, Number of Economics Classes, and Gender

Predictor Variables	Own Behavior and Decisions	Recognition of Economists' Position	Value Conflict	Salience of Money and Enjoyment
Grade Point Average	.50***	.18	.15	− .06
Verbal Score	.03	.39**	.50***	− .06
Economics Classes	.15	.32**	.39**	− .09
Gender	.25*	.15	.43***	− .19

Note. Analyses also control for Math score. *p < .05, **p < .01, ***p < .001, two-tailed.

The measure of academic effectiveness, grade point average, was positively related to choosing the cost-benefit response for own behaviors and decisions. Intelligence, as measured by SAT Verbal score, was positively related to recognition of economists' position on various economic problems. The SAT Verbal measure was also positively related to choosing the economic response for policy choices in which there was a conflict with humanitarian values. A similar pattern was found for the number of economics classes taken. The more economics classes the student had taken, the more likely the student was to recognize what the economists' position is on a variety of problems and to prefer the economic response in policy choices that had a value conflict.

Gender was related to choice of economic responses in own behavior and in choices on policy issues in which there was a conflict between cost-benefit rules and humanitarian values. Because the value conflict effect was of a larger magnitude than the behavior effect and there was no relationship between gender and recognition of economists' reasoning, we believe that the gender difference in behavior may be due to value differences that arise in everyday decisions rather than to differences in the understanding of economic rules. This interpretation is supported by results reported for Study 2 indicating the gender difference for behavior is nonsignificant except when there is a value conflict.

None of the variables was related to our measure of the salience of money and enjoyment. What this indicates most notably is that we find no evidence that economics training is associated with an enhanced concern with money or pleasure. Thus the preference of economically-trained students for economic answers to problems is probably related to their preference for the rule system and not to a greater concern with money or with maximizing pleasure.

It is important to note that the regression coefficients in Table 11.2 are in general quite similar to the zero-order correlations between predictor and outcome variables in Table 11.1. An interesting exception is the correlation between GPA and the own behavior and decisions index, which was .50 — higher than the zero-order correlation of .40. What this discrepancy suggests is the conclusion that students who obtain higher GPAs than would be predicted by their intelligence are particularly likely to use cost-benefit rules in their own behaviors and decisions. The only zero-order correlation that loses significance in the regression analysis is the correlation between gender and salience of money and pleasure (a significant − .24). Female students are more concerned with money and pleasure than male students, though not, for reasons we do not pretend to understand, when their levels on the other predictor variables are taken into consideration.

Our major predictions are well supported by the data. The behavior and decisions of students with higher GPAs were more consistent with cost-benefit rules, and particularly so for students whose GPA exceeded what would be expected on the basis of ability measures. Cost-benefit reasoning was recognized more by more intelligent students and by students with training in economics, reflecting a better understanding of rules endorsed by economists. And cost-benefit reasoning was endorsed more by more intelligent students and more by students with training in economics when there was a policy choice in which there was a conflict between cost-benefit rules and humanitarian considerations. This pattern of results suggests that there may actually be separate behavioral and attitudinal components underlying the use of economic rules that do not necessarily intersect (a distinction similar to the one Wagner and Sternberg (1985) make between practical intelligence and formal knowledge). Neither economics training nor the other predictor variables was associated with greater salience of money or pleasure in decision-making. Finally, the data supported our supposition that females' adherence to economic rules differs from that of males primarily in that it simply takes a backseat to humanitarian values. Females were significantly less likely to give answers in line with economic rules for problems for which the rules gave an answer in conflict with such values.

STUDY 2

In Study 2, we reexamined data collected in a survey of economic reasoning administered to University of Michigan faculty. Professors of economics, biology, and the humanities were asked two types of questions, one type measuring behavior reflecting economic choices and the other type measuring reasoning about university and international policy.

The other variables studied were salary, academic discipline, gender, and age. The study allows us to replicate the training and gender findings of Study 1, and to attempt a conceptual replication of the life consequences finding by examining salary instead of grade point average.

Method

Subjects. All of the professors in the economics, biology, art history, and modern languages departments at the University of Michigan were contacted by telephone and asked to participate in a twenty minute telephone survey on university policy choices and personal choices. Overall, 88% of the professors agreed to participate, yielding a sample of 125 subjects.

Materials. Two types of reasoning questions were included on the faculty survey: reasoning about university policy and about international policy. Several of the questions were identical to those asked of the university seniors. For example, one of the policy questions was the one concerning buying blood from poor Asians. Policy questions were also asked in which economic reasoning led to the same conclusion as would the consideration of a humanitarian value. An example of an opportunity cost problem of this type is:

> Some financial planners for the university anticipate that jobs for young people may soon be much more plentiful than in the recent past, for the simple reason that a much smaller fraction of the population is in the younger age group. One implication is that pay will increase for entry level jobs in all kinds of industries. The argument has been made that the university should respond to this situation by offering more money for scholarships in order to lure low income students away from starting work and toward continuing their education. Do you feel:
>
> (1.00) ___ scholarships should be kept competitive with salaries
>
> (0.00) ___ scholarships should simply maintain pace with inflation and not respond to competitive inducements
>
> (0.50) ___ or you do not have an opinion? (from Larrick et al., 1990)

An analysis of opportunity cost indicates that, if students are expected to forego jobs in an improving market, universities will have to increase their financial aid in order to maintain their attractiveness to students. In this case, the cost-benefit recommendation is consistent with the salient humanitarian consideration that low income students should receive financial assistance for their education.

The policy questions were followed by questions about consumer and time-use choices that subjects had actually made. For instance, the faculty were asked a question similar to the one asked of the university seniors in Study 1: "In the past five years, have you ever started one of the following items and then not finished it?" This was followed by a list of seven consumer items. Discontinuing an activity for which one has already paid is an indication that one is willing to ignore sunk costs. Faculty were also asked, "Have you ever dropped a research project that was not proving worthwhile?" which measures willingness to ignore a sunk cost and to attend to opportunity costs. They were also asked about attempts to save time: "Do you own a microwave? A dishwasher? A VCR?" Freeing up time for other activities by investing in time-saving appliances was considered a measure of attending to opportunity costs.

The questions were subsequently reclassified into three types: no conflict with humanitarian values (for example, the scholarship question), conflict with humanitarian values (for example, the blood purchase question), and money and enjoyment maximization (for example, "do you own a micro-wave?"). It should be noted that the last index is not directly comparable to the salience of money and enjoyment index used in Study 1. The Study 1 index included questions asking subjects to describe the considerations that would enter into different decisions they might make, and then the responses were coded for the mention of financial or of enjoyment concerns. The Study 2 index consisted of questions that asked subjects about how they managed their money and about whether they owned creature comforts.

Subjects also provided demographic information regarding gender and age. Six years of salary data were obtained from published sources at the university.

Results and Discussion

The behavior and policy choice indices were correlated with salary, economics training, gender, and age, and are reported in the left side of Table 11.3.[2] In addition, the analyses were repeated using ordinary least squares multiple regression to assess the independent effects of the predictors. It may be seen that the standardized multiple regression coefficients in Table 11.4 yield very similar conclusions as the correlations, with the zero-order correlations being in general higher.

The results show that higher salaries were significantly related to economic behavior and policy choices. It is important to note that all of these relationships also held when the salary sensitive items were removed from the indices. In addition, the salary results were actually stronger when the

TABLE 11.3
Zero-Order Correlation Coefficients Between Measures of Economic Reasoning
and Salary, Economics Training, Gender, and Age

	Behavior and Policy Indices		Value Indices		
	Own Behavior and Decisions	Combined Policy Choices	No Value Conflict Items	Value Conflict Items	Money- and Enjoyment-Directed Behavior
Salary	.32***	.32***	.29***	.27**	.35***
Economics	.43**	.45**	.36***	.49***	.27**
Gender	.19*	.24**	.09	.21*	.26**
Age	−.11	−.21*	−.06	−.23**	.04

Note. The reasoning and behavior indices and the value indices are different ways of indexing the same items. They are not independent findings. *p < .05, **p < .01, ***p < .001, two-tailed.

TABLE 11.4
Standardized Regression Coefficients for Economic Reasoning Regressed on
Salary, Economics Training, Gender, and Age

	Behavior and Policy Indices		Value Indices		
	Own Behavior and Decisions	Combined Policy Choices	No Value Conflict Items	Value Conflict Items	Money- and Enjoyment- Directed Behavior
Salary	.26*	.33***	.26*	.26**	.30**
Economics	.32***	.27**	.24*	.34***	.16
Gender	.11	.20**	.02	.19*	.17*
Age	−.16	−.30**	−.12	−.27**	−.08

Note. The reasoning and behavior indices and the value indices are different ways of indexing the same items. They are not independent findings. $*p < .05$, $**p < .01$, $***p < .001$, two-tailed.

economists were omitted from the sample. When the sample included only biologists and humanists, the standardized salary coefficients were .28 for behavior and .43 for combined policy choices. There was no effect of discipline among the noneconomists for any of the indices. The salary relationships were of a similar magnitude when examined entirely within a discipline, although the significance levels suffered due to the smaller sample size.

The variables on the right side of Tables 11.3 and 11.4 are recategorizatons of the variables on the left. It may be seen that higher salaries were significantly related to cost-benefit reasoning both when it was and when it was not in conflict with humanitarian values. And, as might be expected, salary was positively related to money- and enjoyment-directed behavior, which included such measures as owning labor-saving devices. The relationships were once again somewhat stronger when the economists were excluded from the sample (standardized regression coefficients of .30 for salary for all three value indices).

Another measure of effectiveness is the average size of raise, which may be regarded as reflecting changes in the rate of effectiveness. Average raise over the past five years, measured as an annual percentage change in salary, was (weakly) related to cost-benefit reasoning for policy choices (regression coefficient $= .15$, $p = .07$) when it was added to the full regression model. Again, the relationship is stronger—though not more statistically significant because of the smaller sample size—when the economists are excluded (coefficient $= .19$, $p = .11$).

As has been reported previously by Larrick et al., economics training was significantly related to economic reasoning and behavior. It may be seen from the right side of Tables 11.3 and 11.4 that economics training was significantly related to cost-benefit reasoning both when it did and when it did not conflict with humanitarian values. Economists, however, were not significantly more likely to engage in the pursuit of money and enjoyment when the other predictors were controlled in the analysis.

Gender was not related to behavior when the other predictors were held constant. Men were more likely to endorse cost-benefit reasoning for the policy index than were women, but this was due entirely to differences when there was a value conflict. It may be seen that men and women showed no difference on the no conflict items, but a significant difference on the conflict items. Men were more concerned with money- and enjoyment-related behavior, and this remained significant when the other variables were controlled.

Age was not related to economic behavior but was significantly related to economic reasoning such that younger subjects employed more cost-benefit reasoning. This difference was confined to problems where cost-benefit reasoning conflicted with humanitarian values. Younger subjects were more likely to employ cost-benefit reasoning only for problems for which there was such a conflict. We cannot tell whether this is a developmental effect, leading us to expect that the younger subjects will eventually come to resemble older subjects, or a cohort effect, reflecting what may be a stable preference in the younger generation for cost-benefit reasoning even when its conclusions conflict with other values. An answer will have to await the arrival of another generation or two of academics.

GENERAL DISCUSSION

The present results greatly expand the empirically-based case for the normativeness of cost-benefit rules. As microeconomic theory predicts, the people who use these rules are more likely to have successful life outcomes. The college seniors who used cost-benefit reasoning in their everyday decisions had higher grade point averages, including higher averages net of their aptitude, and the faculty who used cost-benefit reasoning in their everyday behaviors had higher salaries. These data cannot answer questions of causality and tell us whether use of the rules leads to greater success, greater success leads to use of the rules, or some third factor causes both. However, Study 1 shows at least that the relationship between cost-benefit reasoning and academic effectiveness is independent of intelligence and of economics training.

Additional evidence for the normative claim of cost-benefit reasoning comes from the fact that it was positively related to intelligence in Study 1. As Baron (1985) and others have defined it, intelligence is the set of psychological properties that enable a person to achieve his or her goals effectively. On this view, intelligent people will be more likely to use rules of choice that are effective in reaching their goals than will less intelligent people.

Finally, our results show that people who are familiar with the economic rules use them to a large extent in the way they behave and think in their everyday lives. We found in Study 1 that the number of economics classes taken was positively correlated with cost-benefit reasoning and in Study 2 that economists were more likely to use the rule system both in behavior and expressed choices than noneconomists. Unfortunately, we cannot assess whether these results are due to the effect of training, to self-selection, or some other combination of factors. But it should be recalled that we have elsewhere shown that laboratory-training in the cost-benefit rules has effects on behavior outside the laboratory.

The fact that effectiveness, intelligence, and training were related to cost-benefit reasoning even when it conflicted with certain humanitarian values raises interesting normative questions concerning the conflict between maximizing material well-being for society as a whole and concern with rules of fairness and compassion. These findings suggest that many of the people who know and use the rules in their own decisions believe that they are beneficial when applied to a larger social context, even when there are costs involving important values. On the other hand, the women in both studies and the older faculty in Study 2 tended to favor humanitarian considerations when they conflicted with the economic rules. Younger men seemed to be concerned with issues of maximizing material well-being to society in general. Women and older men seemed to be more concerned with avoiding inegalitarian or debasing outcomes for groups or individuals.

There is some evidence indicating that the age difference reflects at least in part a cohort effect. A fair amount of survey data indicates that members of the present younger generation hold more conservative values related to humanitarian concerns than their elder colleagues who were often found taking action to uphold those values when they were younger (Inglehart and Flanagan, 1987; American Council on Education, 1973–1986). But we also suspect, in this case in the absence of supporting data, that people become more concerned with individual welfare and more dubious of abstract utilitarian principles as they grow older. We close by noting that we are sympathetic with the perspective of our female subjects and our older subjects. We believe that a complete set of normative rules for choice must include rules that can adjudicate between cost-benefit reasoning and moral questions reflecting such considerations as the rights of particular individuals and the avoidance of exploitation.

FOOTNOTES

[1]There were no records of standardized test scores for seventeen subjects who had transferred to the university after their first year. We ran two regressions to test whether the

complete sample of 86 was different from the sample of 69 for whom we had scores on all the predictor variables. We excluded the test scores from these regressions to determine whether the remaining predictors had the same relationship to the outcome measures in both samples. The results were essentially the same, so we report the analyses for the sample of sixty-nine subjects for which we have values for all of the predictors.

²Some of the items in the behavior index (e.g., discontinuing an activity for which a sunk cost was incurred) could be affected by consumption opportunities (e.g., how often the person sees movies, plays, concerts, and so on), so the analysis was repeated with consumption opportunities included as an additional predictor variable. It was not significant (p > .20) and did not change the significance levels of any of the independent variables.

REFERENCES

American Council on Education (1973–1988). *The American freshman: National norms.* Annual report issued by the Cooperative Institution Research Program, Graduate School of Education, University of California.

Arkes, H. R., & Blumer, C. (1985). The psychology of sunk cost. *Organizational Behavior and Human Decision Processes, 35,* 124–140.

Baron, J. (1985). *Rationality and intelligence.* Cambridge: Cambridge University Press.

Becker, G. (1976). *The economic approach to human behavior.* Chicago: University of Chicago Press.

Frank, R. (1988). *Passions within reason: The strategic role of the emotions.* New York: Norton.

Gilligan, C. (1982). *In a different voice: Psychological theory and women's development.* Cambridge, MA: Harvard University Press.

Goldman, A. I. (1978). Epistemics: The regulative theory of cognition. *Journal of Philosophy, 75,* 509–523.

Goldman, A. I. (1986). *Epistemology and cognition.* Cambridge, MA: Harvard University Press.

Heath, J. (1989). An econometric model of the role of gender in economic education. *American Economic Review, 79,* 226–230.

Hirshleifer, J. (1985). The expanding domain of economics. *American Economic Review, 75,* 53–68.

Holland, J. H., Holyoak, K. J., Nisbett, R. E., & Thagard, P. R. (1986). *Induction: Processes of inference, learning, and discovery.* Cambridge, MA: MIT Press.

Hoskin, R. E. (1983). Opportunity cost and behavior. *Journal of Accounting Research, 21,* 78–95.

Inglehart, R., & Flanagan, S. C. (1987). Value change in industrial societies. *American Political Science Review, 81,* 1288–1322.

Jepson, C., Krantz, D. H., & Nisbett, R. E. (1983). Inductive reasoning: Competence or skill? *Behavioral and Brain Sciences, 6,* 494–501.

Larrick, R. P., Morgan, J. N., & Nisbett, R. E. (1990). Teaching the use of cost-benefit reasoning in everyday life. *Psychological Science, 1,* 362–370.

March, J. G. (1978). Bounded rationality, ambiguity, and the engineering of choice. *Bell Journal of Economics, 9,* 587–608.

Mishan, E. J. (1976). *Cost-benefit analysis.* New York: Praeger.

Morgan, J. N., & Duncan, G. J. (1982). *Making your choices count: Economic principles for everyday decisions.* Ann Arbor: University of Michigan Press.

Newell, A., & Simon, H. A. (1972). *Human problem solving.* Englewood Cliffs, NJ: Prentice-Hall.

Nisbett, R. E., Fong, G. T., Lehman, D. R., & Cheng, P. W. (1987). Teaching reasoning. *Science, 238,* 625–631.

Simon, H. A. (1955). A behavioral model of choice. *Quarterly Journal of Economics, 69,* 99–118.

Smith, E. E., Langston, C., & Nisbett, R. E. (in press). The case for rules in reasoning. *Cognitive Science.*

Sternberg, R. J. (1985). *Beyond IQ: A triarchic theory of human intelligence.* New York: Cambridge University Press.

Sternberg, R. J. (1988). *The triarchic mind: A new theory of human intelligence.* New York: Viking.

Stich, S. P. (1990). *The fragmentation of reason: Preface to a pragmatic theory of cognitive evaluation.* Cambridge, MA: MIT Press.

Stich, S. P., & Nisbett, R. E. (1980). Justification and the psychology of human reasoning. *Philosophy of Science, 47,* 188–202.

Thagard, P. R. (1982). From the descriptive to the normative in science. *Philosophy of Science, 49,* 24–42.

Thagard, P. R., & Nisbett, R. E. (1983). Rationality and charity. *Philosophy of Science, 50,* 250–267.

Tversky, A., & Kahneman, D. (1986). Rational choice and the framing of decisions. *Journal of Business, 59,* 251–278.

Wagner, R. K., & Sternberg, R. J. (1985). Practical intelligence in real world pursuits: The role of tacit knowledge. *Journal of Personality and Social Psychology, 49,* 436–458.

Watts, M., & Lynch, G. J. (1989). The principles courses revisited. *American Economic Review, 79,* 236–241.

VI IMPLICATIONS FOR EDUCATION

12 Teaching Reasoning

Richard E. Nisbott
University of Michigan

Darrin R. Lehman
University of British Columbia

Geoffrey T. Fong
University of Waterloo, Canada

Patricia W. Cheng
University of California, Los Angeles

Do people use abstract, domain-independent inferential rules to think about everyday events? Can reasoning be improved by formal instruction in the use of inferential rules? Historically, the answer to both questions was yes. That reasoning makes use of inferential rules and that these rules can be taught by formal discipline shaped a position endorsed by most educators through the end of the 19th century.

In the 20th century two different positions have countered the formal discipline view. The first is that there are no inferential rules, but only highly domain-specific empirical rules dealing with concrete types of events. First presented by Thorndike *(1),* this position is still endorsed by many theorists today. For example, Newell *(2)* stated, "The modern . . . position is that learned problem-solving skills are, in general, idiosyncratic to the task." A second view is that people do use abstract inferential rules, but that these cannot be taught to any significant extent. Instead, such rules are induced by every individual in the normal course of development and cannot be improved by instruction. First put forth by Piaget *(3),* this view is highly influential in cognitive and developmental psychology and in education.

We propose an alternative view that is close to the pre-20th-century one: people do make use of inferential rules and these can be readily taught. In fact, rules that are extensions of naturally induced ones can be taught by quite abstract means. This description does not apply to formal, deductive logical rules or to most other purely syntactic rule systems, however. Instead, the types of inferential rules that people use naturally and can be taught most easily are a family of pragmatic inferential rule systems that people induce in the context of solving recurrent everyday problems *(4)*. These rule systems are abstract inasmuch as they can be used in a wide variety of content domains, but their use is confined to certain types of problem goals and particular types of relations between events. They include "causal schemas" *(5)*, "contractual schemas," such as the rules underlying permission and obligation in the social sphere, and "statistical heuristics," used in the evaluation of evidence, such as qualitative, intuitive versions of the law of large numbers.

We review briefly the history of the formal discipline notion, summarize the views of 20th-century psychologists who opposed it, present evidence from our research that people reason in accordance with abstract inferential rules, present experimental evidence from the laboratory showing that people can be trained to enhance their use of inferential rules for solving everyday problems, and present evidence from studies of higher education showing that something akin to formal discipline is a reality — reasoning can be taught.

FORMAL DISCIPLINE AND ITS CRITICS

Plato stated the doctrine of formal discipline, which holds that the study of abstract rule systems trains the mind for reasoning about concrete problems. Plato wrote that the study of arithmetic and geometry was especially effective in improving reasoning, ". . . [E]ven the dull, if they have had arithmetical training, . . . always become much quicker than they would otherwise have been. . . . We must endeavour to persuade those who are to be the principal men of our state to go and learn arithmetic . . ."*(6)*.

Later, Roman philosophers added the study of grammar and the training of the faculty of memory to the list of exercises that were useful for formal discipline. The medieval scholastics then added an emphasis on logic, particularly the syllogism. Finally, the humanists added to the previous list the study of Latin and Greek *(7)*.

The formal discipline view ultimately became so extreme that a mid-19th-century educator was able to advocate the teaching of a content field strictly for its discipline or exercise properties *(8)*:

> My claim for Latin, as an Englishman and a . . . teacher, is simply that it would be impossible to devise for English boys a better teaching instrument. . . . The acquisition of a language is educationally of no importance; what is important is the process of acquiring it. . . . The one great merit of Latin as a teaching instrument is its tremendous difficulty.

One of the first endeavors of the new discipline of psychology was to provide experimental research that cast doubt on the formal discipline concept. The most effective antagonist was Thorndike, who undertook a program of empirical research on transfer of training effects that remains impressive by today's standards. Thorndike rarely found strong transfer effects. He reached the conclusion that the degree of transfer was a function of the number of identical elements in common to the target task and the trained task, where identical elements were defined at the level of relatively concrete features and relations. By taking this position of extreme domain specificity, Thorndike (9) was as pessimistic about training effects as previous thinkers had been optimistic.

> Training the mind means the development of thousands of particular independent capacities. . . . The amount of identical elements in different mental functions and the amount of general influence from special training are much less than common opinion supposes.

Thorndike's work was enormously effective in destroying the theoretical rationale for the 19th-century curriculum, which consisted mostly of languages and mathematics and other subjects deemed useful for formal discipline and which largely excluded the natural sciences and other fields because of their emphasis on mere content. But Thorndike's work was really more effective than it should have been, inasmuch as it rarely dealt with reasoning per se. Instead, he studied transfer of training from tasks such as canceling letters in a written message to canceling parts of speech, and estimating areas of rectangles of one size and shape to estimating areas of rectangles of another size and shape. In more recent work in the problem-solving tradition, however, the same conclusion has been reached on the basis of tasks that most people would classify as reasoning tasks. For example, solution of the "Towers of Hanoi" problem (requiring people to move objects from one location to another while preserving size relations among the objects at every location at every point during the move) does not generalize to other, formally identical problems (10).

The major psychologist to study reasoning in the period between Thorndike's work and the revolution in thought in the 1960s that saw the shift from a behaviorist viewpoint to an information-processing one was Piaget. Piaget, agreeing with the classical philosophers that everyday reasoning is governed by abstract rules, argued that much reasoning is hypothetico-deductive, handled for the most part by what he called "propositional operations" and by "formal operational schemes." The former are operations in deductive logic; the latter, methods whereby propositional operations are applied to reasoning situations that occur with great regularity in the environment. Formal operations include the probability scheme, an elaborate set of rules for applying probabilistic concepts to uncertain events, such as those produced by randomizing devices.

In Piaget's view, both the propositional operations and the formal operational schemes develop in early adolescence. Before that, children possess only various concrete operations for solving problems, that is, problem-solving rules that are tied to particular content domains. Although Piaget argued that people use inferential rules, he insisted that teaching rules at a high level of abstraction was not possible and that teaching rules in several concrete domains could not accelerate their acquisition in an abstract form. He argued that learning of such rules was dependent on spontaneous cognitive development resulting from active self-discovery.

Piaget's views about both propositional and formal operations have been undermined by recent research *(3)*. Piaget's view of propositional operations is cast into doubt because even adults accept invalid arguments when their world knowledge encourages it. For example, given, "All oak trees have acorns. This tree has acorns. Is it an oak?", many adults insist it must be. Defenders of Piaget point out that errors of this type may reflect only vagaries in the interpretation of the arguments, such as the addition or omission of premises due to implicit knowledge. Our knowledge of oaks and acorns, for example, may invite the assumption that only oaks have acorns. Thus, although the conclusion that the tree is an oak is fallacious according to formal logical principles (it is an instance of the fallacy of "affirming the consequent"), it is actually valid within the context of the invited assumptions.

Although it is reasonable to assume that people often do make mistakes because of invited inferences, such interpretive mistakes cannot account for errors produced by college students on deductive reasoning problems in which arbitrary symbols and relations are used. The best known of these problems is Wason's selection task *(11)*. In this task subjects are informed that they will be shown cards that have numbers on one side and letters on the other, and are given a rule such as, "If a card has a vowel on one side, then it has an even number on the other." Subjects are then presented with four cards, which might show A, B, 4, and 7, and are asked to turn over only those cards that they have to in order to determine whether the rule holds. The correct answer in this example is to turn over the cards showing A and 7. The logical rule used in such problems is a conditional, "if p then q," and the relevant cases are p (because if p is the case it must be established that q is also the case) and not-q (because if it is not the case that q then it must be established that it is also not the case that p). It has been shown with a wide variety of subject populations that when people are presented with such problems with arbitrary relations and no clear semantic interpretation, only a small minority can produce the correct answer.

In the face of evidence that people sometimes seem incapable of using formal logical principles, a view similar to Thorndike's extreme domain specificity has arisen. Since subjects can solve concrete problems in realistic contexts but often cannot solve arbitrary problems, the assertion is sometimes made that all reasoning takes place by domain-specific rules and that more abstract rules play no part in everyday reasoning *(12)*.

Piaget's assertion that people use formal operational schemes such as the probability scheme comes from his work showing that even children can use intuitive versions of the laws of probability to predict the behavior of randomizing devices *(13)*. But the assumption that these rules generalize to everyday events has been buffeted by recent work, especially that of Kahneman and Tversky and others studying problem-solving heuristics *(14, 15)*. These investigators have shown that for many inductive reasoning tasks that require statistical principles, such as the law of large numbers is that the base rate or regression principle, and the conjunction principle, people often fail to use such rules. For example, in one study *(14)* it was shown that subjects did not recognize that a deviant ratio of male to female births was more likely at a hospital with 15 births per day than at a hospital with 45 births per day.

In another study *(14)* subjects were told that 100 people, all of whom were either lawyers or engineers, had been interviewed by psychologists. The subjects were to read what they were told were thumbnail descriptions of the people written by psychologists and asked to guess whether each person described was a lawyer or an engineer. Some subjects were told that the sample of 100 consisted of 70 lawyers and 30 engineers and some were told that the sample consisted of 30 lawyers and 70 engineers. Subjects based their guesses as to occupation almost exclusively on the similarity of the description to their stereotypes for lawyer versus engineer and were little influenced by the frequency of engineers and lawyers in the sample. This was true even when the description was designed to be nondiagnostic with respect to occupation, that is, not suggestive either of an engineer or a lawyer. It should be noted that performance typically is not improved on such problems by various manipulations designed to encourage good work, including monetary incentives for correct answers. Such results have suggested to some that any statistical rules that people may have for the behavior of randomizing devices may not exist at a sufficiently general level to make contact with everyday life problems not involving such devices.

Whether or not these rules exist at a general level, however, both Piaget and theorists who espouse a position of extreme domain specificity are in agreement that teaching abstract rules should be ineffective and that training in a given domain should produce little transfer to other domains. We attempt to show that this pessimistic view of the trainability of inferential rules is mistaken.

TEACHING STATISTICAL REASONING

Our initial work on the use and trainability of inferential rules focused on a set of statistical rules that are derivable from the law of large numbers. We and our colleagues have found that people reason in accordance with the law of large numbers in a wide range of tasks and domains. For example, generalization often proceeds in accordance with the principle that larger samples are required when generalizing about populations that are more variable with respect to a given attribute than when generalizing about populations that are less variable (16).

We did, however, find substantial domain specificity of the use of the law of large numbers. There was a hierarchy of usage such that subjects were very likely to use the law of large numbers for reasoning about the behavior of randomizing devices, less likely to use it for reasoning about objectively measurable events such as athletic performance and job and academic achievement, and unlikely to use it for reasoning about subjective events such as judgments about a person's friendliness or honesty (17). For example, subjects understood that a small sample of a slot machine's behavior is a poor guide to its behavior in general. They were less likely to apply the law of large numbers to a small sample of an athlete's behavior (for example, to assume that performance at a tryout might not be typical of general ability) and still less likely to apply the law of large numbers to social behavior (for example, to assume that friendliness expressed over a brief time period might not be typical of a person's friendliness in general).

It seems to us that subjects' failure to use the law of large numbers reflects not so much the lack of a general rule, but rather the difficulty of seeing its applicability to events of various kinds. Randomizing devices are by definition those whose behavior cannot be understood by application of causal laws; thus causal laws and other rules do not seriously compete with statistical rules for the "right" to analyze the problem. Objectively measurable events such as sports contests and various achievements normally are understood by the use of various rules about causality, but such events are also sufficiently "codable" (often using literally numerical codes) that people can apply a formal rule such as the law of large numbers. But for purely subjective events, it can be difficult to define the appropriate units for events or to code them on the same scale. Whereas it is possible to directly compare Bill's baseball or sales performance to Sam's with respect to a clear metric (for example, batting average, dollar volume, and so on), it is normally not possible to compare Bill's friendliness or honesty or conscientiousness to Sam's with the use of a clear metric. (What metric would one use to compare Bill's and Sam's friendliness? Smiles per minute?)

One implication of the codability interpretation of domain specificity is that manipulations of the codability of events would be expected to affect people's ability to apply the law of large numbers. And in fact, Nisbett *et al.* (15) found that when they made it easier to code events in problems in such a way that their inherent uncertainty was made more apparent, or simply when the events were made easier to compare by suggesting a unit of comparison, a higher proportion of subjects applied the law of large numbers to the problems.

Another finding consistent with the view that people actually possess an abstract version of the law of large numbers is that subjects often justified their statistical answers, across problems having widely varying content, by invoking quite abstract versions of the law of large numbers. This fact demonstrates that people do understand the rule in the abstract and that they know how to describe correctly how it can be mapped onto a solution for a given problem.

One way of providing evidence that people can use purely abstract rule systems would be to teach the rule system in order to see if people can apply it to a wide range of events for which it is applicable. Two different means of teaching would be persuasive on this point: (i) brief formal instruction in the abstract rule system and (ii) brief instruction in use of the rule system in a single domain. If purely formal instruction is effective across a wide variety of content domains, this would suggest a preexisting rule system and an ability to apply improvements to it to many domains. If training in a given domain generalizes substantially to other domains, this would suggest a substantial ability to abstract the rule, or rather, improvements to it, from particular content and would further imply a preexisting ability to apply uninstructed versions of the rule to a broad range of content.

We have examined the effects of teaching the law of large numbers both in the abstract and with examples drawn from a given broad domain *(18)*. Abstract instruction in the law of large numbers consisted of defining the notions of sample, population, and parameter, and illustrating that as sample size increases, the sample usually resembles the population more closely. Training on examples consisted of showing how to use the law of large numbers to solve a number of problems. In one problem, subjects read about the director of a ballet company who uses an audition to select new dancers. "Usually we're extremely excited about the potential of two or three of these young people—a young woman who does a brilliant series of turns or a young man who does several leaps that make you hold your breath. Unfortunately, most of these young people turn out to be only somewhat better than the rest. I believe many of these extraordinarily talented young people are frightened of success." Subjects were invited to appreciate the relevance of the law of large numbers to the problem in addition to the director's exclusively causal view: they were encouraged to think of each ballet dancer as possessing a population of ballet movements and to think of the audition as providing samples of that population; then since the sample is relatively small, the population value might well be different, especially when the sample value is quite extreme. (The measure in this case was simply the director's evaluation of each individual movement.) Examples were drawn exclusively from one of the following broadly defined domains — (i) manifestly probabilistic problems such as those involving random generating devices (for example, a problem in which the first few cards drawn from a shuffled deck in a board game are all from a particular category and subjects must realize that such a small sample result may not be indicative of the overall proportion in the category), (ii) objectively measurable events such as those involving achievements of some kind (for example, a problem about whether the performance of graduates of a particular law school in general could be safely estimated on the basis of the performance of just two particular graduates), or (iii) subjective judgments such as those assessing someone's sense of humor or kindness (for example, a problem in which the subjects must realize that a first impression of a person might not be a good indication of that individual's personality, at least not in comparison to impressions reached after a longer acquaintance).

Some subjects received no training at all, some received abstract rule training only, some examples training only, and some received both rule and examples training *(19)*. Each of the two separate training procedures took less than 30 minutes. All subjects were then tested on their ability to apply the law of large numbers to a variety of problems in all three domains. Subjects in one variant of the experiment were University of Michigan students; subjects in another variant were New Jersey homemakers, most with secondary education only, who were paid for their participation. Results from the two variants were entirely comparable and are reported together.

Subjects' open-ended answers to the test problems were coded and two dependent variables were created. "Frequency" was defined as the overall probability that a subject responded to a test problem by incorporating statistical concepts such as sample size, variability, or uncertainty, without regard to whether the subject used these concepts properly. "Quality" was defined as the conditional probability that a subject gave a "good statistical answer," that is, one in which the subject had made appropriate use of statistical principles, identifying the metric, the sample, the population, and their correct relation to one another.

Three results support the view that people possess an abstract version of the law of large numbers and that improvements to it can transfer to a wide range of problem content. First, purely abstract rule training produced improvement in both the frequency and the quality of statistical answers. Second, the abstract rule training effect was substantial across all three problem domains: training improved statistical reasoning for problems that people rarely think of in terms of probability just as much as it did for problems that people almost always think of in probabilistic terms. On average, rule training increased the percentage of statistical answers from 42 to 56 and increased the percentage of statistical answers judged by coders to be of high quality from 54 to 67 *(20)*. Third, training on examples readily generalized to domains very different from the trained domain. Indeed, generalization across domains was literally as great as generalization within domains. This seems hard to explain without assuming that instruction in the particular examples served to improve the abstract rule system underlying solution of all problems.

A follow-up study with Northwestern University students examined the effect of "examples" training with narrower domains *(21)*. Subjects were taught how to apply the law of large numbers either to a variety of sports problems or to a variety of problems having to do with ability testing. For example, in the sports training condition, subjects were asked to explain the fact that, after the first 2 weeks of the major league baseball season, the top batter typically has an average as high as .450, yet no batter has ever had as high an average as that at the end of the season. After subjects had tried their hands at the problem (usually providing exclusively causal, though not necessarily wrong, answers such as "the pitchers make the necessary adjustments"), they were shown the investigators' analysis which pointed out that, whatever causal factors might be involved, it is also relevant to note that 2 weeks provides a relatively small sample of a batter's ability and that batting averages that are highly discrepant from the average should therefore be more common than they are with a large sample.

Subjects' performance was then examined either in the trained domain or in the untrained domain, either immediately or after a delay of 2 weeks. Figure 12.1 presents the statistical reasoning score, that is, the average quality of the answer for each of five different problems. The remarkable domain independence of training effects is evident for subjects tested immediately. There was no significant advantage to being trained in a given domain: performance was as good for the untrained domain as for the trained domain. After a delay, there was a substantial degree of domain specificity. Even then, however, there remained a significantly greater

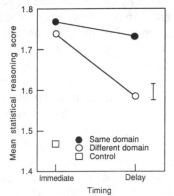

FIG. 12.1 Mean statistical reasoning score as a function of training and problem domain. Vertical bar represents one standard error of the mean ($N = 231$).

ability to apply the rule across domains after the delay than without any training at all.

It should be noted that the full degree of improvement initially observed in the trained domain is still observed after 2 weeks. It is unlikely either that the full retention of training within a domain or the improved performance across domains is due to retention of problem details and consequent mapping of details from the example problems to the new test problems by construction of analogies. In separate studies *(21),* it was found that ability to spontaneously recall details, or even the gist of the training examples, was extremely low after 2 weeks. We suspect that subjects learned improvements to the abstract rule system initially, as well as some specific abilities to apply the rule system to a particular content domain. After a delay, the increments to both general and specific rules were fully retained, and thus performance on the trained domain was as high as it was initially. Only the increments to general rules could be passed along directly to the untrained domain, and thus performance in the untrained domain was poorer after a delay — though nevertheless better than in the absence of training.

TEACHING LOGICAL REASONING

Since highly abstract statistical rules can be taught in such a way that they can be applied to a great range of everyday life events, is the same true of the even more abstract rules of deductive logic? We can report no evidence indicating that this is true, and we can provide some evidence indicating that it is not.

A purely syntactic rule system provides no information about which inferences among infinitely many valid inferences are useful. For example, given the statement, "If a burglar is breaking into one's house, then one should call the police," it is valid though hardly useful to infer, "If it's not the case that one should call the police, then a burglar is not breaking into one's house." In our view, when people reason in accordance with the rules of formal logic, they normally do so by using pragmatic reasoning schemas that happen to map onto the solutions provided by logic.

One type of pragmatic reasoning schema that could mimic the logic of the conditional is the "causal schema" identified by Kelley *(5).* He proposed that, when making causal attributions, people sometimes rely on very abstract rules about the kind of relations that obtain when the particular type of causality in question is of the necessary sort, the sufficient sort, or neither. We have found support for Kelley's contention. For example, people use different procedures for establishing whether a causal hypothesis is true depending on whether they assume that the type of causality they are examining is necessary and sufficient, necessary but not sufficient, sufficient but not necessary, or neither necessary nor sufficient *(22)*. The checking procedure for one of the causal schemas is identical to that for the conditional, namely, the sufficient but not necessary type of cause. To falsify such a hypothesis, one may either establish that the effect q is not present when the putative cause p is present, or establish that the cause p is present when the effect is not. The checking procedures for one of the other causal schemas, namely, the necessary and sufficient schema, are the same as those for the biconditional.

Another type of pragmatic reasoning schema is what might be called the contractual schema. The concept of a permission establishes that one will not be allowed to do action p unless permission q has been obtained. The concept of an obligation establishes that if situation p occurs then one is obliged to do action q. As it happens, the procedures for checking whether an infraction of a permission or obligation has occurred are the same as those for checking whether the conditional obtains. For example, one must establish that q has occurred (permission has been obtained) when one finds that action p has been carried out, and one must establish that action p has not been carried out when one knows that q (permission) has not occurred.

If people actually make use of schemas such as those for permission and obligation, then they should be able to solve problems whose checking procedures are identical with the logic of the conditional when they are encouraged to apply such schemas. Several studies indicate that this is true *(23)*. For example, many subjects who were given no context were unable to solve a simple conditional problem about deplaning airport passengers who were required to show a form. They were required to check whether the rule, "If the form says 'entering' on one side, then the other side includes cholera among the list of diseases," was violated by different instances. Almost all subjects readily solved the problem, however, when they were provided with a "permission" rationale, to wit, they were told that the form listed diseases for which the passenger had been inoculated, and a cholera inoculation was required to protect the entering passengers from the disease.

Another study examined the effects of training in the logic of the conditional on subjects' ability to solve both arbitrary conditional problems and problems evoking permission and obligation schemas *(24)*. Neither abstract rule training nor examples training showing how to use the conditional for solving particular concrete problems was effective. It is not the case that the training procedures were inherently useless, however, because when subjects were given both of the training procedures, this resulted in a very significant improvement in their performance. This is in sharp contrast to the statistical training studies, where both abstract rule training and examples training were effective alone. We believe that abstract logical training by itself was ineffective because the subjects had no preexisting logical rules corresponding to the conditional. (Or, more cautiously, any such rules are relatively weak and not likely to be applied in meaningful contexts.) Showing subjects how to use the rule to solve example problems was ineffective for the same reason. It was only when subjects were given both types of training that they could make use of either. The training procedures and problems used were far from exhaustive of reasonable approaches to teaching the conditional, but the results suggest that it may be difficult to teach logical rules by the straightforward techniques used to teach what we call pragmatic inferential rules.

In marked contrast to the effects of teaching abstract logical rules, training in the obligation schema was highly effective in improving performance both on problems that were suggestive of the obligation rule and on arbitrary problems that could be mapped onto it. We believe that this is the case because the obligation-based training could be attached to a preexisting knowledge structure whereas the purely syntactic training could not.

Our work suggests that the formal discipline view may well be correct in essence, but that it has misidentified the knowledge structures that underlie reasoning about everyday life events. There are abstract rules, and these can be trained abstractly. The rules may not be those of formal logic, however, but instead may be pragmatic inferential rules having to do with particular types of relationships and inferential goals. These structures are more specific than logical rules, but they are abstract in that they are not bound to any content domain.

IMPLICATIONS FOR HIGHER EDUCATION

It appears that inferential rules can be taught in the laboratory, and taught in such a way that they are reasonably enduring. Does higher education serve to teach these inferential rules in the same way, with similar or even greater durability? The answer appears to be yes, for both statistical rules and pragmatic reasoning schemas such as causal schemas and contractual schemas.

Teaching Statistics.   Fong et al. (18) examined the effects of differing amounts of statistical education on answers to a problem asking subjects to explain why a traveling saleswoman is typically disappointed on repeat visits to a restaurant where she experienced a truly outstanding meal on her first visit. Subjects who had no background in statistics almost always answered this problem with exclusively nonstatistical, causal answers such as "maybe the chefs change a lot" or "her expectations were so high that the food couldn't live up to them." Subjects who had taken one statistics course gave answers that included statistical considerations, such as "very few restaurants have only excellent meals, odds are she was just lucky the first time," about 20 percent of the time. Beginning graduate students in psychology, who had taken one to three courses in statistics, gave statistical answers about 40 percent of the time. Doctoral-level scientists at a research institution gave statistical answers about 80 percent of the time. (Though we do not wish to create the impression that these scientists would necessarily think in statistical terms so often in real life contexts! In this case, performance in the laboratory undoubtedly outstrips competence in the world.) Training affected the quality of statistical answers as much as it did their frequency. Subjects with but one statistics course rarely gave an answer that did much more than just point to the chance nature of the quality of any one meal; subjects with many courses often defined meals as the sampling unit, defined the population as all possible meals in the restaurant, invoked the notion of variability in meal quality within a restaurant, and so on.

The study just described was correlational. Another study of higher education by Fong et al. (18) was experimental, and replicated the effects. They conducted a telephone survey of opinions about sports. The subjects were males who were enrolled in an introductory statistics course at the University of Michigan. Some subjects were randomly selected and "surveyed" during the first 2 weeks of the term, the others at or near the end of the term. In addition to filler questions on National Collegiate Athletic Association rules and National Basketball Association salaries, subjects were asked questions for which a statistical approach was relevant. For example, subjects were asked to explain why the rookie of the year in baseball usually does not perform as well in his second year. Most subjects answered this question in a purely nonstatistical way, invoking causal notions such as "too much press attention" and "slacking off." Some subjects answered the question in a partly or completely statistical way, for example, "there are bound to be some rookies who have an exceptional season; it may not be due to any great talent advantage that one guy has over some of the others — he just got a particularly good year." The statistics course markedly increased the frequency and quality of statistical answers to this question and to two of four other questions that were asked.

Teaching Logic. If it is correct that systems of formal deductive logic are alien and hard to teach, then one might expect that even an entire course in formal logic would have little effect on students' ability to deal with problems that can be solved by the use of the conditional or biconditional. To test this, Cheng et al. (24) examined the effects of introductory logic courses given at two different universities, one a highly selective state university and one a less prestigious branch of the same university. The course at the former university was exclusively concerned with teaching formal deductive systems. The course at the latter also dealt with informal fallacies. Quite different texts were used in the two courses. But both courses covered topics in propositional logic, and indeed, both built from an initial foundation on the logic of the conditional, including the biconditional.

A pretest consisting of both meaningful selection problems (for example, ones inviting a causal or permission interpretation) and arbitrary ones (for example, the original Wason card problem) was given in the first week of class before any discussion of the conditional had taken place. A posttest was given in the final week of the semester. Problems on the pretest and posttest, although embodying the same principles as those taught in both logic courses, did not correspond directly to any problems actually presented in either course. The results provided no statistically significant evidence that formal instruction in logic can improve reasoning performance as measured by the selection task. The mean improvement was only 3 percent. The percentage of biconditional problems solved correctly actually decreased trivially.

Effects of Graduate Training.   Graduate programs provide an excellent opportunity to examine the effects of intensive training in particular types of inferential rules. Different fields emphasize different rule systems, and, unlike undergraduate school, where students are exposed to many different disciplines, the narrow focus of graduate programs might make it possible to show distinct patterns of inferential gains.

Lehman, Lempert, and Nisbett *(25)* studied the effects of 2 years of graduate education in four different fields in which inferential rules are taught that are extensions of the naturally induced pragmatic rules we have identified. Graduate students in these fields were tested on several different kinds of inferential skills: (i) statistical reasoning about both scientific content (such as statistically flawed studies in the natural and social sciences) and everyday life content (such as the sports or restaurant meal problems described above), (ii) methodological reasoning dealing with different types of confounded variable problems, for example, self-selection problems *(26)*, sample bias problems, and inferential uses of control groups *(27)*, for both scientific content and everyday life content, and (iii) ability to solve both arbitrary and meaningful problems involving the conditional and biconditional. Four fields at the University of Michigan were examined—psychology, medicine, law, and chemistry. Two different studies were conducted, one with a cross-sectional design (that is, first-year students in each field were compared with third-year students) and one with a longitudinal design (that is, first-year students in each field were tested and, after 2 years of training, tested again). The expectations were that training in the probabilistic sciences of psychology and medicine would result in an enhanced ability to apply statistical and methodological rules to both scientific content and everyday life problems. In addition, because psychology and medicine must deal with all kinds of causal patterns involving necessity and sufficiency, it was expected that training in these fields would also improve ability to solve conditional and biconditional problems. The field of chemistry, dealing as it does primarily with necessary and deterministic causes, was expected to produce little improvement in ability to apply rules for dealing with uncertainty or with the conditional. It was also expected that training in law would produce little improvement in ability to apply rules for dealing with uncertainty. Training in law, however, was expected to produce improvements in the ability to reason about problems that could be solved either by use of the conditional or by use of the biconditional. This is because law students are taught about contractual relations.

Initial differences among the three groups were very slight for all types of reasoning studied. Figure 12.2 shows that the effects of 2 years of training conformed closely to the pattern just described. The effects of training on ability to use statistical rules and confounded variable rules were marked, for both psychology and medical students, both for scientific problems and for everyday life problems. (The effects for both types of rules were almost identical and results were combined in Fig. 12.2.) The change for psychology students was particularly great, resulting in approximately an 80

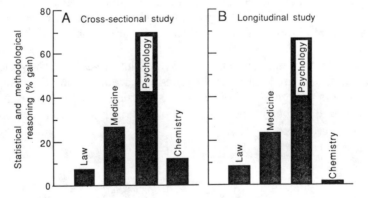

FIG. 12.2 Percentage of change in statistical and methodological reasoning score after 2 years of study as a function of graduate discipline. (A) The cross-sectional study examined first-year students and simultaneously enrolled third-year students. Sample sizes for first-year students were law, 213; medicine, 127; psychology, 25; and chemistry, 31. The sample sizes for third-year students were 50, 48, 33, and 26, respectively. (B) The longitudinal study examined the same students at the beginning of their first year and at the beginning of their third year. Sample sizes were law, 77; medicine, 87; psychology, 24; and chemistry, 18.

percent increase in ability to apply both types of rules for both studies. The change for medical students was also statistically significant for both studies. Neither law students nor chemistry students improved in reasoning using either statistical rules or confounded variable rules, for either type of content, when studied by either type of design.

For problems involving the logic of the conditional, it may be seen in Fig. 12.3 that psychology, medicine, and the law were all effective, and about equally so, producing about a 30 percent improvement. Changes for the cross-sectional study were not statistically significant, whereas all changes for the more sensitive longitudinal study were. Chemistry training had no effect on conditional problems in either study.

To increase generalizability, the cross-sectional version of the study was replicated at the University of California at Los Angeles for psychology and chemistry students. The results were similar. Chemistry students showed no gain for statistical or methodological problems or for conditional problems. Psychology students improved in all three.

THE FUTURE OF FORMAL DISCIPLINE

Taken together, the results of our studies suggest that the effects of higher education on the rules underlying reasoning may be very marked. In fact, the effects may be marked enough to justify the teaching of some rule systems invoking precisely the principles of formal training and general transfer that have long been invoked for logic, grammar, and other formal systems.

Our results also suggest that contrary to the pre-20th-century view of formal discipline, higher education does not train the mind as physical exercise trains the muscles. For example, although law students improved on conditional problems, possibly because of training about contractual

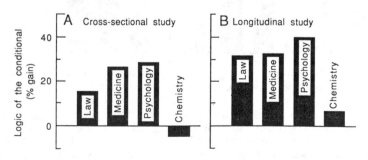

FIG. 12.3 Percent change in ability to solve problems in the logic of the conditional after 2 years of study as a function of graduate discipline.

relations, the improvement did not generalize to statistical rules or confounded variable rules. Thorndike *(1, 9)* was partially correct, after all, in that transfer applies only insofar as there are common identical elements. But the identity lies at a much higher level of abstraction than he suggested, at the level of pragmatic inferential rules such as contractual schemas, causal relations, and the law of large numbers. Furthermore, also contrary to his thesis, transfer does not necessarily occur when problems share identical elements. There is transfer neither for identity as specific as different types of isomorphic Tower of Hanoi problems, nor for identity as general as modus tollens (the contrapositive rule that a logician can use to solve the Wason selection problem). We suggest that transfer in the domain of reasoning may occur only when the identical elements are pragmatic inferential rules.

The results also indicate that Piaget was mistaken in two respects: (i) people may not possess rules of propositional logic at the purely syntactic level (at least in a form such that they are used for meaningful problems), and (ii) it is indeed possible to improve inferential rules through training.

Thus we propose there is such a thing as formal discipline — teaching people how to reason. It should be noted that our optimism is consistent with recent findings indicating that it is possible to train such foundations of reasoning as how to use dimensions to analyze and organize similarities and differences and how to identify the structure of simple propositions *(28)*. Our view is also consistent with process-oriented theories of intelligence that emphasize the pragmatic experiential context in which intelligence evolves in the context of everyday problem solving *(29)*.

Now that there are some clues about the nature of the rules that people actually use and can be taught, we may be able to proceed more efficiently to identify the ones that are most useful and how they can best be taught.

REFERENCES AND NOTES

1. See, for example, E. Thorndike, *The Psychology of Learning* (Mason-Henry, New York, 1913).
2. A. Newell, in *Problem Solving and Education,* D. Tuma and F. Reif, Eds. (Erlbaum, Hillsdale, NJ, 1980).
3. For a review, see C. Brainerd, *Piaget's Theory of Intelligence* (Prentice-Hall, Englewood Cliffs, NJ, 1978).
4. P. Cheng and K. Holyoak, *Cognit. Psychol. 17,* 391 (1985); J. Holland, K. Holyoak, R. Nisbett, P. Thagard, *Induction* (MIT Press, Cambridge, MA, 1986).
5. H. Kelley, *Am. Psychol. 28,* 107 (1973).
6. B. Jowett, Ed., *The Dialogues of Plato* (Oxford Univ. Press, Oxford, 1875), p. 785.
7. L. Mann, *On the Trail of Process* (Grune & Stratton, New York, 1979).
8. B. Tarver, quoted in Mann *(7),* p. 132.
9. E. Thorndike, *Principles of Teaching* (Seiler, New York, 1906), p. 246.

10. J. R. Hayes and H. A. Simon, *Cognitive Theory,* N. J. Castellan, Ed. (Erlbaum, Hillsdale, NJ, 1977).
11. P. Wason, in *New Horizons in Psychology,* B. Foss, Ed. (Penguin, Harmondsworth, England, 1966).
12. R. Griggs and J. Cox, *Br. J. Psychol. 73,* 407 (1982).
13. J. Piaget and B. Inhelder, *The Origin of the Idea of Chance in Children* (Norton, New York, 1975).
14. A. Tversky and D. Kahneman, *Science 185,* 1124 (1974).
15. R. Nisbett and L. Ross, *Human Inference* (Prentice-Hall, Englewood Cliffs, NJ, 1980).
16. R. Nisbett, D. Krantz, C. Jepson, Z. Kunda, *Psychol. Rev. 90,* 339 (1983).
17. C. Jepson, D. Krantz, R. Nisbett, *Behav. Brain Sci. 6,* 494 (1983).
18. G. Fong, D. Krantz, R. Nisbett, *Cognit. Psychol. 18,* 253 (1986).
19. An additional control group received brief "placebic" instruction: the law of large numbers was lauded and defined as the superiority of larger quantities of evidence over smaller quantities of evidence, and subjects were exhorted to use the law in solving test problems. This "demand" control group was not different from completely untrained control subjects in either the frequency or quality of statistical explanations produced.
20. Sample size for the rule training group was 69 and for the control group, 68.
21. G. Fong and R. Nisbett, unpublished data.
22. P. Cheng and R. Nisbett, unpublished data.
23. P. Cheng and K. Holyoak, *Cognit. Psychol. 17,* 391 (1985).
24. _____, L. Oliver, R. Nisbett, *ibid. 18,* 293 (1986).
25. D. Lehman, R. Lempert, R. Nisbett, unpublished data.
26. An example of a problem involving self-selection was drawn from an editorial in the *New York Times* (6 March 1982, p. 23) in which the Learning of Latin and Greek was urged on the grounds that high school students who had done so were found to score a standard deviation higher on the SAT verbal tests. Subjects able to apply the self-selection rule recognized that the difference would be due largely to initial differences in ability between the sorts of students who would take Latin and Greek and those who would not.
27. An example of a problem in which the ability to apply control group concepts to everyday life is examined is one noting that the Mayor of Indianapolis is under pressure to fire his police chief because crime has increased since the chief began his tenure in office. Subjects able to apply control group concepts recognize that a decision to fire should be based in part on the crime rates in comparable cities over comparable periods of time.
28. R. Herrnstein, R. Nickerson, M. de Sanchez, J. Swets, *Am. Psychol. 41,* 1279 (1986).
29. E. Hunt, *Science 219,* 141 (1983); R. J. Sternberg, *ibid. 230,* 1111 (1985).
30. Supported by NSF grants SES85-07342, BNS84-09198, and BNS-8709892, NIMH grant 1 RO1 MH38466, and grant 85-K-0563 from the Office of Naval Research. We thank K. J. Holyoak, L. Novick, and E. E. Smith for comments on an earlier draft.

13

The Effects of Graduate Training on Reasoning: Formal Discipline and Thinking About Everyday-Life Events

Darrin R. Lehman
University of British Columbia

Richard E. Nisbett
University of Michigan

Richard O. Lempert
University of Michigan Law School

A few years ago an article appeared on the Op-Ed page of *The New York Times* urging that Latin and Greek be taught routinely to high school students in order to improve intelligence (Costa, 1982). The justification given for this recommendation was a study showing that students who had taken Latin and Greek in high school scored 100 points higher on the verbal portion of the Scholastic Aptitude Test (SAT) than students who had not studied these languages.

Although the editors of *The New York Times* apparently thought that this argument was worthy of consideration by its readers, it seems likely that most academically trained psychologists would be dubious on two different grounds. First, because of their methodological training, psychologists would be aware of the likelihood of substantial self-selection effects in any study of the kind described: High school students who take Latin and Greek are likely to be more intelligent than students who do not, and schools that include Latin and Greek in their curriculums are likely to have higher academic standards than schools that do not. Second, most psychologists are aware of the bad reputation of the "learning Latin" approach to teaching reasoning. Thus, they believe reasoning cannot be taught by teaching the syntax of a foreign language, by teaching principles of mathematics, or indeed by any "formal discipline" procedure whereby the rules of some field are taught and then are expected to be generalized outside the bounds of the problems in that field.

Psychologists are, no doubt, right in their assertion that self-selection undercuts the argument for teaching Latin and Greek. Are they equally justified, though, in assuming that teaching foreign languages or any other

315

formal discipline has no generalized implications for reasoning? The antiformal discipline view not only conflicts with what people have believed for most of recorded history, but its scientific support is far less substantial than most psychologists realize.

The ancient Greeks believed that the study of mathematics improved reasoning. Plato urged the "principal men of the state" to study arithmetic. He believed that "even the dull, if they have had an arithmetical training . . . always become much quicker than they would otherwise have been" (quoted in Jowett, 1937, p. 785). Roman thinkers agreed with the Greeks about the value of arithmetic and also endorsed the study of grammar as a useful discipline for improving reasoning. The medieval scholastics added logic, especially the study of syllogisms, to the list of disciplines that could formally train the mind. The humanists added the study of Latin and Greek, and the curriculum for European education was set for the next several hundred years (Mann, 1979).

THE 20TH CENTURY CRITIQUE OF FORMAL DISCIPLINE

Although there were objections to the standard curriculum as early as the Enlightenment on the grounds that the rules of mathematics and Latin bear little actual resemblance to the rules necessary to think about most everyday-life events, it was not until the late 19th century that the view came under concerted attack. The attack came from psychologists, and it was utterly effective. In fact, it was one of the first policy victories of the new field. William James was withering in his critique of "faculty psychology," that is, of the view that mental abilities consisted of faculties such as memory, reasoning, and will that could be improved by mere exercise in the way that muscles could. Thorndike (1906, 1913) undertook a program of research, still impressive by modern standards, that showed little transfer of training across tasks, for example, from canceling letters to canceling parts of speech or from estimating areas of rectangles of one size and shape to estimating areas of rectangles of another size and shape. Thorndike declared that "training the mind means the development of thousands of particular independent capacities" (Thorndike, 1906, p. 246). Hence, training in Latin could not be expected to improve people's capacities to perform other very different mental tasks.

Similar conclusions have been reached by contemporary psychologists investigating the transfer of solutions of one problem to solutions of another formally identical problem, for example, between isomorphs of the "Tower of Hanoi" problem (Hayes & Simon, 1977), between homomorphs of the missionaries and cannibals problem (Reed, Ernst, & Banerji, 1974), and between slightly transformed versions of algebra problems (Reed, Dempster, & Ettinger, 1985). Learning how to solve one problem produces no improvement in solving others having an identical formal structure.

The most influential student of reasoning in the middle of the 20th century, Piaget, reinforced already skeptical views of the value of formal training. Piaget believed that there were general rules underlying reasoning—the formal operations and the propositional operations—but that these abstract rules were induced by everyone by virtue of living in the world with its particular regularities (Inhelder & Piaget, 1955/1958). Because learning is mainly by induction, via methods of self-discovery, formal training can do little to extend it or even to speed it up. It is important to note, however, that little research seems to have been conducted examining Piaget's dictum that abstract rules are difficult to teach.

A still more radical view than Piaget's has emerged as a result of studying people's ability to perform certain logical operations. Wason (1966) and other investigators have established that people have great difficulty with abstract problems that follow the form of the material conditional, *if p then q*. This has been done by examining how people respond to selection tasks that embody this logic. For example, subjects are shown four cards displaying an *A*, a *B*, a *4*, and a *7;* are told that all cards have letters on the front and numbers on the back; and are asked to turn over as many as necessary to establish whether it is the case that "if there is a vowel on the front, then there is an even number on the back." Few subjects reach the correct conclusion that it is necessary to turn over the A (because if there were not an even number on the back, the rule would be violated) and the 7 (because if there were a vowel on the front, the rule would be violated). More generally, to determine the truth of a conditional statement, the cases that must be checked are *p* (because if *p* is the case, it must be established that *q* is also the case) and *not-q* (because if it is not the case that *q*, it must be established that it is also not the case that *p*).

Yet subjects have no difficulty solving familiar everyday-life problems formally identical to the Wason selection task. For example, when asked to turn over as many sales receipts as necessary to establish that "if the receipt is for more than $20, it has a signature on the back," subjects readily understand that large amounts and unsigned reverses have to be checked (D'Andrade, 1982). This fact has led some theorists to argue that people do not use inferential rules at all, but rather they use only those rules that are at a concrete, empirical level (e.g., D'Andrade, 1982; Griggs & Cox, 1982; Manktelow & Evans, 1979). This view would be consistent with the most extreme position derivable from Thorndike's findings: Learning does not transfer from task to task, and subjects do not generalize from a set of tasks to the level of abstract rules.

PRAGMATIC INFERENTIAL RULES

Recently, we and our colleagues have argued that the Thorndike tradition is mistaken in asserting the extreme domain specificity of all rule learning. We have identified several naturally occurring inferential rules that people use to solve everyday-life problems and have found that they are improvable by purely formal training (Cheng & Holyoak, 1985; Cheng, Holyoak, Nisbett, & Oliver, 1986; Fong, Krantz, & Nisbett, 1986; Holland, Holyoak, Nisbett, & Thagard, 1986; Nisbett, Fong, Lehman, & Cheng, 1987). These "pragmatic inferential rules" capture recurring regularities among problem goals and among event relationships that people encounter in everyday life. They are fully abstract in that they are not tied to any content domain (much like Piaget's formal operations), but they are not as independent of relationship types and problem goals as formal logical rules (which are included in Piaget's propositional operations) or the purely syntactic rule systems often studied by modern cognitive psychologists.

Contractual Schemas

One type of pragmatic inferential rule system we have studied we call "contractual schemas." These schemas represent situations in which a *permission* is required to perform some action or in which an *obligation* is incurred by virtue of the occurrence of some event. These schemas are of particular interest because the procedures needed to establish whether a permission or obligation has been violated are the same as the checking procedures required by the conditional to establish whether a proposition of the form "if p, then q" obtains.

Cheng and Holyoak (1985) showed that the schema for permissions is useful in performing selection tasks having the form of the Wason card problem. In one of Cheng and Holyoak's experiments, subjects were presented with a selection problem based on an abstract description of a permission situation: "If one is to take action 'A,' then one must first satisfy precondition 'P.' " About 60% of the subjects solved this problem as compared with 20% who solved the original Wason selection task. Cheng and Holyoak also found that providing an explicit purpose for a rule that would otherwise seem arbitrary could serve to cue the permission schema and hence facilitate performance. These findings are incompatible with the extreme domain specificity view stemming from Thorndike's position. The findings also indicate that the selection task, with its arbitrary elements and relations, is difficult because people normally reason using schemas of the permission type rather than the rules of formal logic. When reasoning schemas are invoked, people can solve problems that are formally identical to the card selection task because the schematic rule structures are identical.

It also turns out to be the case that training in formal logic has little effect on people's ability to solve either arbitrary or semantically meaningful versions of the selection task, whereas training in the obligation schema has a substantial effect. Cheng, Holyoak, Nisbett, and Oliver (1986) found that neither an intensive training session on the nature of conditional rules nor even an entire course in logic improved subjects' performance. In contrast, Cheng et al. found that even brief instruction in the obligation schema improved subjects' abilities to solve the selection task, especially more semantically meaningful versions of it that could be understood in terms of the obligation notion.

Causal Schemas

Cheng, Nisbett, and Oliver (1987) have argued that another type of pragmatic reasoning schema, namely causal schemas of the kind defined by Kelley (1971, 1973), may also help people to solve problems that are syntactically identical to the selection problem. Kelley argued that people understand the ideas of necessariness and sufficiency in causality and possess different schemas for checking evidence supporting causal hypotheses that are necessary and sufficient, necessary but not sufficient, and so on. Cheng et al. (1987) found support for this view. They found that subjects tacitly assumed a particular type of causality and then applied evidence-checking procedures appropriate to the type. Interestingly, one of the schemas, namely that for sufficient but not necessary causes, has checking procedures identical to that for the conditional selection task. A hypothesis of the type "A among other things always causes effect B" can be disproved by examining A and finding that not-B was the case, or examining not-B and finding that A was the case. Cheng et al. (1986) found that subjects performed better on selection tasks that had a causal interpretation that might encourage subjects to use the same checking procedures as required by the conditional. The checking procedures for the necessary and sufficient type of causality, as it happens, are the same as for the biconditional *(p if and only if q)* in formal logic. The biconditional requires examining all four cases—*p, not-p, q,* and *not-q*. The other two causal schemas—namely, necessary but not sufficient, and neither necessary nor sufficient—also have distinct checking procedures associated with them. The social sciences, it should be noted, have developed elaborate methodologies for dealing with the completely probabilistic type of causality characterized by the neither necessary nor sufficient type.

Statistical Rules

Another of the inferential rules we have studied is comparable to Piaget's "probability schema." In our view, this is not a single schema but a family of related schemas or heuristics having to do with the law of large numbers; the rule that sample values resemble population values as a direct function of sample size and an inverse function of population variability; and the related regression or base rate principles, for example, the rule that extreme values for an object or sample are less likely to be extreme when the object is reexamined or a new sample observed. We have found that people often use the law of large numbers and relatively simple applications of the regression principle when solving problems in everyday life (Nisbett, Krantz, Jepson, & Kunda, 1983). We have also found that people's solutions of everyday-life problems using statistical rules are greatly enhanced not only by instruction in college statistics courses but even by relatively brief training sessions (Fong, Krantz, & Nisbett, 1986). These training sessions are effective even when the training is highly abstract and formal and does not make any reference to everyday-life content. In addition, training in one domain of events improves reasoning for other quite different domains fully as much as for the trained domain, suggesting that subjects readily abstract what they learn from a given domain (Fong et al., 1986; Fong & Nisbett, 1988).

GRADUATE SCHOOL AND FORMAL DISCIPLINE

The work done to date indicates that people reason using inferential rules at a fairly high level of abstraction and that their ability to use such rules can be improved by formal training procedures. Theorists prior to the 20th century thus were probably correct about the basic notion of formal discipline, although they probably misidentified the particular types of rule systems that are amenable to training and that allow substantial generalization to everyday-life problems. The syntactic rule systems of mathematics and formal logic may be destined to play little role in everyday reasoning even when these have been well-taught; pragmatic rule systems, such as the law of large numbers, causal schemas, and contractual schemas, may play a significant role even prior to formal training.

The work also has some clear implications for understanding the effects of education on the way people reason. Because graduate training in particular is highly specialized with respect to the inferential rules emphasized, the possibility exists that different kinds of graduate training produce different effects on reasoning about various everyday-life events. In particular, we would expect that scientific disciplines teach different rules than non-scientific disciplines and that there might be differences within the sciences themselves having to do with whether the field is at base probabilistic or deterministic. We studied two probabilistic sciences, namely psychology and medicine, a nonprobabilistic or deterministic science, namely chemistry, and a nonscience, namely law.

One would expect that training in the probabilistic sciences would affect statistical reasoning, sensitizing people, for example, to the riskiness of inferences from small samples. One would also expect such training to affect causal reasoning because accurate causal judgments usually require some understanding of the problems posed by confounded variables, the bane of the probabilistic sciences. A methodological education in the probabilistic sciences sensitizes people to problems that arise when studying causes that are neither necessary nor sufficient. It includes rules about when and how to employ control groups, how to avoid sample bias, and how to recognize and avoid the errors that can arise when subjects who are selected or who select themselves for a treatment on the basis of one variable also differ on other variables that are potentially correlated with the dependent variable of interest. In contrast, one might expect that training in a nonprobabilistic science such as chemistry would have less effect on statistical reasoning and on methodological reasoning, which requires sensitivity toward the problems posed by confounded variables. One might also expect training in a nonscience such as the law to have relatively little effect on such kinds of reasoning.

The probabilistic sciences might be expected to improve reasoning on conditional and biconditional problems because these fields distinguish the nature of causality implied by their hypotheses, often in a quite self-conscious fashion. Most hypotheses examined by social scientists are of the neither necessary nor sufficient type. Some hypotheses are of the necessary but not sufficient kind (for example, that only certain kinds of subjects are "at risk" for certain outcomes, although other causes are required for the risk to be manifest). Other hypotheses are of the sufficient but not necessary kind (that is, many different causes may produce a given effect, for example, retardation, although none is required). To the extent that people use these schemas to solve problems for which a logician would use the conditional, we might expect that training in the probabilistic sciences would improve conditional reasoning. Again, one might expect training in a nonprobabilistic science such as chemistry to affect such reasoning less because it focuses primarily on deterministic causality of the necessary and sufficient kind.

We might also expect that training in the law would improve conditional reasoning. The law deals with contractual relations that have the form of the conditional such as permissions and obligations as well as with contractual obligations that have the form of the biconditional, that is, agreements that a certain action may be taken if and only if some event has occurred.

We investigated the effects of different types of graduate education on answers to problems that we thought would be differentially affected by training. As a control, we examined the effects of different training on verbal reasoning of the kind tested by the Graduate Record Examination (GRE). Verbal reasoning ability increases steadily during the young adult years for those involved in mentally challenging work (Share, 1979). We expected that subjects in all four disciplines would improve slightly, and to about the same extent, in verbal reasoning.

The first study was cross-sectional, examining first- and third-year students enrolled at the University of Michigan in the fall semester of 1983. The second study was a longitudinal one that reexamined the first-year students in the cross-sectional sample at the beginning of their third year.

STUDY 1: CROSS-SECTIONAL DESIGN

Subjects

Subjects were first- and third-year graduate students in law, medicine, psychology, and chemistry at the University of Michigan. Because of substantial attrition in the relatively small chemistry program, the "third-year" chemistry group also included all available fourth-year students.

Many educational studies suffer low response rates or high drop-out rates, raising the possibility that any effects reflect selection biases rather than educational effects of interest. The present investigation, except for the chemistry group, suffers very little from these problems. Almost all the enrolled students in the four programs responded, and the drop-out rates were extremely low in all programs but chemistry. Moreover, as will be seen later, the results for chemistry suggest that the drop-out rate for that group does not pose serious problems for interpretation.

The first year response rates were as follows: 213 of 241 law students (88%), 127 of 133 medical students (96%),[1] 25 of 27 psychology students (93%), and 31 of 32 chemistry students (97%).[2]

Due to the different numbers of students in the four disciplines and the cost of sampling third-year students, random samples of 60 third-year law students and 55 third-year medical students were contacted. Samples were based on the populations initially enrolled, so that some of the sampled students had dropped out by the time the study began. All third-year psychology students and third- and fourth-year chemistry students were sampled because these programs were relatively small. The third-year response rates were as follows: 50 of 60 ever-enrolled law students (83%, but the figure for currently enrolled students was 89%), 48 of 55 ever-enrolled medical students (87%), 33 of 36 ever-enrolled psychology students

(94%), and 26 of 52 ever-enrolled chemistry students (50%, but the figure for currently enrolled students was 93%).

Procedure

First-year subjects were given a reasoning test during separate mass orientation meetings at the beginning of their first term in graduate school. Third-year subjects were given the test in one of three settings: group administrations in their home department, in their own offices, or in offices at the Institute for Social Research. In all settings, a relaxed, unhurried atmosphere prevailed. Subjects were instructed to take as much time as necessary to solve each problem: "Please treat each fully, but there is no need to puzzle unduly over any problem. While some questions have right and wrong answers, others do not."

Two forms of the reasoning test were developed so that pre- and posttest versions would be available for the longitudinal study. Approximately half of the subjects in each group filled out Form 1 of the reasoning test, and the other half filled out Form 2. The test took between 40 and 60 minutes to complete. The third-year students were paid $10 for their participation.

Instrument

The reasoning test consisted of four sets of questions, spread evenly throughout the test booklet. One set was intended to measure statistical reasoning; one was intended to measure confounded variable (or methodological) reasoning; one was intended to measure reasoning about problems to which conditional logic could be applied; and one was a standard measure of verbal reasoning of the kind employed in the Graduate Record Examination verbal test.

Statistical Reasoning. The statistical reasoning items were intended to measure the subjects' abilities to apply the law of large numbers and the regression or base rate principle to both scientific problems and everyday-life problems. Scientific problems were those that specifically mentioned a study of some kind within the body of the question, whereas everyday-life problems did not. In one of the scientific problems, for example, subjects were told about a teaching experiment using high school students. They were asked what would be expected to happen to the grades of students in a control condition who had relatively high grades and those who had relatively low grades. A recognition of the regression principle was shown by indicating that the high group could be expected to have lower grades in the subsequent term and the low group could be expected to have higher grades. An everyday-life problem to which the law of large numbers could be applied was identical to one used by Nisbett, Krantz, Jepson, and Kunda (1983): A high school student had to choose between two colleges. The student had several friends, who were similar to himself in values and abilities, at each school. All of his friends at school A liked it on both educational and social grounds; all of them at school B had deep reservations on both grounds. The student visited both schools for a day, and his impressions were the reverse. Subjects could indicate their understanding of the law of large numbers by stating that the student should probably choose A because his "one-day visit can't give him a very good idea of what the school is like, whereas his friends' long-term experience can be informative." An example of an everyday-life problem to which the regression principle (and perhaps the law of large numbers as well) could be applied is presented in its entirety in Appendix A at the end of this article.

Methodological Reasoning. The methodological problems were intended to measure ability to apply various confounded-variable principles to problems having both scientific content and everyday-life content. One of the scientific content problems, for example, presented an assertion that the bald eagle population was on the rise based on the fact that a study showed that sightings of bald eagles by the North American Wildlife Federation's annual watch had increased by 35%. An ability to apply control group concepts was indicated by recognizing that increased sightings of other kinds of birds would undermine the claim (because it would suggest more people involved in the watch, different reporting methods, etc.). Another of the scientific problems presented the claim that students who learned Latin or Greek got higher SAT verbal scores and measured subjects' recognition of the self-selection principle. One of the everyday-life content methodological problems, showing recognition of the need for control groups, is presented in Appendix A.

Conditional Reasoning. Each form contained three problems that could be solved by application of the conditional and one that could be solved by application of the biconditional. The problems were those used by Cheng et al. (1986). One of the conditional problems was arbitrary (for one of the forms, the Wason card selection problem was used), one was couched in language that was expected to encourage causal reasoning, and one was couched in language that was expected to encourage application of the permission schema. An example of a permission-schema version of the conditional problem is presented in Appendix A. The biconditional problem was an assessment of the necessary-and-sufficient checking procedure.

Verbal Reasoning. A fourth set of questions was intended to measure general verbal abilities to recognize arguments, evaluate evidence, and detect analogies. These items were similar to GRE verbal exam items taken by psychology and chemistry students, and to verbal exam items on the LSAT (taken by law students) and the MCAT (taken by medical students). Many items were in fact drawn from practice materials for these verbal exams. An example of a verbal reasoning question is presented in Appendix A.

Scale Construction

Seven items were answered correctly by 90% or more of first-year students in one or more of the disciplines. In order to prevent ceiling-effect problems, all such items were dropped. One additional item was dropped because it correlated negatively with total score, that is, the sum of all items on the test minus the item itself.

Individual statistical reasoning items, as it turned out, were no more highly correlated with the sum of other statistical items than with the sum of methodological reasoning items, nor were individual methodological items correlated more highly with the sum of other methodological items than with the sum of statistical items. These results, together with the fact that the two scales behaved very similarly for each discipline for both the cross-sectional and longitudinal designs, led us to collapse them into a single scale. All but two items on this scale were correlated more highly with the total statistical-methodological reasoning score than with either the conditional reasoning scale or the verbal reasoning scale.[3] All the conditional reasoning items correlated more highly with the conditional reasoning total (minus each item itself) than with either the statistical-methodological total or the verbal total.

STUDY 2: LONGITUDINAL DESIGN

A second study was identical in every respect to the first except that it had a longitudinal design. First-year students were retested at the beginning of their third year of study. All first-year psychology students and chemistry students from the cross-sectional study were asked to be retested. Stratified random samples were drawn of the first-year medical and law students originally tested, with the stratification being based on total scores on the initial test. Only the sampled students were contacted and asked to be retested. Students initially given Form 1 were given Form 2 on the retest and vice versa. Response rates were as follows: 77 of the 88 randomly selected law students (88%), 87 of the 91 randomly selected medical students (96%), 24 of the 25 initially tested psychology students (96%), and 18 of the 31 initially tested chemistry students (58%, but 100% of the 18 still enrolled).

Students were tested under the same circumstances as third-year students in the cross-sectional study and were paid $20 for their participation.[4]

NORMATIVE QUESTIONS ABOUT STATISTICAL-METHODOLOGICAL ITEMS

We have sometimes been asked how it is we know that the answers we endorse for the statistical and methodological questions are the "correct" ones. It would be possible for us to say simply that we are reporting changes and that others may decide whether these changes are for the better. Undoubtedly, others will decide for themselves, regardless of what we say, but we have a normative stance, which applies to the verbal and conditional questions as well, that readers may wish to consider.

Generally speaking, the position that testers take on the question of how to identify "right answers" is that an answer endorsed by a consensus of experts is the correct one. In some cases, this presumption is based on actual polling of experts, but in most cases it is based on an assumed ability to mimic the stance of experts toward test items. We subscribe to this position.

In the present case, we have discussed many of our statistical and methodological items with experts in statistical and methodological reasoning, in several instances at conferences of experts in inductive reasoning, including statisticians as well as epistemologists and cognitive psychologists with substantial statistical expertise. For each of these items, the overwhelming consensus of the experts is that the answer we prefer is the correct one. The other items we used resemble those items to a considerable degree.

Our judgments in these respects are supported by some empirical data. First, it turns out that people who endorse the statistical answers we prefer for questions of the present type are more likely to endorse parallel answers for quite noncontroversial statistical questions involving the behavior of randomizing devices (Jepson, Krantz, & Nisbett, 1983). In addition, people who endorse the answers we prefer receive generally higher scores on intelligence tests than do those who do not. Indeed, a subtest of statistical items correlates about as well with combined verbal and mathematical ability as measured by the SAT as do some standard IQ subtests such as spatial reasoning and analogies (Jepson et al., 1983). In the present study, all of our subtest scores were positively correlated both with full test scores and with the admissions test score, which was the total GRE score (math plus verbal plus analytic test scores) in the case of psychology and chemistry students, the total MCAT in the case of medical students, and the LSAT in the case of law students. Thus, our preferences are in line both with those of experts and with those students in each discipline scoring highest on traditional ability tests.

RESULTS

Cohort Differences

In order to determine whether there were any cohort differences in general ability, we compared the admission test scores of first-year students and third-year students within each discipline. The combined GRE score was used for psychology and chemistry students, the combined MCAT for medical students, and the LSAT for law students. There were no differences between first- and third-year students of even marginal significance for any discipline.

Initial Differences

The first-year students differed marginally by discipline in their initial scores on the conditional reasoning test, $F(3, 395) = 2.2, p = .08.$[5] This was due to the law students scoring slightly higher and the medical students slightly lower than the other two groups. The first-year students differed substantially in both statistical-methodological and verbal reasoning, $F(3, 395) = 6.9, p < .0002, F(3, 395) = 2.93, p < .03$, respectively. These latter two differences were due almost entirely to the relatively low scores of chemistry students (though there was also a slight elevation of law student scores over the scores of others on verbal reasoning). As might be expected, it was disproportionately the low-scoring chemistry students who subsequently left the program. The combined GRE scores for chemistry students who left the program ($M = 1,676$) was also lower than for those who remained ($M = 1,880$), $t(40) = 39.18, p < .01$. As a consequence, when only those first-year students who were included in the longitudinal sample were examined, a different pattern emerged. There were no disciplinary differences in the first-year scores of those in the longitudinal sample in either statistical-methodological reasoning, $F(3, 205) = 1.78, p = .15$ or conditional reasoning, $F(3, 205) = .31, p = .82$. There remained a slight difference in verbal reasoning for this group, $F(3, 205) = 3.04, p < .05$, that was due entirely to the law students having higher scores than psychology, chemistry, or medical students.

This pattern of first-year differences means that the cross-sectional results slightly overestimate improvement for the (self-selected) third-year chemistry students, at least for statistical-methodological reasoning and verbal reasoning. Other than that, the pattern indicates that there was little difference among first-year students in either design except for a slight advantage for the first-year law students in verbal reasoning.

Changes in Reasoning Scores

Verbal Reasoning. The change scores for verbal reasoning for all students, for both the cross-sectional study and the longitudinal study, are presented in Figure 13.1. It may be seen that, as anticipated, all groups show slight improvement in verbal reasoning, ranging from 5% to 17% in the cross-sectional design and from 4% to 14% in the longitudinal design. Only the medical students' improvement reaches statistical significance as measured by t test, $p < .05$, for both the cross-sectional and the longitudinal study. The interaction between discipline and year fell far short of significance. These results provide a base from which to examine the differential change for the four groups in the other two types of reasoning.

Statistical-methodological Reasoning. It will be recalled that statistical and methodological reasoning scores could not be differentiated from one another psychometrically. The two types of scores were also affected in the same way by training in the different disciplines. For these reasons, the scores for statistical and methodological reasoning were combined for purposes of analysis. Change scores for all subjects, for both the cross-sectional study and the longitudinal study, are presented in Figure 13.2. It may be seen that the psychology students changed dramatically from the first year to the third year in statistical-methodological reasoning, $t(56) = 5.00, p < .0001$ in the cross-sectional study, paired-$t(23) = 5.37, p < .0001$ in the longitudinal study. Medical students also changed substantially, $t(173) = 2.73, p < .01$ in the cross-sectional study, paired-$t(86) = 3.09, p < .005$ in the longitudinal study. Law students, in contrast, showed no significant improvement in statistical-methodological reasoning, $t(261) < 1$ in the cross-sectional study, paired-$t(76) = 1.17$, *ns,* in the longitudinal study. Chemistry students also did not improve, ts for both designs < 1.

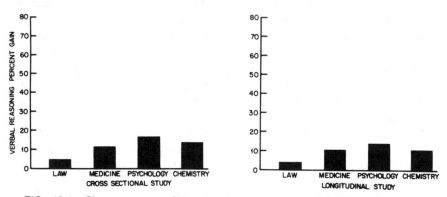

FIG. 13.1   Change scores for verbal reasoning as a function of design, year, and graduate program.

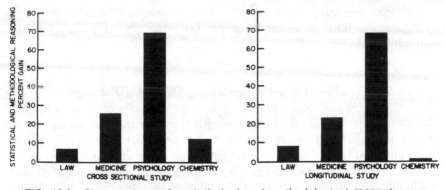

FIG. 13.2 Change scores for statistical and methodological reasoning as a function of design, year, and graduate program.

The interaction between year and discipline is significant for both the cross-sectional design, $F(3, 552) = 5.33$, $p < .001$, and the longitudinal design, $F(3, 202) = 5.62$, $p < .001$.

Conditional Reasoning. Figure 13.3 presents change in conditional reasoning for all students, for both the cross-sectional and the longitudinal design. The students in law, medicine, and psychology all improved in their ability to reason about conditional problems. None of the differences are significant in the cross-sectional study, but all three are significant in the longitudinal study, paired-$t(76) = 2.91$, $p < .005$ for law, paired-$t(86) = 3.22$, $p < .002$ for medicine, paired-$t(23) = 2.29$, $p < .05$ for psychology. It should also be noted that the trend was for all three groups to improve on all four types of questions — arbitrary, causal wording, permission wording, and biconditional. In contrast, chemistry students did not improve in

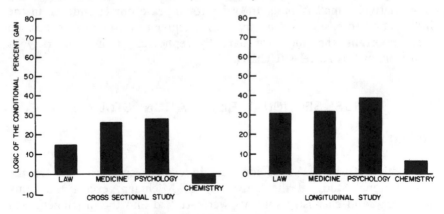

FIG. 13.3 Change scores for conditional reasoning as a function of design, year, and graduate program.

conditional reasoning, both ts < 1. The interaction between year and discipline fell short of significance for both the cross-sectional and the longitudinal design.

DISCUSSION OF STUDIES 1 AND 2

The results are thus quite consistent with the view that reasoning can be taught and that different graduate disciplines teach different kinds of reasoning to different degrees. It appears that the probabilistic sciences of psychology and medicine teach their students to apply statistical and methodological rules to both scientific and everyday-life problems, whereas the nonprobabilistic science of chemistry and the nonscientific discipline of the law do not affect their students in these respects. Psychology, medicine, and the law all seem to teach their students rule systems that increase their ability to reason about problems for which the conditional or the biconditional in logic affords solutions. In our view, this is not because these fields teach the rules of formal logic, but because they teach pragmatic reasoning schemas that provide the same solutions as does the conditional. These reasoning schemas include causal schemas and their associated evidence-checking procedures, and contractual schemas, including the permission and obligation schemas.

The results for the cross-sectional and longitudinal designs are similar enough to give us some confidence that the results are an accurate reflection of true changes produced by training in the various disciplines at the University of Michigan. It would increase our confidence in the generality of the results, however, to have a replication at another institution. This is especially the case for the chemistry results, which amount to a null finding on a relatively small N base. In order to increase our confidence in the findings and to ensure that no features peculiar to a Michigan education were important, the study was partially replicated at the University of California at Los Angeles (UCLA).

CROSS-SECTIONAL REPLICATION: STUDY 3

Method

The method for UCLA was identical in every respect to that for the cross-sectional study at the University of Michigan, except that only psychology and chemistry students were studied and the instrument was shortened to delete items having ceiling effects at Michigan. In addition, an extra biconditional item was added to the conditional-reasoning scale on both forms. A very high response rate was obtained. The *n*s were 27 of 30 first-year psychology students (90%), and 27 of 27 still-enrolled third-year psychology students (100%), 35 of 37 first-year chemistry students (95%), and 28 of 30 still-enrolled third-year chemistry students (93%). The drop-out rates were lower for chemistry at UCLA (22%) than at Michigan (46%). The psychology drop-out rate at UCLA (23%) was virtually identical to that for chemistry.

Results

Cohort Differences.   A comparison of combined GRE scores for first- and third-year students in the two disciplines showed only very slight differences between chemistry cohorts but a nontrivial difference between psychology cohorts, $t(47) = -1.91, p = .06$, with first-year students ($M = 2,002$) scoring higher than third-year students ($M = 1902$). Because GRE scores are correlated with each of the dependent variables, results were subjected to covariance analyses and adjusted means are reported. GRE scores were not available for 12 students, therefore *n*s for the covariance analyses are slightly reduced.

Social Science versus Natural Science Differences Among Psychology Students.   Preliminary analyses revealed that the magnitudes of training effects for psychology students were smaller at UCLA than at Michigan. Subsequent analyses indicated that differences were entirely due to the relatively large fraction of "natural science" psychology students at UCLA. Fully 35% of UCLA psychology students were in the areas of physiological, learning and behavior, or experimental psychology, versus only 12% at Michigan. Analyses revealed that these fields showed little positive change in reasoning scores, whereas the "social science" fields of personality, social, developmental, and clinical showed changes fully comparable to those observed at Michigan. Results are therefore presented separately for social science and natural science psychologists. The *n* for first-year social science psychology students was 17, for third-year social science psychology students 15, for first-year natural science psychology students 8, for third-year natural science psychology students 9, for first-year chemistry students 31, and for third-year chemistry students 25.

Verbal Reasoning.   Table 13.1 presents reasoning scores, reported as percent correct for each scale, for both social science and natural science psychology students, and for chemistry students. It may be seen that the pattern for verbal reasoning is very similar to that observed in Studies 1 and 2, that is, all fields of study show slight and non-significant improvements

TABLE 13.1
Adjusted Means for Reasoning Scores for First- and Third-Year UCLA Psychology and Chemistry Students

Type of reasoning	Social science psychologists		Natural science psychologists		Chemistry	
	1st year	3rd year	1st year	3rd year	1st year	3rd year
Verbal	51.2	55.6	42.4	45.7	50.4	51.1
Statistical and methodological	40.5	64.2	47.4	36.1	29.0	33.8
Conditional	32.7	51.6	53.3	36.1	39.3	31.3

from the first year to the third year, all $ts < 1$. The interaction between year and discipline fell far short of significance.

Statistical and Methodological Reasoning. It may be seen in Table 13.1 that the statistical-methodological reasoning of social science psychologists showed substantial change, amounting to a 59% improvement over two years of study, $F(1, 31) = 11.35, p < .002$. In contrast, neither the natural science psychologists nor the chemistry students improved. The natural science psychologists actually showed a slight but nonsignificant decrease. The interaction between year and discipline is highly significant, $F(2, 104) = 5.61, p < .005$. It should be noted that the difference between social science and natural science psychologists is particularly marked for the questions having everyday-life content, interaction $F(1, 48) = 9.15, p < .005$, and is substantially less for questions having scientific content, interaction $F(1, 48) = 2.84, p = .10$.

Conditional Reasoning. It may be seen in Table 13.1 that conditional reasoning for the social science psychologists improved substantially over two years of study, $F(1, 31) = 3.93, p = .06$. Conditional reasoning for both natural science psychologists and chemistry students actually declined, although the decline is not significant in either case. The interaction between year and discipline is significant, $F(2, 104) = 3.36, p < .05$.

DISCUSSION OF STUDY 3

The results for the replication study lend support to the results, and the interpretation of the results, for Studies 1 and 2. Change in verbal reasoning is positive and slight for all fields. Change in both statistical-methodological reasoning and conditional reasoning is positive and pronounced for social science psychologists and nil or slightly negative for chemistry students and natural science psychologists. The results indicate that the early years of training in the probabilistic sciences can be helpful for reasoning about certain kinds of problems using particular rule systems whereas the early years of natural science training have little effect on those same problems and rule systems.

GENERAL DISCUSSION

The results show that training in both psychology and medicine can affect statistical reasoning about everyday-life problems, methodological reasoning about everyday-life problems employing a number of rules related to the confounding principle, and reasoning about problems that logicians can solve using the material conditional in deductive logic. In addition, training in the law affects conditional reasoning. Training in chemistry does not seem to affect any of these kinds of reasoning.

Why do we find this pattern of results? Psychologists receive statistical training as part of the first two years' research experience; thus, the finding that training in psychology affects statistical reasoning about everyday-life events amounts to an extension of previous results by Fong et al. (1986) showing that statistical training affects thinking about everyday-life events. Most psychologists will not be surprised that training in their field also affects reasoning about confounded variables in everyday life involving methodological principles such as selection and the need for control groups. Particularly in the social science branches of psychology, day-to-day research experience requires students to think about everyday-life events of the kind being studied and to employ such methodological principles. Although the natural science branches of the discipline also teach these rules in a formal way, we believe they provide much less experience in applying them to everyday-life events. Thus, it would not be surprising if further work replicated the results of Study 3, which showed more improvement for social science psychology students than for natural science psychology students, especially in working with everyday-life problems. (For the time being, however, the reader should be warned that this difference was found only at one institution and that the n of natural science psychology students was rather small.)

It may be more surprising to psychologists that medical training increases statistical and methodological reasoning skills as much as it does. Examination of the medical curriculum at the University of Michigan reveals, however, that a great deal of training is geared toward teaching students how to think about uncertain events. For one thing, students are given a pamphlet explaining the basics of statistics and are expected to learn its contents. In addition, they are given original articles to read, with their reports of statistical tests, considerations of variance, sample size, and so forth. Perhaps more important, although most of the course content in the first two years is ostensibly focused on the natural sciences, there is in fact a continual effort to relate such content to complicated everyday medical problems. This attempt contains frequent allusions to the difficulties of making inferences in medical situations and to the uncertainties inherent in medical practice. Students are told of false positive and false negative rates for tests and of costs for tests, and they are asked whether, for a patient with particular presenting symptoms, they would "pay" for a particular test to be done. It is also made clear to students that the confounded variable principle underlies much medical "sleuthing." For example, they are reminded that some behaviors, such as cigarette smoking, are likely to be associated with others, such as coffee drinking. Thus, it is not surprising that two years of medical school affects statistical and methodological reasoning about everyday-life events. Because such training is also likely to require students to think about causal relations of different kinds, including those for which the evidence-checking procedures resemble those for the conditional and those for the biconditional, it is also not surprising that medical training results in improved ability to solve conditional and biconditional problems. Probably for the same reason, training in psychology results in improved ability to solve these problems.

Training in the law does not stress rules for dealing with variability or uncertainty in causal relations, and so it is not surprising that it produces no improvement in the ability to apply the statistical and methodological rules of the probabilistic sciences to either scientific studies or everyday-life events. Legal training does provide substantial instruction and drill in the logic of permissions and obligations, which can be used to solve problems in the conditional, and it provides additional instruction and drill for other contractual relations, particularly those in which an action must be taken if and only if some other event occurs, which can be used to solve biconditional problems.

In our view, training in chemistry provides no improvement in statistical or methodological reasoning because training in that field, especially in the early years, does not deal with events that are probabilistic. Statistics is not taught in the first two years of chemistry, and one would be hard pressed to come up with examples of confounded-variable rules in the curriculum. Similarly, there is little need to differentiate among the various types of causal relations because chemistry deals primarily with necessary-and-sufficient causes. Moreover, to the extent that any statistical or conditional reasoning does occur, it would be in field-specific settings highly abstracted from the problems of everyday life. The chemistry curriculum obviously should not be regarded as deficient, any more than a failure to teach about electrical charges should be regarded as a deficiency of psychological or legal training. However, the luxury of not being confronted with messy problems that contain substantial uncertainty and a tangled web of causes means that chemistry does not teach some rules that are relevant to everyday life.

The present results indicate that 20th century psychologists have been too quick to conclude that formal discipline is not possible and that rule training has little generalized educational potential. The results make it clear that training of some kinds has substantial effects on the way people reason about some sorts of problems. The error of psychologists in this century, in our view, has been to assume that because some kinds of rule systems do not generalize readily from problems having certain features to problems having another set of features (for example, rules for estimating the area of rectangles or rules for solving the Tower of Hanoi problem), *all* rules show equally poor transfer and generalization properties. The failure, in other words, amounts to a willingness to endorse the null hypothesis on the basis of a limited amount of research on a relatively small set of rules. Importantly, none of the studies that have led to the pessimistic perspective on the value of formal discipline have examined situations in which people learn through immersion in a field of study and have numerous occasions to apply the rules of the discipline to problems that arise both inside and outside their course of study. Yet this seems to be how disciplinary learning naturally occurs.

What types of inferential rules can be taught in such a way that they will be graceful additions to the rule systems that people already use? We think that a major class of such rules are those that people have induced, though only partially, in the course of their daily existence. Rules about assessing causality, rules for generalizing, rules for determining argument validity, and rules for assessing the probativeness of evidence are the kinds of rules that people must have in some measure in order to live effectively in the world.

Our work predisposes us to be optimistic about the possibility of identifying abstract rule systems underlying solutions of real-world problems and about the ability of educators to teach these rule systems. This optimism parallels that stemming from recent work by Herrnstein, Nickerson, de Sanchez, and Swets (1986) and others (see Nickerson, Perkins, & Smith, 1985, for a review) who have shown that strategies of reasoning can be taught to elementary school children. These investigators have taught such foundations of reasoning as how to use dimensions to analyze and organize similarities and differences, how to recognize and extrapolate different types of sequences, how to see the structure of simple propositions and analyze complex arguments, how to evaluate consistency, and so on. Such training not only improves performance on IQ tests but also improves the quality of open-ended written arguments.

The truth is that we know very little about reasoning and how to teach it.

The one thing we thought we knew—namely, that formal discipline is an illusion—seems clearly wrong. Just how wrong, and therefore just how much we can improve reasoning by instruction, is now a completely open question.

FOOTNOTES

[1]An additional 62 first-year medical students were given a different test for the purposes of another study. The total class N was 195.

[2]Students with English language problems were omitted throughout. This exclusion procedure significantly affected only the chemistry samples. Approximately 18% of chemistry students were excluded as compared to fewer than 3% of those in the other three disciplines.

[3]Of the two exceptions, one correlated .12 with the statistical-methodological total (minus itself) and .18 with the conditional total, and the other correlated .09 with the statistical-methodological total and .12 with the conditional total. Because the manifest content of these items was so similar to the other statistical-methodological items, we decided to treat these small discrepancies as measurement error and to leave the items on the statistical-methodological scale.

[4]A separate study was done of the effect of retesting on scores on each of the subscales. The study included 129 medical students, none of whom had participated in either Study 1 or Study 2. The two test administrations were approximately six weeks apart. The group posttest score was not higher than the group pretest score for any of the three reasoning subtests of interest. A similar "retest" study was done with approximately 80 law students with identical results. These findings mean that any changes registered for the longitudinal study are due to something associated with two years of education in the respective disciplines rather than with the effect of retesting per se.

[5]All p values reported are based on two-tailed tests. Means (and more detailed summaries) of the data are available upon request from the first author.

REFERENCES

Cheng, P. W., & Holyoak, K. J. (1985). Pragmatic reasoning schemas. *Cognitive Psychology, 17,* 391–416.

Cheng, P. W., Holyoak, K. J., Nisbett, R. E., & Oliver, L. M. (1986). Pragmatic versus syntactic approaches to training deductive reasoning. *Cognitive Psychology, 18,* 293–328.

Cheng, P. W., Nisbett, R. E., & Oliver, L. M. (1987). *The use of causal schemas in the evaluation of evidence for hypotheses.* Unpublished manuscript, University of California, Los Angeles.

Costa, R. M. (1982, March 6). Latin and Greek are good for you. *The New York Times,* p. 23.

D'Andrade, R. (1982). Paper presented at the Symposium on the Ecology of Cognition: Biological, Cultural, and Historical Perspectives, Greensboro, NC.

Fong, G. T., Krantz, D. H., & Nisbett, R. E. (1986). The effects of statistical training on thinking about everyday problems. *Cognitive Psychology, 18,* 253–292.

Fong, G. T., & Nisbett, R. E. (1988). *Domain specificity and domain independence of statistical training: The effects of time.* Unpublished manuscript, Northwestern University.

Griggs, R. A., & Cox, U. R. (1982). The elusive thematic-materials effect in Wason's selection task. *British Journal of Psychology, 73,* 407–420.

Hayes, J. R., & Simon, H. A. (1977). Psychological differences among problem isomorphs. In N. J. Castellan, Jr., D. B. Pisoni, & G. R. Potts (Eds.), *Cognitive theory* (pp. 21–41). Hillsdale, NJ: Erlbaum.

Herrnstein, R. J., Nickerson, R. S., de Sanchez, M., & Swets, J. A. (1986). Teaching thinking skills. *American Psychologist, 41,* 1279–1289.

Holland, J. H., Holyoak, K. J., Nisbett, R. E., & Thagard, P. T. (1986). *Induction: Processes of inference, learning, and discovery.* Cambridge, MA: Bradford Books/MIT Press.

Inhelder, B., & Piaget, J. (1958). *The growth of logical thinking from childhood to adolescence.* New York: Basic Books. (Original work published 1955)

Jepson, C., Krantz, D. H., & Nisbett, R. E. (1983). Inductive reasoning: Competence or skill? *Behavioral and Brain Sciences, 6,* 94–101.

Jowett, B. (1937). *The dialogues of Plato.* New York: Random House.

Kelley, H. H. (1971). Causal schemata and the attribution process. In E. E. Jones, D. E. Kanouse, H. H. Kelley, R. E. Nisbett, S. Valins, & B. Weiner (Eds.), *Attribution: Perceiving the causes of behavior.* Morristown, NJ: General Learning Press.

Kelley, H. H. (1973). The process of causal attribution. *American Psychologist, 28,* 107–128.

Manktelow, K. I., & Evans, J. St. B. T. (1979). Facilitation of reasoning by realism: Effect or non-effect? *British Journal of Psychology, 63,* 395–400.

Mann, L. (1979). *On the trail of process.* New York: Grune & Stratton.

Nickerson, R. S., Perkins, D. N., & Smith, E. E. (1985). *The teaching of thinking.* Hillsdale, NJ: Erlbaum.

Nisbett, R. E., Fong, G. T., Lehman, D. R., & Cheng, P. W. (1987). Teaching reasoning. *Science, 238,* 625–631.

Nisbett, R. E., Krantz, D. H., Jepson, D., & Kunda, Z. (1983). The use of statistical heuristics in everyday inductive reasoning. *Psychological Review, 90,* 339–363.

Reed, S. K., Dempster, A., & Ettinger, M. (1985). Usefulness of analogous solutions for solving algebra word problems. *Journal of Experimental Psychology: Learning, Memory and Cognition, 11,* 106–125.

Reed, S. K., Ernst, G. W., & Banerji, R. (1974). The role of analogy in transfer between similar problem states. *Cognitive Psychology, 6,* 436–450.

Share, K. W. (1979). The primary mental abilities in adulthood: An exploration in the development of psychometric intelligence. *Life Span Development and Behavior, 2,* 67–115.

Thorndike, E. L. (1906). *Principles of teaching.* New York: A. G. Seiler.

Thorndike, E. L. (1913). *The psychology of learning.* New York: Mason-Henry.

Wason, P. C. (1966). Reasoning. In B. M. Foss (Ed.), *New horizons in psychology.* Harmondsworth, England: Penguin.

APPENDIX A: EXAMPLES OF ITEMS USED

(Correct answers are denoted by †)

Statistical Reasoning — Everyday Life

After the first two weeks of the major league baseball season, newspapers begin to print the top ten batting averages. Typically, after two weeks, the leading batter has an average of about .450. Yet no batter in major league history has ever averaged .450 at the end of a season. Why do you think this is?

†(a) A player's high average at the beginning of the season may be just a lucky fluke.

(b) A batter who has such a hot streak at the beginning of the season is under a lot of stress to maintain his performance record. Such stress adversely affects his playing.

(c) Pitchers tend to get better over the course of the season, as they get more in shape. As pitchers improve, they are more likely to strike out batters, so batters' averages go down.

(d) When a batter is known to be hitting for a high average, pitchers bear down more when they pitch to him.

(e) When a batter is known to be hitting for a high average, he stops getting good pitches to hit. Instead, pitchers "play the corners" of the plate because they don't mind walking him.

Methodological Reasoning — Everyday Life

The city of Middleopolis has had an unpopular police chief for a year and a half. He is a political appointee who is a crony of the mayor, and he had little previous experience in police administration when he was appointed. The mayor has recently defended the chief in public, announcing that in the time since he took office, crime rates decreased by 12%. Which of the following pieces of evidence would most deflate the mayor's claim that his chief is competent? †(a) The crime rates of the two cities closest to Middleopolis in location and size have decreased by 18% in the same period.

(b) An independent survey of the citizens of Middleopolis shows that 40% more crime is reported by respondents in the survey than is reported in police records.

(c) Common sense indicates that there is little a police chief can do to lower crime rates. These are for the most part due to social and economic conditions beyond the control of officials.

(d) The police chief has been discovered to have business contacts with people who are known to be involved in organized crime.

Conditional Reasoning — Permission Schema

You are a public health official at the international airport in Manila, capital of the Philippines. Part of your duty is to check that every arriving passenger who wishes to enter the country (rather than just change planes at the airport) has had an inoculation against cholera. Every passenger carries a health form. One side of the form indicates whether the passenger is entering or in transit, and the other side of the form lists the inoculations he or she has had in the past six months. Which of the following forms would you need to turn over to check? Indicate only those forms you would have to check to be sure.

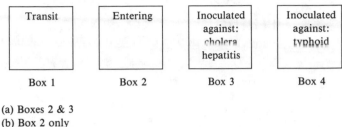

Transit	Entering	Inoculated against: cholera hepatitis	Inoculated against: typhoid
Box 1	Box 2	Box 3	Box 4

(a) Boxes 2 & 3
(b) Box 2 only
(c) Boxes 2,3 & 4
†(d) Boxes 2 &4
(e) Box 3 only

Verbal Reasoning

The new miracle drug Amotril has caused unforeseen side effects of a devastating nature; therefore, no new drugs should be released for public consumption without a thorough study of their effects.

Which of the following arguments most closely resembles the argument above?

(a) Because exposure to several hours of television a day has been shown to undermine children's interest in reading, children should be prevented from watching television.

(b) Because it is difficult to predict whether the results of pure research will be of practical benefit to human beings, the amount of money spent on such research should be sharply curtailed.

(c) The 1977 model of this compact station wagon has been shown to have a faulty exhaust system; therefore, it is urgent that this model be recalled immediately.

†(d) Some of the worst highway accidents have been caused by teenagers between the ages of 16 and 18; therefore, only carefully screened members of this age group should be granted driver's licenses.

(e) Rising medical costs have put many routine medical procedures out of the reach of low- and middle-income families; therefore, doctors should prescribe only the most essential laboratory tests.

14

A Longitudinal Study of the Effects of Undergraduate Training on Reasoning

Darrin R. Lehman
University of British Columbia

Richard E. Nisbett
University of Michigan

Does an undergraduate education improve reasoning about everyday-life problems? Do some forms of undergraduate training enhance certain types of reasoning more than others? These issues have not been addressed in a methodologically rigorous manner (Nickerson, Perkins, & Smith, 1985). We consequently have little knowledge of whether reasoning can be improved by instruction, yet this question has long been regarded as central to theories of cognitive development.

FORMAL DISCIPLINE AND OPPOSING VIEWS

Until the 20th century, most educators endorsed the concept of *formal discipline,* initially formulated by Plato. This is the notion that reasoning can be improved as a result of teaching rules within a particular field, which then generalize outside the bounds of that field. This view is consistent with the optimistic hypothesis that instruction in abstract rule systems can affect reasoning about everyday-life events (Lehman, Lempert, & Nisbett, 1988; see also Fong, Krantz, & Nisbett, 1986; for a general summary, see Nisbett, Fong, Lehman, & Cheng, 1987). The formal discipline concept was countered initially by Thorndike (Thorndike, 1906, 1913; Thorndike & Woodworth, 1901), who concluded that people use only highly domain-specific rules dealing with concrete types of events to solve problems. Many current theorists endorse Thorndike's view. For example, Newell (1980) holds that "the modern . . . position is that learned problem-solving skills are, in general, idiosyncratic to the task." Piaget (see, for example, Inhelder & Piaget, 1955/1958) put forth a highly influential theory suggesting that people do use abstract inferential rules, but because learning of these rules comes mainly through self-discovery (constrained by level of cognitive development), formal training can do little to extend it. Thus, much contemporary theorizing has suggested that reasoning is either domain-specific or quite difficult to teach. Such theorizing gives us little reason to expect that higher education would have much effect on reasoning abilities.

Our previous results (Lehman et al., 1988), however, suggest that a version of the formal discipline view is correct. We reported on the effects of graduate training in law (a nonscience), medicine and psychology (two probabilistic sciences), and chemistry (a nonprobabilistic or deterministic science) on statistical and methodological reasoning and on reasoning about problems in the logic of the conditional. We found that graduate students in the probabilistic sciences improved in statistical and methodological reasoning and that students in both the probabilistic sciences and in the law improved in conditional reasoning. Chemistry students did not improve in any of the types of reasoning examined.

STATISTICAL AND METHODOLOGICAL REASONING

Statistical reasoning includes a family of related schemas or heuristics that are derivable from the law of large numbers. These include the rule that, all things being equal, larger samples are more representative of the population they are drawn from than are smaller samples and that this difference is greater the greater the variability inherent in the population. The related rule of regression to the mean and the base-rate principle are derivable directly from the law of large numbers and the concept of variability (Nisbett, Krantz, Jepson, & Kunda, 1983). For example, regression to the mean occurs because extreme values for an object or sample are due partly to observational error and therefore are less likely to be extreme when the object is reexamined or a new sample is observed.

The sort of methodological reasoning examined in our previous work included judgments requiring an understanding of problems posed by confounded variables. These reasoning skills are particularly helpful when thinking about causes that are neither necessary nor sufficient (Kelley, 1971, 1973). They include rules about when and how to use control groups, how to avoid sample bias, and how to recognize and avoid errors that can arise when subjects who are selected or who select themselves for a treatment on the basis of one variable also differ on other variables that are potentially correlated with the dependent variable of interest (third-variable problems).

CONDITIONAL REASONING

Conditional reasoning, or reasoning using the material conditional in formal logic, is a form of deductive logic based on modus ponens and the contrapositive or modus tollens rule. Wason (1966) established that people typically have great difficulty with abstract problems that follow the form of the material conditional "if p, then q." He examined how people respond to abstract selection tasks that embody this logic. For example, subjects are shown four cards displaying *A, B, 4,* and *7;* are told that all cards have letters on the front and numbers on the back; and are asked to turn over as many cards as necessary to establish whether it is the case that "if there is a vowel on the front, then there is an even number on the back." Few subjects reach the correct conclusion that it is necessary to turn over the A (because if there was not an even number on the back, the rule would be violated) and the 7 (because if there was a vowel on the front, the rule would be violated). More generally, to determine the truth of a conditional statement, the cases that must be checked are *p* (because if *p* is the case, it must be established that *q* is also the case) and *not-q* (because if it is not the case that *q,* it must be established that it is also not the case that *p*).

Recently, Cheng, Holyoak, and their colleagues (Cheng & Holyoak, 1985; Cheng, Holyoak, Nisbett, & Oliver, 1986) argued that, instead of using the rules of formal logic to solve conditional problems, people use pragmatic inferential rules, or pragmatic reasoning schemas, which capture recurring regularities among problem goals and among event relations that people encounter in everyday life. These rules are fully abstract in that they are not tied to any content domain, but they are not as independent of relation types and problem goals as formal logical rules or the purely syntactic rule systems often studied by modern cognitive psychologists.

One type of pragmatic inferential rule system is the *contractual schema.* Contractual schemas include rules about situations in which a *permission* is required to perform some action or in which an *obligation* is incurred by virtue of the occurrence of some event. These schemas map onto the conditional in formal logic. That is, the procedures needed to establish whether a permission or obligation has been violated are the same as the checking procedures required by the conditional to establish whether a proposition of the form "if p, then q" holds. Subjects can solve problems invoking the obligation schema that map directly onto the conditional. For example, most subjects know how to check whether the rule "if X occurs, then you must do Y" has been violated. In addition, research (Cheng & Holyoak, 1985; Cheng et al., 1986) has shown that whereas training in formal logic has little effect on people's ability to solve either arbitrary or semantically meaningful versions of conditional problems, training in pragmatic reasoning schemas has substantial effect.

Cheng, Morris, and Nisbett (1990) argued that another type of pragmatic reasoning schema, namely, causal schemas of the kind defined by Kelley (1971, 1973), may also help people to solve problems that are syntactically identical to the selection problem. Kelley argued that people understand the ideas of necessity and sufficiency in causality and possess different schemas for checking evidence supporting causal hypotheses that are necessary and sufficient, necessary but not sufficient, and so on. It is interesting that one of the schemas, namely, that for sufficient-but-not-necessary causes, has checking procedures identical to those for the conditional selection task ("if p, then q"). A hypothesis of the sufficient-but-not-necessary type, "Factor A always (though not exclusively) causes Effect B," can be disproven by examining A and finding that not B was the case or by examining not-B and finding that A was the case. Cheng et al. (1986) discovered that subjects performed better on selection tasks that had a causal interpretation that might encourage subjects to use the same checking procedures as required by the conditional. The checking procedures for the necessary and sufficient type of causality, it turns out, are the same as for the biconditional (p *if and only if* q) in formal logic. The biconditional requires examining all four cases: *p, not-p, q,* and *not-q.* The conditional reasoning materials used in this study include (a) classic, arbitrary material conditional problems of the Wason type; (b) biconditional problems; and conditional problems having (c) permission or (d) causal interpretations.

EFFECTS OF GRADUATE TRAINING

The results of Lehman et al. (1988) showed improvement on different types of reasoning tasks by graduate students, in terms of rule systems taught by the various fields. Lehman et al. argued that psychology and medicine improve statistical and methodological reasoning about a wide range of problems because both fields teach their students how to think about uncertain events, in part through instruction in statistics. In addition, in the case of psychology, students are instructed in methodology and given day-to-day hands-on research experience. In the case of medicine, a concerted effort is made to have students read research articles and understand the complicated statistical and methodological connections to everyday medical problems. Because neither training in law nor chemistry stresses rules for dealing with variability or with uncertainty in causal relations, it was not surprising that these two disciplines did not improve students' abilities to apply statistical or methodological rules to the range of problems.

Lehman et al. (1988) argued that students of psychology and medicine improved on conditional reasoning because their graduate training in the probabilistic sciences required them to think about causal relations of different kinds, including those for which the evidence-checking procedures resemble those for the conditional. They argued that law students improved in conditional reasoning because law provides substantial instruction in thinking about contractual relations that have the form of the conditional, such as permissions and obligations. Finally, Lehman et al. argued that chemistry students did not improve in conditional reasoning because chemistry provides neither contractual training nor training in how to reason about the wide variety of types of causal relations encountered in the probabilistic sciences.

IMPLICATIONS FOR THE EFFECTS OF UNDERGRADUATE TRAINING

In this undergraduate study, we again wanted to include probabilistic sciences, nonprobabilistic (or deterministic) sciences, and nonsciences. Social science training, in addition to psychology, included anthropology, economics, political science, and sociology. Natural science training included biology, chemistry, microbiology, and physics. Humanities training included communications, English, history, journalism, linguistics, and philosophy. We used a longitudinal design, following subjects through 4 years of undergraduate training. This allowed us to remove the possibility of alternative explanations such as differential attrition rates.

We anticipated that psychology, and, more generally, social science training, at the undergraduate level would parallel the relative improvement in statistical and methodological reasoning of psychology training at the graduate level. We anticipated that training of this sort would alert people to consider sample sizes when making inferences and would also affect methodological reasoning.

In contrast, we anticipated that undergraduate training in the deterministic sciences and in the nonsciences would have less effect on statistical and methodological reasoning. The natural sciences focus primarily on deterministic causes and consequently should produce less improvement in rule usage concerned with uncertainty and self-selection. The humanities, with their emphasis on language, history, and philosophy, should also produce less improvement on these statistical and methodological reasoning abilities.

Lehman et al. (1988) discovered improvements in conditional reasoning among graduate students in the probabilistic sciences and attributed these improvements to extensive experience with causal relations of various kinds (e.g., sufficient but not necessary causes). Cheng et al. (1990) have recently found that psychology graduate students do indeed improve in their ability to reason causally, whereas chemistry and philosophy graduate students do not. Should we expect the same sort of improvement in conditional reasoning for social science majors at the undergraduate level? It seems unlikely that the training in causal reasoning at the undergraduate level is nearly as intensive as it is at the graduate level. For example, undergraduate training in psychology usually does not involve large doses of experimental research. Thus, although graduate students in the probabilistic sciences improve in conditional reasoning (presumably because of their improved ability to reason about formally different types of causal relations), it is not clear that similar improvements should occur for social science undergraduates.

What about predictions concerning improvements in conditional reasoning for natural science and humanities undergraduates? Lehman et al. found no improvement in conditional reasoning for chemistry graduate students. Similarly, Cheng et al. (1990) discovered that graduate training in chemistry did not improve students' abilities to reason causally. On the other hand, recent research has suggested a specific prediction concerning improvements in conditional reasoning that probably applies to undergraduates in the natural sciences. Jackson and Griggs (1988) found a significant effect of mathematics training on ability to solve conditional problems. They found that subjects trained in mathematics performed better than subjects trained in computer science, electrical engineering, and the social sciences. Jackson and Griggs reasoned that mathematics students, with their experience in proof by contradiction ("if p were the case, q would have to be the case; not q, therefore not p"), are quite familiar with the basic material conditional relation. In effect, Jackson and Griggs argued, proof by contradiction is a pragmatic reasoning schema for students with training in math. Given that the conditional task maps onto this schema, it is possible that mathematics students would perform at a higher level on conditional problems. Therefore, natural science undergraduates, because of the greater number of mathematics courses in their curriculum, may improve significantly in conditional reasoning. Moreover, it should follow that the more math courses natural science majors take, the more they will improve in conditional reasoning. We have no reason to expect that humanities undergraduates will gain much in conditional reasoning because they are not taught extensively about causal schemas or contractual relations, and they do not take an abundance of mathematics courses.

To help test these hypotheses, we obtained the transcripts of our undergraduate subjects and recorded a number of types of courses taken by them. These included all of the course theoretically relevant to gains in either statistical, methodological, or conditional reasoning, namely, computer science, logic, mathematics, natural science lab, psychology lab, social science lab, and statistics courses.

To ensure that improvements in statistical, methodological, and conditional reasoning by particular groups of subjects were not observed because these groups were improving in all aspects of reasoning, we examined the effects of different undergraduate training on verbal reasoning of the kind tested by the Scholastic Aptitude Test (SAT). Because verbal reasoning ability increases slightly during the young adult years for those involved in mentally challenging work (Share, 1979), we expected subjects in each of the disciplines to improve slightly, and to about the same extent, in verbal reasoning.

The above predictions regarding improvements in statistical, methodological, and conditional reasoning contradict much of the current thinking on reasoning and cognitive development. The notion that reasoning is domain-specific or that abstract rule systems cannot be taught suggests that education would have little effect on people's abilities to apply formal rules of inference to everyday-life problems. To the extent that such improvements in reasoning are discovered, a version of the pre-20th century formal-discipline theory would gain plausibility. The Piagetian view that inferential rules are learned essentially just by self-discovery would lose plausibility.

METHOD

Subjects

Subjects were University of Michigan undergraduates tested in the first term of their 1st year of school and again in the second term of their 4th year of school. Subjects were contacted initially through a random selection of first-year students from a university-wide roster. Virtually all of them had recently graduated from high school. The subjects were phoned and asked if they had a tentative selection for their major of study (none of them had declared their major officially at this point). Those who reported a major that fell into one of the disciplines under investigation were then invited to participate in the study. The first-year response rates were as follows: 39 of 42 randomly sampled natural science students (93%), 46 of 50 randomly sampled humanities students (92%), 38 of 42 randomly sampled social science students (90%), and 42 of 45 randomly sampled psychology students (93%).

We attempted to recontact all of the pretest subjects approximately 3½ years later (in the middle of their senior year). Subjects were phoned, reminded about the study, and asked about their current major. If their major fell into one of the four disciplines, they were invited to participate a second time. As might be expected, by the middle of their fourth year, a number of students had switched majors and consequently were reclassified. Of the original 165 subjects who completed the pretest in their first year, 121 still had majors that we had targeted for study, and completed the posttest (73%). The sample sizes were as follows: 29 natural science students, 39 humanities students, 30 social science students, and 23 psychology students. An additional 44 subjects who took the pretest did not complete the posttest because of the following reasons: were not located (20); were repeated no-shows (11); were living out of the country (2); refused (3); and had switched to majors not included in the study (e.g., business; 8). Of the 29 natural science subjects, only 7% had switched majors since their first year. Of the 39 humanities subjects, 31% had switched majors, approximately half from psychology and half from other social sciences. Of the 30 social science subjects, 43% had switched majors, spread evenly throughout the other three categories. Finally, of the 23 psychology subjects, 22% had switched majors, approximately half from natural science and half from the humanities.

Procedure

Subjects were administered reasoning tests (one during their first year and a second during their fourth year) in a relaxed atmosphere in offices at the Institute for Social Research. They were instructed to take as much time as necessary to solve each problem: "Please treat each fully; but there is no need to puzzle unduly over any problem. While some questions have right and wrong answers, others do not."

Two forms of the reasoning test were developed so that pre- and posttest versions would be available. Approximately half of the subjects in each group completed Form 1 of the reasoning test at the pretest, and the other half completed Form 2. Subjects initially given Form 1 were given Form 2 on the retest and vice versa.[1] The test took between 45 and 70 min to complete. Subjects were paid $5 for their participation in the pretest and $10 for their participation in the posttest.

Instrument

The reasoning test consisted of three sets of multiple-choice questions, with items spread evenly throughout the test booklet. One set was intended to measure statistical and methodological reasoning, one was intended to measure reasoning about problems to which conditional logic could be applied, and one was a standard measure of verbal reasoning of the kind used in the SAT Verbal test.

Statistical and Methodological Reasoning. The statistical reasoning items were intended to measure subjects' abilities to apply the law of large numbers and the regression or base rate principle. These problems were embedded in either scientific or everyday-life contexts; scientific questions were those that specifically described a study of some kind in the natural or social sciences, whereas everyday-life problems did not. Examples of a "scientific-law-of-large-numbers" problem and an "everyday-life-regression-principle" problem are presented in their entirety in the Appendix.

The methodological problems were intended to measure subjects' knowledge of selection or attrition effects, the need for control group data, problems with confounded variables, and sample bias effects. These questions were also embedded in either scientific or everyday-life contexts. Examples of a "scientific-attrition" problem and an "everyday-life-sample-bias" problem are presented in the Appendix.

Conditional Reasoning. Each form contained three questions that could be solved by application of the conditional and one that could be solved by application of the biconditional (used by Cheng et al., 1986). One of the conditional problems was arbitrary (e.g., the Wason, 1966, card-selection problem), one was couched in language that was expected to encourage causal reasoning, and one was couched in language that was expected to encourage application of the permission schema. An example of a "conditional-causal schema" problem is presented in the Appendix.

Verbal Reasoning. A third set of questions was intended to measure general verbal abilities to recognize arguments, evaluate evidence, and detect analogies. These items were similar to SAT Verbal exam items, and some were taken from practice materials for these exams.

Scale Construction. Information about the psychometric properties of the three sets of items came from the Lehman et al. (1988) study of graduate students. Individual statistical reasoning items were no more highly correlated with the sum of other statistical items than with the sum of methodological reasoning items, nor were individual methodological items correlated more highly with the sum of other methodological items than with the sum of statistical items. Consequently, these items were collapsed into a single scale. All but two items on this scale were correlated more highly with the total statistical-methodological reasoning score (minus each item itself) than with either the Conditional Reasoning scale or the Verbal Reasoning scale. All of the conditional reasoning items correlated more highly with the conditional reasoning total than with either the statistical-methodological total or the verbal total. In the two forms of the reasoning test, there were 11 and 9 statistical-methodological items, 4 and 4 conditional items, and 8 and 7 verbal items, respectively.

RESULTS

Initial Differences

There were no disciplinary differences in first-year scores in verbal reasoning, $F(3, 117) = 1.04$, $p = .38$, statistical-methodological reasoning, $F(3, 117) = 0.42$, $p = .74$, or conditional reasoning, $F(3, 117) = 0.64$, $p = .59$.[2] These data were grouped on the basis of subjects' eventual majors of study.

To determine whether there were any disciplinary differences in general ability, we compared the admission test scores of subjects in the various disciplines. There were no statistically significant differences among the disciplines on either the Verbal or Quantitative sections of the Scholastic Aptitude Test. However, marginal trends were found for each of the tests ($p < .10$ for Verbal, $p < .11$ for Quantitative). The Verbal SAT score means indicate that the humanities students scored highest ($M = 582$), followed by the natural science students ($M = 560$), the social science students ($M = 540$), and the psychology students ($M = 524$). The Quantitative SAT score means indicate that the natural science students scored highest ($M = 621$), followed by the social science students ($M = 583$), the humanities students ($M = 558$), and the psychology students ($M = 553$).

Changes in Reasoning Scores

Verbal Reasoning. The change scores for verbal reasoning for all groups of subjects are presented in Fig. 14.1. It may be seen that all of the groups except social science majors showed slight improvements in verbal reasoning, ranging from 6% to 16%. The social science group actually decreased trivially (-5%). None of the differences reached statistical significance, and the interaction between discipline and year fell far short of significance, $F(1, 117) = .82$, *ns*. These results provide a base from which to examine the differential change in the other two types of reasoning.

Statistical-methodological Reasoning. The change scores for statistical-methodological reasoning for all groups of subjects are presented in Fig. 14.2. It may be seen that the psychology and social science students changed dramatically from first year to fourth year in statistical-methodological reasoning, $t(22) = 3.96$, $p < .001$, for psychology students, and $t(29) = 4.10$, $p < .001$, for social science students. The improvement in statistical-

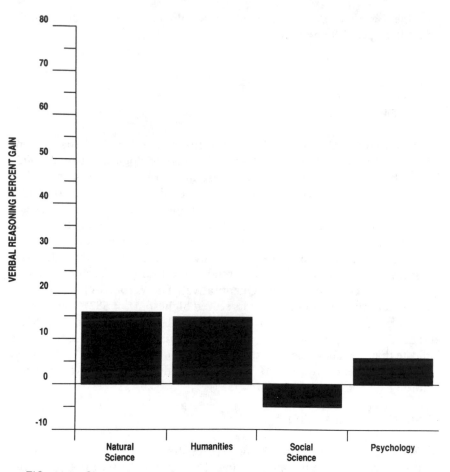

FIG. 14.1 Change scores for verbal reasoning as a function of year and undergraduate studies.

methodological reasoning for natural science and humanities students, although much smaller than for psychology and social science students, was still marginally significant (both ps < .10). Pooling the probabilistic sciences (psychology and social science) and the nonprobabilistic sciences and non-sciences (natural science and humanities) produces a significant interaction between year and type of discipline, $F(1, 119) = 5.96, p < .02$.

Conditional Reasoning. Figure 14.3 presents change in conditional reasoning for all subjects. As anticipated, students in the natural sciences improved in their ability to reason about conditional problems, $t(28) = 2.63, p < .02$. Surprisingly, humanities students also improved, $t(38) = 3.41, p < .003$. In contrast, psychology and social science students did not

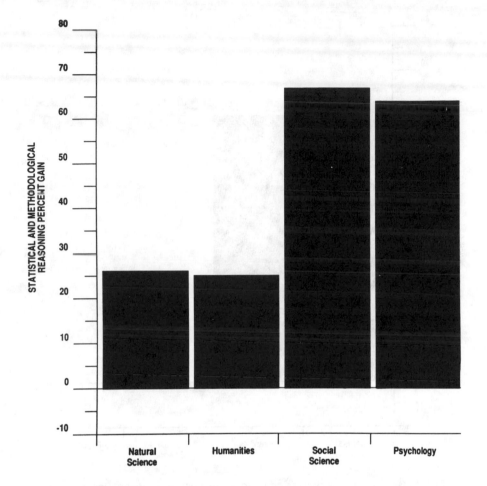

FIG. 14.2   Change scores for statistical and methodological reasoning as a function of year and undergraduate studies.

improve in conditional reasoning, both $ts < 1$. The interaction between year and discipline was significant, $F(3, 117) = 2.64$, $p = .052$.[3]

Correlations Between Courses Taken and Improvements in Reasoning

We were able to examine correlations between the number of courses taken of various types and improvement scores (posttest score minus pretest score) on the three types of reasoning skills. Sample sizes are reduced because of missing transcript data. The only significant correlations were between (a) statistical-methodological reasoning improvement and number

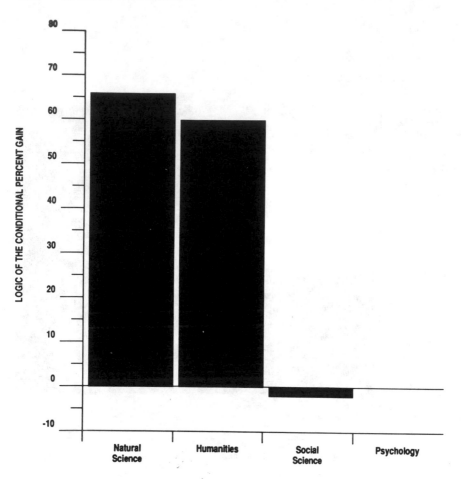

FIG. 14.3 Change scores for conditional reasoning as a function of year and undergraduate studies.

of statistics courses taken, and (b) conditional reasoning improvement and number of math and number of computer science courses taken.

The correlation between statistical-methodological reasoning improvement and number of statistics courses taken was .17 ($p < .05$) in the overall sample ($N = 103$). The correlations for psychology, social science, and natural science students were .23, .23, and .28, respectively. Only 15% of humanities students took any statistics courses, and the sample was therefore regarded as too restricted to compute a correlation.

The correlations between conditional reasoning improvement and number of math and number of computer science courses taken were .31 ($p < .002$) and .27 ($p < .005$), respectively, in the overall sample. The correlation between conditional reasoning improvement and math courses taken just for the natural science majors, who took most of the math courses, was .66 (p < .001). The correlation between conditional reasoning improvement and computer science courses taken again just for the natural science students (who took the bulk of the computer science courses) was .45 (p < .02).

The correlation between conditional reasoning improvement and computer science courses taken was largely spurious because of the correlation between taking math and computer science courses. For the overall sample, the correlation between conditional reasoning improvement and number of math courses taken (partialing out number of computer science courses taken) was .20 (p < .03). The same correlation for computer science courses taken (partialing out math courses taken) was .12 *(ns)*. For the natural science group, the correlation between conditional reasoning improvement and number of math courses taken (partialing out number of computer science courses taken) was .55 (p < .005). The same correlation for computer science courses taken (partialing out math courses taken) was −.11 *(ns)*.

Correlations Between Admission Test Scores, GPA, and Improvements in Reasoning

We were able to examine relations between verbal and quantitative SAT scores and grade point average (GPA), on the one hand, and improvements in the three kinds of reasoning, on the other. The possible patterns of data were many, of course, but we expected a "rich gets richer" pattern. That is, on the basis of a frequent pattern of differential gain found in educational research, we believed it likely that subjects with higher SATs and GPAs would also show the largest improvements in the various reasoning skills. Hence, we expected a significant percentage of strong, positive correlations.

The data did not support this prediction. For the overall sample, only two of the possible nine correlations approached significance. Quantitative SAT score was marginally and positively correlated with improvement in statistical-methodological reasoning, $r(96) = .16$, $p < .06$, and verbal SAT score was marginally and positively correlated with improvement in verbal reasoning, $r(96) = .16$, $p < .06$. Although some correlations for particular majors were higher than these, the pattern was inconsistent and not interpretable.

DISCUSSION

These results are consistent with the view that reasoning can be taught and with the presumption that different undergraduate disciplines teach different kinds of reasoning to different degrees.

Undergraduate training in psychology, and, more generally, the social sciences, can affect statistical and methodological reasoning about a wide range of problems to a very large degree. Students majoring in the natural sciences and the humanities did not improve in statistical-methodological reasoning nearly as much but still showed marginally significant improvements.

The results also indicate that the natural sciences and humanities can affect conditional reasoning. Undergraduate training in the social sciences does not seem to affect this kind of reasoning. We believe that the latter type of training had little effect because, unlike graduate training in the probabilistic sciences, undergraduate training does not emphasize types of causality and the methodologies that are appropriate to each type. The positive effect of the natural sciences in improving conditional reasoning appears to be due to the greater number of math courses natural science students take. We discovered that the more mathematics courses natural science majors took, the more they improved on conditional reasoning, a finding that supports previous work by Jackson and Griggs (1988) indicating that the proof-by-contradiction schema generalizes to problems outside mathematics. We lack an explanation for the gain in conditional reasoning by humanities students.

With the relatively minor gains in verbal reasoning as a backdrop, the percent gains in statistical-methodological reasoning by the social science students, and the percent gains in conditional reasoning by the natural science and humanities students, are quite large. Subjects showed between 60% and 70% improvement, on average, on these classes of problems.

The findings regarding statistical-methodological reasoning seem especially significant. We view these reasoning skills as important for an ability to think critically (see also Ennis, 1987). When deciding what to believe or how to act in everyday life, people must often reflect on the available data and determine their meaning. Accurate assessments frequently require consideration of statistical and methodological questions.

The fact that an undergraduate education can change the way people (a) think about uncertainty in everyday-life events, (b) assess the reliability of information they have before them, and (c) solve logical problems lends support to the premodern formal discipline hypothesis. Our results show that, contrary to much contemporary theorizing about reasoning, highly general inferential rules can be taught and that the quality of people's everyday reasoning can be improved. Given that universities attempt to hone critical abilities and see this in fact as one of their major tasks, our results paint an optimistic picture.

FOOTNOTES

[1]Separate studies were conducted of the effect of retesting on scores on each of the reasoning scales. Over 200 subjects were administered the two forms of the test approximately 6 weeks

apart. The group posttest scores were not higher than the group pretest scores for any of the reasoning subsets of interest. These findings mean that any changes registered for this study were due to something associated with 4 years of undergraduate education in the respective disciplines rather than with the effect of retesting per se.

[2]All p values reported are based on two-tailed tests.

[3]The mean percent correct for the pre- and posttests on verbal reasoning was, respectively, 42 and 49 for natural science, 46 and 52 for humanities, 50 and 48 for social science, and 45 and 47 for psychology subjects. The mean percent correct for the pre- and posttests on statistical-methodological reasoning was 26 and 33 for natural science, 27 and 34 for humanities, 23 and 39 for social science, and 25 and 41 for psychology subjects. The mean percent correct for the pre- and posttests on conditional reasoning was 28 and 46 for natural science, 28 and 44 for humanities, 32 and 31 for social science, and 35 and 35 for psychology subjects.

REFERENCES

Cheng, P. W., & Holyoak, K. J. (1985). Pragmatic reasoning schemas. *Cognitive Psychology, 17,* 391–416.

Cheng, P. W., Holyoak, K. J., Nisbett, R. E., & Oliver, L. M. (1986). Pragmatic versus syntactic approaches to training deductive reasoning. *Cognitive Psychology, 18,* 293–328.

Cheng, P. W., Morris, M., & Nisbett, R. E. (1990). *Schemas for causal deduction.* Unpublished manuscript, University of California, Los Angeles.

Ennis, R. H. (1987). A taxonomy of critical thinking dispositions and abilities. In J. B. Baron & R. J. Sternberg (Eds.), *Teaching thinking skills: Theory and practice* (pp. 9–26). New York: Freeman.

Fong, G. T., Krantz, D. H., & Nisbett, R. E. (1986). The effects of statistical training on thinking about everyday problems. *Cognitive Psychology, 18,* 253–292.

Inhelder, B., & Piaget, J. (1958). *The growth of logical thinking from childhood to adolescence.* New York: Basic Books. (Original work published 1955)

Jackson, S. L., & Griggs, R. A. (1988). Education and the selection task. *Bulletin of the Psychonomic Society, 26,* 327–330.

Kelley, H. H. (1971). Causal schemata and the attribution process. In E. E. Jones, D. E. Kanouse, H. H. Kelley, R. E. Nisbett, S. Valins, & B. Weiner (Eds.), *Attribution: Perceiving the causes of behavior.* Morristown, NJ: General Learning Press.

Kelley, H. H. (1973). The process of causal attribution. *American Psychologist, 28,* 107–128.

Lehman, D. R., Lempert, R. O., & Nisbett, R. E. (1988). The effects of graduate training on reasoning: Formal discipline and thinking about everyday-life events. *American Psychologist, 43,* 431–442.

Newell, A. (1980). One final word. In D. T. Tuma & F. Reif (Eds.), *Problem solving and education: Issues in teaching and research* (pp. 175–189). Hillsdale, NJ: Erlbaum.

Nickerson, R. S., Perkins, D. N., & Smith, E. E. (1985). *The teaching of thinking.* Hillsdale, NJ: Erlbaum.

Nisbett, R. E., Fong, G. T., Lehman, D. R., & Cheng, P. W. (1987). Teaching reasoning. *Science, 238,* 625–631.

Nisbett, R. E., Krantz, D. H., Jepson, C., & Kunda, Z. (1983). The use of statistical heuristics in everyday inductive reasoning. *Psychological Review, 90,* 339–363.

Share, K. W. (1979). The primary mental abilities in adulthood: An exploration in the development of psychometric intelligence. *Life Span Development and Behavior, 2,* 67–115.

Thorndike, E. L. (1906). *Principles of teaching.* New York: Seiler.

Thorndike, E. L. (1913). *The psychology of learning.* New York: Mason-Henry.

Thorndike, E. L., & Woodworth, R. S. (1901). The influence of improvement in one mental function upon the efficiency of other functions. *Psychological Review, 8,* 247–261, 384–395, 553–564.

Wason, P. C. (1966). Reasoning. In B. M. Foss (Ed.), *New horizons in psychology.* Harmondsworth, England: Penguin.

APPENDIX: EXAMPLES OF ITEMS USED

In one of the "scientific-law-of-large-numbers" problems, for example, subjects were told about a study showing that noise harms plants. In the study, two identical coleus plants were transplanted from the same greenhouse and grown under identical conditions, except that the first plant was exposed to about 100 dB of noise (approximately the same as a person would hear while standing on a busy subway platform) while the other plant was grown in quiet conditions. After 1½ weeks of continuous exposure, only the sound-treated plant wilted. A recognition of the law of large numbers was shown by indicating that a larger number of coleus plants should have been used in each of the two conditions. An everyday-life problem to which the regression principle could be applied was identical to one used by Fong, Krantz, and Nisbett (1986): Subjects were asked why rookies of the year in major-league baseball tend not to do as well in their second year. Understanding of the regression principle was demonstrated by indicating that these rookies' performances are unusually good, even for them, and thus it is unlikely that they will have two such unusually good years in a row.

A "scientific-attrition" problem described a study conducted to assess the effects of a weight-loss club. All new members who joined the club during a 1-year period had their weight recorded over time. Out of 138 people who started to attend meetings, 81 kept attending for at least 3 months. In fact, the average amount of weight lost by these people was 14.7 pounds. Appreciation of the attrition principle was indicated by answering that those who enroll in the program and stick to it will on the average be better off, although it is impossible to say whether the techniques used in the program are generally effective. An everyday-life question tapping sample bias effects told of a television debate about a temporary proposal that Alberta, Canada was considering: the taxing of all people with incomes above $18,000 to deal with a budget imbalance. The debate was followed by a viewer telephone poll in which, for 50 cents, viewers could register their opinion by calling one of two numbers. The final result showed that 64% of the callers wanted the proposal to be defeated, whereas 36% wanted it to pass. Subjects were asked what they thought the results of the election 3 days later would be. Awareness of sample bias was indicated by the answer

"I am very uncertain about how the election came out." Note that this question bears a resemblance to the famous poll predicting Landon to beat Roosevelt in the 1936 U.S. presidential election. Because the sample came from lists of owners of automobiles and telephones, the "poor person's candidate" was not given a fair chance.

A "causal schema conditional" problem read, "As part of your job as a quality control inspector at a shirt factory, you have the task of checking fabric and washing instruction labels to make sure that they are correctly paired. Fabric and washing instruction labels are sewn back to back. Your task is to make sure that all silk labels have the 'dry clean only' label on the other side." Subjects were shown four labels ("machine wash in warm water," "silk," "cotton," and "dry clean only") and were asked to turn over only those labels they would have to check to be sure the labels were correct. The answer is that one must turn over the "machine wash in warm water" label to make sure the other side does not say "silk," and the "silk" label to make sure the other side does not say "machine wash in warm water."

VII IMPLICATIONS FOR COGNITIVE SCIENCE

15 The Case for Rules in Reasoning

Edward E. Smith
Christopher Langston
Richard E. Nisbett
University of Michigan

One of the oldest views about the nature of thought is that reasoning is guided by abstract rules of inference. This view has its origins in Plato's theories of reasoning and education, and was the rationale behind "formal discipline" approaches to education ranging from the medieval scholastics' teaching of the syllogism to the English "public school" curriculum of Latin and mathematics. In modern times, abstract inferential rules have played important roles in some of the most influential theories of cognition, including those of Newell and Simon (e.g., 1972) and Piaget and Inhelder (e.g., 1958). This blue-blood intellectual history notwithstanding, the role of abstract rules has recently come under attack from a variety of sources.

Part of the attack stems from the development of alternatives to rule-based models of thought. One class of alternatives is *instance* models, which assume that solving a problem involves the retrieval of specific instances from memory, one or more of which is then used as an analog for the current problem. Sophisticated instance models were first developed in the study of categorization, and the key ideas of the approach have been extended to reasoning (see Medin and Ross, 1989, for a review). Thus numerous researchers contend that deductive reasoning is more a matter of retrieving examples than of applying rules (e.g., Manktelow and Evans, 1979; D'Andrade, 1982; Griggs and Cox, 1982; Reich and Ruth, 1982). A related development in artificial intelligence is the emergence of *case-based* reasoning models. These models assume that knowledge about a topic is partly represented by particular cases, which are stored with a relevant generalization and which figure centrally in reasoning processes (e.g., Schank, 1982; Kolodner, 1983). Still another theoretical development that eschews rules is *connectionism*. Connectionist models contain only simple processing units, each of which sends excitatory and inhibitory signals to other units, with nothing like a rule in sight. Yet these neural-like models can often produce the same behavior as rule models (e.g., McClelland and Rumelhart, 1986).

In addition to the challenge of rival models, the rule-based approach to reasoning is at odds with certain broad intellectual movements that affect psychology. One is the evolutionary approach to behavior, which holds that much of cognition may be attributable to specific mechanisms rather than to general-purpose ones like applying abstract inferential rules (for example, Buss, 1991). Along different lines, the heuristic approach to choice and decision making that is gaining strength in decision theory and economics contends that people lack the rules necessary for normatively correct reasoning, such as the base-rate and regression principles (for example, Kahneman and Tversky, 1973; Tversky and Kahneman, 1971; 1986). Work in this tradition shows, for example, that people often substitute judgments about similarity for normatively-required rule-based reasoning. Although these broad trends lack the "bite" of alternative models, they have contributed to the tarnishing of the rule-based approach to reasoning.

The case for abstract rules, then, appears debatable. In this paper, we try to give some direction to the debate. We propose eight criteria for deciding whether a given abstract rule is applied, where each criterion essentially embodies a phenomenon that is more readily explained by a rule-based approach than by an alternative model. We argue that use of these criteria indicates there is substantial evidence for people's use of several deductive and inductive inferential rules, all of which have in common that they are widely considered to be normatively required for correct reasoning.

TWO CONTROVERSIAL ISSUES ABOUT RULE FOLLOWING

Abstraction and Application

To appreciate what is involved in the debate about rules we need to say what it means to claim that a person is following a rule. Note first that our interest is in a person *following* a rule, not in a person's behavior merely *conforming* to a rule. When we fall down, for example, our behavior conforms to certain rules of physics, but no one would want to claim that we are actually following these rules. For rule following to occur, there must be a correspondence between the rule and a mental event; indeed, there should be a one-to-one correspondence between the symbols of the rule and the components of a mental event (Pylyshyn, 1990).

As a paradigm case of following an abstract rule, consider the situation where a reasoner is presented the statements, "If Abner is over 18, then he can vote; Abner is over 18", and tries to determine what follows from these statements by using the propositional logic rule *modus ponens — If p then q; p; therefore q,* (Quotes indicate specific statements, italics rules.) To say that the reasoner "follows" or "uses" modus ponens requires that the reasoner:

(1) recognize that the input is of a certain abstract kind (the input is of the form *If p then q;*), and as a consequence it is subsumed by a certain rule (modus ponens); and

(2) applies the rule to the input (instantiates *If p then q* with "If Abner is over 18 then he can vote;", *p* with "Abner is over 18," and concludes *q,* that "Abner can vote").

Step (1) establishes that *the input can be coded as an instantiation of an abstraction.* Step (2) establishes that *the rule itself is applied;* that is, the variables stated in the rule (*p* and *q*) are instantiated with constants from the input (such as, "Abner is over 18"), and then another process inspects this instantiated representation and draws the appropriate conclusion. Some opponents of rules have taken issue with the claim about abstraction, whereas others are troubled by the claims about applying a rule.

Consider first the abstraction issue. A code or representation can be abstract in several different senses. It can:

(i) contain relatively few meaning components (this is the sense in which *color* is more abstract than *red*)
(ii) contain variables (such as *p* and *q* in modus ponens)
(iii) have a high degree of generality
(iv) be relatively non-perceptual

The four meanings are clearly interrelated. In particular, a rule that contains variables must contain relatively few meaning components (since the variables have replaced some components), and must have some degree of generality (since the variables range over certain values). In this paper, we generally use the term *abstract* to mean *contains variables,* with the other three meanings typically being implied as well (exceptions to this usage will be explicitly noted).

Given this interpretation of abstraction, we note that many of those who favor instance models, and some who champion case-based models (e.g., Lewis, 1988), object to the claim that inputs are coded and processed as instantiations of abstract structures. They would not, for example, believe that our miniproblem about Abner is ever coded in terms of anything as abstract as modus ponens. And if the problem is not coded abstractly, it cannot be assimilated to an abstract rule. Hence the contrast between rules on the one hand versus instances and cases on the other, comes down in large part to the question of how abstractly we represent problems (see Barsalou, 1990).

We can further illustrate this contrast with a task that has been widely used in reasoning research and that will figure prominently in this paper, Wason's (1966) 4-card problem (also known as the "selection" task). In the standard version of the problem, four cards are laid out displaying the symbols "E," "K," "4," and "7." Each card has a letter on one side and a number on the other. The task is to determine which of these cards needs to be turned over to determine the truth or falsity of the hypothesis "If a card has a vowel on one side then it has an even number on the other." In another version of the problem, the four cards read "beer", "coke", "22", and "16", and the hypothesis to be tested is "If a person is drinking beer, s/he must be over 18." Though the two versions are formally identical, people do much better on the drinking version than on the standard version. (The correct answers are "E" and "7" in the standard version, and "beer" and "16" in the drinking version.) According to proponents of abstract rules, people solve the 4-card problem by applying rules that, though less general than propositional-logic rules, still are general enough to cover various kinds of relations; in this case, the rules concern the relations involved in *permission*. Because rules concerned with permission are likely to apply to drinking but not to alphanumeric symbols, people do better on the drinking version than on the standard version of the problem (Cheng and Holyoak, 1985). In contrast, according to the proponents of instance models, people solve the 4-card problem by retrieving from memory either specific episodes or domain-specific rules (like rules about drinking in particular bars) that are applicable to the problem. The drinking version of the problem is likely to retrieve either a domain-specific rule that is applicable to the current problem or a specific episode that can be analogized to the current problem, whereas the standard version is not likely to do so. That is why the drinking version leads to better performance (Griggs, 1983; Manktelow and Evans, 1979).

Unlike instance models, connectionist models are not hostile to the notion of stored abstractions per se. Some connectionist models (for example, Hinton and Sejnowski, 1984) include units that represent entities like *animate* and *metallic,* which are abstract in the senses of containing few meaning components, being very general and being relatively nonpercept-ual. Other connectionist models embrace abstractions in that they deal with the representation of variables and variable binding (for example, Smolensky, 1988). However, connectionist models are incompatible with the claims that a rule can be represented *explicitly* as a separate structure, and that this structure is inspected by distinct processes. This seems to be the most widely held interpretation of rule following, and it is the one we will pursue for most of this paper.

Thus the two major issues that fuel the anti-rule movement concern how abstractly we represent problems, and how explicitly we represent rules. At this time there is comparatively little empirical data on reasoning that can be brought to bear on the rule-application issue. The abstraction issue is a different story; in this case there is a large body of relevant data on reasoning. The bulk of this paper is concerned with these data, in particular with determining how well the data line up with a set of proposed criteria that can be used to distinguish abstract representations from concrete, specific ones. In the final section we return to the rule-application issue.

Need for Criteria in Dealing With the Debate

Many researchers would agree that people can reason both ways — by applying abstract rules and by analogizing to stored instances. But to go beyond this bland and uninformative generalization we need to know how to determine when people reason in each way. That is, we need agreement about what counts as evidence for abstract-rule use and what counts as evidence for instance use. In this paper we will propose eight such criteria and apply them to proposals about rule systems in deductive and inductive reasoning. We claim that the criteria taken together will often suffice to resolve controversy about a given case of reasoning concerning whether abstract rules are or are not being used. Furthermore, we will argue that the existing evidence concerning these criteria establishes that people often use abstract rules when reasoning about everyday problems. Before considering the criteria, however, several constraints on the scope of the discussion and several ground rules need to be spelled out.

First, we are concerned with the use of rules in *reasoning* (that is, evaluating a hypothesis in light of evidence). Many arguments have already been advanced for the use of abstract rules in language comprehension and production (e.g., Chomsky, 1985; Pinker and Prince, 1988), but in view of the possibility that language may be a special skill we cannot generalize this evidence to the case of reasoning.

Another constraint is that, within the realm of reasoning, we are concerned with *inferential* rules, which by definition apply to multiple content domains (where content domains are different areas of knowledge that have specific properties — areas like chess or physics or adult social relations). Rules at this level include logical rules, rules for causal deduction dealing with necessity and sufficiency, contractual rules including rules for permission and obligation, statistical rules such as the law of large numbers, and decision rules such as cost-benefit rules. They are to be distinguished from empirical rules, no matter how general, which describe events in some content domain. Inferential rules are also to be distinguished from *operating principles* (Holland, Holyoak, Nisbett, and Thagard, 1986), which are immutable principles that work automatically in running the cognitive system. An example is the similarity principle, which holds that objects that share known properties tend to share unknown ones as well. This principle plays a substantial role in reasoning but it is not clear that use of the principle involves following an explicit rule (for contrasting views on this, though, see Collins and Michalski, 1989, and Smith, Lopez, and Osherson, in press). Throughout the rest of this paper, when we refer to "abstract rules" we mean "abstract inferential rules".

A related constraint is that most of the abstract rules of interest are, in some sense, *natural* ones. We have in mind the kind of rule that *could* be induced by any cognitively-mature human given normal experience with the environment. That is, exemplars of the rule are plentiful in everyday experience, and inducing the rule from these exemplars would not require excessive demands on any relevant processing mechanism (short term memory, for example) nor require coding of events in ways that are uncongenial (for example, disjunctions, as in "a red circle or a loud tone"). Furthermore, natural rules are such that they lead to many pragmatically useful inferences. We realize that all this does not amount to a definition, but we take comfort in the fact that the notion of a natural rule, or the related notion of a natural concept, has proven exceptionally difficult to characterize formally (see, for example, Goodman, 1955; Murphy and Medin, 1985).

Another ground rule is that we do not assume that there is always conscious awareness of the use of inferential rules. Some inferential rules may be applied only unconsciously (Nisbett and Wilson, 1977). Others may be applied some of the time with a concomitant recognition that the rule is being used.

In our discussion we will make no attempt to distinguish a specific instance ("Abner being told that he must be over 21 to drink at Joe's Bar") from an instance-specific rule *(If Abner wants to drink at Joe's bar, he must be over 21)*. We neglect this distinction in part because our concern for most of the paper is with the abstraction issue, not the rule-application issue, and in part because it is not clear what empirical evidence could be brought to bear on the distinction.

Our final ground rule concerns the criteria themselves. We do not believe that any single criterion provides iron-clad evidence for the use of an abstract rule (nor does negative evidence for a single criterion establish that the rule does not operate). Rather, it is the use of multiple criteria in converging operations that can make a strong case for or against the use of a particular rule. We also make no claim that the criteria are exhaustive of those that would provide evidence for or against the assertion that an abstract rule is used for some task. They exhaust only our knowledge of criteria that actually have been examined.

EVIDENCE FOR CRITERIA OF RULE FOLLOWING

In this section we will defend the use of eight different criteria for establishing whether reasoning makes use of abstract rules and apply each criterion to relevant evidence. Three of the criteria derive from psycholinguistics, where more than in any other area an effort has been made to establish that behavior is based on rule following. Three of the other criteria involve the performance measures of speed, accuracy and verbal report that are routinely used by experimental psychologists to examine cognitive processes. The remaining two criteria make use of training procedures to establish that highly general rules can be "inserted" by abstract training methods. We list the criteria below and then present a rationale for each of them and a discussion of its use to date.

Eight Criteria for Rule Use

Criteria Stemming from Linguistics

1. Performance on rule-governed items is as accurate with unfamiliar as with familiar material.
2. Performance on rule-governed items is as accurate with abstract as with concrete material.
3. Early in acquisition, a rule may be applied to an exception (the rule is overextended).

Performance Criteria

4. Performance on a rule-governed item or problem deteriorates as a function of the number of rules that are required for solving the problem.
5. Performance on a rule-governed item is facilitated when preceded by another item based on the same rule (application of a rule primes its subsequent use).
6. A rule, or components of it, may be mentioned in a verbal protocol.

Training Criteria

7. Performance on a specific rule-governed problem is improved by training on abstract versions of the rule.

8. Performance on problems in a particular domain is improved as much by training on problems outside the domain as on problems within it, as long as the problems are based on the same rule.

We note in advance that the criteria vary among themselves with respect to the strength of evidence they provide for rule use. This variation will become evident as we discuss the criteria. We note further that the criteria also vary with respect to how many different abstract rules they have been applied to. Consequently, for some criteria, such as 1, we will consider numerous rules, whereas for other criteria we will discuss but a single rule.

Criterion 1: Performance on Rule-Governed Items is as Accurate with Unfamiliar as With Familiar Items.

Rationale.   The logic behind Criterion 1 stems from the idea that an abstract rule is applicable to a specific item because the item can be represented by some *special abstract structure* that also defines the rule (the special structure is the antecedent of the rule). Since even novel items can possess this special structure, they can be assimilated to the rule (see Rips, 1990). Consider the phonological rules for forming plurals of English nouns. One of the rules is (roughly) of the form, *If the final phoneme of a singular noun is voiced, then add the phoneme |z| to it.* This rule identifies the special structure, *singular noun whose final phoneme is voiced,* and any noun—familiar, unfamiliar, or nonsense—that can be represented by this structure can be assimilated to the rule. This is why the fact that any English speaker can tell you the plural of the nonsense item "zig" is "zigz" (as in "cows") has been taken by many psycholinguists as evidence that people do indeed possess the phonological rule in question (e.g., Berko, 1958).

To see how this criterion can be applied to reasoning rules, consider again modus ponens *(If p then q; p; therefore q).* Clearly this rule can be applied to novel items, even nonsense ones. If someone tells you that "If gork then flum, and gork is the case," you no doubt will conclude that "flum" follows. To the extent you can draw this conclusion as readily as you can with familiar material, the rule should be attributed to your repertoire.

To make the argument for rule following even stronger, it is useful to consider a sketch of a prototypical rule model (which is just an amplification of our previous comments about rule following):

When a test item or problem is presented, it is coded in a form that is *sufficiently abstract* to lead to access of an abstract rule. Once accessed, if need be, the rule can be used for further abstract coding of the test item. The next stage is to instantiate, or bind, the variables in the rule with entities from the input. Finally, the rule is applied to yield the desired answer; that is, inspection of the instantiated representation reveals that the antecedent of the rule has been satisfied, thereby licensing the conclusion. There are therefore four stages—coding, access, instantiation (variable binding), and application.

We can illustrate the model with our "If gork then flum; gork; ?" example. When presented with this item, you might code it, in part, as an "If X, then Y" type-item. This would suffice to access modus ponens. Next you would instantiate p with "gork" and q with "flum". Then you would apply the rule and derive "flum" as an answer. Note that had you initially coded the item more superficially—say, as an "If-then claim"—this might still have sufficed to activate modus ponens, which could then have been used to elaborate the abstract coding. Though this is merely a sketch of a model, it is compatible with the general structure of rule-based models of deductive and inductive reasoning, (for example, Rips, 1983; and Collins and Michalski, 1989).

With this sketch in hand we can be more explicit about how our criterion of equivalent accuracy for familiar and unfamiliar items fits with rule-following. If we assume that there is no effect of familiarity on the likelihood of coding an item sufficiently abstractly, then there will be no effect of familiarity on the likelihood of accessing an abstract rule. Similarly, if we assume there is no effect of familiarity on instantiating a rule or inspecting an instantiated representation, there will be no effect of familiarity on applying a rule. Both assumptions seem plausible, which makes the criterion plausible (that is, familiar items should not lead to greater accuracy). Indeed, if anything, the more familiar an item is, the *less* likely it is to be coded abstractly. This is because familiarity often rests on frequency, and frequent presentations of an item might lead one to represent it in terms of its specific content.

For a criterion to be truly useful, of course, the phenomenon it describes must also be difficult to account for by a non-rule based explanation. The major alternatives to rule models are instance models, and Criterion 1 is indeed hard to explain in terms of instances. To appreciate this point, consider a rough sketch of a prototypical instance model:

When a test item or problem is presented, it is first coded, and this representation serves to activate stored instances from memory. The basis for access is the similarity of the test item and stored instances. One or more of the stored instances then serve as an analog for the test item. More specifically, a mapping is made between certain aspects of the retrieved instance and known aspects of the test item; this mapping then licenses the transfer of other aspects of the retrieved instance to unknown aspects of the test item. There are therefore three major stages—coding, access, and mapping.

This sketch of a model captures the general structure of current analogy models (for example, Gentner, 1983; Holyoak, 1984; Holyoak and Thagard, 1989). In applying the sketch to the phenomenon captured by Criterion 1, two critical questions arise. The first is whether the representation of an instance codes the special structure of the rule, or is instead restricted to more concrete information. To illustrate, suppose you have stored an instance of the statement "If you drive a motorcycle in Michigan, then you must be over 17"; the question of interest amounts to whether your stored instance includes information equivalent to *If p implies q; p; therefore q*. If an instance representation does include such information, then it essentially includes the rule. This strikes us not only as implausible, but also as contrary to the intended meaning of "instance". In particular, one does not think of an instance as containing variables. In what follows, then, we will assume that instances do not encode the abstraction they instantiate, though often they may encode features that are correlated with the abstraction. Thus instance models differ from rule models not just in whether the test item accesses an instance or a rule, but also in how abstractly the test item is coded to begin with. (A possible exception to this principle arises when people are explicitly encouraged to process the instances deeply. In experimental situations like this, there is evidence that abstractions are indeed coded, though the abstractions that have been studied are different from the inferential rules that we discuss — see Hammond, Seifert, and Gray, 1991).

The second critical question for an instance model is how to compute the similarity between the test item and the stored instance. If the similarity is computed over all features, then the model cannot explain the phenomenon of equal accuracy for familiar and unfamiliar items. For there is no guarantee that the stored instances most similar to "gork implies flum" will be useful in dealing with the test item. Perhaps "glory and fame" will be retrieved, and this conjunction is of no use in dealing with the test item. A comparable story holds for our phonological example. If overall similarity is what matters, "zig" may retrieve "zip" from memory, and the latter's plural will not work for the test item.

To salvage an instance model we must assume that the similarity between the test item and stored instance is computed over very restricted features, namely those correlated with the special structure of the rule. Consider again a stored instance of the regulation "If you drive a motorcycle in Michigan, then you must be over 17". The representation of this instance may well contain features corresponding to the concepts *if* and *then,* where these features are correlated with modus ponens. If such features were given great weight in the similarity calculation, a useful analog might be retrieved. There are, however, three problems with the assumption of differential weighting. First, it is ad hoc. Second, it may be wrong, as a growing body of evidence indicates that the retrieval of analogs is influenced more by concrete features, like appearance and taxonomic category, than abstract ones (e.g., Gentner and Toupin, 1986; Holyoak and Koh, 1986; Ross, 1987). Third, for some rules there may be no obvious features correlated with the rule's special structure (a good example is the law of large numbers, as we will see later). In short, when it comes to explaining the phenomenon that accuracy is as high for novel rule-based items as for familiar ones, an instance model seems to be either wrong or ad hoc. As we will see, the same conclusion holds for many of the other phenomena we consider.

Evidence About Modus Ponens.   Criterion 1 supports the hypothesis that people use modus ponens. Our "if gork then flum" example suggests that we can perform extremely well on unfamiliar rule-based items.

Surprisingly, we have had difficulty locating a published experimental report that permits a comparison between performance with familiar and unfamiliar instances of modus ponens. Perhaps the closest to the mark is a study by Byrne (1989; Experiment 1). In this study, subjects were given statements of the form, *If p then q* and *p,* and had to decide which of three possible conclusions was correct, one of them of course being *q.* Subjects' performance—which was extremely close to perfect—showed no difference between the very familiar item, "If it is raining, then we'll get wet. It is raining. ?", and the seemingly less familiar item, "If she meets her friend, then she will go to a play. She meets her friend. ?" For these data, modus ponens passes Criterion 1.

Evidence About Modus Tollens.   Modus tollens is a rule in propositional logic that states, *If p then q; not q; therefore not p.* Unlike modus ponens, subjects seem to have more difficulty in applying modus tollens to unfamiliar than to familiar items. Some critical evidence comes from a study by Cheng and Holyoak (1985), which used the 4-card problem described earlier. Recall that in this paradigm subjects decide which of four cases must be checked to determine the truth or falsity of a hypothesis. Cheng and Holyoak used the hypothesis, "If a letter is sealed, then it must carry a 20 cent stamp", along with four cards corresponding to "sealed", "unsealed", "20 cent", and "10 cent". Note that the hypothesis has (part of) the special structure of modus tollens with the "10 cent" card instantiating the role of *not q.* Cheng and Holyoak presented the hypothesis and choices to two groups of subjects, with one group being familiar with the hypothesized regulation and the other group not being familiar with the regulation. There were more choices of the *not q* card in the group familiar with the hypothesized regulation than in the group that was not. Hence modus tollens fails Criterion 1, suggesting that it is not a rule that most people naturally follow.

Evidence About Contractual Rules.   Cheng and Holyoak and their colleagues (1985; Cheng, Holyoak, Nisbett, and Oliver, 1986) proposed that people have sets of abstract rules (often referred to as "schemas") that characterize contractual relations of various types. Thus people have a set of abstract *permission* rules, which they use to understand that a certain action may be carried out only when a precondition of some kind is established. The permission rules include:

(1) If action A is taken, precondition P must be satisfied.
(2) If action A is not taken, precondition P need not be satisfied.
(3) If precondition P is satisfied, action A can be taken.
(4) If precondition P is not satisfied, action A must not be taken.

Note that this set of rules carries with it an indication of the checking procedures necessary to establish whether a permission contract has been violated: examine cases where an action has been carried out (to establish that the precondition obtained — rule (1)), and cases where the precondition does not obtain (to establish that the action was not carried out — rule (4)). Presumably people also have a set of abstract *obligation* rules, which they use to understand that when a certain precondition obtains a particular action must be carried out. The rules include:

(1′) If precondition P is satisfied, action A must be taken.
(2′) If precondition P is not satisfied, action A may be taken.
(3′) If action A is taken, precondition P may or may not be satisfied.
(4′) If action A is not taken, precondition P must not be satisfied.

Again, the rules specify checking procedures to establish whether violations of an obligation contract has occurred (see rules (1') and (4')).

The major line of evidence establishing that people use such abstract rules comes from studies using the 4-card problem. One important finding is that as long as the hypothesis being tested can be assimilated to the permission rules, the familiarity of the hypothesis has no effect on performance. For example, Cheng et al. (1986) presented subjects with the relatively unfamiliar hypothesis "If a passenger wishes to enter the country then he or she must have had an inoculation against cholera", along with the choices "entering", "not entering", "inoculated", and "not inoculated"; subjects were also presented with the relatively familiar hypothesis "If a customer is drinking an alcoholic beverage, then he or she must be over 21," along with the choices "drinking", "not drinking", "over 21", and "under 21". Subjects performed as well with the unfamiliar hypothesis as the familiar one. Subjects correctly identified which cases must be checked ("entering", "not inoculated" "drinking", "under 21") and avoided checking the other cases which could not establish a violation of the hypothesis, and did so to the same extent whether the rule was familiar or not. (Note that selecting "not inoculated" or "under 18" counts as evidence for a permission rule but not for modus tollens, because other items that fit modus tollens but not the permission rule were handled poorly.)

There is similar evidence for the use of obligation rules. Again using the 4-card problem, Cheng et al. (1986) presented subjects with relatively unfamiliar hypotheses that could be assimilated to the obligation rules, such as "If one works for the armed forces, then one must vote in the elections", along with choices like "armed forces", "not armed forces", "vote", and "not vote." They also presented subjects with somewhat more familiar hypotheses that could be assimilated to obligation, such as "If any miner gets lung cancer, then the company will pay the miner a sickness pension," along with choices like "lung cancer", "not lung cancer," "pension," and "no pension". Again subjects performed as well with the unfamiliar hypothesis as with the familiar one.

The evidence just cited has some weaknesses. There was no independent check on the variation in familiarity, and very few items were used. Still, the evidence is suggestive. Furthermore, as noted earlier, it is difficult to construct an account of these results in terms of an instance model. Such an account has to explain why it is that whatever instances are dredged up from memory by the intersection of events like "entering a country" and "having an inoculation" are just as likely to key the appropriate checking procedures as the direct memory of actual cases of drinking though less than 21 years old, not being able to drink because of being less than 21 years old, and so on.

Evidence About Causal Rules.   Morris, Cheng and Nisbett (1991) have investigated a version of Kelley's (1972) causal schema theory. Kelley's theory assumes that people have different rule sets (often referred to as "schemas") for causal situations that differ with respect to the necessity and sufficiency of the causes involved. For example, people understand that some types of causes are both necessary and sufficient (e.g., 100 C temperature causes water to boil), some types are necessary but not sufficient (exposure to the Hong Kong flu virus, together with other preconditions, causes Hong Kong flu), some types are sufficient but not necessary (lack of fuel, among other factors, causes a car to be inoperable), and some types are neither necessary nor sufficient (smoking, together with other preconditions, and among other factors, causes lung cancer).

Using the 4-card problem and related paradigms, Morris and colleagues (1991) have provided evidence that people follow such causal rules. They showed that subjects usually performed appropriate checking procedures to establish whether a given case could overturn a particular causal hypothesis. Moreover, this was true even when the hypothesis was an unfamiliar one, involving entities never encountered before by the subjects. For example, for the hypothesis "Temperature above 1500 C causes the element Floridium to turn into a gas", most subjects understood that all four possible events ("temperature above 1500 C", "temperature below 1500 C", "Floridium in gaseous form", "Floridium in liquid form") should be checked in order to see whether the hypothesis was overturned. If we focus on the data from the more sophisticated subjects (advanced graduate students), more than 70% of their tests of unfamiliar hypotheses were completely correct whereas only 6% of the tests would be expected to be completely correct by chance alone. Although the study lacks a comparison with the testing of familiar hypotheses, the obtained level of performance is sufficiently high to suggest that subjects (particularly sophisticated ones) were using the rules.

Evidence About the Law of Large Numbers.   Nisbett, Krantz, Jepson, and Kunda (1983) argued that people have an intuitive appreciation of the law of large numbers and an ability to apply it to real-world situations. The central notion in the law of large numbers is that sample parameters approach population parameters as a direct function of the number of cases in the sample, and as an inverse function of the degree of variability associated with the parameter. In the limiting case of no variability for the parameter, a sample of one case is adequate for an induction to the population value.

To show that people appreciate these notions as an abstract rule, Nisbett et al. asked subjects to imagine that they were visitors to a South Pacific island who were being introduced to a range of local phenomena they had never seen before. They were to imagine that they saw an unusual bird called a "shreeble", which was blue in color, and asked to estimate what percent of shreebles on the island were blue. Other subjects were asked the same question after being told to imagine they had seen either 3 or 20 shreebles, all of which were blue. Subjects' estimates were systematically affected by the number of cases. They believed that a higher fraction of shreebles were blue when examining 20 cases than when examining 3 cases, and believed that a higher fraction were blue when examining 3 cases than 1 case. In contrast, the number of cases did not affect the percentage estimates when the entities in question were members of the "Barratos" tribe and the parameter was skin color. (The modal estimated percentage to the skin-color question was 100%, even with only one case.) This pattern of findings is consistent with subjects' reports of their assumptions about variability, as they generally assumed that bird kinds are variable with respect to color whereas isolated tribes are uniform with respect to color. Again we see a high level of performance with relatively unfamiliar material, so high as to suggest the use of rules even though the study lacks an explicit comparison with familiar material.

Finally, it should be noted that it is difficult to explain the high level of performance by direct application of an instance model. Presumably such a model would assume that, when told about shreebles, subjects retrieve similar instances, some particular tropical birds for example, examine their variability with respect to color, and qualify their generalizations as a function of the presumed variability. This still leaves unexplained, however, why subjects recognize that they have to qualify generalizations more for small samples than for large ones. And it is extremely unlikely that subjects retrieve a prior problem that they had solved by applying the law of large numbers, because there are no obvious features of the shreeble problem that are correlated with that rule.

Criterion 2: Performance with Rule-Governed Items is as Accurate with Abstract as With Concrete Materials.

Rationale. This criterion is similar to our first one. However, whereas Criterion 1 was concerned with unfamiliar or nonsensical items, Criterion 2 is concerned with abstract items that may in fact be very familiar. To appreciate Criterion 2, note that intuition suggests that the rule modus ponens can readily be applied to a totally abstract item, such as "If A then B; A; therefore B." (This item is abstract in the sense of containing few features, and, possibly, in the sense of containing variables.) Good performance on this item fits with the sketch of a rule model we presented earlier. For there is no reason to expect that abstract items are less likely than concrete ones to access the modus ponens rule, and no reason to expect abstract items to fare less well than concrete ones in instantiating the rule or inspecting an instantiated representation. If anything, we might expect abstract items to be both more likely to access the rule and easier to instantiate, because abstract items are more similar to the rule than are concrete items. Note further that good performance on abstract items is quite difficult to explain in terms of an instance model. For the only thing that an abstract item and a retrieved instance can possibly have in common is the special structure of the rule. That is, the use of abstract items allows one to strip away all content but the special structure, and consequently performance must be based on the special structure alone (Rips, 1990). For these reasons, Criterion 2 is among the most diagnostic ones we will consider.

Evidence About Modus Ponens. As for Criterion 1, intuitive evidence alone makes it plausible that modus ponens passes Criterion 2. But it is worth considering some experimental results. Evans (1977) presented each of 16 subjects four modus ponens problems of the following abstract sort:

If the letter is L, then the number is 5
The letter is L
Therefore the number is 5.

The task was to decide whether the conclusion (the statement below the line) was valid or invalid. Performance was perfect: all 16 subjects got all four questions right. Modus ponens passes Criterion 2 with flying colors.

Evidence About Modus Tollens.   Comparable research shows poor performance on modus tollens using abstract material. This was the striking finding of the classic Wason (1966) paper that introduced the 4-card problem. Given cards labeled "A", "B", "4" and "7", and asked to turn over enough cards to test the hypothesis "If there is an A on the front then there is a 4 on the back", even highly intelligent subjects rarely turn over the "7" card (finding an A on the other side would establish the falsity of the hypothesis). This is the chief evidence against people using modus tollens.

We note in passing that this sort of negative evidence was overgeneralized by many to become evidence against formal rule systems in general, and is another component in the current popularity of instance models. The studies on contractual and causal schemas by Cheng and her colleagues amount to a demonstration that there has been such an overgeneralization. Subjects solve problems that are syntactically identical to the Wason 4-card problem so long as the content of the problem suggests a contractual or causal interpretation allowing an appropriate, abstract rule to be applied.

Evidence About Contractual Rules.   Some of Cheng's work just alluded to shows good performance on the permission rule using abstract materials. In the 4-card problem, Cheng and Holyoak (1985) presented subjects with the hypothesis "If one is to take action A, then one must first satisfy precondition P", along with choices like "A", "not A", "P", and "not P". Performance on this abstract problem (61% correct) far exceeded performance on a control problem ("If a card has an A on one side, it must have a 4 on the other") that could not be assimilated to the permission rule (19% correct). While the study lacks a direct comparison with concrete materials, the level of performance is sufficiently high to suggest the use of a rule. (See also Cheng and Holyoak's 1989 study of an abstract precaution rule.)

Evidence About Causal Rules.   Morris, Cheng and Nisbett (1991) provide some evidence that people can accurately apply causal rules to purely abstract material. They presented subjects with causal hypotheses that were qualified with respect to necessity and sufficiency, and asked subjects to indicate whether particular states of affairs could overturn the hypotheses. For example, subjects were told that a scientist believes that

"Event A causes event B", and further believes that "The occurrence of event A is the only cause of event B, and that event A only sometimes causes event B." When presented with possible patterns of events — namely, "A and B", "A and not B," "not A and B", and "not A and not B" — subjects were highly accurate in selecting those patterns that could refute the hypothesis ("not A and B"). Furthermore, a change in the causal hypothesis — say, "A causes B, but A is not the only cause of B, and A always causes B" — led to marked changes in the subjects' choice of a refuting pattern ("A and not B"). Although the study again lacks an explicit comparison to concrete materials, the high level of performance seems difficult to account for by an instance model: over 60% of the tests of abstract hypotheses were completely correct, whereas the percentage expected by chance is only 6%.

Criterion 3: Early in Acquisition. A Rule May be Applied to an Exception (A Rule is Overextended).

Rationale.   In psycholinguistics this criterion has figured prominently in studies of how children master the regular past-tense form of English verbs. The relevant rule is to add "ed" to the stem of verbs to form the past tense, such as "cook"-"cooked". A finding that has been taken as evidence for following this rule is the tendency of young children to overextend the rule to irregular forms, such as "go-goed," even though they had previously used the irregular form correctly (Ervin, 1964). The rule specifies a special structure — the stem of a verb — and the phenomenon arises because children apply the rule to items containing the special structure even though the items should have been marked as exceptions. In terms of our sketch of a rule model: early in acquisition, exceptional verbs are likely to be represented in a way that accesses the relevant rule, and once the rule is accessed it is instantiated and applied.

Perhaps for more than any other criterion, there has been a concerted effort to formulate non-rule-based accounts of overextension. Thus, Rumelhart and McClelland (1987) have offered a connectionist account of the overextension of the past-tense "rule", and others have offered instance-based accounts of apparent overextensions of classification rules (see for example, Medin and Smith, 1981). In general, then, this criterion seems less diagnostic than the previous two we considered. We include it, though, because it may prove to be diagnostic in specific cases. Indeed, with regard to overextension of the past tense rule, critiques of the Rumelhart and McClelland proposal by Pinker and colleagues (Pinker and Prince, 1988; Marcus, Ullman, Pinker, Hollander, Rosen and Xu, 1990) suggests that a rule-based theory still provides the fullest account of the data. The critics note, for example, that children are no more likely to overgeneralize an irregular verb that is similar to many regular ones than to overgeneralize an irregular verb that is similar to few regular ones. Yet in most connectionist models, as in instance models, generalization is based on similarity. The lack of similarity effects fits perfectly with a rule-based account, of course. Thus, in situations where the likelihood of overgeneralizing an exception does not depend on the similarity of the exception to the regular cases, the criterion is indeed diagnostic.

Evidence About the Law of Large Numbers. The overextension criterion has rarely been applied to abstract rules. An exception is the law of large numbers. Fong, Krantz, and Nisbett (1986) trained subjects on this rule, and found they sometimes applied it to cases in which it was inappropriate. For example, in one problem presented after training, subjects were told about a basketball talent scout who watched a particular prospect through two games and concluded that he had excellent skills but a tendency to misplay under extreme pressure. The former inference was based on nearly two hours of play, the latter on a single episode. Trained subjects were more likely than controls to assert correctly that the "pressure" diagnosis was based on too little evidence, but were also more likely to assert incorrectly that the global judgment of excellent skills was similarly based on too little evidence. Thus trained subjects sometimes overextended the rule to cases where it was not appropriate. The fact that this kind of overextension occurred lends credibility to the claim that a rule corresponding to the law of large numbers was indeed being followed, especially since virtually no control (untrained) subjects expressed the view that a larger sample would have been helpful in assessing the prospect's skills.

An instance model has difficulty explaining this specific phenomenon. According to such a model, an overextension would occur whenever the basketball problem retrieves a stored problem that just happened to utilize the law of large numbers. But such problems might be very diverse, with few if any sharing content with the basketball problem. Therefore the only way to insure that the basketball problem retrieves a useful analog is to make the problematic assumption that retrieval is heavily based on the features correlated with the special structure of the rule.

Criterion 4: Performance on a Rule-Governed Problem Deteriorates as a Function of the Number of Rules that are Required to Solve the Problem.

Rationale. Criterion 4 essentially holds that rules provide the appropriate unit for measuring the complexity of a problem. We can illustrate the criterion by considering problems that vary in the number of times they require application of the rule modus ponens. Even after equating for reading time, deciding that argument (2) is valid presumably would take longer and be more error prone than deciding that (1) is valid, because (2) requires one more application of modus ponens:

(1) If it's raining, I'll take an umbrella
    It's raining
    _____
    I'll take an umbrella

(2) If it's raining, I'll take an umbrella
    If I take an umbrella, I'll lose it.
    It's raining
    _____
    I'll lose an umbrella

(Our example might suggest that the phenomenon is due to the premises being more complex in (2) than (1); however, using correlational techniques, Rips, 1983, found no evidence that premise complexity per se affects the accuracy of reasoning.)

The phenomenon of interest follows from our sketch of a rule model as long as one or more of the stages involved—coding, access, instantiation, and application—is executed less efficiently when it has to do n + 1 things than just n things. As many theorists have pointed out, this vulnerability to sheer number may disappear with extended practice. In Anderson's (1987) rule-based model of cognitive skills, for example, rules that are frequently applied in succession come to be "compiled" or chunked into a single rule; in such a case, performance would be rule-based yet fail to meet Criterion 4. The diagnosticity of this criterion is further reduced by the fact that the basic phenomenon involved seems roughly compatible with an instance model: what needs to be assumed is that problems that supposedly require more rules are really just problems that generally have fewer or less accessible analogues in memory. Again, though, we include the criterion because it may prove very diagnostic in certain cases, for example, in cases where there is a *linear* relation between the number of rules that a problem requires and the reaction time needed to solve the problem. Also, the criterion has a history of use in evaluating rule-based hypotheses. For example, in psycholinguistics it figured centrally in testing the hypothesis that the complexity of a sentence was an increasing function of the number of transformational rules needed to derive the surface form of the sentence (Miller, 1962).

Evidence About Modus Ponens.   We know of no direct application of Criterion 4 like our double modus ponens example. Rather than being applied to a single rule used a varying number of times, the criterion has been applied to a set of rules. Osherson (1975), Rips (1983), and Braine, Reiser, and Rumain (1984) have all applied the criterion to proposed sets of logical rules that include modus ponens along with a dozen or so other rules from propositional logic (such sets are capable of determining the validity of most arguments in propositional logic and hence constitute relatively complete theories of people's logical capabilities). The work of these investigators shows that there is a monotonic relation — and sometimes a linear one — between the number of rules needed to determine whether an argument is valid and the reaction time and accuracy of the final response. In so far as modus ponens is a rule in the systems of all three investigators, there is indirect evidence for the use of modus ponens.

Criterion 5: Performance on a Rule-Based Item is Facilitated when Preceded by Another Item Based on the Same Rule (Application of a Rule Primes its Subsequent Use)

Rationale.   The rationale for this criterion is that, once used a mental structure remains active for a brief time period and during this period the structure is more accessible than usual. In terms of our rule model, the access stage has been facilitated. (Anderson, 1983, makes a similar assumption relating recency of rule use to ease of subsequent access.) Our sketch of an instance model would be able to account for the phenomenon to the extent that successively presented rule-based items are also similar in content; but as we will see, the plausibility of this account depends on the specific findings involved.

Evidence About Contractual Rules.   As far as we know the priming criterion has been applied only to contractual rules. In a study we performed recently (Langston, Nisbett, and Smith, 1991), subjects were presented on each trial with a different version of the 4-card problem. Sometimes the version conformed to a permission rule *(If precondition P is satisfied action A can be taken),* whereas other times it conformed to an obligation rule *(If precondition P is satisfied, action A must be taken).* It was therefore possible to have successive trials in which the permission rule would be used twice, as illustrated in (3) below, as well as successive trials in which the permission rule is used only once, as in (4):

(3) a. If a journalist has a press pass, she can cross a police line
    b. If a journalist gets a statement on the record, she can quote her source
(4) a. If a journalist is a member of the union, she must pay dues

b. If a journalist gets a statement on the record, she can quote her source

Subjects made more correct responses in testing the rule in (3b) than in (4b). The same permission rule was involved in both cases, but was primed only in (3b). (Repetition of the rule was confounded with repetition of the word "can", but as we will see below, repetition of "can" alone has no effect.)

It might seem that an instance model can readily explain these results. All that need be hypothesized is that subjects use the previous item as an analog for the current problem they are working on. This would lead to a correct response for 3b and an incorrect one for 4b. This predicts, however, that errors on permission (obligation) problems would be correct responses had the problems in fact been obligation (permission) problems. This prediction was not supported. There is, however, another aspect of the Langston et al. results that does suggest a role for instances. Langston et al. found priming effects only for items similar in content (as in (3)). If the priming item shared little content with the target item, there was no improvement either in accuracy or latency (even though the word "can" was repeated). Nisbett (unpublished data) found a similar failure of semantically unrelated items to produce priming of the law of large numbers in an untimed problem-solving situation. The fact that rule-priming depends on the similarity of the prime and target items suggests that both rules and instances may be involved in these tasks (hence the criterion is not very diagnostic). We return to this issue in the final section.

Criterion 6: A Verbal Protocol may Mention a Rule or its Components

Rationale. The rationale for this criterion is based on the standard interpretation of protocol analysis. Presumably the protocol is a direct reflection of what is active in the subject's short-term or working memory (Ericsson and Simon, 1980), and if a particular rule has been in working memory then it may have been recently used. Or to put it in terms of our sketch of a rule model, the products of the access, instantiation, or application stages may reside (perhaps only briefly) in working memory, which makes them accessible to report. There is no reason to expect an instance model to yield such reports. However, the protocol criterion is still of limited diagnosticity, given that there are cases of apparent rule following in which the rules cannot be reported (namely in language), as well as cases of reported rules for tasks for which there is independent evidence that the rules were not followed (Nisbett and Wilson, 1977).

Evidence About Modus Ponens. In Rips' (1983) studies of deductive reasoning, he had subjects talk aloud while solving some problems. He found some clear parallels between the successive statements in a protocol and the sequence of propositional rules needed to solve the problem. Since one of these rules is modus ponens, these findings provide some indirect evidence for modus ponens meeting our protocol criterion. Similarly, Galotti, Baron, and Sabini (1986) collected verbal protocols while subjects tried to generate conclusions to syllogistic arguments. They concluded that the protocols ". . . provide direct evidence of the existence of deduction rules" (the protocols also provide evidence of the existence of non-rule-like entities).

Evidence About the Law of Large Numbers.   In Piaget and Inhelder's (1951/1975) classic study of the child's conception of chance, they found surprisingly clear paraphrases of the law of large numbers even from children aged 10 to 12. For example, in one situation a child is presented with a pointer that could stop on one of 8 different colored locations, and is asked if there is more likely to be an equal number of stops on each color if the pointer is spun 15 times or 800 times. One child replied:

"It will be more regular with 800 because that's larger. For a small number (of chances) (the outcome) changes each time and it depends on the number of times, but with a larger number of tries it has more chances of being more regular."

Although the above protocol provides some prima facie evidence for the use of the law of large numbers, a skeptic could easily claim that the reasoning revealed in the protocol is not what is actually mediating the problem solving and that people are merely inventing plausible stories to explain their behavior. What is needed to strengthen protocol evidence is a linking of it to performance measures. This is exactly what Nisbett and his colleagues have done. They found evidence that some people can articulate an abstract version of the law of large numbers, and that those who invoke it in justification of their answers to problems covered by the rule are in fact more likely to give correct answers. For example, in the isolated-island problem discussed earlier, Nisbett et al. (1983) found that subjects often justified their willingness to make strong generalizations from a single case on the basis of assumptions about low variability and the resulting generalizability even from small samples. Subjects who explicitly gave such justifications were more likely to reason in accordance with the law of large numbers in general. Similarly, Jepson, Krantz and Nisbett (1983), and Fong, Krantz, and Nisbett (1985) found that some subjects often articulated quite general versions of the rule in justifying answers to specific problems. For instance, one subject said "The more examples you have, the better the conclusion you can draw". Subjects who provided such articulations of the rule gave answers in accordance with the rule on a higher proportion of problems than did other subjects.

Criterion 7: Performance on a Specific Rule-Based Problem is Improved by Training on an Abstract Version of the Rule

Rationale. The idea behind this criterion is that, because rule following is presumably what underlies performance on specific problems, practice on an abstract version of the rule (abstract in all senses we have considered) can improve performance on specific problems. In part, this should be true because training improves the rule — clarifies it, renders it more precise, and even changes its nature so as to make it more valid. From the perspective of our sketch of a rule model, practice on the rule in the abstract could also benefit performance by increasing the accessibility of the rule and perhaps also by facilitating the application of the rule. (To the extent that there were *any* examples in the training, there could be a facilitation of the instantiation stage as well.) From the perspective of an instance model, there is no obvious reason why such abstract training should have any effect on performance. Criterion 7 is therefore quite diagnostic.

Evidence About Modus Tollens. Cheng et al. (1986) showed that training on rules from propositional logic, particularly modus tollens, did not lead to any improvement in performance on the 4-card problem, specifically on selection of the choice corresponding to *not q*. Training was of two forms. One form was an extensive laboratory session describing the rule and its application in Venn diagrams, truth tables, and an illustrative conditional statement. The other was an entire course in introductory logic that was centered on conditional logic, including the modus tollens rule. Criterion 7 therefore speaks against the use of modus tollens. (Abstract instruction also did not improve performance on the component of the 4-card problem that could be solved by application of modus ponens — selection of the *p* choice — but errors were sufficiently infrequent for ponens as to raise the possibility that there was a ceiling effect.)

Evidence About Contractual Rules. In another study, Cheng et al. (1986) showed that comparable training on an abstract statement of the obligation rule ("If precondition P is satisfied, action A must be taken") did improve performance on the 4-card problem. Training included drill in the checking procedures required to establish whether an obligation had been violated. Subjects were then asked to solve various versions of the 4-card problem, including versions to which an obligation interpretation could be applied relatively easily, and arbitrary versions such as the original Wason letter-and-number problem. We performed a reanalysis of the Cheng et al. results and found that the abstract training improved performance on those versions of the problem that could possibly be interpreted in obligation terms ("If a house was built before 1979, then it has a fireplace"), and did not improve performance on problems for which an obligation interpretation seemed out of the question (such as the original Wason problem).

We mentioned earlier that there is no obvious way in which an instance model can handle these results, but a non-obvious way might proceed as follows: although the training involved only abstractions, subjects may have generated their own examples and subsequently retrieved these examples during the 4-card problem. What is wrong with this account is the usual set of difficulties. It seems most unlikely that the examples generated during training would have anything in common with the test items in the 4-card problem other than that they involved the notion of obligation. Again the account rests on the ad hoc assumption that retrieval is primarily based on whatever is correlated with the special structure of the rule.

Evidence About the Law of Large Numbers.   Fong, Krantz, and Nisbett (1985) have shown that training on the law of large numbers affects the way people reason about a wide range of problems involving variability and uncertainty. They taught their subjects about the law of large numbers using purely abstract concepts and procedures. They defined for them the notions of *sample, population, parameter,* and *variability,* and showed by urn-problem demonstrations that larger samples are more likely to capture population parameters than smaller samples. (These demonstrations, according to our sketch of a rule model, might have influenced the instantiation stage). Subjects were then asked to solve problems involving random generating devices, such as slot machines and lotteries, problems dealing with objective, quantifiable behavior, such as athletic and academic performances, and problems dealing with subjective judgments or social behaviors that are not normally coded in quantifiable terms. For example, one objective problem referred to earlier, required subjects to recognize that a basketball talent scout's assessment of a potential player was based on a relatively small sample of behavior and might be mistaken. A subjective problem described a head nurse's assertion that the most compassionate nurses, as judged from the first few days on the job, generally turn out to be no more concerned than the others, together with her attribution that this was probably the case because the most caring nurses build up a shell to protect themselves. A statistical answer to this problem recognized that a few days' observation of nurses' behavior might not be a large enough sample for a stable estimate of an attribute like compassion. In line with a rule model, the abstract-rule training produced a substantial increase in the number and quality of statistical answers, and did so to about the same degree for all three problem types.

Further Evidence on the Law of Large Numbers and Other Rules.   An extensive set of studies by Nisbett and his colleagues on the effects of undergraduate and graduate training on reasoning is relevant to Criterion 7. They found that undergraduate training in psychology and the social sciences (Lehman and Nisbett, 1990) and graduate training in psychology (Lehman, Lempert, and Nisbett, 1988) markedly increased the degree to which students call on statistical principles (like the law of large numbers) in reasoning about everyday events involving uncertainty. Fong et al. (1986) found that a single course in statistics had a marked effect on the way students reason about sports. These results speak to Criterion 7 to the extent that statistics is typically taught as a highly abstract set of rules.

Similarly, Morris, Cheng and Nisbett (1990) found that graduate training in psychology improved students' abilities to apply causal rules to both unfamiliar and purely abstract material. In contrast, training in philosophy or chemistry had no effect on students' causal reasoning, presumably because neither of these fields emphasizes the reasoning required for inferences about various types of causality. Again the work is relevant to Criterion 7 to the extent that instruction about causality in psychology is quite formal and owes little to detailed work with concrete examples.

Finally, work by Larrick, Morgan and Nisbett (1990; Larrick, Nisbett, & Morgan, in press) shows that formal training in cost-benefit rules affects people's reasoning about an indefinitely large number of problems involving choice in everyday life.

Criterion 8: Performance on Problems in a Particular Domain is Improved as Much by Training on Problems Outside the Domain as on Problems Within it, as Long as the Problems are Based on the Same Rule.

Rationale.   If a major product of training is an abstract rule that is as applicable to problems from one domain as to those from another, then subjects taught how to use the rule in a given content domain should readily transfer what they have learned to other domains. To put it in terms of our sketch of a rule model: the major products of training are increases in the accessibility of the rule and in the consequent ease with which the rule can be instantiated and applied, and all of these benefits should readily transfer to domains other than those of the training problems. The upshot is that domain-specificity effects of training might be relatively slight. To the extent such effects are slight, instance models are embarrassed because they naturally predict better performance for test problems that resemble training ones. Hence, Criterion 8 is very diagnostic of rule following.

Evidence About the Law of Large Numbers.   This criterion has thus far been applied only to the law of large numbers. Fong et al. (1986) trained subjects in one of three domains—random generating devices, objectively measurable abilities and achievements, or subjective judgments. Then subjects worked on test problems from all three domains. Performance on the test problems—as measured by the frequency of mention of statistical concepts and laws, and by the quality of the answers—was improved by the training. Most importantly, the degree of improvement for problems in the untrained domains was as great as for problems in the trained domain. For example, training on probabilistic-device problems improved performance on objective and subjective test problems as much as it did for probabilistic-device test problems.

The domains employed by Fong et al. (1986) are very broad ones, leaving open the possibility that two problems from the same domain shared very little in the way of content, perhaps little more in fact than two problems from different domains. But this possibility is ruled out by a more recent study. Fong and Nisbett (1990) examined two different objective attribute domains—athletic contests and ability tests. They taught some of their subjects to apply the law of large numbers to one domain, and some to apply this rule to the other domain. When subjects were tested immediately, again there was no effect at all of training domain on performance. This is strong evidence for rule following. When subjects were tested after two weeks, however, there was some effect of domain on performance, although there was still a significant training effect across domains as well. The domain-specificity effect after a delay should probably not be attributed too quickly to retrieval of examples from memory. Performance at the later testing time was unrelated to the ability to recall details of examples, but was related to the ability to recall the abstract rule. The latter findings suggest that, during training, subjects may have learned how to code the elements of a given domain in terms of the rule, which could result in domain-specific coding and access processes. Such processes would lead to an advantage for problems in the trained domain after a delay when access was more problematic.

It is worth emphasizing that the utter lack of domain specificity effects, when testing takes place immediately, is particularly problematic for an instance model. Such a model requires that the more similar the content of the test and training problems, the more likely a test problem will retrieve a training problem, which will culminate in better performance when the test and training problems are from the same domain. The only way to salvage the model is to posit that retrieval is heavily based on only those features correlated with the special structure of the rule. Yet it is not even clear that there are any content features of a problem that are correlated with the law of large numbers. As usual, then, the assumption in question seems ad hoc, and likely wrong.

A Possible Ninth Criterion.   Criterion 8 says that after training, performance on a rule-governed item is unaffected by its similarity to items encountered during training. A generalization of this phenomenon yields a new criterion: *Performance on a rule-governed item is unaffected by its degree of similarity to previously encountered items.* This is a very diagnostic criterion, since the hallmark of instance models is their sensitivity to similar items stored in memory.

We have not included the preceding as one of our criteria because we have not been able to find a study in which it has been successfully used to bolster the case for abstract rules in reasoning. Perhaps one reason the proposed similarity criterion has not been used in that it is exceptionally sensitive to any use of instances whatsoever. But we may be being too pessimistic here. For there are psycholinguistic studies where the proposed similarity criterion has been met, thereby providing very strong evidence for rule use. Consider again research on phonological rules showing that people can supply the plurals of nonsense nouns. The fact that people can as readily supply the plural for "zamph" as for "zig"-even though "zamph" does not rhyme with any English word and hence is not very similar to any known instance—is an indication that performance is unaffected by the similarity of the test item to previous instances (Pinker and Prince, 1988). A comparable story holds for the rule for forming the past tense of regular verbs. Young children are no more likely to produce the correct past tense for regular verbs that are similar to many other regular verbs, than they are to produce the correct past tense for regular verbs that are similar to few other regular verbs (Marcus et al, 1990). Perhaps this kind of evidence can be obtained with abstract reasoning rules.

GENERAL DISCUSSION

In this final section, we begin by summarizing our results, and then take up a number of outstanding issues. One such issue concerns reasoning mechanisms that involve both rules and instances; a second issue concerns the possibility of a type of rule following other than the explicit sort we have considered thus far; the final issue deals with the implications of our findings and arguments for connectionist models of reasoning.

Summary

Throughout most of this paper we have been concerned with two interrelated matters—possible criteria for rule following and possible rules that are followed. Let us first summarize our progress regarding the possible criteria, then turn to what we have found out about rules.

Criteria. We have presented and defended a set of criteria for establishing whether or not a rule is used for solving a given problem.

Satisfaction of the less diagnostic of these criteria—those concerned with overextension, number of rules, priming, and protocols—adds something to the case that a given rule is used for solving a given problem. Satisfaction of the more diagnostic criteria—those concerned with familiarity, abstractness, abstract training effects, and domain-independence in training—adds even more to the case for rule-following. And satisfaction of most or all of these criteria adds greatly to the case for rule-following. These criteria can serve to put the debate between abstraction-based and instance-based reasoning into clearer perspective.

Table 15.1 presents each of the eight criteria crossed with the five different rule systems that we have examined in detail. Table 15.1 makes it easy to see a pair of points concerning the criteria. One is that most of the criteria have been underused. It is clear that application of the criteria has been relatively haphazard, with many tests of a particular criterion for some rules and only one or two tests of a smattering of the other criteria. We suspect that the criteria used have been chosen relatively arbitrarily, and that investigators often have tested less powerful criteria than they might have simply because they were not aware of the existence of other, more powerful ones. Our overview of criteria and the rationales behind them should help to organize and direct research on the use of rules.

The other point about the criteria that is readily apparent from Table 15.1 is that the criteria converge. That is, if a rule passes one criterion it generally passes any other criterion that has been applied. Conversely, if a rule fails one criterion it generally fails other criteria that have been applied. We have only one case of this convergence of failures—modus tollens—because our main concern has been with abstract rules that are likely to be in people's repertoires. If we turn our attention to unnatural rules, which are unlikely to be in people's repertoires, we should see other failures to satisfy the criteria. Consider, for example, work by Ross (1987), in which people were taught relatively unnatural rules from probability theory, such as the rule that specifies the expected number of trials to wait for a particular probabilistic event to occur (the "waiting time" rule). Ross observed a strong violation of our domain-independence-of-training criterion; that is, performance on a test problem markedly depended on its similarity to a training problem. Recent results by Allen and Brooks (1991), who taught subjects artificial rules, makes exactly the same point. These failures of unnatural rules to pass the criterion attest to the validity of the criteria.

Three qualifications of the criteria are also worth mentioning. First, for purposes of clarity we have stated some of our criteria in an absolute or all-or-none fashion, but probably it would be more useful to treat each criterion in a relative fashion. We can illustrate this point with Criterion 1, *Performance on rule-governed items is as accurate with unfamiliar as familiar items.* Taking the criterion literally, there is evidence for rule-

TABLE 15.1
Criteria for Use of Abstract Rules for Reasoning and Evidence Base Relating to Them

CRITERIA	RULE TYPES				
	Modus Ponens	Modus Tollens	Contractual (Permissions & Obligations)	Causal	Law of Large Numbers
1. Good performance on unfamiliar items	Byrne (1989)	~~Cheng & Holyoak (1985)~~ / ~~Numerous others~~	Cheng, Holyoak, Nisbett, & Oliver (1986) / Cheng & Holyoak (1985)	Morris, Cheng, & Nisbett (1991)	Nisbett, Krantz, Jepson & Kunda (1983)
2. Good performance on abstract items	Evans (1977)	~~Wason (1966)~~ / ~~Numerous others~~	Cheng & Holyoak (1985)		
3. Overextension early in training					Fong, Krantz, & Nisbett (1986)
4. Number of rules and performance	Osherson (1975) Rips (1983) Braine, Reiser & Rumain (1984)				
5. Priming effects			Langston, Nisbett, & Smith (1991)		
6. Protocols identify rules	Rips (1983)				Piaget & Inhelder (1951) Jepson, Krantz, & Nisbett (1983) Nisbett et al. (1983) Fong et al. (1986)
7. Abstract training effects	~~Cheng, Holyoak, Nisbett & Oliver (1986)~~	~~Cheng, Holyoak, Nisbett & Oliver (1986)~~	Cheng, Holyoak, Nisbett & Oliver (1986)	Morris, Cheng, & Nisbett (1991)	Fong, Krantz, & Nisbett (1986) Lehman & Nisbett (1990) Lehman, Lempert & Nisbett (1989)
8. Domain independence of training					Fong, Krantz, & Nisbett (1986) Fong & Nisbett (1991)

Note. Cross-hatching indicates that the evidence shows that the rule fails the criterion.

following only when there is absolutely *no* difference between unfamiliar and familiar items. But surely the phenomenon that underlies the criterion admits of degrees, perhaps because of moment-to-moment variations in whether an individual uses a rule. Given this, Criterion 1 is better stated as *The less the difference in performance between unfamiliar and familiar rule-governed items, the greater the use of rules.* Similar remarks apply to Criterion 2 (good performance on abstract items), Criterion 7 (abstract training effects), and Criterion 8 (domain independence of training). It is noteworthy that actual uses of these criteria tend to employ the relative interpretation (see, for example, the Allen and Brooks, 1991, use of domain-independence-of-training effects).

A second qualification of the criteria stems from the fact that their diagnosticity has been measured in terms of how difficult they are to explain by models based on *stored* instances. But Johnson-Laird (1983) has championed a theoretical approach which holds that people reason by generating *novel* instances (in his terms, "reasoning by means of mental models"). To illustrate, suppose someone is told, "If gork then flum." They would represent this conditional in terms of the following sort of mental model:

gork1 = flum 1
gork2 = flum 2
        (flum 3).

The equal sign indicates that the same instance is involved, and the parentheses indicates that the instance is optional. If now told there exists a gork, one can use this mental model to conclude there also exists a flum, and in this way implement modus ponens. What is important about this for our purposes is that a theory based on such novel instances seems more compatible with our criteria than theories based on stored instances. For example, there is no obvious reason why one cannot construct a mental model as readily for an unfamiliar item as for a familiar one, or as readily for an abstract item as a concrete one.

The final qualification is simply that the application of our criteria does not provide as definitive data on the rule-vs-instance issue as does a contrast of detailed models. Our criteria are needed mainly in situations where detailed reasoning models have not been developed—the usual case as far as we can tell. (An exception is Nosofsky, Clark, and Shin, 1989, who do contrast detailed rule and instance models, but who consider rules that are not abstract by our definitions.) Our criteria also provide useful constraints in developing detailed rule models—for example, any rule model that is concerned only with abstract rules ought to produce comparable performance for unfamiliar and familiar items, for abstract and concrete items, and so on.

Rules.   Table 15.1 also tells us about what rules are followed. We believe that the applications of the criteria to date serve to establish that people make use of a number of abstract rules in solving problems of a sort that occur frequently in everyday life. In particular there is substantial evidence for at least three sorts of rule systems.

For modus ponens, there is evidence that people: (a) perform as well — that is, make inferences in accordance with the rule — on unfamiliar as on familiar material; (b) perform as well on abstract as on concrete material; (c) perform better if they must invoke the rule fewer rather than more times; and (d) sometimes provide protocols suggesting that they have used the rule. (On the other hand, there is some evidence that the rule cannot be trained by abstract techniques, but this evidence may merely indicate that the rule is already asymptotic.)

For contractual rules, namely permission and obligation rules, there is evidence that people: (a) perform as well on unfamiliar as on familiar material; (b) perform as well on abstract as on concrete material; (c) show priming effects of the rule, at least within a content domain; and (d) benefit from training in their ability to apply the rule to any material that can plausibly be interpreted in terms of it. There is also some evidence of a comparable kind for formally similar causal rules.

For the system of statistical rules under the rubric of the law of large numbers, it has been shown that people: (a) perform well with unfamiliar material; (b) overextend the rule early in training; (c) often mention the rule in relatively abstract form in justification of their answers for particular problems; (d) improve in their ability to apply the rule across a wide number of domains by purely abstract training on the rule; and (e) improve their performance on problems outside the domain of training as much as on problems within it.

The demonstrations that people follow modus ponens and the law of large numbers are of particular interest in view of the fact that these two rules are normative and promote optimal inferential performance. Evidence for people following certain abstract inferential rules thus amounts to evidence for people manifesting aspects of rationality. Although there is less data about causal rules, what evidence there is suggests that people also follow these rules (see Table 15.1), which again are normative. And there is some recent evidence for the use of still another set of normative rules, those governing economic choices (Larrick et al., 1990; in press).

In contrast to the positive evidence summarized above, there are three lines of negative evidence on the question of whether people use modus tollens. It has been shown that people perform poorly: (a) with unfamiliar items; (b) with abstract items; and (c) even after formal training in the rule. We therefore believe that the consensus among students of the problem that most people do not use modus tollens is justified in terms of the criteria studied to date. This demonstration indicates that application of our criteria can cut both ways: negative evidence relating to the criteria can cast substantial doubt on the use of a rule, just as positive evidence can buttress the case for its use.

Of course modus ponens, modus tollens, contractual rules, and the law of large numbers are just a handful of the many possible seemingly-natural rules that people may follow in reasoning about everyday problems. There are, for example, numerous rules in propositional logic other than ponens and tollens that have been proposed as psychologically real (see, for instance, Braine et al., 1984). One such rule is *and introduction*, which states *If p is the case and if q is the case then p and q is the case.* The obvious question is: How does and-introduction stack up against our eight criteria? The same question applies to other rules from propositional logic, and to rules that have figured in Piagetian-type research (including transitivity, commutativity, and associativity), as well as to rules that come from other bodies of work. The point is that all we have done in the present paper is sample a rule or two from a few major branches of reasoning—deduction, statistics, and causality—and there are other rules of interest in these and other branches of reasoning.

A final point to note about the evidence for rules is that the work to date shows not merely that people *can* follow rules when instructed to do so in artificial problem-solving situations, but that they *do* follow quite abstract inferential rules when solving ordinary, everyday problems. For example, in their studies of the law of large numbers, Fong et al. (1985) performed not merely laboratory experiments but field studies in which subjects did not even know they were being tested. In one study, male subjects were called in the context of an alleged "survey on sports opinions." Subjects were enrolled in introductory statistics courses and were called either at the beginning of the course or at the end. After being asked a few questions about NBA salaries and NCAA rules, it was pointed out to them that while many batters often finish the first two weeks of the baseball season with averages of .450 or higher, no one has ever finished the season with such an average. They were asked why they thought this was the case. Most subjects responded with causal hypotheses such as "the pitchers make the necessary adjustments." Some, however, responded with statistical answers such as "there are not many at-bats in two weeks, so unusually high (or low) averages would be more likely; over the long haul nobody is really that good." There were twice as many statistical answers from subjects tested at the end of the term as from subjects tested at the beginning.

Similarly, Larrick et al. (1990) found that subjects who were taught cost-benefit rules came to apply them in all sorts of life contexts, from consumer decisions about whether to finish a bad meal or bad movie, to professional decisions about whether to pursue a line of work that was turning out to be disappointing, to hypothetical questions about institutional policy and international relations.

Thus the work reviewed here establishes not merely that people can follow abstract rules self-consciously in appropriate educational, experimental or professional settings, but that such rules play at least a limited role in ordinary inference.

Combining Rule and Instance Mechanisms

Our review indicates that pure instance models of reasoning and problem solving are not viable. There is too much evidence, stemming from the application of too many criteria, indicating that people use abstract rules in reasoning. On the other hand, there is also abundant evidence that reasoning and problem-solving often proceed via the retrieval of instances (for example, Kaiser, Jonides, and Alexander 1986; Ross, 1987; Medin and Ross, 1989; Allen and Brooks, 1991). At a minimum, then, we need to posit two qualitatively different mechanisms of reasoning. While some situations may involve only one of the mechanisms, others may involve both.

In addition to *pure-rule* and *pure-instance* mechanisms, hybrid mechanisms may be needed as well. In particular, hybrid mechanisms may be needed to account for the situations noted earlier in which people process instances deeply enough to encode some information about the relevant abstraction as well as about the concrete aspects of the instance. These are the situations that are the concern of most case-based reasoning models (for example, Schank, 1982; Kolodner, 1983; Hammond et al, 1991). In such situations, people have essentially encoded both an instance and a rule, so a hybrid mechanism must specify how the two representational aspects are connected. We consider two possibilities.

One possibility is that a retrieved instance provides access to a rule. That is, when an item is presented it first accesses similar instances from memory, which the reasoner uses to access a rule. Then the final stages of rule processing — instantiation and application — ensue, though the instance may serve as a guide for these two stages. We can illustrate this mechanism with the drinking version of the 4-card problem. When presented the problem, presumably a subject uses this item to retrieve from memory an episode of a drinking event; this representation may contain the information that people below the drinking age are in violation of the law, and the concept of *violation* may be used to access the permission rule; from here on, processing would continue as specified in our sketch of a rule model except that the retrieved instance can be used to guide the instantiation and application stages. This hybrid process, which we will refer to as *instance-rule mechanism,* captures the intuition that we often understand an abstract rule in turns of a specific example.

The other possibility is that a rule provides access to a relevant instance (a *rule-instance* mechanism). That is, when an item is presented it is coded abstractly, and this abstraction accesses the appropriate rule (these are the first two stages of our sketch of a rule model). The rule then provides access to some typical examples, and these instances control further processing. Again we can illustrate with the drinking version of the 4-card problem. When presented the problem, a subject codes the item in terms of *permission,* and uses this code to access the permission rules. Associated with these rules are typical examples of *permission* situations, and one or more of these instances is used as an analogue for the present problem (that is, it is used for the mapping stage).

A few comments are in order about these mechanisms. Note that we are not proposing the two hybrid mechanisms as alternatives to the two pure mechanisms (rule and instance). Rather, we suspect that all four mechanisms can be used, albeit with different situations recruiting different mechanisms. (The experimental situations we reviewed in this paper likely involved either the pure-rule or the rule-instance mechanism.) In situations where more than one mechanism is involved, presumably the processes operate simultaneously and independently of one another. Thus the final answer may be determined by a kind of "horse race" between the operative mechanisms, with the mechanism that finishes first determining the final judgment.

Note further that our hybrid mechanisms allow room for instance-type effects should they occur. Consider again Criterion 1, that novel rule-based items are treated as accurately as familiar ones. The available evidence is consistent with this criterion, but the criterion deals only with accuracy. Perhaps if one were to measure reaction times, familiar rule-based items might be processed faster than novel ones. Such a result could be handled easily by our instance-rule mechanism. Familiar items should be faster in accessing a relevant instance because familiar items are themselves likely to be instances. In addition, we have already seen an indication of instance effects even for accuracy. Such an effect appeared in connection with Criterion 5, that application of a rule primes its subsequent use. Recall that in the 4-card problem Langston et al. (1991) found evidence for priming of contractual rules only when the prime and target were similar in content. This pattern of results also fits nicely with the instance-rule mechanism. Only when the target and prime are similar in content does the target retrieve the prime instance, and only when the prime is retrieved does one gain access to the relevant rule. Thus, instance-type effects do not imply that rules were not involved.

Finally, another case of instance-type effects during rule use is provided by Ross (1987). Ross trained subjects on the waiting-time rule of probability theory and then had them solve new test problems with the rule present. Even though the rule was present, subjects appeared to rely on training problems when determining how to instantiate the rule. These results indicate that instances are used not just to access a rule but also to help instantiate it, as in the instance-rule mechanism. (These results, however, may depend in part on the fact that the rule involved was not a natural one).

In short, the dichotomy between pure rules and pure instances is too simple. Hybrid mechanisms seem plausible, particularly in light of the role they play in current versions of case-based reasoning.

Two Kinds of Rule Following

Up till now we have acted as if explicit rule following is the only kind of rule following. But a critical observation suggests the need to consider a second kind. The observation (due to Douglas Medin) is that, when *linguistic* rules are stacked up against our eight criteria they seem to consistently fail three of them, namely verbal protocols, abstract training effects, and context independence in training. That is, people are notoriously unable to verbalize the linguistic rules they purportedly use, and they fail to benefit much from explicit (school) instructions on these rules. If linguistic rules meet only five of our criteria while reasoning rules (generally) meet all eight, perhaps the kind of rule followed involved in language is different from that involved in reasoning.

Presumably there is a kind of rule following that is *implicit* rather than *explicit;* that is, the rule is never explicitly represented, which accounts for why it cannot be reported nor affected by explicit instruction. The rule might be implemented in the hardware, and is essentially a description of how some built-in processor works (see Pinker and Prince, 1988, Section 8.2). Implicit rules are close to what we earlier characterized as operating principles of a system (see pp. 8–9), and rules like this may be part of our basic cognitive architecture. Such notions fit nicely with Pylyshyn's (1984) concept of *cognitive penetrability*. His basic idea is that anything that is part of the fixed cognitive architecture cannot be altered (penetrated) by goals, context, or instruction. If some linguistic rules are part of our basic architecture, they should not be affected by instruction, which means that our two instructional criteria should fail, as they in fact do. (The seeming imperviousness of modus ponens to instruction leaves open the possibility that this rule too may be represented implicitly.)

Implications for Connectionist Models

While we know of no in-principle limit on the ability of connectionist models to code abstractions, the evidence we have presented for abstract rules does not fit well with the connectionist program.

For one thing, what seems to be the most straightforward account of much of the evidence involves concepts that are anathema to connectionism. The account we have in mind is that of explicit-rule following: the rule and input are mentally represented explicitly, and application of the rule to the input involves an inspection of the input to determine whether the antecedent of the rule has been satisfied. Notions of *explicit data structures* and *inspection of explicit structures* simply lie outside the ontology of connectionism. Of course, connectionists may be able to develop alternative accounts of the data, but there is no reason to believe the resulting connectionist models will be as parsimonious as the sort of rule-based model we advocate. This is particularly the case given that the abstract rules that have to be modeled all involve variable bindings, which remains a difficult issue in connectionist work (for discussion, see Holyoak, 1990). In short, rule-based models provide a simple account of the data, and no comparable connectionist alternatives are thus far in sight.

In constructing alternative models of the evidence, connectionists face another difficulty. The evidence indicates that people can use two qualitatively different mechanisms in reasoning—which we have termed "rules" and "instances"—while connectionist models endorse a uniform architecture. Connectionist models can either blur the rule-instance distinction, in which case they are simply failing to capture a major generalization about human cognition, or they can somehow mark the distinction, in which case they may be merely implementing a rule-based model in a connectionist net. We say "merely" because it is not clear that such an implementation will yield any new important insights about reasoning.

The preceding points have been programmatic, but the remaining one is more substantive. According to rule models, the rationale for some rules hinges on a *constituency relation*—like that which holds between *If p then q* and *p*—but most current connectionist models lack true constituency relations. In discussing this issue, we need to keep separate *localist* connectionist models, in which a concept can be represented by a single node, and *distributed* models, in which a concept is represented by a set of nodes. We consider localist models first.

To understand the constituency issue, consider modus ponens. Given *If p then q* and *p,* the fact that the latter is a constituent of the former is part of why we can conclude *q*. To take an even simpler example, consider again and-introduction, *If p is the case and if q is the case then p and q is the case.* Here it is clear that the basis of the rule is a constituency relation—the rule essentially states *If each of its constituents is the case then a conjunction is the case.* In contrast, localist connectionist models lack constituency relations, so such relations can never serve as the bases for rules.

The reason localist connectionist models lack constituency relations is that their nodes (their representations) lack any internal structure, including a part-whole structure. In a localist model for and-introduction, for example, there might be separate nodes for *p, q,* and *p and q,* which are connected in such a way that whenever the nodes for p and q are both activated the node for p and q is activated. Importantly, the node for p and q has no internal structure, and in no sense contains the node for p or that for q. Hence the relation between the p and q nodes on the one hand, and the p and q node on the other, is strictly causal (as opposed to constituency). That is, activation of p and q causes activation of p and q in exactly the same way that activation of a node for *fire* might cause activation of a node for *smoke*. Although we know of no data on whether constituency relations are perceived as the bases of some rules, our intuitions suggest they are, which favors the rule account. (For a fuller discussion of these issues, see Fodor and Pylyshyn, 1988).

Distributed connectionist models seem better able to accommodate constituency relations because they at least have a part-whole structure. Thus if p and q is represented by a set of nodes, then some part of that set can in principle represent p and another part q. Such a part-whole structure, however, is not equivalent to a constituent structure, as Fodor and McLaughlin (1990) point out. The latter authors take up a proposal of Smolensky's (1988), in which a concept (rule) is represented in terms of a vector whose components represent the activity levels of the members of the relevant set of nodes. According to Smolensky, vector a is a constituent of vector b if there exists a third vector — call it x — such that $a + x = b$. Clearly a is a part of b, but Smolensky's proposal permits of the possibility that b may be activated without a being activated. In the case of *and introduction,* this means that p and q could be activated without p being activated. Such a thing should be impossible if p is a true constituent of p and q. Again, to the extent some rules are based on constituent structure, the rule account is favored over current connectionist rivals.

None of this is to suggest that connectionist models do not have an important role to play — they have been very successful in capturing aspects of perception, memory, and categorization, for example — but rather to suggest that some aspects of reasoning may be inherently rule-based, and hence not naturally captured by connectionist models. Of course, a rule-based model, unlike a connectionist one, will not look like a biological model. Thus, to pursue rule-based models of reasoning is to give up the wish that all mental phenomena be expressive of biological phenomena rather than merely emergent on them. It has always been hard to make the leap from mere neural connections to abstract rules which seem metaphorically to sit astride the hustle and bustle of biological activity in the brain, altering and managing the results of such activity, and being modified by the mere words of outsiders and the ministrations of educators. We do not pretend to be able to make the leap from the known facts of the behavior of the nervous system to a plausible, emergent set of highly modifiable abstract rules. We claim merely that a correct theory of mind may have to do so.

REFERENCES

Allen, S. W. & Brooks, L. R. (in press). Specializing the operation of an explicit rule. *Journal of Experimental Psychology: General.*

Anderson, J. R. (1982). Acquisition of cognitive skill. *Psychological Review, 89,* 369–406.

Barsalou, L. W. (1990). On the indistinguishability of exemplar memory and abstraction in category representation. In T. K. Srull & R. S. Wyer (Eds.), *Advances in social cognition,* Vol. 3. Hillsdale, NJ: Erlbaum Press.

Berko, J. (1958). The child's learning of English morphology. *Word, 14,* 150–177.

Braine, M. D. S., Reiser, B. J., & Rumain, B. (1984). Some empirical justification for a theory of natural propositional logic. In G. H. Brown (Ed.), *Psychology of learning and motivation, 18,* 313–371. Orlando, FL: Academic Press.

Buss, D. (1991). Evolutionary personality psychology. *Annual Review of Psychology, 42,* 459–491.

Byrne, R. M. J. (1989). Suppressing valid inferences with conditionals. *Cognition, 31,* 61–83.

Cheng, P. W., & Holyoak, K. J. (1985). Pragmatic reasoning schemas. *Cognitive Psychology, 17,* 391–416.

Cheng, P. W., Holyoak, K. J., Nisbett, R. E., & Oliver, L. M. (1986). Pragmatic versus syntactic approaches to training deductive reasoning. *Cognitive Psychology, 18,* 293–328.

Cheng, P. W., & Holyoak, K. J. (1989). On the natural selection of reasoning theories. *Cognition, 33,* 285–314.

Chomsky, N. (1985). *Knowledge of language.* New York: Praeger.

Collins, A. M., & Michalski, R. (1989). The logic of plausible reasoning: A core theory. *Cognitive Science, 13,* 1–50.

D'Andrade, R. (1982). Reason versus logic. Paper presented at the Symposium on the Ecology of Cognition: Biological, Cultural, and Historical Perceptions, Greensboro, North Carolina.

Ericsson, K. A. & Simon, H. A. (1984). *Protocol analysis: Verbal reports as data.* Cambridge, MA: MIT Press.

Ervin, S. M. (1964). Imitation and structural change in children's language. In E. H. Lenneberg (Ed), *New directions in the study of language.* Cambridge, MA: MIT Press.

Evans, J. St. B. T. (1977). Linguistic factors in reasoning. *Quarterly Journal of Experimental Psychology, 29,* 297–306.

Evans, J. St. B. T. (1982). *The psychology of deductive reasoning.* London: Routledge & Kegan Paul.

Evans, S. H. (1967). A brief statement of schema theory. *Psychonomic Science, 8,* 87–88.

Fodor, J. A., & Pylyshyn, Z. (1988). Connectionism and cognitive architecture: A critical analysis. *Cognition, 28,* 3–72.

Fodor, J. A., & McLaughlin, B. P. (1990). Connectionism and the problem of systematicity: Why Smolensky's solution doesn't work. *Cognition, 35,* 183–204.

Fong, G. T., Krantz, D. H., & Nisbett, R. E. (1986). The effects of statistical training on thinking about everyday problems. *Cognitive Psychology, 18,* 253–292.

Fong, G. T., & Nisbett, R. E. (1990). Immediate and delayed transfer of training effects in statistical reasoning. *Journal of Experimental Psychology: General.*

Galotti, K. M., Baron, J., & Sabini, J. (1986). Individual differences in syllogistic reasoning: Deduction rules or mental models? *Journal of Experimental Psychology: General, 115,* 16–25.

Gentner, D. (1983). Structure mapping; A theoretical framework for analogy. *Cognitive Science, 7,* 155–170.

Gentner, D., & Toupin, C. (1986). Systematicity and surface similarity in the development of analogy. *Cognitive Science, 10,* 277–300.

Gluck, M. A. & Bower, G. H. (1988). Evaluating an adaptive network model of human learning. *Journal of Memory and Language, 27,* 166–195.

Goodman, N. (1955). *Fact, fiction and forecast,* chapter 3. Cambridge, MA: Harvard University Press.

Griggs, R. A. (1983). The role of problem content in the selection task and in the THOG problem. In J. St. B. T. Evans (Ed.), *Thinking and reasoning* (pp 16–43). London: Routledge & Kegan Peul.

Griggs, R. A. & Cox, J. R. (1982). The elusive thematic-materials effect in Wason's selection task *British Journal of Psychology, 73,* 07–420.

Hammond, K. J., Siefert, C. M., & Gray, K. C. (1991). Functionality in analogical transfer: A hard match is good to find. *The Journal of the Learning Sciences, 1,* 111–152.

Hinton, G. E., & Sejnowski, T. J. (1984). Learning semantic features. *Proceedings of the 6th Annual Conference of the Cognitive Science Society* (pp. 28–30). Boulder, Colorado, June.

Holland, J. H., Holyoak, K. J., Nisbett, R. E., & Thagard, P. T. (1986). *Induction: Processes of inference, learning, and discovery.* Cambridge, MA: Bradford Books/The MIT Press.

Holyoak, K. J. (1984). Analogical thinking and human intelligence. In R. J. Sternberg (Ed.), *Advances in the psychology of human intelligence,* Vol. 2., Hillsdale, NJ: Erlbaum Press.

Holyoak, K. J. (1990). Symbolic connectionism: Toward third-generation theories of expertise. In K. A. Ercsson & J. Smith (Eds.), *Toward a general theory of expertise: Prospects and limits.* Cambridge, MA: Cambridge University Press.

Holyoak, K. J., & Koh, K. (1987). Surface and structural. similarity in analogical transfer. *Memory & Cognition, 15,* 332–340.

Holyoak, K. J., & Thagard, P. T. (1989). Analogical mapping by constraint satisfaction. *Cognitive Science, 13,* 295–355.

Jepson, C., Krantz, D. H., & Nisbett, R. E. (1983). Inductive reasoning: Competence or skill? *Behavioral and Brain Sciences, 6,* 94–501.

Johnson-Laird, P. N. (1983). *Mental models.* Cambridge, MA: Harvard University Press.

Kahneman, D., & Tversky, A. (1973). On the psychology of prediction. *Psychological Review, 80,* 237–251.

Kaiser, M. K., Jonides, J., & Alexander, J. (1986). Intuitive reasoning on abstract and familiar physics problems. *Memory and Cognition, 14,* 308–312.

Kelley, H. H. (1972). Causal schemata and the attribution process. In E. E. Jones, D. E. Kanouse, H. H. Kelley, R. E. Nisbett, S. Valins, & B. Weiner (Eds.), *Attribution: Perceiving the causes of behavior.* Morristown, NJ: General Learning Press.

Kelley, H. H. (1973). The process of causal attribution. *American Psychologist, 28,* 107–128.

Kolodner, J. L. (1983). Reconstructive memory: A computer model. *Cognitive Science, 7,* 281–328.

Langston, C., Nisbett, R. & Smith, E. E. (1991). Priming contractual rules. Unpublished Manuscript, University of Michigan.

Larrick, R. P., Morgan, J. N., & Nisbett, R. W. (1990). Teaching the normative rules of choice. *Psychological Science, 1,* 362–370.

Larrick, R. P., Nisbett, R. E., & Morgan, J. N. (In press). Who uses the normative rules of choice? *Organizational behavior and human decision-making.*

Lehman, D. R., Lempert, R. O., & Nisbett, R. E. (1988). The effects of graduate training on reasoning: Formal discipline and thinking about everyday life events. *American Psychologist, 43,* 431–443.

Lehman, D., & Nisbett, R. E. (1990). A longitudinal study of the effects of undergraduate education on reasoning. *Developmental Psychology, 26,* 952–960.

Lewis, C. (1988). Why and how to learn: Analysis-based generalization of procedures. *Cognitive Science, 12,* 211–256.

McClelland, J. L. & Rumelhart, D. E. (1986). *Parallel distributed processing:* Vol. 1. Cambridge, MA: MIT Press.

Manktelow, K. I., & Evans, J. St. B. T. (1979). Facilitation of reasoning by realism: Effect or non-effect? *British Journal of Psychology, 70,* 477–488.

Marcus, G. F., Ullman, M., Pinker, S., Hollander, M., Rosen, T. J., & Xu, F. (1990). Overextensions. MIT Center for Cognitive Science, Occasional Paper #41.

Medin, D. L., & Ross, B. H. (1989). The specific character of abstract thought: Categorization, problem solving, and induction. In R. J. Sternberg (Ed.), *Advances in the psychology of human intelligence,* (vol. 5). Hillsdale, NJ: Erlbaum Press.

Medin, D. L., & Smith, E. E. (1981). Strategies and classification learning. *Journal of Experimental Psychology: Human Learning and Memory, 7,* 241–253.

Miller, G. A. (1962). Some psychological studies of grammar. *American Psychologist, 7,* 748–762.

Morris, M. W., Cheng, P., & Nisbett, R. E. (1991). Causal reasoning schemas. Unpublished manuscript, University of California, Los Angeles.

Murphy, G. L. & Medin, D. L. (1985). The role of theories in conceptual coherence. *Psychological Review, 92,* 289–317.

Newell, A., & Simon, H. A. (1972). *Human problem solving.* Englewood Cliffs, NJ: Prentice-Hall.

Nisbett, R. E., Fong, G. T., Lehman, D. R., & Cheng, P. W. (1987). Teaching reasoning. *Science, 238,* 625–631.

Nisbett, R. E., Krantz, D. H., Jepson, D., & Kunda, Z. (1983). The use of statistical heuristics in everyday inductive reasoning. *Psychological Review, 90,* 339–363.

Nisbett, R. E., & Ross, L. (1980). *Human inference: Strategies and shortcomings of social judgment.* Englewood Cliffs, NJ: Prentice Hall.

Nisbett, R. E., & Wilson, T. D. (1977). Telling more than we can know: Verbal reports on mental processes. *Psychological Review, 8,* 231–259.

Nosofsky, R. M., Clark, S. E. & Shin, H. J. (1989). Rules and exemplars in categorization, identification, and recognition. *Journal of Experimental Psychology: Learning, Memory, and Cognition, 15,* 282–304.

Osherson, D. (1975). Logic and logical models of thinking. In R. Falmagne (Ed.), *Reasoning* Representation and process. New York: Wiley.

Piaget, J. & Inhelder, B. (1958). *The growth of logical thinking from childhood to adolescence.* New York: Basic Books.

Piaget, J., & Inhelder, B. (1951/1975). *The origin of the idea of chance in children.* New York: Norton.

Pinker, S. & Prince, A. (1988). On language and connectionism: Analysis of a parallel distributed processing model of language acquisition. *Cognition, 28,* 73–194.

Reich, S. S., & Ruth, P. (1982). Wason's selection task: Verification, falsification and matching. *British Journal of Psychology, 73,* 395–405.

Rips, L. J. (1983). Cognitive processes in propositional reasoning. *Psychological Review, 90,* 38–71.

Rips, L. J. (1990). Reasoning. *Annual Review of Psychology, 41,* 321–353.

Ross, B. H. (1987). This is like that: The use of earlier problems and the separation of similarity effects. *Journal of Experimental Psychology: Learning, Memory, and Cognition, 13,* 629–639.

Plyshyn, Z. (1984). *Computation and cognition: Toward a foundation for cognitive science.* Cambridge, MA: MIT Press.

Plyshyn, Z. (1990). Rules and representations: Chomsky and Representational Realism. In ? (Ed.), *The Chomskyian Turn,* Blackwell.

Rumelhart, D. E., McClelland, J. L. (1987). Learning the past tenses of English verbs: Implicit rules or parallel distributed processing. In B. MacWhinney (Ed.), *Mechanisms of language acquisition*. Hillsdale, NJ: Erlbaum Press.

Rumelhart, D. E., McClelland, J. R., & the PDP Research Group. (1986). *Parallel distributed processing: Explorations in the microstructure of cognition,* Vol.1. Cambridge, MA: MIT Press.

Schank, R. C. (1982). *Dynamic memory: A theory of learning in people and computers.* Cambridge, England: Cambridge University Press.

Smith, E. E., Lopez, A., & Osherson, D, N, (in press) Category membership, similarity, and naive induction. In A. Healy, R. Shiffrin, & S. M. Kosslyn (Eds.), *Essays in honor of W. K. Estes.* Hillsdale, NJ: Erlbaum Press.

Smolensky, P. (1988). On the proper treatment of connectionism. *Behavioral and Brain Sciences, 11,* 1–23.

Tversky, A., & Kahneman, D. (1971). Belief in the law of small numbers. *Psychological Bulletin, 2,* 105–110.

Tversky, A., & Kahneman, D. (1986). Rational choice and the framing of decisions. *Journal of Business, 59,* S251–S278.

Wason, P. (1966). *Reasoning.* In B. Foss (Ed.), *New horizons in psychology* (pp. 135–152). Harmondsworth: Penguin Books.

Author Index

Subject Index

U